THE

BLACK
AVENGER

IN

ATLANTIC
CULTURE

THE

BLACK AVENGER

IN

ATLANTIC CULTURE

GRÉGORY
PIERROT

THE UNIVERSITY OF
GEORGIA PRESS
ATHENS

Part of this book originally appeared, in a different form, as "*Droit du Seigneur*, Slavery, and Nation in the Poetry of Edward Rushton," in *Studies in Romanticism* 56, no. 1 (Spring 2017), published by the Trustees of Boston University; as "Writing over Haiti: Black Avengers in Martin Delany's *Blake*," in *Studies in American Fiction* 41, no. 2 (2014), copyright © 2014 The Johns Hopkins University Press; and as "Our Hero: Toussaint Louverture in British Representations," in *Criticism: A Quarterly for Literature and the Arts* 50, no. 4 (2009), published by Wayne State University Press.

Set in 11/13.5 Garamond Premier Pro by
Graphic Composition, Inc.

Most University of Georgia Press titles are
available from popular e-book vendors.

Printed digitally

Library of Congress Cataloging-in-Publication Data

Names: Pierrot, Grégory, author.
Title: The black avenger in Atlantic culture / Grégory Pierrot.
Description: Athens : The University of Georgia Press, [2019] | Includes
    bibliographical references and index.
Identifiers: LCCN 2018036508| ISBN 9780820354910 (hardcover : alk.
    paper) | ISBN 9780820354927 (paperback : alk. paper)
Subjects: LCSH: Blacks in literature. | Revenge in literature. | Heroes in
    literature.
Classification: LCC PN56.3.B55 P54 2019 | DDC 809/.93352—dc23
    LC record available at https://lccn.loc.gov/2018036508

CONTENTS

ACKNOWLEDGMENTS

Accounting for all the people I'm indebted to is a daunting task.

At different times along the way I relied on funds from the Institute for the Arts and Humanities Graduate Student Summer Residency, Sparks Fellowship, George and Barbara Kelly Fellowship in Nineteenth-Century English and American Literature, Africana Research Center Research Grant, Center for American Literary Studies Graduate Travel to Research Collections Award, Philip Young Memorial Endowment in American Literature. Sandy Stelts at Pennsylvania State University, Phara Bayonne and Nancy Dryden at the library of the University of Connecticut at Stamford, and Richard Bleiler at Storrs. The publication of this book was made possible by the University of Connecticut's Humanities Institute Book Fund, for which both the press and I are grateful.

All thanks to Paul Youngquist: accepting his challenge a decade (!) ago set me off on this journey. I learned all things as I went and made one crucial discovery: somewhere along the way I had become a scholar. Not a Romanticist per se, but I think Paul will forgive me. I could not have done it without Claire Maniez, Aldon Nielsen, Linda Selzer, Shirley Moody Turner, all models of excellence, humility, and collegiality who showed me ways to do this work that would not jeopardize my soul.

There were jeopardies aplenty on the long way out of school, along with tight ranks of soul defenders, fellow students now grown older, friends now near or far who through the Pennsylvania years listened more or less patiently to this or that and gave helpful advice, read and commented, suggested and doubted, laughed and raged: the vegfest crew, Dustin Kennedy, Nancy Cushing, Hannah Abelbeck, Kristin Shimmin, Moura McGovern, Phyllisa Deroze, Micky New, Emily Sharpe, Mark Sturges, Rachel Bara, Jesse Hicks, David Green, Angela Ward, Kevin Browne, Krista Eastman, Ersula

Ore, Josh Tendler, Manolis Galenianos, Steven Thomas, and in memory of Michael DuBose. I'll go to Texas yet.

Sometimes the voices that compel us belong to the people who compel us: at different times and in different ways, words from the mouths of Paul Gilroy, Vron Ware, Sibylle Fischer, Laurent Dubois, and Chris Bongie confirmed all the good things I had glimpsed on the page. I found a home at the University of Connecticut and warm welcoming people, generous with support and advice: Fred Roden, Pam Brown, Serkan Gorkemli, Ingrid Semaan, Annamaria Csizmadia, and Monica Smith. Along the years I had the chance to benefit from the remarks and feedback of many insightful scholars: Talissa Ford and the P19 Faculty Seminar at Temple University, Anne Eller, Marlene Daut, and Michael Drexler, inspired me through their own work and generously offered invaluable input that helped me sharpen my arguments at different stages of writing—so did Bhakti Shringapure, Lily Saint, and Miles Grier, who managed to juggle patience, curiosity, understanding, and advice without ever dropping one.

There are people we meet just so we can ponder topics such as destiny: this project was one thing, then I met Tabitha McIntosh again, and it became a book. This book evolved in the light of her brilliant mind, wit, insight, and friendship. I typed much, deleted as much, and argued and fought tooth and nail for unnecessary plot summaries, as she patiently read and reread and helped me birth this monster: nothing I can write could accurately describe how grateful I am to have her as a friend and chapter whisperer.

I want to thank Germaine and François Pierrot, without whom I would not be; without their influence this book would never have been. Stories and histories started in the living room and kitchen. *Vous ne lirez pas ce livre, mais je vous le raconterai.*

Thanks also go to Peggy and Philippe, who were in the same living room and kitchen and everywhere else and with whom I started everything, read everything, argued about everything, and wrote about everything. Caliméro vous embrasse.

Nothing would have happened without Kate's love, care, and patience. I can't promise I won't do it again, but I'm confident you'll make it possible.

And, finally, I dedicate this book to Chloë. This project began before you were born; I wrote part of it carrying you on my chest, and you're now old enough that you could read it. I'll answer all the questions when you do.

THE
BLACK
AVENGER
IN
ATLANTIC
CULTURE

PRELUDE

This is a story about the stories men tell one another.

A woman is brutalized by men. Her pain and suffering, inscribed in her flesh, become public—a *res publica*—after she commutes them into words to testify. She dies. Her ordeal becomes a pretext for men's speeches and political material. Watching over her dead body, men renew a brotherhood premised on a gendered, othering gaze, a community that polices the women who belong and dehumanizes the people who do not. Soon a man who does not quite belong takes a principled stand—against the utter unfairness of this community's rules, for hope of a better system—and leads a movement that, for a time, seems likely to topple the order. The movement fails; the lone man dies; the brotherhood oppresses on.

This is the story of a repeated balancing act, where the revolutionary potential of gendered, racial, and cultural otherness threatens to—but never quite does—outweigh its usefulness as a notion that belongs to and helps maintain the old order. This is a history of the stories that cement the cultural walls by which civilizations mean to keep out so-called barbarian invasions, the story of the cost one pays for living on the margins of Western civilization and casting a shadow within. This story structures the order of Man, who appears as a palimpsest in the tales of the birth of nations accreted in Western tradition, a body of work composed by contrast to bodies whose fleshly inadequacy is regularly reassessed.[1]

This is the story of these bodies, the *not-quite-humans* necessary to define Man, and the tropes Man uses to represent them so that they can serve this purpose. This story has a history, a palimpsestic constellation of points connecting past and present, women then and women now, the enslaved of Rome and the enslaved of America.

This story always starts with rape.

Rape, as a legal definition, has long rested on the specific gendering and physical actions set out in English common law as "the carnal knowledge of a woman by force and against her will." The law and its upholders shift the burden of proof squarely onto the shoulders of victims, who are expected to demonstrate that force was employed, that they were unwilling. Narrative and rhetoric play a paramount role in a system where "women believe the word of other women. Men do not."[2] In a court of law, rape is a story before it can be considered a criminal act. What counts as rape serves to define the borders of the order of Man. It tells us what bodies get their say and what flesh will remain silenced.

Three figures emerge in ancient tales that provide the original patterns for our story: Lucretia, the citizen woman; Spartacus, the slave who revolted; and, hiding in the shadows, the anonymous slave used against Lucretia. They are presented to us by servants of the order of Man, the order that brutalized them and that they challenged. They come to us as necessary but dangerous, threatening pieces in a tale the Roman nation tells about itself. Passed on to the nations of modern Europe by way of classical culture, Lucretia and the anonymous slave, Spartacus and slave revolt, and the issues they face, raise, and embody become crucial—if often obfuscated—figures in Western conceptualizations of nationhood during and after transatlantic expansion. They reappear throughout the modern era in a variety of declensions, in different guises, in narrative structures by which Western societies not only make sense of themselves as racial assemblages but also maintain the fictions of their imagined communities.

According to the Roman historian Livy, during Rome's early years as a monarchy, Sextus Tarquinius, son of Lucius Tarquinius Superbus, the king of Rome, assaulted Lucretia, the wife of the Roman nobleman Collatinus. She was known as a paragon of virtue, and that was precisely the reason the prince decided to go into her house and rape her. He blackmailed Lucretia into compliance: if she did not surrender to his lust, he would kill her, then kill a slave, put the slave's body in her bed, and claim that he had caught them in the act. His ability to write and control the narrative with which her body would be read is of the essence: Lucretia surrendered to him to save her husband's reputation, which would be forever tainted by allegations of her dalliance with a slave. Were Lucretia to choose death, Sextus would not have had her body, but he would have control over her story: "At this dreadful prospect," Livy tells us, "her resolute modesty was overcome, as if with force, by his victorious lust." Lucretia "chooses" rape because death would preclude her ability to tell her tale. The day after the rape, she denounces Sextus to her husband and other Roman aristocrats. She secures from them the promise that they will avenge her and declares, "Though I acquit myself of the sin, I do not absolve myself from punishment; not in time to come shall ever unchaste woman live through the example of Lucretia," before stabbing herself to death.[3] Even this death leaves her body and her story in the hands of others: they are appropriated by Collatinus's fellow nobleman Brutus, and the communal vow to avenge Sextus's wrongs becomes a solemn oath to overthrow the royal family. Brutus and his companions take Lucretia's body and story to the forum and muster a movement that leads to the birth of the Roman Republic.

Lucretia's story belongs to a corpus of Western texts pertaining to the birth of nations. It has been the subject of hundreds of paintings, legal disquisitions, plays, and poems. In the modern era it has been both a reference and a model narrative tying, in rather obvious ways, *patria* to patriarchy. Yet for all the emphasis in Western art on the rape of Lucretia, the Latin word from which this term derives evoked different crimes in Roman law. The original meaning of *raptus* was "forcible abduction"—as it happens, the very act by which "an obscure and lowly multitude . . . a miscellaneous rabble, without distinction of bond or free, eager for new conditions," gathered by Rome's founder, Romulus, first became a nation in abducting the daughters of the neighboring Sabine tribe.[4] With time the term evolved to cover aspects of sexual assault that had previously fallen under *stuprum*, a legal category that "referred at base to sex in which one person was used by the other to gratify his lust. . . . The archaic notion of *stuprum* seems to have been one of pollution, so that the victim, however innocent of causing the act, was nevertheless irreparably tainted."[5] Slaves, foreigners, and even citizens, male or female, in circumstances where their legal status as persons was challenged could only ever suffer *raptus*—a crime consisting essentially in taking away another man's property.[6] Only full-fledged Roman citizens could suffer *stuprum*, as one needed to have honor—a noble masculine quality extended to related female citizens—for it to possibly be tainted. Lucretia's suicide occurs at the gendered, social, and ethnic confluence of *stuprum* and *raptus*. She kills herself only after obtaining the promise that the men will bypass the law and avenge her. This oath implicitly threatens the very order of Man that made Lucretia's rape possible in the first place: to enact revenge on Sextus would be to recognize the worth of Lucretia's word over that of a powerful man. But they never do—the impetus of vengeance for Lucretia's violation is transcended into a political movement.

Lucretia's story offers a model of citizenship neither she nor any woman can fully access—except maybe posthumously—but that sets the standards for the Roman nation to come. The words Livy puts in her mouth—"not in time to come shall ever unchaste woman live through the example of Lucretia"—justify the sternness of laws punishing adultery in Livy's time rather than in Lucretia's.[7] In modern times Lucretia's gesture has gradually been interpreted as a bid for sexual and racial purity; still, the political radicalism of her speech and subsequent suicide remain. The rape of Lucretia "evidently defines women as property," but it also suggests "the expropriability of all property" and other earth-shattering possibilities.[8] Not only does it present righteous death as a way out of moral—and by extension sexual, gendered, and racial—servitude; it also justifies violent retribution for all forms of injustice. "What is it to be raped?" asks Peter French. "It is to be enslaved."[9] Sextus implied as much. In return Lucretia's response offers a logic of absolute equivalence apt to destroy the system. If a tyrant can lower a Roman woman to the level of a not-quite-human slave, is it not possible that all slaves could have been similarly wronged? If a citizen turned slave is warranted in seeking revenge on her oppressor, would not all slaves be equally justified in doing the same? Endlessly, Rome must find ways to say no.

A few years before Livy's birth, the former gladiator Spartacus threatened to topple the republic during the Third Servile War. Previous servile wars had taken place off the mainland, in Sicily. In 73 BCE Spartacus and a band of gladiators escaped bondage in Capua and took to the countryside, their group growing larger as each of their victories over Roman militias drew more escaped slaves, as well as "many of the herdsmen and shepherds of the region" (like those who had followed Romulus centuries before).[10] Romans grew anxious and sent professional legions led by Crassus after the resilient rebels, pushing them toward the southern coast to force a battle. The rebels made their last stand at the Battle of the Trenches. Spartacus was never found and is believed to have died in the battle. Six thousand of his companions "were captured and crucified along the whole road from Capua to Rome."[11] This gruesome punishment could not quite erase the fact that slaves had ridiculed Roman citizens.

Imagining a community necessarily implies imagining those who are not part of it; building a racial assemblage is as much about designating those who belong as it is about designating those who do not, and to conceive of themselves ethnic groups may crush the potential of others to constitute themselves into nations. Such destruction happened in the material world as in literature, in as extreme and ostentatious a manner as Crassus's lines of bodies. To think that slaves were "not content with merely having escaped, but were eager to take vengeance on their masters" seemingly baffled the antique historian Florus.[12] This proved that the rebels imagined themselves equal to their Roman foe. Worse yet, it suggested that such a thing might indeed be true. As Aristotle asserts, revenge "is the bond of union of the body politic," as men "demand that they shall be able to requite evil with evil—if they cannot, they feel they are in the position of slaves."[13] Slaves acting like full-fledged men threatened to dissolve the body politic as it was known. Romans hung thousands to rot on the sides of the Appian Way as a visual and material reminder of the hierarchy essential to Roman society: the enslaved were owned and disposable flesh unless deemed otherwise by their masters. Yet for lack of the revolt's alleged figurehead body to put on display, the mass crucifixion also tacitly recognized the revolt as a mass political movement.

The rebels' worth could not easily be diminished in the light of their incredible military accomplishments. The narrative solution was to separate Spartacus from his companions, thus allowing for the recognition of his extraordinariness without having to challenge the injustice of the social system that caused the revolt in the first place. Spartacus, and Spartacus only, is revealed as a citizen in disguise. About a century after the fact, the Greek-born Roman historian Plutarch thus claims Spartacus for civilization, asserting that he was a "Thracian of Nomadic stock, possessed not only of great courage and strength, but also in sagacity and culture superior to his fortune, and more Hellenic than Thracian."[14] In doing so he channels Aristotelian understandings about social hierarchy as an expression of nature: the Greek philosopher posits, "There are cases of people of whom some are freemen and the others slaves by nature."[15] Spartacus's alleged nobility accounts for his actions and, by extension, the entire revolt: no mere natural slave could have so threatened the glory of Rome. If freedom is what separates citizens from slaves, then the thought of freedom, and the struggle for it, must be productions of Man. Within these strictures the unthinkable (not-quite-humans demanding human status) can acceptably be thought.

Spartacus and his companions were trapped in hostile territory and seemingly met their demise after failing to achieve their plan of sailing away from the mainland. By comparison, slave revolts across the settler colonies of the early modern Atlantic world suggested the possibility of different outcomes in radically different circumstances: the slave uprising of 1526 at San Miguel de Guadalupe in Mexico and other successful Maroon communities in the first century of settlement, thwarting European efforts to destroy them, forced colonial authorities to recognize the rebels as distinct, autonomous sociopolitical entities and to treat them at times as independent nations.[16] By the mid-seventeenth century such communities peppered Spanish America, Brazil, Suriname, and the Caribbean—notably in the mountains of Jamaica, wrested from Spain by England in 1655. For the most part Maroons were formerly enslaved African people who had escaped European control and fled to remote locations, but their resilience, imperviousness to assault, and at times ability to force European authorities to acknowledge their political agency cast a shadow on the European settlement of the Americas. How long until they fought for more than merely being left alone? What might be done, what tale might be spun, to help preserve the order of Man?

Enter the black avenger.

INTRODUCTION

Be it ancient Rome or modern-day America,
you're either citizen or slave.

—Paul Beatty, *The Sellout*

BLACK SPARTACUS AND BLACK LUCRETIA
IN HOLLYWOOD, 2012

Few U.S. films generated more discussion in 2012 than Quentin Tarantino's *Django Unchained*. The tale of Django—an enslaved African American man setting out to free his wife, Broomhilda, from the clutches of evil slave owner Calvin Candie—was a finely honed entertainment machine sprinkled with Tarantino's usual mix of offensive talk, blood-drenched slapstick, virtuoso montage, and referential mise en abyme. Early conversations about the film predictably focused on its extensive use of racial slurs. Critics later moved on to debating the historical soundness of Tarantino's view of the slaveholding South in 1858, when the story takes place. Tarantino tends to be more faithful to his cinematic inspirations than to historical sources. *Django Unchained* self-consciously evokes the aesthetic and atmosphere of spaghetti Westerns and blaxploitation films: it notably borrows its title and title song from the Sergio Corbucci's 1966 spaghetti Western *Django* and, like the original and other Westerns, it "takes homicidal vengeance as the highest— if not the only—form of justice."[1] That's no surprise, from a director who has made no secret of his love for these genres throughout his career.

Yet, for A. O. Scott, Tarantino innovates with *Django Unchained*. His film "exposes and defies an ancient taboo.... Vengeance in the American imagination has been the virtually exclusive prerogative of white men." Vengeance in the American imagination is closely related to the Western genre;

it constitutes an essential element of what Robert Jewett and John Shelton Lawrence have dubbed the "American monomyth," in which "a community in a harmonious paradise is threatened by evil" and saved by a "selfless superhero" who "restores the community to its paradisal condition" before riding in the sunset.[2] Variations on this myth involving people of African descent have generally left them on the outskirts looking in. African Americans might be actors in classic American revenge stories, but, according to Scott, "The sanctification and romanticization of revenge have been central to the ideology of white supremacy." In presenting an African American in a role traditionally reserved for whites, Tarantino "expose[d] and defie[d] an ancient taboo" concerning revenge as much as the motive for revenge: the subjection and sexual abuse of Django's wife, Broomhilda, a form of gendered, racialized terror that has also long undergirded reflections on freedom in the Atlantic world. Audiences cheering Django could feel they were supporting the righteous righting of wrongs history so sorely lacks. Why, oh why, did slaves not fight back? This is the question Tarantino's evil planter Calvin Candie asks in a tense dinner scene. Candie reminisces about "growing up the son of a huge plantation owner in Mississippi . . . surrounded by black faces." This entire time, he asserts, he had only one question in mind regarding the slaves around him: "Why don't they kill us?" Old Ben, the slave, shaved Candie's father on the porch for decades but never bothered to slash his throat.

The scene will seem familiar: it mirrors an iconic moment in Herman Melville's "Benito Cereno," a novella published in *Putnam's* in 1855, a few years before *Django Unchained*'s fictional present. As to Candie's question, the answer, quickly: in the real world, slaves did kill, time and again. In fiction they might, but only in very specific circumstances. In any case Candie does not distinguish between fact and fiction and appears to know precious little about both. He thinks most slaves are naturally submissive. He has phrenology—the racist pseudoscience that pretends to read the characteristics of people in the shapes of their skulls—on his side and demonstrates on the bleached skull of old Ben, the slave who raised his father and grandfather before him and served as their manservant. Like all black people, Candie argues, Ben has three dimples in an area of his skull conveniently associated with servility. Candie's belief in phrenology and ignorance of history go hand in hand with his theory about slave revolt: "There is a level above bright, above talented, above loyal that a nigger can aspire to. Say, one nigger that just pops up in ten thousand: the exceptional nigger." "Bright boy," he adds, pointing at Django, "you are that one in ten thousand."

Django is a familiar anomaly: though he must be spoken of in tones of wonder and disbelief, the extraordinary black leader who would lead his fellow enslaved to deliver righteous retribution on their white oppressors has been a fixture of Western culture for the best of three hundred years. The second edition of French philosophe and political economist Guillaume-Thomas Raynal's gigantic, best-selling study of European colonization, *Histoire philosophique et politique des établissements et du commerce des Européens dans les deux Indes* (1774) thus asks virtually the same question as Candie, albeit in a distinctively more anxious tone: "Where is this great man to be found, whom nature, perhaps, owes to the honour of the human species? Where is this new Spartacus, who will not find a Crassus? Then will the *black code* be no more; and the *white code* will be a dreadful one, if the conqueror only regards the right of reprisals."[3] The Western world heard echoes of Raynal's words in every slave revolt, but after the French colony of Saint-Domingue erupted in a slave revolt in 1791, it "recognized" the new Spartacus in the insurgents' most prominent leader, Toussaint Louverture. These are but two salient points in the long—if systematically obfuscated—history of an essential trope of Atlantic modernity. This trope is the topic of my book.

The American monomyth elaborates on an older "race plot of freedom," originated in revolutionary-era Great Britain: the "Anglo-Protestant liberty story," rooted in depictions of the English Revolution that present "freedom as a racial inheritance and . . . revolution as racial renewal." According to Laura Doyle, in this narrative developed throughout the modern era, freedom is equated with whiteness.[4] An essential node in the genealogy of the race plot of freedom is Aphra Behn's 1688 novella *Oroonoko* and its eponymous hero, an enslaved African prince who leads an ill-fated slave revolt in the Americas. The novella has long been seen as a crucial point in modern Western treatments of race, perhaps to a fault. It remains useful for the way it connects a long tradition of reflection on freedom and citizenship rooted in classical culture to the new conditions and circumstances of the Atlantic slave trade.

For all its apparent novelty, the black avenger narrative draws on classical literary motifs attached to the subject of national belonging, oppression, vengeance, justice, race, and gender. The black avenger himself draws essential characteristics from the figure of Spartacus, leader of slaves who revolted and almost overthrew the Roman Republic not long before it became an empire. By this lineage the black avenger trope systematically expresses a critique of the terms of national self-definition, but also reflects on matters of racial and social hierarchy, justice, and revolution in an expanding Western world. In its multiple versions—much like original tellings of Spartacus's story—it echoes the ancient Roman story of the rape of Lucretia and through it rehearses conversations and anxieties concerning what Alexander Weheliye has called "racial assemblages"—the gendered, ethnic, social terms by which nations define themselves against outsiders.[5]

Audre Lorde famously declared that "the master's tools will never dismantle the master's house": the house that the slave trade built in the West rests in no small part on literary, narrative foundations.[6] In an unforgettable scene in Stanley Kubrick's 1960 film *Spartacus*, when given the chance to be spared if they identify "the body or the living person of the slave called Spartacus," his defeated companions stand each in turn to declare "I am Spartacus," dissolving the individual hero into the collective. This vision of the gladiator at the service of the people owes much to Marxist analysis and has become "arguably the most pervasive in the modern world," but for most of its existence as a modern Western icon, Spartacus served exactly the opposite purpose as the individual hiding collective action.[7] Antique figures linger in the bones of this narrative construct, but its shape was molded in the crucible of the Black Atlantic. The black avenger trope, used as it has long been in the service of resistance to racist oppression, always simultaneously contributed to maintain this system by promoting extraordinary, individual black heroism to the detriment of collective agency.

The core of this study is the Haitian Revolution, arguably the most formidable achievement of black collective agency in the Americas: the black avenger trope was designed in preparation for such an event, and ever since it occurred has played a central role in what Michel-Rolph Trouillot has called the "silencing" of the revolution's history. The link between Raynal's text and characterizations of Louverture has been the topic of many studies: mine is the first to explore in detail exactly how the identification of the textual figure to the man was carefully constructed in specific political circumstances the trope itself was designed to blur. The black avenger trope allows for the simplification of politics through race: this treatment, applied to Louverture, impacted portrayal and understanding of black politics throughout the Atlantic world. Organized in concentric layers around this beating heart, my book traces the genealogy of the trope from the early modern period to the turn of the twentieth century, from Europe to the Americas, and exposes its impact on Western conceptualizations of race, racism, and resistance.

Part of the novelty of the black avenger trope is precisely how this narrative downplays its cultural origins to emphasize the alleged newness of the cultural clash on which it focuses. African characters were not unheard of in European drama and fiction of the late seventeenth century. Behn's creation breathed into a stock character inherited from the revenge tragedy tradition the novelty of modern racial relations as revealed in such brutal, head-on encounters as portrayed in the novel. Following in the path of their early incarnation, Prince Oroonoko, later black avengers appear, time and again, at the crossroads of African (and the African diasporic) cultures and Western culture, always extraordinary, always implied as new. The erasure of precedents is central to the black avenger tradition. It operates through, and is most obvious in, the treatment of female characters. Thus, Oroonoko's wife, Imoinda—in many ways the heart of Behn's novella, the reason for Oroonoko's every action—mostly lurks in the background, twice removed, her acts and words always reported through one or two intermediary voices. In Thomas Southerne's 1696 stage adaptation, she is quite literally erased as a black woman, as she turns white. The silencing of Imoinda is performed by the female voice of Behn's narrator, which covers some of its effects. Behn's narrative allows for an assertion of citizenship by a Western female voice at the expense of black voices, masculine and feminine. Behn's narrator becomes a white American by contrasting herself with both Imoinda and Oroonoko. She also does this by reversing a pattern of racial and national definition as old as the tale of Lucretia's rape.

Rape was a common weapon of the regime of terror Django and Broomhilda attempt to escape; it hovers over the entire film, but it never lands. Unlike most female characters in Tarantino's films, Broomhilda in *Django Unchained* is quasi-silent. Echoing in this literal silence is what the film figuratively passes under silence, although it is essential to the plot: the sexual abuse Broomhilda suffers at the hands of slaveholders. This is a peculiar choice on Tarantino's part, all the more so that the issue featured prominently in *Django Unchained*'s original script. In fact, it was presented there in such fashion that when the script was leaked, many took exception to the graphic treatment it promised, as it called for several graphic instances of sexual abuse all perpetrated on Broomhilda.[8] Rape is almost entirely erased in the final version of the film. When indirectly evoked, as when Candie gleefully mentions Broomhilda's role as a "comfort girl," the camera zooms in on Django. We see how he copes with violence wrought on Broomhilda. She is a perpetually passive recipient, a pretext for his revenge, an object lesson in Django's education in becoming a model westerner. For him to reach this status demands literacy in, mastery of, and compliance with Western narratives of agency, age-old formulas by which his existence can be deemed (narratively) acceptable. It demands he become a black avenger, following a scenario as old as Atlantic slavery, predicated on the silencing of black women.

Laura Doyle asserts that the Anglo-Saxon myth of freedom on display in *Oroonoko* was the model by which later American myths of freedom—including African American variations—were developed.[9] I argue that, in fact, this myth was constructed as a prevention, a literary exorcism of sorts against the threat of a black nation. The narrator's citizenship comes about only to cancel out the possibility of citizenship for the enslaved, taking all of the novel's political ground and leaving none of it to the population whose political agency would most profoundly threaten the new American order. From *Oroonoko* on, the silencing of the enslaved and their political agency is enabled specifically through the silencing of enslaved women. Behn's narrator raises Oroonoko to a heroic pedestal and simultaneously unmans him, a piece of theater that deflects attention from a foundational phenomenon—the silencing of Imoinda. If this book offers a theatrical genealogy for the black avenger, it cannot do so without simultaneously excavating how the pattern of silencing and erasing black femininity was built and normalized over four centuries in the crucible of the Atlantic.

BACKGROUND

The black avenger first appeared under this moniker in studies in the early 1970s, the last time the notion of a new black American nation was discussed as a viable—if fantastical—political possibility; the term fit many contemporary protagonists in literature and film channeling (or at the very least paying lip service to) the concerns and attitudes of the Black Power movement.[10] Interest in these "new" characters can also be tied to the militant introduction of black studies on American campuses around the same period.[11] Catherine Juanita Starke notably exposed the black avenger figure as one of the standout representations of blackness in American and African American literature, offering a genealogy of black avengers with roots extending to the two protagonists of Sutton Griggs's *Imperium in Imperio* (1899).[12] Jerry H. Bryant's *Victims and Heroes* (1997) extended this genealogy to the character of Picquilo in William Wells Brown's *Clotel* (1853), and, more recently, Céleste-Marie Bernier's *Characters of Blood* (2012) explored a "cultural tradition of black male and female heroism both within and beyond the United States."[13] Bernier's genealogy, though it opens up to the wider Black Atlantic, nevertheless remains very U.S.-centric.

In turn, studies on black presence in early modern English drama such as Anthony G. Barthelemy's *Black Face, Maligned Race* (1987) or Derek

Hughes's *Versions of Blackness* (2007) demonstrate that the genealogy of black avengers must be extended across the Atlantic. Hazel Waters's *Racism on the Victorian Stage* (2007) notably focuses on the black avenger tradition in British culture. Yet, while Waters does reveal the close ties binding nineteenth-century British theater to American culture and politics, her conclusions are also constrained by their historical and cultural focus.[14] This issue was recently addressed in convincing fashion by Elizabeth Maddock Dillon's *New World Drama: The Performative Commons in the Atlantic World* (2014) and Jenna Gibbs's *Performing the Temple of Liberty: Slavery, Theater and Popular Culture in London and Philadelphia, 1760–1850* (2014). Both studies demonstrate how the opinions and concerns transpiring in theatrical performances circulated far and wide in the English-speaking Atlantic and how they contributed to building a complex network of self-understanding and self-representation. For Dillon, theatrical performances and spaces around the Anglophone Atlantic world saw the development of "performative commons" engaging the plays themselves, the actors performing them, and their audiences, articulating together "emergent possibilities and foreclosures of popular sovereignty by means of embodiment and representation, and in the promiscuous interaction between the two," in and between the great cities of Great Britain and its U.S. empire: London, Kingston, Charleston, or Philadelphia.[15] Gibbs's focus on the figure of the Genius of America and her argument—"theater did not simply reflect political events and debates; rather, it played an active role in steering them and shaping how they were understood"—are directly relevant to my work.[16]

Studies on such scale have to find their borders, and often these have followed national or linguistic lines, both in design and in inspiration. Although scholars take for granted that intertextuality prior to the nineteenth century was routinely—and, one might argue, necessarily—multilingual, following these patterns in practice can be very difficult. Léon-François Hoffmann's survey *Le Nègre romantique: Personnage littéraire et obsession collective* (1973) has seldom been considered outside of French studies, where its influence can be felt in such recent work such as *Colonialism, Race, and the French Imagination* (2009), in which Pratima Prasad discusses the influence of French Romantic fiction on discourses of race. My book shares with these studies a sense of the essential role played by literature and literary tropes in spreading racialized notions of citizenship and nationhood, yet I believe that a clearer assessment of the impact of racial thinking in the modern era demands that these concepts be considered in wider frames. There are undeniably unique elements to French, English, or U.S. American approaches to citizenship and race—and to such approaches within the groups of the African diaspora and between them—but they have developed in constant conversation to one another. Race as a global concept circulated by way of such literary tropes as the black avenger, in translation, exchange, and—to use Brent Hayes Edwards's cross-linguistic terminology—*décalage*, working around "the kernel of precisely that which cannot be transferred or exchanged, the received biases that refuse to pass over when one crosses the water."[17] The necessity and benefit of looking across linguistic lines appear clearly in *Tropics of Haiti* (2015), Marlene L. Daut's study of the intertwined histories of race and of representations of the Haitian Revolution in the Atlantic world. My book is in direct conversation with Daut's, which explores what she calls the "mulatto/a vengeance narrative" of the Haitian Revolution. I discuss further how the black avenger predated the mulatto vengeance narrative, this scenario rising to match developments in racial thinking stemming from a specific Caribbean context before spreading to the broader Western world.

I am especially interested in the constitution of this black avenger concept and in its transnational existence and dynamics: it is a product of the acceleration of the Atlantic slave trade in the late seventeenth century, and as such it has developed in the cultures of the two main European actors in this acceleration, Great Britain and France, and in their colonial extensions in the Americas that would become the two first independent countries there, the United States and Haiti. I contend that, in these cultures, black avenger narratives have systematically been used to reflect on the slave trade, but also more subtly to imagine national singularities in the light of the slave trade. As Great Britain, France, the United States, and Haiti faced crises of self-definition, authors in each country summoned the literary trope of the black avenger as either a model or a foil to design national visions and project them into the world. In these processes, even as black avenger narratives expressed national anxieties toward the potential collapse of slave colonies, they also contributed to deny, stifle, and obfuscate the portrayal of black collective agency and its very reality.

The black avenger trope has been a transnational print phenomenon with ramifications in historical writing, newswriting, and philosophy. The Atlantic slave trade was a global system of exchange with local specificities; black avenger texts in turn were produced in historical and geographic circumstances dependent on the slave trade—but were never bound to them. The black avenger trope is a tree with distinct branches: its trunk is the fact of the Atlantic slave trade and slaveholding societies' anxieties in the face of potential revolt. As it grew, local and individual particularities impacted related but distinct expressions of a similar trope, each branch in turn potentially intertwined with the next and growing new shoots throughout the years. In choosing certain texts and events to focus on, I have ignored or missed others. I do not claim this to be an exhaustive study. *The Black Avenger in Atlantic Culture* follows a path along early English and French engagements with the trope in the seventeenth and eighteenth century, then from the event horizon of the Haitian Revolution bifurcates into U.S. variations, studying important articulations of the traditions, moments, places, and texts in which the figure shifted significantly.

Chapter 1 focuses on the transition from the black villains of English revenge drama by way of heroic romance to Aphra Behn's protoavenger *Oroonoko*, in the context of France's and England's expansion into the Americas and increasing involvement in the Atlantic slave trade at the end of the sixteenth century. Characters of revenge drama—most notably for our purpose here, black villains—were instrumental to the portrayal and expression of political dissent in England and budding notions of what defined the English national spirit in the revolutionary period. Before writing *Oroonoko*, Behn adapted the 1601 revenge drama *Lust's Dominion* into *Abdelazer*, whose eponymous black villain in turn inspired crucial elements of *Oroonoko*. The other reigning literary genre of the time, the French-inspired heroic romance, also influenced the making of the black avenger trope through conventions of characterization deeply marked by the concerns of courtly literature. The chapter highlights *Oroonoko*'s overlooked conversation with Roger Boyle's *Parthenissa* (1676), a successful English heroic romance and perhaps the earliest treatment of Spartacus in the modern period. Behn's hero channels the antique slave rebel, but the novella at large also rearranges and adapts elements of the story of Lucretia, the essential myth of nation making, to foreclose the possibility of a black American nation. The silent Imoinda is an anti-Lucretia, and Oroonoko a Spartacus caught alive and executed. His person strips the revolt of collective agency, and his death symbolically dismembers the black body politic in the Americas, whose purpose becomes to mark the boundaries of a white colony.

Chapter 2 looks at black avengers in the eighteenth century, at a time when Great Britain and France were the two most prominent powers in the Atlantic world and were both engaged in debates over national identity in a widespread, colonial world. France and Great Britain defined themselves against each other and in relation to colonials. Authors from both countries and their colonies were in constant conversation, notably over the seemingly unavoidable prospect of major (and successful) slave revolts. English national sentiment, as expressed in drama that revisited episodes of Roman history (notably the aftermath of Lucretia's death), inspired such French authors as Voltaire to ponder the characteristics of Frenchness in the light of classical history and increasingly influential notions of racial and national belonging. These efforts coincided with a trend in literary black avenger narratives—including rival adaptations of *Oroonoko* in English and French—that purported to measure national worth against the practice of slavery. Rising in the late eighteenth century, abolitionism both drew on and further inspired literary treatments of slavery in the Americas. I also explore the introduction of the figure of Spartacus in Bernard-Joseph Saurin's popular play *Spartacus* (1760) into France's rising sense of national spirit at the dawn of the French Revolution and the rise of the motif of slave revolts in the abolitionist poetry of Thomas Chatterton and Edward Rushton. Their texts portray and lament the violence wrought on the enslaved and envisaged black avengers' reaction to the sexual abuse of their companions, but they struggle to imagine a black politics in response.

In chapter 3 I explore the ways in which the main actors of the Haitian Revolution, a complex conflict that opposed former slaves and free people of color to Spanish, French, and English colonial forces between 1791 and 1804, engaged with the figure of the black avenger in forms of print discourse directed toward the French revolutionary public and the global stage. At the heart of my chapter is the 1796 speech in which French general Etienne Laveaux allegedly dubbed Toussaint Louverture the "black Spartacus," inspired by a figure famously developed in Louis-Sébastien Mercier's *L'An 2440, rêve s'il en fût jamais* (1770) and Abbé Raynal's *Histoire philosophique et politique des établissements et du commerce des Européens dans les deux Indes* (1774). My close study of the records of the "Affair of 30 Ventôse Year IV," the coup attempt that led to Laveaux's speech, shows for the first time how the famous and traditionally unquestioned phrase was carefully crafted to serve in the war of words of the revolution. This chapter reveals how local actors Etienne Laveaux, Toussaint Louverture, and later the first ruler of independent Haiti, Jean-Jacques Dessalines, made use of essentialist racial arguments tied to the black Spartacus figure to attract European support—a political act that ironically contributed to giving credibility to a literary trope that channels and constrains black political agency into a romantic hero figure.

In chapter 4 I look at the impact of the black avenger trope on U.S. racial politics in the nineteenth century before the Civil War, beginning with David Walker's *An Appeal to the Coloured Citizens of the World* (1830), which introduced and adapted the black avenger trope for American public discourse. Walker's effort serves as a counterpoint to the use of the trope in antebellum abolitionist texts written by white authors in which they present themselves as discoverers of the extraordinary Haitian Revolution and necessary translators of its significance for the broader American public. I focus on Martin R. Delany's effort to claim it for African Americans in *Blake* (1859–1861), where Delany works to bend heroic representation to serve the demands of collective political action. Delany recognizes race-based nationalism as a function of the black avenger tale and is interested in designing a U.S. American version of a tale then attached to Haiti. In this innovative novel, Delany also attempts to adapt the Lucretia myth to African American experiences of slavery.

U.S.-centric developments of the black avenger trope at the turn of the twentieth century occupy chapter 5. With the normalization of white supremacist terror in the post-Reconstruction South and the rise of Jim Crow, at a time when the United States launched into colonial expansion in the Pacific and the Caribbean, African American authors strove to imagine a place for African Americans in a white supremacist republic. Sutton Griggs's *Imperium in Imperio* explores alternative approaches to this conundrum, transposing schemes for the creation of a black nation entirely within the United States, geographically and politically. Griggs's novel ends in abeyance, trapped in its equation of black agency with black masculinity. Looking at Charles Chesnutt's rejection, in *The Marrow of Tradition* (1901), of the very idea of a black American nation outside the boundaries of the United States, the chapter ends with Robert Lewis Waring's little discussed novel, *As We See It* (1910). Waring adopts a rugged, masculine individualism notably popularized in the Western genre and declares support of an ideal, elitist United States, in which deserving African Americans would be given a chance to thrive like their white peers, in separation and equality. Waring's novel is a declaration of U.S. patriotism. His main character's bid to citizenship rests on the silencing of black women and on accepting conventions that effectively make him an honorary white man.

In his review of *Django Unchained*, A. O. Scott asserts that "the idea that regenerative violence could be visited by black against white instead of the reverse . . . has been almost literally unthinkable."[18] Though it is likely an accident, Scott's words significantly echo the phrase Haitian scholar Michel-Rolph Trouillot uses to describe a pattern of historiographic obfuscation in the reception, portrayal, and understanding of the Haitian Revolution in the white West. According to Trouillot, the complex events that made the Haitian Revolution "were unthinkable facts in the framework of Western thought . . . made to enter into narratives that made sense to a majority of Western observers and readers." He is concerned with unraveling the complex legends of the revolution itself and offers a logic that might account for the ways in which the Haitian Revolution was made to be unthinkable even as it was occurring. As he further notes, "The successive events within that chain [which constitutes the Haitian Revolution] were systematically recast by many participants and observers to fit a world of possibilities. That is, they were made to enter into narratives that made sense to a majority of Western observers and readers": framed, boxed, and stored away on the shelves of exotic history so efficiently as to make the world forget, for ages, that this, Sire, was not a revolt, but the revolution that most challenged the political and moral conventions of its time.[19] In the light of Trouillot's analysis, Scott's statement is revealed as the byproduct of a long cultural tradition by which black retributive violence and the politics that underlay it were systematically undermined in incredulous representations. These narratives remain active, framing not only the Haitian Revolution itself but also broader understandings of black collective agency. Some time ago, in conversation with a friend and colleague, this not-so-innocent question came up: How is it that an event as crucial to Western modernity as the Haitian Revolution keeps getting "discovered"?[20]

Let us find out.

CHAPTER I

STILLBIRTH OF A NATION

Roots of the Black Avenger

PETTING THE FAMILIAR

A gallant African prince is treacherously kidnapped by European slave traders to whom he had previously sold slaves and brought to Suriname, where he miraculously rejoins the lover he thought dead. The governor of the colony lusts after the beautiful woman, now pregnant with the prince's child, and the couple realize that slavery is a constant threat on their future family's welfare. The prince rouses the slave population into revolt, but they quickly surrender to the European colonists, and he is caught and whipped. Rather than suffer further humiliation and see his wife and future child at the mercy of the ruthless slavers of the Americas, the prince resolves to kill his wife, take revenge, and kill himself. Paralyzed by grief after killing her, he is captured again and gruesomely executed.

The plot of Aphra Behn's 1688 novella *Oroonoko; or, The Royal Slave* has become such a staple of literary studies that a willfully bare summary such as this cannot obfuscate it as the source. The text itself has been presented as a turning point in literary history, a transition between Old and New Romance; the link between romance and the novel; or, indeed, the first modern English—and possibly American—novel.[1] Behn's self-inscription in the text has generated its own tradition of scholarly engagement. Attempts at separating the true, the false, and the embellishments in between still occupy readers: scholars study the details of the book against averred historical facts about Behn's life and her potential stay in Suriname.[2] *Oroonoko* has also been analyzed as an early example of militant feminist art, the blurring of fact and fiction at play in the text participating in a broader engagement with issues of female agency, autonomy, and independence at the confluence of private and public life.[3] Finally, it is often seen as originating an ambivalent "paradigm of slavery" by straddling antislavery sentiments and loyalty to the plantocracy, echoes of which carried into eighteenth-century abolitionism notably by way of a theatrical tradition derived from the text.[4] Two decades ago Srinivas Aravamudan warned against echoing in criticism the "logic of pethood" at work in Behn's text, which he analyzed as an "authorial act of self-portraiture." What African servants were to aristocrats of the seventeenth century, "flesh-and-blood status symbols," *Oroonoko* was to Aphra Behn: an exotic accessory of charming shape, a commodity, evidence of economic and cultural wealth, and a source of entertainment rendered in literary form.[5] When rubbed the right way, *Oroonoko* still proves friendly to a variety of theoretical arguments that single it out as both expression and originator of new trends paralleling in literature the profound social, economic, and political changes felt in late seventeenth-century England. The risk, then, is to reproduce in criticism Behn's commodification of her own subject—the cameoed memory of Behn's much admired pet *Oroonoko* giving birth to myriad pet theories.

Yet I want to argue, tongue firmly in cheek, that, rather than a pet, Oroonoko might be better thought of as a familiar, the fabled evil companions of witches taking animal or human shape. A specificity of English visions of witchcraft, familiars served as "the witch's personal helper," notably providing "demonic aid to help a witch take revenge."[6] *Oroonoko* is not just a pet: it wreaks havoc in the service of the author and, beyond her, Englishness as a whiteness. Behn suffered as a woman writer routinely vilified by jealous peers and foes for her independence, her success, and also her politics—not as a literal witch but certainly a figurative one. *Oroonoko* is her "familiar" in that, as "Behn's reclamation of her eyes and ears, her witnessing and her voice," the novella allowed for "the avenging of the fifteen-year-old silenced subject, her life and politics in retrospect." Moira Ferguson points out the problematic fact that objectifying Africans is a process central to this personal vengeance, but she does little more than point to the presence of revenge in the text itself.[7] Yet the pattern in which vengeance appears in *Oroonoko* is essential to her point and crucial to mine. Oroonoko clamors for retribution from the novella's early pages, when he promises to "revenge . . . with the certain Death of him that first enters," but does not act on his threat.[8] The prince's revenge is systematically deflected or deferred, most glaringly when Oroonoko kills Imoinda as the first step of a revenge plan he finds himself unable to complete in his grief. This may explain why scholarship on *Oroonoko* has generally ignored the theme of vengeance in the novella.

I argue here that vengeance is an important element of the text, not only for the way it ties *Oroonoko* to English literary tradition but also for the framing it provides on issues of race constitutive of modern notions of English-ness and whiteness. Behn's "drawing on race membership to authorize her freedom to write" depends on simultaneously dangling the threat of alterna-tive racial assemblages and thwarting it.[9] The prince is designed to be threat-ening: Behn characterizes him with the vocabulary of gender, class, race, and retribution made common in England by a century of revenge drama. She taints her royal slave with attributes this chapter traces in villainous Moors of the Elizabethan stage such as Eleazar in Thomas Dekker's 1601 *Lust's Do-minion* or Behn's Abdelazer in her 1676 revision of Dekker's play, *Abdelazer or the Moor's Revenge*, dangling the terrifying possibility of black autonomy in America. Oroonoko delivers only off the page and in the service of the author, as an abstracted literary thrill conceptualizing slave revolt as racial failure, the stillbirth of a black American nation. In turn, this failure is ex-pressed in terms owing to heroic romance and beyond it to classical culture. Behn rewrites the foundational Lucretia tale not for a new American Rome but to contrast it to the story of Spartacus as modernized in Roger Boyle's *Parthenissa* (1676), a text never evoked in relation to the novella, but that, I argue, was a crucial influence on it. Behn's treatment of slave revolt strips it of political intent and naturalizes it. The narrator's access to white citizen-ship is dependent on her black protagonists' incapacity to follow the narra-tive path toward the nation modeled in the Lucretia myth. To that end, she undoes it, putting revolt before rape, merging revenge and suicide, and eras-ing nation making in the process. Seen in the light of the literary treatments of black resistance that preceded and inspired it, *Oroonoko* reveals itself as a utilitarian exposé on the political uses of the metatheater of race.

REVENGERS OF OLD

Aphra Behn did not write *Oroonoko* as a play, yet her command of the stage certainly contributed to its novelty.[10] Notably, the "new holistic pattern of narrative" on which the novel relies was first developed by Behn at the crossroads of dramaturgy and fiction writing; "her main claim to histori-cal significance . . . is to having refined the *dramatic scene* for the purpose of narrative."[11] When it comes to relations with the theater, *Oroonoko* has been studied mostly in the light of heroic drama; however, reading it in the light of the revenge drama tradition clarifies how it indirectly engages with the po-litical and cultural debates of its time.

Revenge has been a central element of tragedy since its birth in antiquity. Tragedy is concerned with portraying societal crises, moments when a com-munity's social and moral values are challenged, generally from within. Justice does not eradicate revenge so much as it *"rationalizes* revenge and succeeds in limiting and isolating its effects in accordance with social demands."[12] Like revenge, justice is reactive and punitive, based on a notion of fit in which an original act of violence is balanced by a response adequate enough to deter private revenge. Yet revenge never disappears. Ancient Greece saw revenge as "order itself in its original and vital form."[13] For René Girard, Greek tragedy betrays a fundamental fear not of violence itself but of the absolute, millennial equivalence violence promises. Tragedy yearns for a return to hierarchical order. By contrast, on the modern English stage tyranny was inseparable from the hierarchies of social inequity. Elizabethan audiences may well have received stage revenge with a "tacit disapproval" based on Christian values; it is likely they simultaneously saw how it responded to injustice based on economic disparity.[14] In the plays they saw, as in the world they knew, "It was the rich whose guilt went unpunished, the poor who were harshly penalized."[15] That the revengers are generally members of the elite as well is tempered by the fact that they also tend to resort to revenge when they are at their lowest: disgraced, forsaken, banished, wronged, or harmed. Revenge plays on individual trajectories, but because characters are generally crowned heads, high officers, magistrates, and courtiers, their deeds necessarily have political dimensions that often spread the cycle of violence beyond the scale of immediate, personal feuds into broader conflicts: wars, coups, and revolutions. Villains and heroes tend to be easily distinguished, but no one is safe from the pollution of retaliatory violence. Revenge is both literal and symbolic mirroring, an enforcement of the very reciprocity Girard considers a threat to social order.

This pattern is made excruciatingly clear in Shakespeare's *Tragedy of Titus Andronicus* (1593), notably, where the titular Roman general executes Goth queen Tamora's eldest son, triggering a cycle of revenge in the process. He does so by ignoring Tamora's plea, expressed in the language of reciprocity: "And if thy sons were ever dear to thee, / O, think my son to be as dear to me!" she cries out, to no avail, before deciding on revenge.[16] Tamora, her sons, and her lover, Aaron the Moor, are the villains of the play, barbarians in the heart of civilization. Yet it is Titus's deed that initiates the cycle of violence, and later, as he is faced with a slew of personal injustices, Titus eventually resorts to revenge himself. Wrongs suffered here are not righted within the purview of the law, and personal feuds spill out into all-out war: ironically, it is at the head of a Goth army that Titus's son marches on Rome. The equality of peoples denied throughout the play obtains here, for a time, in the whirlwind of revenge. Romans and Goths find common ground in their hatred for Aaron the Moor.

Aaron was one among the Moors that took to the English stage in the late sixteenth century, in the wake of contemporary Barbary states disputes in which European rulers, including Elizabeth I, also got involved. Thus George Peele's "barbarous Moore, / the Negro" Muly Mahamet in *The Battle of Alcazar* (1594) was a fictionalized version of Abdallah Mohammed, sultan of Morocco; and Thomas Dekker's Eleazar in *Lust's Dominion* (1601)—in the play the son of the former king of Fez, Catholic convert, and grandee of Spain—evokes Abdallah Mohammed's son Muley Xeque, who after his father's defeat at the Battle of Alcazar lived for some time at the court of King Philip II of Spain, converted to Catholicism, and was renamed Don Felipe. The real Xeque was notoriously on friendly terms with King Philip II of Spain and well integrated in Spanish society, but Dekker's Eleazar is a poisonous snake in the bosom of Spain, characterized by utter and unrequited evil.[17] Like Shakespeare's Aaron and later stage Moors after him, he is a stranger in a foreign land, isolated even as he shows his ability to blend.

The black villains of English revenge tragedy are outsiders within the societies in which they live. Though they may have the support of other villains or lovers and friends unable to see them as evil, by the time it comes their unrepentant death bothers no one and marks a return, if not to normal, at least to order, as the final verses of *Titus Andronicus* make clear:

> See justice done on Aaron, that damn'd Moor,
> By whom our heavy haps had their beginning:
> Then, afterwards, to order well the state,
> That like events may ne'er it ruinate.[18]

They are the perfect embodiment of the human scapegoats described by Girard. Their sacrifice puts an end to the cycle of revenge and gives society an opportunity to recover from crisis. However, the motives they offer to justify the violence they unleash on others are often undistinguishable with those given by heroic characters. They echo arguments lamenting society's unjust hierarchical system made by heroes in plays where revenge is "a strategy of survival resorted to by the alienated and dispossessed." The rhetoric of revengers both echoed and inspired an increasing number of thinkers who, from the Tudor era on, developed theories that "in the absence of peaceable means of redress ... advocated violent overthrow of rulers."[19] Contrary to antique plays, modern English revenge tragedies challenge more than they support social conventions and hierarchy. English revenge plays pave the way for the wave of discontent and the political and religious upheaval that eventually swelled into the English Revolution. The rhetoric of revenge notably reached a peak in the pamphlets and broadsides published in the period before the trial and execution of the "tyrant" Charles I in 1649.[20] At the forefront of the "decentered malcontents" of early seventeenth-century drama, we find Moor archvillains.

In their ambiguous status as both anomaly and familiar presence, early Moors of the English stage testify to how undefined the borders of English cultural, political, and racial life remained at the turn of the seventeenth century. Moors—Africans or Arabs, Muslim or not, black or not—provided a handy canvas on which to "expose cultural identity and cross-cultural exchange as a dynamic work in progress, always contingent on the unpredictable intricacies of circumstance and always therefore vulnerable to change, a thing perpetually in the making and never quite the thing made."[21] Indeed, the black bodies increasingly visible in the streets of London throughout the sixteenth century also influenced anxieties of identity related to budding notions of Englishness.[22] In 1596 Queen Elizabeth I produced an "Edict Arranging for the Expulsion from England of Negroes and Blackamoors," followed in 1601 by a proclamation in which she granted the merchant Casper van Senden the right to transport "Negars and blackamoores" living in England to sell them in Spain and Portugal. The language of her letters displayed "a discontinuous but persistent scripting of [the black person] as an already formed illicit pathology marked for the outside of English cultural and political life," and her decisions suggested a broader inclination "toward discrimination against blacks as a racial group."[23] Racial thinking in the modern era brewed through contact in Europe as much as in Africa and America. In this sense, black presence in European culture must also be thought of as reflecting local occurrences, however anomalous.

Common Africans are likely to have had close influence on early modern English drama: in London they tended to live in "neighborhoods dominated by the theatre industry," near the playhouses and the homes of playwrights and actors of the time.[24] Most of them were pariahs in the lower rungs of English society—many arrived in England as the servants of foreign traders and noblemen—and they might have struggled to see much of themselves in the aristocratic, outsized outsiders of the English stage. The discrepancy between the Moor onstage and the Moors of England (and possibly in the audience) is essential to the parallel racializations of Englishmen and Africans in the seventeenth century. *Lust's Dominion* is a case in point.

LUST'S DOMINION

Eleazar has lived at the court of the Spanish king Philip since the latter defeated and killed his father, the king of Fez, years before. Married to the noblewoman Maria, sister of Hortenzo, he has converted to Christianity and served Spain in its wars. Yet Eleazar harbors the secret ambition of avenging his father and ruining Spain. He has been having an affair with the queen, who poisoned her husband to keep Eleazar's affection. The rest of the play sees Eleazar scheming to take the throne from Prince—now King—Fernando and his brother, Prince Philip. With the help of the queen mother, Eleazar successfully dispatches his wife, Maria, and King Fernando. But Eleazar's ambition is his downfall: although he could become king consort, he rejects the queen and attempts to seduce Princess Isabella, who is promised to Eleazar's brother-in-law, Hortenzo. With "the *Moors* Habits on" and "with the oil of hell" on their faces, Hortenzo and Philip meet Eleazar and kill him as he is clapped and manacled in an "Iron engine."[25] Philip claims the Spanish throne.

Assessing villain tragedy, Ashley Thorndike declares that "all or nearly all of the active characters [of villain tragedy] are black with sin."[26] Thorndike speaks metaphorically, and so do characters throughout *Lust's Dominion*, as when Eleazar describes two friars he bribes to do his bidding and declares that "sin shines clear, / When her black face Religions masque doth wear" (2.2.966–968). Where blackness is a moral measure calculated through deed more than melanin, Eleazar's black skin conveniently happens to match the blackness of his soul. Evil is distributed widely among the surviving characters: "Lustful Spaniards... behaving like the Moor, help to create an environment conducive for him 'to carry black destruction to the world.'"[27] For Derek Hughes, although *Lust's Dominion* is "dominated by explicit contempt for the black African," it shows little moral difference between the villains—Eleazar and his Moor guards—and the "good" characters, Prince Philip, Hortenzo, and the cardinal.[28] Yet the notion that black skin is a clear mark of evil is also one of its recurrent puns. Like gender, race on the Elizabethan and Jacobean stage was a matter of clothing and makeup. In the final act, Prince Philip and Hortenzo exert their cowardly revenge in blackface, and Philip remains in blackface when he utters his first royal decree banishing the Moors from Spain.

Lust's Dominion; or, The Lascivious Queen was likely written between 1599 and 1600 and possibly performed then under the title *The Spanish Moor's Tragedy*.[29] We know it in a text possibly revised to reflect the expulsion of the Moriscos (Muslims converted to Catholicism who had remained in Spain after the Reconquista) ordered by King Philip III in 1609 and published only in 1657, at a time when theatrical performances were officially banned by English authorities.[30] Yet theater endured: in published pamphlet plays, closet dramas, and secret performances, as well as a few officially sanctioned performances.[31] Much of the theatrical production under the republic adopted and exaggerated the characteristic elements of revenge drama, amplifying the cruelty and graphic nature of crimes, the salacity and sadism of villains, and the violence of the rhetoric itself, applying to the magistrates of the republic the treatment once given to the king and his administrators.

Official censorship of the theater softened in the last years of the republic. Former court playwright William Davenant notably argued that theatrical performances could be used to political ends: spreading visions of "the Spaniards' barbarous conquests in the West Indies" was thought politically sound enough to warrant official sanction of private performances at Davenant's Rutland House.[32] Davenant offers his play as a piece of what would come to be known as the "Black Legend," "the legend of inquisitorial Spain — ignorant, fanatical, incapable . . . of being considered among the civilized nations."[33] England, like other European rivals of the Spanish Empire, actively contributed to tarnish its reputation. English revenge plays illustrate how they did so along distinctively racial lines. As Walter Mignolo explains, "No British men or women of letters confused the Spaniards with the Moors or the Turks," but play after play entertained this illusion, inaugurating in the process "a racialized discourse within, that is, internal to, capitalist Empires of the West" that presented Spaniards as tainted.[34] Spaniards were not black nor Muslim, but they were implied to be black*er*, more African than other Europeans, owing notably to the long period of Moorish presence in the Iberian Peninsula, but also to what was presented as particularly barbaric behavior in the conquest of America. Such a portrayal hinged on the notion that Spaniards and Englishmen shared "a subterranean fraternal bond . . . defined by rivalrous antipathy."[35] The extent to which such notions were closely related to the theater, notions of honesty, role-playing, and race is illustrated in *Lust's Dominion*.

Discussions of race within the play are intertwined with reflections on acting, as when Eleazar declares, tongue in cheek:

> Black faces may have hearts as white as snow
> And 'tis a generall rule in morall rowls,
> The whitest faces have the blackest souls. (5.6.3608–3610)

The play expresses at times seemingly contradictory views on race and acting. Focusing on the utter deviousness of Eleazar, Anthony Barthelemy judges that "in the dramatic world of *Lust's Dominion* . . . blackness and role-playing define the spiritually deficient state of the Moors."[36] Yet, as often in revenge plays, role-playing is part of the plot itself, and everyone onstage is a player. Some, of course, are better than others: Eleazar is singled out as the villain of the play early on, by virtue, so to speak, of his skin or, rather, the paint covering it. Indeed, while "blackface functioned as a polyphonic signifier"—notably mixing negative views of the color itself partly influenced by medieval Christian lore but also by impressions of Africans inspired by current events, diplomacy, and propaganda—audiences were aware of the fictional nature of the spectacle at hand. The white actor in blackface "is not the thing he pretends to be and his audience knows it, his gestures and attitudes suggest that his identity is adopted, not inherited."[37] The play does not condemn Eleazar's role-playing so much as it suggests that role-playing is the rule of this Spanish court. Eleazar performs deviousness and barbarity, but it is ultimately unclear how much of it should be blamed on his blackness and how much he learned from the evil characters that surround him.[38]

Eleazar outwits Spaniards throughout the play, but he is bested in the final scene, when he fails to recognize Philip and Hortenzo as they impersonate Zarrack and Baltazar in blackface. The play within the play is a common motif in revenge drama, where "revenge seeks justice by mimicking injustice."[39] It is especially significant here, when Spanish actors don blackface to mirror Eleazar's acting, a skill he learned from them in the first place. For Emily Bartels, the scene reveals that Spain's "inherent permeability and malleability" is more of an issue than Eleazar's potential for evil deeds.[40] Yet the scene also depicts European victory through performance and metatheatrical consciousness. Hortenzo and Philip manage to outdeceive Eleazar in a role one might think he would control. Yet he falls for Hortenzo and Philip's act like the most naive and unsophisticated of theater spectators. Eleazar's ultimate lack of sophistication as a spectator, his inability to step back and off the stage, is ultimately what defines him as non-European.

The play ends with the banishment of all Moors by King Philip, but it is his brother, Fernando, who first evokes "banish[ing] by a law all *Moors* from Spain" (3.2.1534) during his short term as king of Spain, as he attempts to woo Eleazar's wife, Maria. Fernando proposes this measure as a means to separate her from her lawful husband. Earlier in the scene, Fernando, meaning to assert his good intentions, utters these lines:

> Though thus in dead of night, as I do now
> The lustful *Tarquin* stole to the chast bed
> Of *Collatines* fair wife, yet shalt thou be
> No *Lucrece*, nor thy King a Romane slave,
> To make rude villanie thine honours grave. (3.2.1471–1475)

In this vision Fernando is sufficiently aware of his own lust to know he plays the role of Tarquin. Yet, as he admits, the parallel has its limits. Maria may be a paragon of virtue in a den of vice, but she is no Lucretia: contrary to the Roman woman, her husband is a foreigner held in contempt and wariness. Sextus's devious assault on Lucretia proved how un-Roman he was, and he coerced her by threatening to ruin the Collatinus name with a false story of her dalliance with a slave. Maria is an inverted Lucretia. Shame is already with her, as she is married to a "slave," and her duty as a Spaniard woman, Fernando argues, is to wash this shame by accepting his advances: "Thy husband is no Spaniard, thou art one, / So is *Fernando*; then for countries sake / Let mee not spare thee" (3.2.1495–1498). For the king, Eleazar's mere existence and presence in Spain's court is a greater wrong than this indecent proposal.

Fernando's shuffling of the Lucretia myth is complete when the king threatens to kill himself if Maria does not accept him. It also illustrates the issue at hand: Fernando's Spain is out of joint by comparison to Rome. In Spain a slave can marry a noble Spanish woman. Worse yet, Fernando's own mother killed his father for the love of Eleazar. Moors are desirable. Fernando's awareness is not enough, because he is blinded by his own lust: he does not see Eleazar and Maria's union as a national issue of racial purity so much as an obstacle to his schemes. The political solution he offers—"it shall be death for any *Negroes* hand / To touch the beauty of a Spanish dame" (3.2.1537–1539)—is a maneuver to hide the personal under the more broadly political. Significantly, Fernando describes his plans in theatrical terms:

> The tragedy I'le write with my own hand:
> A King shall act it, and a King shall dye,
> Except sweet mercies beam shine from thine eye.
> If this affright thee it shall sleep for ever,
> If still thou hate me, thus this Noble blade,
> This Royall purple temple shall invade. (3.2.1485–1492)

Lucretia proved her Romanness in killing herself to erase the shame of rape by a tyrant marked as foreign: in this "tragedy" the victim is a king wounded in his pride because the woman he lusts after freely chooses union with a slave. With him, it is all of Spain that might symbolically kill itself if it allows Maria to thus threaten the Spanish racial assemblage. Nothing goes the way Fernando hoped or feared. Maria's chastity saves her from him but leads to ignominy, though not of the kind Fernando implied: she dies after being wrongly accused of killing a momentarily incapacitated Fernando. Fernando indeed dies from a stab wound, though it is Eleazar who performs the deed, killing the king for assaulting his late wife. Fernando lost control of a play of national (re)birth, but his idea of separating righteous Spaniards from false ones along racial lines survives him and is finally realized in Hortenzo and Philip's play within the play.

Eleazar is singled out as the archvillain in a community of reprobates for his final inability to recognize the different levels of acting at work in the play he believes he is directing. He falls one level short in the metatheatrical game of the play: he is capable to speak of blackness as an act, with irony, yet the joke is on him. He fails to recognize Spaniards acting as Moors, the very people to whom he is throughout the play alleged to be—culturally, phenotypically, and protoracially—closest. Crucial elements of Fernando's dreamed national play, such as the absolute separation of Spaniards from Moors and the banishment of the latter, are enacted in the play's coda. None of the survivors are shocked that the new king might do so while sporting blackface: they are a knowing audience, and they own the cultural conventions of racialized representation. It is the new king's prerogative to reassert the very notion whose truth-value was challenged throughout the play: evil is a foreign trait and a physical mark that can be seen, diagnosed, and expunged. The black body can "serve as a one-dimensional symbol against which white society can coalesce." For Virginia Mason Vaughan, the play's "semantic complications" are in that moment set aside to pit an English national audience against "black Moors constituted as 'true'—not fictional at all."[41] Yet I argue that the audience's recognition of the utterly fictional aspect of the moment is essential to its success. For Bartels, the relief brought about by the final banishment "emerges not *despite* the Moor's legitimacy as a Spanish subject but necessarily *through* it": I would add that it also retroactively makes that legitimacy moot.[42] With utter cynicism the final scene offers the fiction of race as the solution. Eleazar proved a formidable player by Spanish rules; he demonstrated, as Vaughan notes, that he could act in both senses of "playing a role" and "also taking action and assuming agency," a threat to Spain as vivid as miscegenation.[43] The metatheatrical spectacle in this last scene binds the audience and the actors themselves in a fiction that doubles as a racial pact: if viewers cannot tell a true Moor from a pretend one, maybe they are not true Europeans.

Eleazar, of course, is not: his revenge is rooted in European conquest. The poisoned king Philip indeed "made warr in *Barbarie*, / Won *Tunis*, conquered *Fesse* and hand to hand, / Slew great *Abdela*, King of *Fesse*, and father / To that *Barbarian* Prince" (5.1.2968–2972). It is from that vantage point, and with the bitterness of the noble born made to suffer the indignity of being called "a *Moore*, a Devill, / A slave of *Barbary*, a dog" (1.2.227–229) that Eleazar calls Philip a "Spanish tyrant" (1.2.236) and vows to "make all Spain a bonefire" (1.2.284). Eleazar words his resentment in the vocabulary of national and cultural difference, yet, much like Fernando, he speaks only of himself. He is staunchly individualistic and has no sense of community. The Moorish community is indirectly evoked throughout the play, notably when Eleazar's anonymous Moor guards appear onstage, but Eleazar only ever sees them as inferiors who can serve him. Like the Spaniards, he uses "slave" and "Moor" as synonyms. His kindest words to a Moor come as he speaks to the body of a soldier killed in a battle against Philip: "But thou didst well, thou knew'st I was thy Lord; / And out of love and duty to me here, / Where I fell weary, thou laidst down thy self / To bear me up, thus: God a-mercy slave" (4.3.2282–2287). Eleazar resents the conquest of the kingdom that was to be his, as well as the Spaniards' scorn for him, but he feels a Moor *Prince*, not a *Moor* Prince. He excels in political intrigue but is unable to act out the politics of community necessary to his success.

Eleazar also emulates Fernando in casting himself as actor and director of his own play: rebuked by Isabella, he imagines he will "new-mould" Spain and make a throne with the bones of Spaniards (5.5.3501). "The scene wants Actors" (5.5.3509), he exclaims, before he rudely orders Zarrack to do his bidding. Eleazar takes his servant for granted throughout the entire play and never imagines that Zarrack might resent his tyrannical behavior. He thinks Zarrack, like the other Moors, is nothing but a useful tool and never considers that Zarrack might resent Eleazar's abuse much like he himself resents the ill-treatment he receives from the Spaniards. That is unfortunate: Zarrack "scorn[s] these blows and these rebukes to bear" (5.5.3521) and offers his services to Isabella. What separates Eleazar from the Spaniards and comes to define him as a Moor is not a capacity for evil he shares with most of them but indeed his inability to master an old Western rhetorical trick and broaden the scope of personal grievances and family feuds to the level of community politics. When Hortenzo and Philip reveal themselves, Eleazar allows that "their subtil policie hath blasted my ambitious thoughts" (5.6.3765–3766). Their revenge is politics.

For being blasted, Eleazar's ambitious thoughts are also certainly shot through with the resistance rhetoric of revolution permeating English late sixteenth-century political discourse. In spite of his status in court, Eleazar has been dispossessed of his rightful throne in Fez. Yet by the same token, he feels he has more in common with Spanish grandees than with his Moorish servants. Indeed, Eleazar explains his outrage to his father-in-law in the following terms: "Although my flesh be tawny, in my veines / Runs blood as red and royal as the best / And proud'st in Spain" (1.2.231–233). Tyranny, for Eleazar, is not in the treatment reserved for other Moors, but in the fact that the insults heaped on him throughout the play ignore his social status.

Spaniards use with Eleazar the same insults they use with his servants, in effect suggesting that in this worldview, racial belonging trumps social caste. This hierarchy is essential to seventeenth-century English politics.

The rhetoric of slavery was not used by opponents to monarchy and radicals alone. Indeed, if English revolutionary rhetoric often pitted enslaved citizens against a tyrant king, it also spread the understanding that English citizens could not possibly be slaves, by law but also by nature.[44] If the most radical Dissenters saw this as a universal rule applying to all humankind, the rhetoric soon devolved to being used by different factions in internal politics and therefore attached to an elusive English racial assemblage. The political grammar that issued from the English Revolution evolved quickly, especially in print, where theater thrived even during its ban under the republic. The radical democratism of Dissenter politics met royalist elitism in 1650s English print culture, by way of revenge narratives in drama and fiction. One such text, Roger Boyle's heroic romance *Parthenissa*, focused on a character from antiquity that until then had all but been ignored in references to classical history and culture: Spartacus, the leader of the Third Servile War.[45]

BOYLE'S *PARTHENISSA* AND THE RETURN OF SPARTACUS

Parthenissa, a thick volume written by Roger Boyle, Earl of Orrery, was published over the first half of the 1650s. It is considered "the first English language imitation of the French heroic prose romance."[46] A writer, Boyle is also remembered for his role in British politics: coming from an Anglo-Irish family of repute, he fought on the English side during the Irish rising of 1641. Seeking the help of Parliament, he eventually joined Oliver Cromwell in his war in Ireland, in spite of personal royalist leanings. While his brothers chose exile to France during Cromwell's rule, Boyle was elected in Parliament and defended Anglo-Irish interests there, becoming a necessary link between central power and the colony. Although he was among the group who pushed—to no avail—the "Humble Petition and Advice" for Cromwell to become king, he was elected in the Restored Parliament after King Charles II's return in 1660 and continued to play an important political role in the new monarchy, even as he gained a certain amount of fame as a playwright, poet, and fiction writer.[47]

Heroic romances tend to be read as expressions of royalist sentiment. Romance heroes, princes burdened with their natural propensity for honor and courtly love, face villains whose evil is generally linked to moral and equally "natural" failings.[48] *Parthenissa* shows the implications of such worldviews, notably in matters of freedom and slavery. This rollicking tale set in antiquity follows the adventures of the Persian prince Artabanes.[49] On his way to Rome, the prince falls victim to pirates, then is enslaved and poised to become a gladiator. But rather than comply, Artabanes rouses his companions to revolt. Following their first victory over Romans, they elect him as their leader, "thenceforwards call[ing] him Spartacus." In *Parthenissa*, all characters are narrators telling one another adventures often weaved around known episodes of antique history. Boyle thus elaborates on the stages of the War of Spartacus as they have been passed on from antique historians, adding dialogue here and fictional secondary characters there. Thus, "'twas not Crassus, but perfidy" that beat Spartacus at the Battle of the Trenches: two of his lieutenants defect to the Roman side and doom the revolt.[50] A wounded Spartacus chances on an old acquaintance, who secretes him away from the battlefield and Roman history and into another adventure, where he becomes Artabanes again.

Like other heroic romances, *Parthenissa* evokes contemporary politics and figures: much in Boyle's retelling of the Spartacus story appears to echo his own pragmatic approach toward the English Revolution, a decidedly aristocratic worldview infused with meritocratic values.[51] Before he is sold into slavery, Artabanes meets the Roman senator Pompey, who upon seeing him exclaims, "Either all the rules of physiognomy are false, or that slave . . . is not what his present habit speaks him."[52] Pompey expresses a notion informed by Aristotle's theories on slavery. The Greek philosopher posited two regimes of slavery: one following the law of nature in which people are born either "freemen" or slaves ("and for these slavery is an institution both expedient and just") and one following the law of society. This type of slavery is more ambiguous:

Some persons, simply clinging, as they think, to principle of justice (for the law is a principle of justice), assert that the enslavement of prisoners of war is just; yet at the same time they deny the assertion, for there is the possibility that wars may be unjust in their origin and one would by no means admit that a man that does not deserve slavery can be really a slave — otherwise we shall have the result that persons reputed of the highest nobility are slaves and the descendants of slaves if they happen to be taken prisoners of war and sold. Therefore they do not mean to assert that Greeks themselves if taken prisoners are slaves, but that barbarians are. . . . And the same applies also about nobility: our nobles consider themselves noble not only in their own country but everywhere, but they think that barbarian noblemen are only noble in their own country—which implies that there are two kinds of nobility and of freedom, one absolute and the other relative.[53]

Aristotle points to the essence of the moral quandary of legal slavery: it can be morally acceptable only if it mirrors a naturalized hierarchical order. The terms of modern discussions of slavery in the Americas were essentially those he described here, the "principle of justice" being bolstered by Christian precepts, even as the encounter of the Christian and pagan worlds, in the Americas and Africa especially, was increasingly seen in Europe as a meeting of natural masters and natural slaves.[54] The misfortune that befalls Prince Artabanes in his exile in turn illustrates the final movement of Aristotle's demonstration. Artabanes has vowed to travel incognito: he does not want his name or station to be known and repeatedly refuses to share this information. But in heroic romance, heroes *know* one another. Pompey the Great recognizes a nobleman in Artabanes, but the "barbarous Batiatus" cannot: when Artabanes refuses to identify himself, Batiatus sends him to be "kept with his other common slaves."[55]

Among the enslaved gladiators, Artabanes delivers a speech the first chance he gets:

> Friends and companions in misery, that Fortune has made us slaves is her fault, that we should continue so will be ours, since a quiet submission to her cruelty tacitly acknowledges that we deserve it and makes that which is an effect of her blindness appear a confession of her justice. You have assur'd me often that you are all Gentlemen, that title obliges you sooner to wear death's livery than Batiatus's; let us therefore by some gallant attempt shew how worthy we were of liberty, or by dying handsomely, how unworthy we are of chains: Death is the worst that can befall us, yet it is a comparative happiness to our present condition. . . . This is the way if we cannot reach for our liberty, yet as least to reach revenge, which will be as pleasing as the irons we now wear are insupportable.[56]

Aristotelian logic is on full display: freemen can be wrongfully enslaved, but they should not be slaves. Being by nature driven to refuse slavery, they will not accept subjection passively. Aristotelian freedom—not unlike the related notion of nobility that occupied discussions from the Middle Ages to the Renaissance—is a paradoxical notion: it claims to be expressed in social hierarchy, but it is not equivalent to it. It is understood to be a natural quality, yet it can be lost; it is expressed mostly in deed, but some recognize it on sight. The text strongly implies that a slave who revolts was likely a natural freeman all along. Plutarch described Spartacus as a "Thracian of Nomadic stock, possessed not only of great courage and strength, but also in sagacity and culture superior to his fortune, and more Hellenic than Thracian."[57] Boyle's Spartacus is Persian rather than Hellenic, but he is undeniably cultured, a true and honorable prince, naturally and legally marked for freedom. Injustice here is not in the institution of slavery but specifically in its application to Artabanes. In turn, the revolt he leads has ultimately little to do with slavery: the heartbroken Artabanes was truly hoping to die but, being a hero, could do so only in heroic fashion. In *Parthenissa* the largest slave revolt in Roman history is but the expression of an aristocrat's natural extraordinariness, the fruit of a prince's lovelorn whimsy.

Boyle's romance is no political program, but it illustrates how revolt and its rhetoric could be adopted and redirected from above. Boyle reclaims the history of Spartacus for nobility, much like Plutarch once did. Though a work of fiction, Boyle's romance can be considered the first major written work to discuss Spartacus at length since antiquity. As such, it reintroduced Spartacus in English collective awareness and initiated a movement completed in the following century, also around works of fiction and drama. The treatment of Spartacus in *Parthenissa* reminds us that one could summon the topic of slavery and even the profoundly rebellious language of freedom and—or possibly to—ignore all or part of its egalitarian implications. Boyle's writings tend to be read in relation to political oppression in the immediate context of the English Revolution. Seen in the light of actual slavery, a system beginning to play an essential role in England's imperial endeavors, their meaning changes.

After leading the brutal campaign that put an end to the Eleven Years' War in Ireland in 1652, Cromwell launched his ambitious Western Design against Spanish possessions in the Americas. The campaign was overall a failure, but it brought the island of Jamaica under English dominion. When the English invaded in 1655, the population formerly enslaved by the Spaniards in Jamaica escaped en masse to the mountains, where they founded strongholds, or *palenques*. Now free, the Maroons offered their help to the Spaniards in their guerilla war against the English. It was only after the latter offered interesting terms to the Maroons in 1658 that they turned against the Spaniards, eventually allowing the English to take over the island. English colonial authorities were later forced to strike treaties with the Maroons as early as 1663.[58] There were enslaved Africans in English colonies of the West Indies and North America already, but the 1660s saw England's involvement in the slave trade grow drastically.[59] By then the discourse of slavery and freedom had become part of the political landscape, yet England's slaves in the colonies did not register in political discourse. Supporters and opponents of the Stuarts alike made money in the slave trade and in American colonies resting on slave labor. Among those thinkers and politicians opposed to the Stuarts' absolutist tendencies was Anthony Ashley Cooper, Earl of Shaftesbury, one of the foremost proponents of free trade and a lord proprietor of the province of Carolina.[60] The freedom-wielding rhetoric of the Whigs was fueled both literally and figuratively by slavery.[61] In the late 1660s he designed with his secretary John Locke the colony's Fundamental Constitutions, which, among other things, infamously regulated slavery in the territory. The constitutions posited America as a state of exception, where the comparatively progressive politics Shaftesbury and Locke advocated for England had no place. In his discussion of civil society in *Two Treatises on Government* (1690), Locke declares "slaves . . . being captives taken in a just war, are by the right of nature subjected to the absolute dominion and arbitrary power of their masters. These men . . . cannot in that state be considered as any part of civil society."[62] Whereas Aristotle pointed out the problem in adopting a moral position on the issue of slavery, Locke has no qualms tying slavery to "just war." Depriving a man of his freedom, Locke says, is acceptable only as retaliation for an unjustified attempt on this man's part at subjugating another: fit revenge, in a way.

Slavery provides the strong vocabulary he needs to make a point against absolutist monarchy: "Nobody can desire to have me in his absolute power unless it be to compel me by force to that which is against the right of my freedom—i.e., make me a slave."[63] John Locke, Royal African Company shareholder, does not directly address Atlantic slavery in his *Treatises*. The slavery he evokes is the political oppression weighing over Englishmen under the Stuart dynasty.[64] Yet by arguing for the moral obligation of revolt against slavery, he provides rhetorical tools applicable to that international form of slavery he blatantly ignores throughout his text. As C. B. MacPherson notes, in attempting to fuse natural law and market morality, Locke is unable "to surmount an inconsistency inherent to market society. A market society generates class differentiation in effective rights and rationality, yet requires for its justification a postulate of equal rights and rationality."[65] Atlantic slavery is the shameful engine of Locke's market society, and it provides the foundation of inequality on which Locke can build his theory of civil society. It is perpetually a crisis in the making, as it demands the suspension of the very values argued to be fundamental to the form of society advocated by Locke. For the Whigs the possibility of a Catholic king accessing the throne of England spelled political and religious tyranny. But "slavery" would also be economic: an absolutist Catholic king would deny his subjects their property rights, which Whigs deemed the keystone to a liberal society.[66] That these rights included the rights to own human beings was a crucial paradox that, if ignored by Locke, nevertheless echoed throughout English cultural production.

To reconcile English scorn for slavery and the increasing practice of it overseas, more drastic ways of separating natural slaves from natural freemen were needed. If Locke avoided addressing the crisis underlying his paradoxical position, these debates played out less coyly in literature. Behn's personal politics were drastically opposed to those of Shaftesbury—whom she caricatured in *The City Heiress* (1682)—and Locke. Yet her *Oroonoko* completes Locke's text in explaining how Englishmen downplayed their participation in the slave trade. In *Oroonoko* Behn conflates approaches of issues of political subjugation marked by the resistance rhetoric of revenge drama and English politics, seen through the filter of late seventeenth-century slavery. The black avenger figure rising in *Oroonoko* may seem like just another exotic prince of heroic romance, but he also takes after the black villain of revenge drama. *Oroonoko* is the expression of modern Western anxiety over the potential for moral and civilizational collapse contained in the practice of Atlantic slavery. With increasing levels of trade came increasingly elaborate justifications for racial slavery, but the utter immorality and injustice of it all could never be completely erased. Injustice holds the potential of a righting of wrongs, a blood feud of potentially gigantic proportions. The threat of widespread, African vengeance hung over modern European culture, and the revenge drama tradition provided ready terms with which to express the issue. In the transition from the black villains of revenge drama to Oroonoko, the tragic black avenger, we must look at Behn's rewriting of *Lust's Dominion*.

BETWEEN VILLAIN AND AVENGER

Oroonoko is generally presented as a fictional text that "evokes and subverts the convention of French heroic romance."[67] Yet, after years of closing under Puritan rule, the theater of the Restoration period first looked into older British drama for inspiration. The Restoration trend of French-style heroic drama was short-lived, and English dramatists soon fell back on the long national tradition of "tragedy of blood." So did Behn with *Abdelazer; or, The Moor's Revenge* (1676), her one and only tragedy and a rewriting of *Lust's Dominion. Abdelazer* retains all the characteristics of the villain tragedy that inspired it: "the arch-villain ... ruthlessly devoted to crime ..., the accomplice assiduous in revolting baseness."[68] Behn's Abdelazer, much like Eleazar, vows to "set all *Spain* on fire" to avenge his father's demise, but, contrary to his model, Abdelazer makes his case in so convincing a manner "as to seem almost justified."[69] He attempts to achieve this goal through increasingly immoral schemes, wreaking havoc on any and all standing in his way. Ultimately, Abdelazer's revenge is jeopardized by his moral shortcomings: with the Spanish Crown at hand, he ruins his chances out of lust for Leonora. Abdelazer acts on the same hypermasculine, patriarchal impulses as the Spaniards around him, and his blackness certainly serves as a defamiliarizing tool in exposing a very familiar behavior.[70] Yet Behn's revision of *Lust's Dominion* shows how the racial politics emerging in Dekker's play had become more entrenched close to a century later. Behn turns Abdelazer into a more credible, and possibly more sympathetic, villain and avoids equating his evil ways with his blackness. In the process she denies political valence to the black racial identity she delineates.

Scholars have taken exception to Barthelemy's assessment of the play as following the "traditionally disparaging representation of Moors," in which Abdelazer and his officer Osmin are cast as distinct black types.[71] For Derek Hughes, "Abdelazer is an individual rather than a type," and, contrary to Eleazar, his "villainy arises from a confluence of specific circumstances, not from the universal wickedness of black-skinned people."[72] Susie Thomas in turn argues that Behn avoids facile black-white symbolism and overall reduces the original play's emphasis on color, "an attempt to minimize the emphasis on blackness as evil."[73] Yet Behn's modifications bury rather than erase the themes of the original play. She characterizes Abdelazer's religious and cultural otherness in ways that *Lust's Dominion* did not: thus, when the cardinal strips Abdelazer of his titles, he calls him an unbeliever and questions his sense of cultural belonging:

> ALONZO. Why should you question his Religion, Sir?
> He does profess Christianity.
> CARDINAL. Yes, witness his habit, which he still retains
> In scorn to ours.—
> His Principles too are as unalterable. (1.2.43)

As proof of Abdelazer's otherness, the cardinal points to "the constructed features of [Abdelazer's] culture—his religion and dress—rather than to any essential racial character."[74] Onstage, clothing as much as blackface designates Abdelazer as the outsider, both suggesting that his otherness is constantly visible. Moors cannot hide from the knowing European gaze. The cardinal's objections evoke essentialism. Once a Muslim, always a Muslim: for the cardinal, Abdelazer can only ever pretend to be a Christian. His appearance is but the outward expression of his interior deviousness, precisely the expression of the "Principles" one has learned to expect from black Muslim villains. Here, as in *Lust's Dominion*, appearances are telling. If Behn seemingly makes less of the villain's skin color, there is also little of *Lust's Dominion*'s irony on this topic to be found in *Abdelazer*.

Abdelazer regrets his being black when rebuffed by Leonora for his "Person":

> And curst be Nature, that has dy'd my skin
> With this ungrateful colour! Cou'd not the Gods
> Have given me equal Beauty with *Alonzo*! (5.1.104)

In the corresponding scene in *Lust's Dominion*, Eleazar rings a slightly different tone:

> I, I may curse his praises, rather ban
> Mine own nativity, why did this colour,
> Dart in my flesh so far? Oh! Would my face
> Were of *Hortenzo*'s fashion, else would your
> Were as black as mine is. (5.3)

Eleazar would be content with being the same skin color as his love interest. Such nuance is absent from Abdelazer's lines. Behn takes direct references to color out of her text, but they are no secret to spectators. What remains is a complaint in which Abdelazer himself merges beauty and that unstated—but hardly invisible—"grateful" skin color, in a monologue from which the metatheatrics of *Lust's Dominion* have completely disappeared. Behn's play certainly gains in coherence, but it also appears to integrate as a given what its model painstakingly showed as a useful fiction: race.

Good morals are respected: villains die with their "sins unpardon'd" and avenged (5.2.112), the narrative closing in a demonstration of poetic justice. Here was a notion in which English tragedy was seriously lacking, according to Behn's contemporary Thomas Rymer. Two years later he critiqued the eccentricities of villain tragedies, notably *The Bloody Brother; or, Rollo, Duke of Normandy*. He lamented the inexplicable and unexplained evil of its titular villain and the lack of equilibrium between his deeds and his punishment: "so many lives taken away, and but the life of one guilty person to answer for all."[75] Finding exception with Rymer's opinion, John Dryden countered that "the punishment of Vice, and reward of Virtue, are the most adequate ends of Tragedy because [they are] most conducing to good Example of Life. . . . The suffering of innocence and punishment of the offender is of the nature of English tragedy." The English shared the same moral goals as the ancients, but they used every tool to reach it: "Rollo committing many murders, when he is answerable but for one, is too severely arraigned by him; for, it adds to our horrour and detestation of the criminal; and poetick justice is not neglected neither; for we stab him in our minds for every offence which he commits."[76] In Dryden's opinion poetic justice is also roused in the very minds of spectators, and outrageous acts of violence on the stage are balanced by making each of them a potential avenger.

Following such notions Behn does away with metatheatrics and cynicism and adds a healthy dose of poetic justice to the plot.[77] The lustful queen, notably, is betrayed and killed by her own lover, Abdelazer, who in turn dies in a much less revolting manner than Eleazar. Behn's "good" characters remain morally unstained: Prince Philip, though still brash and fiery, no longer enjoys slaughtering his chained foe. His counterrevenge is morally justified, a fitting punishment for Abdelazer's ignominies. Once Abdelazer is punished, balance is restored with little of the moral ambiguity of *Lust's Dominion*. This is all the easier that *Abdelazer* almost entirely erases Abdelazer's potential claims to belonging to a community. Moors were seldom visible in *Lust's Dominion*, but they were a recurrent point of discussion: in Behn's play the Moors are reduced to Abdelazer and Osmin. Abdelazer's second officer, Zarrack, comparatively plays a bit part and has little influence on the plot. Behn does away with *Lust's Dominion*'s final banishment of all blacks from the kingdom, but in her version of the play Philip has little reason to banish them: they are utter anomalies.

In *Lust's Dominion* Princess Isabella takes advantage of Zarrack's ambition to trick him into freeing Philip.[78] In Behn's play Osmin interrupts Abdelazer as he is about to rape Leonora, for which his master stabs him in the arm. Rushing offstage, Abdelazer leaves his servant with Leonora, who exclaims: "Sure *Osmin* from the Gods thou cam'st, / To hinder my undoing; and if thou dy'st, / Heaven will almost forgive thy other sins, / For this one pious deed!— / But yet I hope thy wound's not mortal." Leonora's pity moves Osmin to vow to "live to do [her] service" (5.2.106). Her pity even seems to affect the narrative retroactively, as we find out only at that moment that Osmin helped Philip and the cardinal escape three acts previously. Osmin pledges allegiance to Leonora and becomes the most crucial obstacle to Abdelazer's revenge. Until then he has been known as the captain of a "Guard of Moors" that appears onstage but once, standing silent, never again to be seen. The guards influence the play only as potential armed extensions of Abdelazer and Osmin. But, contrary to Abdelazer's, Osmin's agency is in fact proof of his status as natural slave: "There is no revolutionary potential in Osmin" or his guards, who are but sentient tools. By acting honorably in the service of Leonora, Osmin puts in relief what Adam R. Beach argues is Behn's outlook on slavery: royal slaves—that is, natural freemen—cannot muster the support of the natural slaves, yet they are the only people likely to foment revolt in the first place. In subscribing to this logic permeated by antique theories of natural slavery and freedom, Behn alters deeply the dynamics of the original play. Whereas *Lust's Dominion* focused on containing a cultural and racial threat to Europe, *Abdelazer* downplays local, Mediterranean affairs for a reflection on global slavery that fully exorcizes the threat of Moor political agency. Eleazar's self-centeredness kept him apart from his Moor supporters. Similarly, "in pursuing . . . 'the Moor's revenge,' Abdelazer fails to encourage 'the Moors' revenge.'"[79] But there is no need to banish other Moors here: in effect, when Osmin and Abdelazer die one after the other in the final act, all Moors *have* been killed. The rest of them can go back to serving as props on the Western stage, in Europe and abroad. Abdelazer in turn is an abstracted stage Moor, a theatrical convention without a hint of metatheatrical self-consciousness. This transition from failed director in *Lust's Dominion* to merely failed actor in *Abdelazer* is essential to make sense of the innovations at work in Behn's 1688 novel *Oroonoko*.

OROONOKO

In the "Epistle Dedicatory" to *Oroonoko*, Aphra Behn claims her novella to be a "true Story" of her "Travels to the other World," told in the first person by an otherwise unnamed female narrator. She claims to have "receiv'd from the mouth of the chief actor in this History" the parts of the story about Oroonoko's life before Behn's arrival in Suriname.[80] Use of theatrical terminology is not innocent or unexpected, coming from a playwright for whom "the theatre had been life and a metaphor for life."[81] Behn's narrator regularly connects the story to drama: directly, when she mentions wreaths of feathers later donated to the King's Theatre to be "the dress of the *Indian Queen*," and less directly, when *Oroonoko* takes place in locations typical of revenge plays: "private chambers, a room of state, a tent, a grove, a prison."[82] The visual elements of the theater transpire constantly in the text; "clothing, fashion, costume, and disguise mattered" to Behn.[83] Marta Figlerowicz sees in *Oroonoko* "a highly creative, consistent attempt at recreating in the medium of prose fiction the dramatic effects generated by the interactions between an actor and his audience." If, according to Figlerowicz, the theater gives the novella its "overarching structure," I would add that Behn also makes her narrator see with the keen eye of a theater aficionado.[84] She plays but a bit part in the events she describes and appears mostly as a spectator among spectators. But she is a sophisticated spectator: she can read people's faces, specifically skin color. In this she both refers to, and departs from, theatrical conventions of representation and interpretation.

The narrator makes a point of declaring that "'tis a very great error in those who laugh when one says, a Negro can change colour: for I haven seen 'em as frequently blush, and look pale, and that as visibly as ever I saw in the most beautiful white."[85] Blushing is "virtue's color," a sign mentioned time and again onstage as proof of the moral superiority of whites over blacks, a crucial visual clue for a good spectator. Indeed, such effect was not rendered only in makeup onstage: "By the seventeenth century, red and white had become a national obsession, and cosmetic-wielding women seem to have made it the national complexion as well."[86] The narrator's comment sets her apart as a discerning observer, but it does not undermine the visual conventions of the theater it indirectly summons here. Consider the narrator's infamous description of Oroonoko given earlier in the text: "His face was . . . a perfect ebony, or polished jett. . . . His nose was rising and Roman, instead of African and flat. His mouth the finest shaped that could be seen; far from those great turn'd lips, which are so natural to the rest of the Negroes."[87] Unlike "the rest of the Negroes," Oroonoko seems very much an actor in blackface—not an African but "a projection of what the English dramatist . . . thought a black person of African descent should be" through the prism of English representations of blackness and within their tight bounds.[88]

For Figlerowicz, *Oroonoko* "straddles" the theater and the novel.[89] I would argue more specifically that in Behn's text two different registers collide: the conventions of revenge drama and heroic romance. This is made clear in the treatment of Oroonoko's nobility in his new status as a slave. Time and again Behn's narrator suggests that Oroonoko exudes greatness, in classic heroic romance form. Even stripped of his royal garments, "the Royal Youth appeared in spite of the slave, and people cou'd not help treating him after a different manner, without designing it." Enslaved Africans and Europeans alike recognize in Oroonoko an aristocrat, while "he was received more like a governour than a slave" by most Europeans on the plantation and "endured no more of the slave but the name." Though the colony is full of uncouth, despicable colonists and lowly African slaves, they seem as capable of acknowledging his nobility on sight, as Pompey did Artabanes's. On first meeting him, even Trefry, a "Man of great Wit, and fine Learning" was alerted to Oroonoko's singularity by his rich clothes. But even after Oroonoko discards them, his nobility shines through. Then again it is expressed in other, less disposable visual signs. Further on the narrator expands rather awkwardly Oroonoko's outward signs of nobility: "I had forgot to tell you, that those who are Nobly born of that Country, are so delicately Cut and Rac'd all over the fore-part of the Trunk of their Bodies. . . . Some are only Carv'd with a little Flower, or Bird, at the Sides of the Temples, as was Caesar."[90]

Oroonoko and Imoinda bear their social status on their faces. Indeed, the narrator mentions that, even before Oroonoko confirmed it, she and her fellow Britons "took [Imoinda] to be of quality" because of the similar scarifications they had noticed on her body. Behn surreptitiously undermines the notion of natural nobility her own narrator introduced, as she exposes it as a kind of cosmetic, theatrical trick. The noble makeup that Oroonoko wears—unaware—is a European creation. Behn wields the language of heroic romance and simultaneously undermines it by letting her narrator expose its workings. In heroic romance "greatness of soul . . . true honour . . . [and] absolute generosity" are part of the natural virtues of a hero. We learn that Oroonoko owes these to "the care of a Frenchman of wit and learning" who taught the prince "morals, language and science" but also to his dealings with English and Spanish gentlemen and his knowing their languages.[91] Plutarch had emphasized the alleged Greekness of Spartacus; Behn's African prince is similarly a product of Western civilization, raw African material refined by European culture.

Oroonoko's French upbringing taught him something of the references and values of Europe, but discernment and skepticism were seemingly not part of the program, as is demonstrated in the description of the English captain:

> [He was] a Man of a finer sort of Address, and Conversation, better bred, and more engaging, than most of that sort of Men are; so that he seem'd rather never to have been bred out of a Court, than almost all his Life at Sea. This Captain therefore was always better receiv'd at Court, than most of the Traders to those Countries were; and especially by *Oroonoko*, who was more civiliz'd, according to the *European* Mode, than any other had been, and took more Delight in the *White* Nations; and, above all, Men of Parts and Wit.[92]

Englishmen around him read Oroonoko's looks even when he means to hide them. He, in turn, puts too much stock in appearances that can be faked. Quality, like blushing, can be imitated. Susan Andrade argues that Behn portrays Oroonoko as an "ideal Reformation courtier," a point that deserves closer scrutiny.[93] In Baldassare Castiglione's *Courtyer*, the classic treatise on courtly behavior first translated into English by Thomas Hoby in 1561, Castiglione's speakers subscribe to Aristotle's notion of natural nobility, but Count Ludovico Canossa introduces an important caveat: "Betwene thys excellent grace, and that fonde foolyshnesse there is yet a meane, and they that are not by nature so perfectly furnished, with studye and diligence maye polishe and correct a great part of the defaultes of nature." In turn, natural noblemen should also be endowed with "a certain grace, and (as they saie) a hewe, that shall make him at the first sight acceptable and lovyng unto who so beholdeth him."[94] Castiglione famously introduces the concept of *sprezzatura*, "the quality which makes the courtier seem a natural nobleman," and the related idea that those lacking in natural nobility can ally personal skill, imitation, and artifice to fake it 'til they make it.[95]

Hoby's translation of Castiglione worked in concert with rising dissident views against the infallibility of clergy and aristocracy. Its success was partly owing to the fact that the book was "not intended to confirm the natural status of the old nobility . . . but to bring about the ennoblement of his 'inferior' countrymen."[96] Skepticism toward nobility was by the end of the seventeenth century well ingrained in English popular views and culture. *The Book of the Courtier* made "quality" an ideal for which to strive rather than simply a natural asset. It made it an act, a fiction with which one could decide to play along. The women of the colony of Suriname know this well, who try to distract the prince with "diverting adventures" that replicate the "nonracialized and abstractly gendered world of gallant knights and courtly ladies."[97] Natural nobility is a familiar fiction within the diegesis of Behn's narrator, but Oroonoko comes from a world where that fiction is truth: a Coromantien trained in European nobility by the most learned French teachers, an African dreamed by an English narrator. In crossing the Atlantic Oroonoko was drawn from heroic romance into this "true Story" but not made privy to its rules, especially regarding revenge.

Revenge in drama and romance is acceptable for heroes only as a response to initial harm and even then must follow the basic rules of fit: the punishment must match the wrong. Throughout *Oroonoko* the villains themselves expect Oroonoko to resort to revenge, implicitly recognizing that their actions against him would warrant it: when Oroonoko's grandfather tells him that he has ordered Imoinda to be executed, the old man also begs the prince not to react too harshly against him and to turn his anger toward battle. He can be assured "that Death, that common Revenger of all Injuries, wou'd soon even the Account between him and a feeble old Man." Oroonoko's grandfather evidently knows that Imoinda is not dead but has been sold into slavery, "the greatest Revenge, and the most disgraceful of any."[98] Surmising that Oroonoko would not forgive him the ignominy of this act, he lies to him. Oroonoko's grandfather knows that the prince respects the social conventions of his country, which he disobeyed only out of love. When he finally learns the truth, in Suriname, the potential target of his revenge is thousands of miles across the ocean and virtually forgotten by an Oroonoko too happy to have recovered his lover.

The English captain not only deceives Oroonoko with his looks; he lies through his teeth, and Oroonoko takes him at his word every time. On the voyage to the Americas, the captain offers new lies to Oroonoko, swearing that he will let Oroonoko go free at the next harbor they reach. Yet when Oroonoko asks to be unchained, the captain answers that "he durst not trust him with Liberty while he remain'd in the Ship, for fear lest by a Valour natural to him, and a Revenge that would animate that Valour, he might commit some Outrage fatal to himself." Oroonoko promises not to retaliate. Bound by his word, he even convinces his men that they must remain chained "since 'twas all the Security the Captain (his Friend) could have against the Revenge . . . they might possibly justly take." The captain then betrays him again and sells them as soon as they reach Suriname, making sure to separate the "noble Slaves in Fetters," "not daring to trust 'em together, lest Rage and Courage shou'd put 'em upon contriving some great Action, to the Ruin of the Colony."[99] The slavers, it seems, are familiar with *Parthenissa*.

The prince's standards of honor are too high for the Atlantic world: he believes that one's word is sacred, a notion his foes violate over and over again, without scruples. Oroonoko is well treated and receives promises that he will be freed, but he soon despairs. At that point the narrator is delegated by the English to try and placate Oroonoko. She, like the others, "fear'd a Mutiny," and in spite of his assurances she "neither thought it convenient to trust him much out of our View, nor did the Country who fear'd him."[100] The narrator plays courtly games to divert the prince's attention and remind him of the activities that occupied him in his heroic world. Contrary to Oroonoko, she knows this is all an act. In this "true Story," villains come out virtually unscathed, and they read Oroonoko like an open, familiar book.

As shown by James Grantham Turner, New Romance was differentiated from its older variation by its attachment to "neoclassic verisimilitude."[101] Authors generally found their subject matter in ancient history and exotic locales. Behn's novella not only focuses on the recent past: some of its characters—first among them Behn's narrator—are real, sometimes still living people. Their fictional world, then, is presented as inseparable from our world, seemingly with none of the chronological distance that allows for the lofty creative license at work in *Parthenissa*, for example. In the "real" world where Oroonoko finds himself transported, matters of revenge are not beholden to the rules of honor. Oroonoko's enemies are masters of narrative and time. Oroonoko begins to understand the order of this world on the crossing of the Atlantic, as he discusses with the ship captain the validity of his professed Christian beliefs. The slaver captain claims that his belief in the afterworld binds him: having "sworn in the name of a Great G O D; which if he shou'd violate, he would expect eternal Torment in the World to come." Oroonoko is nonplussed: "Punishments hereafter are suffer'd by ones self; and the World takes no cognizances whether this *God* have revenged 'em, or not, 'tis done so secretly, and deferred so long: While the Man of no Honor suffers every moment the scorn and contempt of the honester World, and dies every day ignominiously in his Fame, which is more valuable than Life."[102] Oroonoko sounds like a malcontent from a revenge play, but he lacks the related cynicism: his sole measure is honor, a currency dependent on audience. Where he is going, the audience enjoys the spectacle of honor but does not partake in its performance. These spectators wholly separate words and deeds: the twain can be expected to meet only in the theater.

The captain's averred Christian values rule the discourse of the world in which Oroonoko now finds himself, but not its actions. His reflection on Christian eschatology reveals how it literally distorts time, taking hold of the idea of universal justice that lies at the heart of revenge and wielding an egalitarian version of it. The Christian God is no respecter of persons and announces justice for all, no matter their social station, a radical view of justice conveniently postponed to the afterlife.[103] Oroonoko exposes this rhetorical sleight of hand, echoing in this the terms of Rymer's and Dryden's exchange over poetic justice from within the diegesis. Oroonoko the theatrical hero is unable to mete out revenge in timely—that is, dramatic—manner: after the failed revolt and his punishment at the hands of the authorities, he and Imoinda agree to "his Design, first of Killing her, and then his Enemies, and next himself." But the sight of her dead body overwhelms him: "A thousand times he turned the Fatal Knife that did the Deed toward his own Heart, with a Resolution to go immediately after her; but dire Revenge, which was now a thousand times more fierce in his Soul than before, prevents him: and he would cry out, No, since I have sacrificed Imoinda to my Revenge, shall I lose that Glory which I have purchas'd so dear, as the Price of the fairest, dearest, softest Creature that ever Nature made? No, no!" Yet killing Imoinda affects Oroonoko so badly that he remains incapacitated for two days, after which he feels that "the Deaths of those Barbarous Enemies were deferr'd too long," echoing drearily the words uttered earlier on the topic of divine retribution. They have no such qualms: capturing Oroonoko at the brink of death after he disemboweled himself, his many enemies in the colony eventually quarter and burn him in the presence of a "rude and wild . . . rabble." They make sure to set up "frightful Spectacles of a mangl'd King," thus no longer aligning Oroonoko with heroes of romance but indeed with the black villains of revenge drama.[104]

The British mass is time and again presented as despicable by Behn's narrator. Yet they form the ethnic group she eventually enters, even as she may seem to side with Oroonoko at times.[105] There is no contradiction between her appreciation of Oroonoko and her ultimately siding with the British, of course. The prince is doomed, but, further yet, he is a European creation. Oroonoko is not just a hero "caught between Old and New Romance"; he is also, *within the text*, a theatrical embodiment of Castiglione's perfect grace surrounded by "novel"—read "real, realistic"—spectators educated in the art of reading performance.[106] The crux of Oroonoko's performance is revenge and, more specifically, his inability to approach it in the two ways made available to him: by performing it himself or by transcending it into political action. In the last stages of his story, the sympathy of Behn's narrator notwithstanding, Oroonoko takes on characteristics usually reserved for black villains.

The failed revolt is evidently a crucial moment in the novella, if only because it is the closest Oroonoko ever gets to actual, though indirect, revenge on his foes. He does so by attempting to do what "good" avengers of drama—Europeans all—usually do: attaching his fate to that of a community, in this case African slaves, with whom he had little contact until then. It is meaningful that Oroonoko is led to consider revolt as he ponders the future: Imoinda is pregnant, and their child will be born a slave unless they free themselves, as the English, though they promised Oroonoko his wrongful enslavement would be righted, cannot be trusted to do it. As European settlers wallow in their drink on a Sunday night, Oroonoko delivers a rousing speech to the assembled slaves. It is rendered as follows by Aphra Behn's narrator:

He told 'em, [slavery] was not for Days, Months or Years, but for Eternity; there was no end to be of their Misfortunes . . . ; but Men, Villanous, Senseless Men, such as they, Toyl'd on all the tedious Week till Black *Friday*: and then, whether they Work'd or not, whether they were Faulty or Meriting, they promiscuously, the Innocent with the Guilty, suffer'd the infamous Whip, the sordid Stripes, from their Fellow *Slaves*, till their Blood trickled from all Parts of their Body; Blood, whose every drop ought to be Reveng'd with a life of some of those Tyrants, that impose it; And why, said he, my dear friends and Fellow-Sufferers, shou'd we be Slaves to an unknown People? Have they Vanquish'd us nobly in fight? Have they Wone us in Honourable Battel? And are we, by the chance of War, become their Slaves? . . . No, but we are Bought and Sold like Apes, or Monkeys, to be the Sport of Women, Fools, and Cowards.[107]

Oroonoko's speech points to themes central to the novella: the novelty of the Atlantic slave system and the terrible violence it generates and relies on; slavery's morals, or lack thereof; and the related question of the moral valence of violent retaliation. Add to this a nascent movement toward racial definition: the men and women Oroonoko addresses were originally victims of Oroonoko himself, who sold them to Europeans after winning them, one can only assume, in what he deems to be "Honourable Battel." But, deported in America, these former neighbors and enemies, hailing from different and often antagonistic groups, are all part of a new homogeneous group, united by their general background and their immediate living circumstances. Oroonoko and Imoinda's unborn child embodies perhaps a bit too obviously this embryo of a community, Africans of an America run, and run over, by Europeans. As Imoinda's pregnancy becomes more apparent, the colony and its residents slide more or less successfully into new understandings of themselves. This change appears in the novel's narrative itself, when it "shifts from an English 'us' aligned with Oroonoko to a white 'us' aligned against him."[108] The claim to whiteness made by Behn's narrator demands that, in turn, all Africans be lumped together under the banner of blackness. Whiteness is only possible as an absolute contrast. If Behn's narrator shifts from an English "us" to a white "we," Oroonoko becomes black in the act of leading a revolt. And this is an act. He pretends to ignore his social station, feigning that it is less important than what he has in common with his fellow slaves: the injustice that brought them all there, which can be summed up in their skin color. Framing it in these terms is the only way to unite slaves in the same struggle as Oroonoko. But in this fictional world, such summary union is useless to his ilk: contrary to the Europeans around him, Oroonoko does not get to dictate the terms of the fiction he inhabits.

Tellingly, Oroonoko's speech evokes two related speeches: Nathaniel Lee's dramatic rendering of Brutus's speech to the Roman populace after Lucretia's death and Artabanes's in *Parthenissa*. In Lee's *Lucius Junius Brutus*, Brutus, standing in the forum, asks of his audience:

> You that were once a free-born People . . . Oh Rome! Oh Glory!
> What are you now? What has the Tyrant made you?
> The Slaves, the Beasts, the Asses of the Earth,
> The Soldiers, of the Gods Mechanic Laborers,
> Drawers of Water, Taskers, Timber-fellers,
> Yok'd you like Bulls, his very Jades for luggage,

Drove you with Scourges down to dig in Quarries,
To cleanse his Sinks, the Scavengers o'th Court:
While his lewd Sons, tho not on work so hard,
Employ'd your Daughters and your Wives at home.[109]

This rhetoric was successful to rouse fellow Roman citizens—both nobles and commoners—into overthrowing their king in their own city. Tarquin's tyranny calls for sacred union transcending social divisions; Romans high and low all have in common that they are a "free-born People." Boyle's Artabanes uses similar revolutionary rhetoric, with a crucial difference: he is a foreigner enslaved in a foreign land. He and the core of gladiators with whom he begins his revolt have in common that they are gentlemen down on their luck; they cannot possibly be kept enslaved because they would sooner choose death.

The slaves around Oroonoko do not agree, to the notable exception of Tuscan, "a tall *Negro* of some more Quality than the rest." Oroonoko leads the slaves on a plan evocative of Maroon communities, but also of Spartacus—he means for them to "Plant a New Colony, and Defend it by their Valour; and when they cou'd find a Ship, either driven by stress of Weather, or guided by Providence that way, they wou'd Seize it, and make it a Prize, till it had Transported them to their own Countries; at least, they shou'd be made Free in his Kingdom." No such luck: the anonymous mass of the enslaved of Suriname are servile and simple-minded, incapable of self-rule. They are easily convinced to rebel, but they as easily surrender when colonial troops meet them in the jungle. They are, as Oroonoko expresses in unmistakably Aristotelian accents, "by Nature *Slaves*."[110] The black racialized assemblage lurking threateningly in *Lust's Dominion* and *Abdelazer* finally moves to collective action, only to prove itself of little consequence. The contagious threat of a black nation in the Americas is cured through narrative, by way of a seemingly unexpected tool: a black hero. *Dosis sola facit venenum*: the dose makes the poison, says the principle of toxicology credited to the sixteenth-century Swiss man of science Paracelsus. Filtered through European conventions of black representation, African freedom did not simply fail to be deadly: it proved beneficial, narrative immunization against black agency for the new white body politic being created in the Americas.

Oroonoko's death comes through the intercession of Tuscan. Not unlike *Abdelazer's* Osmin, Tuscan is no aristocrat, nor is he a "natural slave." He occupies the in-between that Behn allows honorable, faithful slaves. Tuscan and the party of Englishmen find Oroonoko weakened almost unto death after wasting away for days in the forest. Oroonoko remains a hero: he kills the first Englishman who attempts to seize him and would likely—and gladly—die in battle but for Tuscan, who "took him in his Arms; but, at the same time, warding a Blow that *Cæsar* made at his Bosom, he receiv'd it quite through his Arm; and *Cæsar* having not the Strength to pluck the Knife forth, though he attempted it, *Tuscan* neither pull'd it out himself, nor suffer'd it to be pull'd out."[111] The English capture Oroonoko again and eventually execute him. An apt reader would recognize in this scene and its outcome a peculiar reflection of act 5, scene 2, of *Abdelazer*, when, after Osmin interrupts Abdelazer's rape attempt on Leonora, the prince stabs his guard. Behn's narrator and "all the females of us" play a part in the narrative, "incentives or witnesses for almost all of Oroonoko's exploits," yet are repeatedly presented as part of an audience used to theatrical conventions and logic.[112] When Oroonoko explains his motive in killing Imoinda to the English ladies, "(however Horrid it first appear'd to us all) when we had heard his Reasons, we thought it Brave and Just."[113] Behn's narrator and her fellow white spectators appreciate Oroonoko's soliloquy—Behn's creation—because they "recognize" in Oroonoko's choice a streak patterned after revenge play protagonists. Oroonoko's killing of Imoinda is the act of a villain, and so is his death. But where black villains were foiled in their attempt at running their own show, Oroonoko never had a clue: for all his heroics he is a passive creation, a character rather than an actor, a tool in the hands of a narrator and her knowing audience.

In her analysis of the role of torture in Thomas Southerne's adaptation of *Oroonoko* for the stage, Ayanna Thompson argues that staging the torture as a spectacle reinforces "an implicitly empowered *and* erased (white) gaze." This is true of Behn's novella at large: while eyes are lovers' favorite means of communication, they are also the medium by which Westerners control the action and ultimately deliver it to readers. Gaze in *Oroonoko* is the property of the narrator, the "eye-witness." What they describe is what they own: Governor Byam's understanding of this rule is only slightly distorted when, through torture, he attempts to physically possess Oroonoko, to "'mark' the African prince as his own."[114] Oroonoko rightly understands his flogging as the ultimate mark of shame, an external, visual sign of humiliation. Yet Oroonoko's owner is unmistakably the narrator. Taking control of the eminently sexual threat Oroonoko represents in the text is for Behn's narrator the key to entering American whiteness. Much like *Lust's Dominion*'s Fernando, she does so by reorganizing the mechanics of the Lucretia myth. She is in a position to make extradiegetic connections that Oroonoko himself cannot; she channels literary conventions and tropes but also writes beyond them toward historiography, or a semblance of it. Thus, we learn that of the "notorious villains" who constitute Byam's council, "some of 'em were afterwards Hang'd when the *Dutch* took possession of the place." She connects their fate to Oroonoko's when she declares that they "after paid dearly enough for their Insolence."[115]

The narrator alone can make a connection between unrelated events and indeed rewrites the death of the British colonists in the Anglo-Dutch War as poetic justice. One might read further proof of cynicism in the narrator's suggestion that the Dutch invasion also vindicated her, leaving her the only witness capable of retelling Oroonoko's story: "His Misfortune was, to fall in an obscure World, that afforded only a Female Pen to celebrate his Fame; though I doubt not but it had lived from others Endeavours, if the *Dutch*, who immediately after his Time took that Country, had not kill'd, banish'd, and dispers'd all those that were capable of giving the World this great Man's Life, much better than I have done."[116] Behn's female narrator demonstrates her mastery of the narrative codes of white patriarchy. She recreates the dangerous sexual and racial dynamics of revenge drama at a safe distance: Imoinda "prevents the white woman from committing miscegenation, and then becomes the willing martyr whose death protects the narrator from the fate of Desdemona."[117] Imoinda's death, though, protects not just the white woman: it protects white people at large. Indeed, if "to be raped by an outsider . . . signifies nothing less than an act of aggression against the body politic itself," Oroonoko's killing Imoinda to prevent her rape suggests and immediately erases the parallel. In describing the killing, the narrator devolves to harmless metaphor to gloss over Imoinda's pregnancy, simply noting that she was "pregnant with the fruits of tenderest love." Oroonoko kills Imoinda and their unborn child. He finds himself alone. René Girard declares that communities in the throes of crises "instinctively seek an immediate and violent cure for the onslaught of unbearable violence and strive desperately to convince themselves that all their ills are the fault of a lone individual who can be easily disposed of."[118] There will be no black body politic here, only a former prince turned scapegoat, serving the purposes of white supremacy in the Americas. Much of the credit goes to Behn's narrator: she thwarted revolt and stilled the birth of a black nation by the modest power of her "Female Pen."

Derek Hughes states that when Behn wrote *Oroonoko*, "attitudes could be combined in ways that are impossible today. Defenders of black Africans could accept slavery."[119] It may be more accurate to say that defenders of slavery could accept *an* African, a singular character damning the mass of his enslaved fellows through his very exemplarity. In this, Behn's "Royal Slave" truly is the reflection of her other "slave" king, Abdelazer. Both must die: the black villain's malevolence makes him unfit for civilized life, while the black hero's very existence is a moral challenge to slavery. The Middle Passage renders him virtually irrelevant, a model nobleman unaware that his world is a stage.

Considered through the prism of theatrical conventions, the lessons *Oroonoko* suggests are especially disturbing. The narrator can lament the irrelevance of notions of honor in a world shamelessly driven by material gain, but she does so from the comfort of her position as a spectator profiting from the way this world functions. Under her words lurks the notion that all this horror, these "frightful spectacles of a mangled King," are quite a popular spectacle, and a sign of the times. The demise of the black hero and the disappearance with him of the potential for his revenge to trigger a "universal onslaught of reciprocal violence" are necessary to sustain the system on which England's economic success is poised. Oroonoko is indeed "the last of his Great Race": Behn's narrator casts him as the last of the old black avengers of British revenge theater, a character that embodies European anxieties of racial and cultural self-definition carried over from Europe to the Americas.[120] This spectacle warns against black agency as much as it titillates: the black avenger is a highly sexualized threat against racial and national purity, a promise of lust. Transposing European literary conventions to the American context opens up possibilities: the wilderness is dangerous, but it can be made into a narrative safe space. The Moors of European drama came uninvited: the Africans of American fiction come coerced, tools in human form. With Oroonoko, Behn's narrator introduces the new black avengers: directly involved in the death of the promise of black agency in the Americas, they are left to embody the black body politic only to be dismembered, sacrificial fodder necessary to exorcize the threat of black autonomy in the Americas.

CHAPTER 2

GENII OF THE NATIONS

*The Black Avenger between
England and France*

ROMANS ONSTAGE

How, when, and why national audiences should watch like Romans as slaves died like Romans were questions that consumed France and Britain in the eighteenth century. Two spectatorial scenes, though separated by language, geography, and politics, point to the function of slave roles in the romanization of the great national rivalry between France and England. They also hint at deep connections between the two countries, as throughout the eighteenth century national sentiments developed that were in no small part built on mutual scorn and articulated around the figures of Lucretia, Spartacus, and black avenger figures in the wake of Oroonoko.

In his 1732 poem "On a Young Lady's Weeping at Oroonoko," John Whaley presents his readers with a scene from the theater:

> At Fate's approach whilst Oroonoko Groans
> *Imoinda*'s Fate, undaunted at his own;
> Dropping a gen'rous tear *Lucretia* sighs
> And views the Heroe with *Imoinda*'s eyes
> When the Prince strikes, who envy's not the Deed?
> To be so Wept, who wou'd not wish to Bleed?[1]

Lucretia, Whaley's "Young Lady," is attending a performance of the thirty-seven-year-old *Oroonoko*, a play so popular it was staged almost continuously throughout the eighteenth century either in Thomas Southerne's version or one of several later rewritings.[2] In every version collective action, in the form of the slave uprising, fails, denounced by Oroonoko himself. Oppression becomes a side effect of the individual feud opposing the evil governor and the one obstacle to his overwhelming desire for Imoinda: Prince Oroonoko.

The prince and his beloved Imoinda ultimately die for, and because of, love in an outpouring of feelings evidenced by their stage lamentations. Slavery is part of the decor, "a dramatic context for exploring more refined concerns of feeling and sensibility" shown to be essential to the play: a hero's tears— proof of true love and grief—are well worth a stabbing.[3] Whaley's Lucretia watches Oroonoko pay "the tribute of [his] Grief" as he sheds "A few sad Tears" over Imoinda's dead body near the end of the play.[4] The prince's plight generates tears, whose purpose is to move Lucretia to tears.

Some sixty years after Whaley published his poem, in the aftermath of the Thermidorian reaction against Maximilien Robespierre and proponents of the Terror, theatergoers in Paris rushed to attend performances of *Spartacus*, a tragedy about the gladiator who almost destroyed Rome, written by Bernard-Joseph Saurin and first performed three decades earlier, in 1760. Marie-Émile-Guillaume Duchosal, writer at the *Journal des Théâtres*, had few compliments for what he considered a "mediocre tragedy" or for the equally questionable lead actor in the production. Still, the audience praised this performance, as it had the previous reprises already staged in several theaters of revolutionary Paris and as it would again the following year.[5] "What prestige could have produced such enthusiasm? How can a play received coldly some forty years ago now obtain so many suffrages?" asked a befuddled Duchosal.[6] It must have been the praise heaped on the play throughout the years by the likes of Jean-François Marmontel and Nicolas de Condorcet, but most of all Voltaire, "who imposed upon the multitude. . . . They put in print that *Spartacus* was an *estimable work*, and all the superficial men, all the ignorant, all the dunces, all the enthusiasts repeated and repeat to this day: *Spartacus is an estimable work*."[7] The play's undue reputation, Duchosal asserted, rested solely on its endorsement by illustrious supporters who, by 1794, formed part of revolutionary France's intellectual pantheon. Their fame was enough to trump *Spartacus*'s utter lack of merit.

In 1732 Britain, Lucretia, the English citizen-spectator, watches the death of an American slave while simultaneously performing as her namesake, the mother of the Roman Republic. Whaley's Young Lady embodies the contemporary cultural axiom that the English government—a parliamentary monarchy born of one regicide, two revolutions, and the ouster of another king—was a modern version of a political system modeled on the Roman Republic. The sympathetic Lucretia weeps over a fallen noble slave as only the model citizen of a moral polity can. The cost of this performance is the lived experience of actual enslaved bodies under English ownership, forced into silence by Lucretia's ostentatious sensibility. In 1794 France the audience at the Théâtre de l'Egalité modeled the performative commons of the new-born French nation. While France had long seen itself as a cultural heir to Rome, the revolution gave it its turn to identify with the Roman Republic. Republicanism was channeled into French popular culture by way of English theatrical conventions and themes. Performances of republican nationhood on both sides of the Channel carried with them the paradox of contemporary slavery, the most absolute denial of freedom, actively practiced by both countries.

The simultaneous evocation and silencing of enslavement through slave avenger figures was no mere creative happenstance: it was crucial to the emergence of English and French national discourse. The role of *Oroonoko* in framing budding notions of whiteness and Englishness has long been known and discussed. Edward D. Seeber and Léon-François Hoffmann discuss its popularity and influence on later French texts, highlighting English lineage to hone in on French literature.[8] In this chapter I focus on tracing the public and critical reception of Oroonoko's different incarnations and the fortunes of his literary descendants from England to France and back again, to show how instrumental race at large and the black avenger figure in particular were in defining related and rival notions of Englishness and Frenchness in the eighteenth century. If the Lucretia myth helped to define ideal English citizenship, black avenger texts served to delimit and test the values and morals of Englishness. These texts propose ways to navigate the contradiction between Englishmen's wonted love of freedom and their widespread practice of slavery. National sentiment in France developed along with increasingly radical opposition to absolutism in ways similar to, and often directly influenced by, England. The Lucretia myth found singular parallels in droit du seigneur plots in which aristocrats performed ignominious feudal tyranny through sexual assault, but it is Spartacus who came to embody French strivings for freedom.

Rooted in drama and performance, these tropes seeped into poetry with the rise of abolitionist sentiment in England. By the end of the eighteenth century, English authors reproduced and subverted elements of both the Lucretia and Spartacus plots in addressing the issue of Atlantic slavery and its potential incidence on English might and morals. English abolitionist poets used the vocabulary central to European nationalism to approach slave revolt. As the works of radical abolitionist poet Edward Rushton demonstrate, the use of increasingly raced rhetoric of freedom rendered imagining black political agency profoundly difficult on the eve of the French and Haitian Revolutions.

The Roman Republic was a cultural and political model for all of Europe, but developing national sentiment demands belief in local and cultural singularity. In Great Britain this process took nothing short of a "virtual cultural revolution aimed at 'rediscovering' a native English tradition and cleansing it of impure foreign accretions" and later finding what drew English, Scots, and Welsh together more than it separated them.[9] This rediscovery notably comprised a movement initiated during the English Revolution that equated the struggle for an egalitarian society with the restoration of the principles that had allegedly animated England before the Norman invasion.[10] In these visions the English social order, a profoundly hierarchical organization derived from feudalism, was an intrinsically foreign system to be extirpated. British princes, Sextuses all, imposed tyranny on true Britons in their own land. English aristocrats, consumers and sponsors of high culture, saw themselves as cosmopolitan and European perhaps more than strictly English. At the turn of the eighteenth century, France was the European reference in matters of taste, fashion, and art, and sophisticated people behaved in accordance. Englishness was defined in relation to and against French influence in both high and low society. The Francophilia characteristic of the wealthy became a problematic status symbol at a time when English commoners increasingly reviled the aristocracy. The question of the influence of France also entered debates surrounding the proper forms and goals of theater that raged during the Restoration and in the aftermath of the Glorious Revolution among English artists eager to find a balance between the unique elements of English drama and forms of refinement represented and dictated by French drama. "A Dream," a poem allegedly written by Roger Boyle, warned Charles II against heeding the advice of the "Genius of France," who strove to encourage the monarch to "promote the Interest of that Kingdom, and to act upon *French* principles."[11] The ghost of Charles I then appeared to impart on his son that "a King's chief Treasure, and only real Strength, is *The Affections of his People*." To the Genius of France should be opposed the "Genius of True English-men," defined by their honesty, principles and dedication to freedom; "The free-born English, generous and wise, / Hate chains, but do not government despise," boasted an anonymous broadside published in 1680.[12] The native qualities "rediscovered" in this cultural turn made cultural and political differences between England and France a matter of essence.

Indeed, highlighting differences was becoming essential: Great Britain and France found themselves in a state of quasi-constant war throughout the eighteenth-century—the period that saw the birth of the United Kingdom. The country's collective identity was forged between the Acts of Union with Scotland in 1707 and Ireland in 1802 in geopolitical opposition to France: the War of the Spanish Succession (1702–1715), the War of the Austrian Succession (1740–1748), the Seven Years' War (1754–1763), the American War of Independence (1776–1783), and a new round of conflict when the French Republic declared war on Britain in 1793. These circumstances contributed to intensifying the push for Britons to "define themselves collectively . . . against the French as they imagined them to be, superstitious, militarist, decadent and unfree."[13] By contrast, the true Englishman was defined by honesty, originality, frankness, and moral independence. The principal characteristic of the true Englishman was *Sincerity*, "a composite personality which supposedly was 'given' in the nation's past and which allegedly still belonged in some immanent way to its simpler inhabitants."[14] By contrast, French artistic refinement increasingly came to be seen as derivative and artificial in contrast to the sincerity of English productions. British and French critics alike concurred in finding evidence of this most English of qualities in English literary works—which of course had contributed to spread this notion in the first place. Texts focused on characters more radically foreign than the French were especially instrumental in this process. Throughout Europe fictional native Americans and Africans "provided a radical standard of alien and primitive behavior (of otherness) that could be used . . . to measure other European people against, thereby contributing to the construction of a new, and more specifically national, self-image."[15] In England the "Noble Savage" so central to Enlightenment thinking "was gradually nationalized and parochialized by the literati and hence made the noble bearer of values supposedly distinctively English."[16] Not least among the works of literature involved in this process was *Oroonoko*.

For Joseph Roach, Thomas Southerne's *Oroonoko* is one of the plays by which "the English theater helped British subjects to imagine a community for themselves by making a secular spectacle out of the deeply mysterious play of ethnic identity and difference."[17] In the complex structure of the story, Oroonoko's body and mind become a battlefield for Europe's modern nationalisms: in him, ideal values of European culture are tested at their purported limit—the uncivilized—and yield a man unfit to live in the world the West made for itself in the Americas. Englishness and later Frenchness constituted themselves over the bodies of Oroonoko and Imoinda, the Africans' flesh serving not as the res publica Lucretia's body was to Rome but rather as the raw material on which England and France built their imperial incarnations. National sentiment and nations are works of imagination, and one can see how, in the constant circulation of translations and adaptations of *Oroonoko* on both sides of the Channel, French and English national sentiment sometimes used as narrow a channel as one specific story to define and redefine themselves and each other. Elizabeth Maddock Dillon argues that the era opened by the English Revolution saw "a 'virtualization' of the commons," where "the collectivity of the commons that was once embedded in material and economic practices [was] increasingly understood as an abstraction—as a virtual body that appear[ed] less in material than figurative terms." The theater played a crucial role in this dynamic, as a space where "audience and actors together form an assemblage that both embodies and represents the collectivity of the people."[18] This virtualization of the commons was both generative of, and generated by, the rise of English national sentiment into which English class resentment was diluted, precisely because, contrary to the Houses of Parliament, theatrical houses welcomed both the rabble and the elite. The story of Oroonoko helped build European nationalisms by attaching fictions of Africanness to them. Fictional Africans became all the more useful as standards, as notions of ethnoracial singularity grew to be essential to nationalism.

Southerne's additions to Behn's plot in his 1696 play make clear the significance of the Oroonoko legend to the "continually tested terrain" of Englishness: he infamously introduced a completely new comic plot involving two English sisters, Charlotte and Lucy Welldon, coming to Suriname to find men to marry. The Welldon plotline "radically condenses the circum-Atlantic crucible of sex and race into an imagined community of the dispossessed."[19] In the process what of the story might otherwise have been specifically African blends into the English. If, generally speaking, Oroonoko is akin to a European courtier, he is also made to endorse values of "Candour, Sincerity, and Love of LIBERTY, which," according to Philip, Duke of Wharton, "are the distinguishing Characteristicks of every TRUE BRITON."[20] No doubt Whaley's English Lucretia recognizes in him an honorary compatriot. Onstage Oroonoko's tragic bride has the "luxury" of being spared rape and suicide by a hero kind enough to kill her. The original Lucretia was not so lucky: she had to take her responsibilities as a wife and citizen and kill herself, and in the process she was given, beyond death, the even weightier responsibility of birthing a polity. The citizenly behavior that the antique Lucretia modeled demands that honor and patria come before physical welfare; the modern Lucretia shares these values, but the ability to sympathize with the pain of others—heathens though they may be—and the ostentatious display of sensibility become essential elements of her performance.

FRENCH ANGLOPHILIA

By the eighteenth century, sensibility became a major concern in English society, and the stage a privileged space for defining national and imperial identities. Eighteenth-century readers and spectators were engaged in a "theatrics of virtue": as they watched the suffering of others, they made a spectacle of expressing the sympathetic emotions righteous citizens are expected to feel in such circumstances.[21] But they were still consuming a performance, and the distance between gazing subject and suffering object allowed for the pain on display to be "unacceptable but simultaneously . . . alluring, 'delicious'" to spectators—enjoyable to the extent that it creates an opportunity for sentiment.[22] In this distance modern, free English citizens found space to simultaneously perform deeds of sympathy for, and rational reflection over, the lives of less civilized men (in Europe and elsewhere). In defining their own relation to standards of civilization, the English saw themselves as heirs to Rome and purported to improve on the ancient model. This notion found ready ears among French literati, who saw in England a sense of initiative they found lacking in France. Thus in Baron de Montesquieu's *Persian Letters*, the fictional Persian visitor Rica is dumbfounded at the fact that France, "the oldest and most powerful kingdom in Europe," would substitute Roman laws for "the old laws made by their first kings in the general assemblies of the nations."[23] A decade later he praised the wisdom of the English system: "The government of Rome was admirable in this—that from its origin its constitution was such . . . that all abuses could be corrected. . . . The government of England is wiser; for it contains a body which continually inspects it, and which as continually inspects itself."[24] The French philosophe recognized and admired the rival nation's ability to emulate and improve Roman principles of self-correction and adaptability.

Much like English Francophilia, French Anglophilia was a high-class phenomenon. It coalesced in the 1730s to later grow into the Anglomania of the 1770s, when "the elite and then their many imitators began to underline their threatened superiority by aping foreigners, especially *the English*."[25] Until the beginning of the eighteenth century, when notable intellectuals began praising English culture, the French had mostly ignored and roundly despised it. Some among the French literati saw in English theater a commendable expression of candor on which they might improve with French refinement, to the point that "the English came to be substituted for the example of the ancients."[26] If the ancients had long inspired French literature, then by way of England their protodemocratic legacy made an impression over France's most visible and influential Anglophile: Voltaire.

In the early 1720s a young Voltaire met Lord Bolingbroke—a Tory leader exiled in France after the accession of George I to the English throne—who introduced him to English culture and politics. Facing potential imprisonment in the Bastille in 1726, Voltaire was offered exile in England as an alternative. He chose to leave, crossing the sea to immerse himself in English culture for two years. He met with the cream of high society, but he especially sought the company and conversation of men of letters, discovering and translating works of English literature into French, as well as writing his own poetry and drama, much of it inspired by these new sources. During his stay he published the *Henriade*, the epic poem on King Henry IV of France that made his reputation. He also completed, in English, the first act of *Brutus*, a play he eventually finished writing and staged in France in 1730. In this take on the early days of the Roman Republic, Voltaire also introduced English theatrical trends into French drama.

Brutus takes place after the overthrow of Tarquin and follows closely the deposed king. In his preface Voltaire expounds the play's "English character," alluding to a conversation with Bolingbroke in which both men agreed that the birth of the Roman Republic "seems peculiarly adapted to [English] theatre."[27] There was indeed something distinctly English about treating rape, which had since the English Revolution been used heavily as a vehicle for political propaganda from all sides, a trend that repeated around the Exclusion Crisis and the Glorious Revolution.[28] As Jennifer L. Airey demonstrates, the story of Lucretia in particular was notably used in "the battle between those who would affirm the divine power of hereditary monarchy and those who would establish limits to monarchical power."[29] Voltaire asserted that "no Englishman had ever treated this subject."[30] Yet his *Brutus* evokes Nathaniel Lee's 1681 play *Lucius Junius Brutus*—later adapted and rewritten with drastic cuts by Charles Gildon as *The Patriot* (1703)—notably in its focus on a fictional tryst between Brutus's son Titus and a fictional Tarquin daughter.[31] Ignoring Lee—disingenuously or not—allowed Voltaire to present his play as a novel application of his idea that "the perfection of this art should consist in a due mixture of the French taste and the English energy."[32] "English energy" is prevalent in characterization: by contrast to Lee's morally ambivalent Brutus, Voltaire's is a man entirely given to the reason of state, and in this sense the perfect embodiment of the "true Briton" extolled in pamphlets for the previous half century. Titus's actions suggest no lesser love of Rome: though he loves Tarquin's daughter, his only failing in the face of difficult circumstances is merely to consider choosing love over patria, or fatherland. Titus never actually betrays Rome, yet having wavered in his love of country, he declares himself deserving of punishment. Rome suffers no doubting Thomas: "Rome wants an example, and demands my life: / By my deserved fate she may deter / Those of her sons, if any such there be, / Who might be tempted to a crime like mine."[33] Titus's words are reminiscent of Lucretia's parting words in Lee's play: "And that my life, tho well I know you wish it, / May not hereafter ever give example / To any that, like me, shall be dishonored, / To live beneath so loathed an infamy; / Thus I for ever lose it, thus set free / My Soul, my Life and honor all together."[34] Yet Voltaire chooses—no doubt at least in part to try and follow the rule of theatrical unity—to completely elide Lucretia's role in the birth of Rome. In *Brutus*, politics is strictly man's play, defined specifically in contrast to—and as superior to—emotional commitment marked as feminine. The only love republican politics suffers is love of patria.

Growing admiration for England among French aristocrats and literati paralleled the rise of French nationalism; yet a crucial difference between English and French national sentiment can be found in the way each approached patria, a concept with antique roots and religious connotations denoting "a community that was essentially closed" but also a vision of history whereby the future always carried the threat of decline from a glorious, purer past. By the eighteenth century this vision of patria had become characteristic of an English nationalism in which "the Protestant (and particularly Calvinist) sense of a terrible and impassable boundary between the elect and the damned paralleled the classical republican theme of the radical difference between citizens and foreigners." By contrast, France had long defined itself in an international context as an extension of its monarch, and the country's tendency to "minimize the connotations of exclusivity and fatality that had been associated with the concept of *patrie* since antiquity" mirrored "the Catholic commitment to a universal human community."[35] What national sentiment existed prior to the eighteenth century increasingly paled in the face of the aggressively exclusionary British form of nationalism. Modern French nationalism developed in the crucible of war against England—the Seven Years' War in particular—yet it retained some of its cosmopolitan, universalist components even as it merged with a mass movement predicated on anti-English xenophobia. The popular nationalist sentiment expressed in plays, poems, and imagery bolstered by governmental propaganda invoked a fuzzy and broad sense of Frenchness, inviting disparate groups and individuals to gather in opposition to the common enemy.

Voltaire pioneered an Anglophile movement that took hold among French literati in the aftermath of Louis XIV's long, ruinous reign, at a time when writers reflected on alleged national characteristics, which they estimated could be seen in drastic relief in French and English literature. Thus for Francophone Swiss writer Béat-Louis de Muralt writing in 1725, if "the Englishman ... depends but little on Public Opinion, and in Conversation he favors the pleasure of telling the Truth to his interlocutors to that of telling them obliging things," the French by contrast "puts great stock in the Opinion of others and seeks to give a good Opinion of himself, as much as he tries to make others happy with themselves; thence come the many Sweet and Flattering Things he utters in Conversation." Muralt finds the same contrast in literature: French theater is characterized by refinement but plagued with preciosity, flaws lamented in earlier works of British self-definition. "England," Muralt continues, "is a Land of Freedom and Impunity; each is what he wants to be, whence come, undoubtedly, the many extraordinary Characters, the many Heroes—good or evil—one finds among the English. This also gives them a certain Freedom of Thought and Sentiments, which contributes significantly to the Good sense one finds in them fairly generally, to set the difference between this Nation and most others."[36] Muralt's empirical observations are paralleled in his artistic analyses: reality echoes art, and art echoes reality. In this wonderful feat of circular thinking, Muralt participates in a movement of naturalization of cultural behavior that announces Johann Gottfried Herder's *Volk* theory: in this vision, each nation's unique spirit breathes in everything they do and produce—but then, that breath is stronger in some things than in others.[37]

In English writings Muralt found originality, independence, and sincerity, to a fault: good theater should "imitate Nature so well that Art does not show, and one forgets the Poet," but in English comedy, Muralt asserts with a condemning tone, "The Poet can always be heard over the Actor ... constantly disabusing the Spectator with his profound thoughts and forcing him against his will to notice that he is watching a Comedy." What—and how—good is art without artifice? English tragedy fares barely better in Muralt's eyes. While the themes English playwrights choose show the English genius for seriousness, their productions suffer from many excesses. They are interspersed with base comedy bits; they relish in blood and gore. Worse than the plays are the playwrights themselves, whom Muralt sees as shameless and ungrateful plagiarists: "It seems English Poets are used to making game of Honesty and Virtue, whose only place they believe to be on the Theater stage." That English playwrights and their practices would contradict a definition of Englishness Muralt pieced out from English literature does not seem to bother the Swiss author. He blames it entirely on authors whom he appears to loathe. The fact that they "try their hardest to please the Populace" is further proof of their infamy for Muralt.[38] Yet it does little to account for the fact that, for all their Francophilia, English aristocrats were also known to appreciate English drama. Though Muralt himself appears impervious to it, his text posits national sentiment as a staged fiction whose success can be measured by the extent to which its own fictionality is bypassed by observers—even, or perhaps especially, in the face of metatheatrical insistence. The resounding success of the staging of English nationalism explains at least in part why French authors were increasingly treating English theater with the same kind of reluctant admiration English playwrights had once reserved for French drama.

At one point in his reflection, Muralt fumes about an unnamed play in which he "watched a man on a cross tortured with pincers for half an hour onstage. It seems to me," Muralt continues, "that Poets of true Genius, who know how to move their audience, should not resort to pincers."[39] There is a distinct possibility that the man he saw tortured onstage was none other than Southerne's Oroonoko.[40] Two decades after Muralt, at the height of Anglomania, Abbé Le Blanc—though himself "a kind of propagandist for England"—voiced similar repugnance at English playwrights' general "lack of taste" and at Southerne's play in particular, arguing that it would never be allowed on French stages for "the low Comedy with which it is variegated."[41] Le Blanc, however, considered *Oroonoko* an example of the "fidelity in depicting Nature," which, contrary to Muralt, he thought characteristic of "English Tragic Poets" and saw in it a depiction of "the first of all virtues; and, let it be said in praise of Englishmen, that which best characterizes their Nation; humanity."[42] As Dillon argues, "The specific contours of the British *people* were never entirely clear": in the eighteenth century *Oroonoko* might be performed on stages thousands of miles apart around the Anglophone Atlantic to spectators in wildly different surroundings and circumstances. Stage representations—or lack thereof—of the legend of Oroonoko played a role in the formation of "performative commons," nodes of communal self-definition by which the audiences of plays in England, North America, and the Caribbean responded "as a 'people' according to the new dispensations of popular sovereignty in the eighteenth-century Atlantic arena." *Oroonoko*, in a novel of theatrical form, could teach readers how to perform, recognize, and reproduce behavior marked as English. Among the audiences of the

Anglophone Atlantic "new forms of popular sovereignty take shape that are articulated in relation to colonial, and not simply national, geographies," but plays performing race such as *Oroonoko* also were vectors for "reproducing Englishness in the New World" on and offstage.[43]

Still, in adapting Behn's novel in 1745, Antoine de Laplace meant to test the possibility not merely of translating but indeed of gallicizing the quint-essentially English text. "*Oronoko* [*sic*] entertained London dressed in the English fashion," he declared in the preface of *Oronoko, ou le prince nègre*; "in order to entertain Paris, I believed he needed French vestments." Laplace took Behn's original text out of its Restoration dress "to better connect certain events, soften others and enhance the interest of the whole."[44] Series of intertwined paradoxical networks of meaning are revealed in the process: systems of national definition dependent on the (re)interpretation of foreign literature, itself focused on the portrayal of foreigners; taxonomies of authentic national behavior resting on stage acting and reception. Laplace's bon mot hints at a deeper truth about the development of modern national sentiment in Europe: if national spirit could drape a narrative like a garment, Englishness and Frenchness depended on colonized, commodified African bodies and on fictionalized American plantation life for material to weave this national cloth. *Oronoko* was among the first French works of fiction to focus on the slave trade and plantation life, but it did so as a derivation of, and reflection on, English literature.[45] As such, it demonstrates how what Christopher Miller calls "triangular texts . . . representing the French Atlantic and its slave trade" always involved more than just France; more fundamentally, in their very reference to national difference they implied the modern Atlantic world.[46]

Laplace's adaptation retains the general plot and other structural elements of Behn's work and its female narrator, but it also borrows elements from Southerne's *Oroonoko*, notably the playwright's emphasis on Oroonoko's sentimental and cultural debt to France. Like Southerne's, Laplace's Imoinda is the daughter of a Frenchman turned general in chief of the Coromantien army, thanks "to his bravery and experience."[47] In this function he tutored Oronoko in the refined ways of Europe, notably showing him how to die nobly (one of Laplace's additions): the unnamed Frenchman voluntarily put his head in the way of an arrow destined for the prince. Among Laplace's other seemingly small changes is lieutenant governor Byam's attempt to rape Imoinda as Oronoko leads a party of English people to Indian towns in the forest. Oronoko's friend Jamoan intervenes and would kill Byam, but for Imoinda's call to spare him: "Let this cruel man live. . . . Let him know that one can be a slave, and be virtuous!"[48] This call to humanity, absent in

Behn's and Southerne's works, announces the drastically novel ending crafted by Laplace: Oronoko reluctantly prepares to stab Imoinda but is prevented from doing so by Byam. He kills Byam instead and is left for dead by the lieutenant governor's henchmen, as Imoinda disappears in the scuffle. Oronoko survives and recovers from his wounds, and he is reunited with Imoinda in the safety of an Indian village. Eventually, the benevolent absentee governor finally appears to find the lovers and their newborn son. He arranges for the new family to return to Africa, where the prince's grandfather, delighted by his return, abdicates in his favor. The royal couple and their child live happily ever after, one must assume, in a location where their race appears to be no issue.

Phenotype and race feature heavily in the original novel. Yet if Laplace translates literally Behn's infamous description of the prince, he erases all her references to Imoinda's skin color and never explicitly defines her racial status. As in Southerne's play, Imoinda is the daughter of a Frenchman, but nothing is ever said of her mother, so "we must reach the absurd conclusion that Laplace made Imoinda both white and black, that is, neither one nor the other."[49] Laplace's "unracing" of Imoinda follows Southerne's whitening of her. More crucially, it is a drastic gallicization of the text. The brave and desirable Imoinda is French more than she is white, at a time when understanding of the two notions was in flux. As a Frenchwoman she cannot be suffered to die, and neither can her noble savage of a husband. Laplace exacerbates the black hero's connection to French culture: his sense of bravery and honor are highlighted as a specifically French legacy. Thus, when Imoinda's father dies to save Oronoko, the narrator exclaims, "Such an admirable model of love and gratitude for his benefactor's kin! Judge how his deed moved Oronoko!"[50] The French tutor's deeds, his performance, move but also impress the African prince, which points to *Oroonoko*'s status as circum-Atlantic text and spectacle. The adaptation's ending further evokes the stage: the eleventh-hour appearance of the governor is a textual deus ex machina that allows for an awkward happy ending.

Laplace's adaptation went through seven editions in five decades and was among the most popular books in France in the eighteenth century, inspiring a spate of novels and broader discussions on the morals of slavery.[51] The different versions of Oroonoko and their critiques thus form a Franco-English conversation about each growing Atlantic superpower's self-definition in relation to the other's, in which the African hero—not unlike other popular exotic figures of the time such as the Indian, the Persian or Ottoman ambassador, and so on—functions essentially as a kind of photographic developer. He is an agent necessary to a process by which the latent images of European national sentiments—here English, there French—taken at each nation's colonial margins are made visible. The African hero acts to differentiate what might be generally human, or more narrowly refined and cosmopolitan, from what might be more specifically English or French. The French for photographic developer is *révélateur*; that its English *faux-ami* (revelator) would carry religious connotations is a convenient and useful coincidence. The word of God is not far from authors who—certainly in the case of the English—regard religious beliefs as an essential aspect of their national identity, allegedly essential truths about which are purportedly revealed here.

TO RACE THE NATIONS

The eighteenth century was indeed a time for revelation, racial and national: the Seven Years' War, a conflict with global repercussions waged on three continents, was a military disaster for France that triggered a deep wave of Anglophobia but also of self-questioning. Anti-English resentment spread among the populace, notably by way of successful plays such as Pierre-Laurent Buirette de Belloy's *Le siège de Calais* (1765), "the most popular historical play of the eighteenth century."[52] The play, extolling the spirit of the "true citizen" who would die for his country, is "the inheritor of ten years of patriotic literature," with a difference: instead of dignified aristocrats, the heroes are commoners, bourgeois ennobled by their love of country. This flurry of performances and publications singing the glory of French citizens played an important part in an intensifying movement by which France began to conceive of itself as a nation "and more so, as a nation which could mobilize itself, instead of simply flocking behind a king."[53] The French equivalent to the English performative commons was constructed in no small part around rising notions of racial essence rooted in pseudoscientific writings.

The decade of patriotic literature had also seen drastic developments in scientific theories about race, more specifically on the issue of what caused blackness of skin in Africans. Buffon's 1749 *Histoire naturelle* and the unified, monogenetic theory of the origins of humans it proposed—positing "the white race [as] the prototype" and the black race as a degeneration—profoundly impacted Western science. It also set a standard by "scientifically" equating the concept of blackness with skin tone. As a "measurable blackness criterion," skin color simultaneously offered "a counterpoint to new, latent definitions of whiteness" and became "a decisive factor in the classification of humans living on the African continent."[54] Buffon's *Histoire naturelle* influenced throughout the Western world an increasing number of reflections on the place of Africans within the whole of humanity, even as their place in

Western economy and culture had become paramount. In turn, the use of racialized Others was crucial to nationalist rhetoric, though in a distinctly different way for the emergent rhetoric of Frenchness than for the rhetoric of Englishness. French writers tended "to describe even the worst enemies as 'savages' who might yet improve themselves enough to join a civilized world community," favoring the relatively new and more open concept of civilization over the more hermetic of patria. In the drastic nationalist turn France took during the Seven Years' War, propaganda "decried turbulent English 'barbarians' and compared them unfavorably with non-European peoples," native Africans and Americans presented as people closer to the state of nature and potentially ameliorable, where lack of civilized behavior in socialized barbarians was evidence of their willful moral corruption.[55] Similar developments took place on the other side of the Channel.

In Whaley's poem the performance onstage, to the extent that it presents the Other, is passive, while the spectators' performance is understood and presented in terms of agency. Educated, civilized spectators sit with Lucretia at a moral balcony—even the rowdy, working-class crowds of the London theater—looking down. Their vantage point allows for a better view and understanding of the Others on display than the Others have of themselves. In recognizing this position, Lucretia appears to suggest that she has the ability to see herself as both sufferer and observer simultaneously. You might call it double consciousness, were not the characters onstage figments of the Western imagination. Thus, not without irony, Whaley's Lucretia envies Imoinda her comparatively carefree death: to die for love alone rather than be weighted with birthing a nation! This contrast becomes essential in the literature of slavery in the eighteenth century, notably as it develops along with abolitionism. In literature the abuse suffered by enslaved women evokes that suffered by Lucretia but works an inverted pattern: it pushes heathen men to look for vengeance but not for collective political agency. Through the noble figure of the black avenger, Africans in the Americas are shown to be unable to graduate from emotional behavior—marked as understandable but primitive—to rational, civilized behavior.

Over a decade after Laplace published his adaptation, Southerne's *Oroonoko* was thoroughly revised in its country of origin: in 1759 John Hawkesworth excised the secondary, comic plot from Southerne's play, justifying his work in terms reminiscent of Laplace. While the merit of *Oroonoko*'s tragic plot was "Universally acknowledged . . . these Scenes were degraded by a Connexion with some of the most loose and contemptible that have ever disgraced our Language and our Theatre."[56] Though reminiscent of Laplace's adaptation of Behn, Hawkesworth's adaptation from Southerne asserted

English moral superiority over the perpetual rival on the Continent. Propriety, sincerity, and sentiment were all of a piece at the dawn of the 1760s. Might makes right, but it also makes virtue: England's crushing victories over France were to the English so much proof of moral and cultural superiority intrinsically attached to a nation increasingly defined in racial terms. A period of "rampant racialism" opened in the 1760s, during which "year by year the vision of a 'truly' English or British racial community with a common past and a common moral, social, cultural and political makeup was pieced together from a maze of scholarly and pseudoscholarly research, and then fitted with tremendous emotional appeal by associating it with the idealized moral qualities of the Saxon ancestors," by contrast to the necessarily tyrannical Norman French.[57] By the same token the debauchery of the late seventeenth century was broadly understood as a result of French influence; if Laplace modified Behn to meet literary conventions, Hawkesworth meant to match Southerne's text with England's self-proclaimed Saxon purity. In a prologue that echoes Whaley's then almost forty-year-old poem, Hawkesworth asserts that the true value of Southerne's play was obscured by the conventions of his time: "Slave to Custom in a laughing Age, / With ribbald Mirth he stained the sacred Page." Hawkesworth's editing not only veils "a Father's Shame"; it also emphasizes that with *Oroonoko* Southerne "touch'd your Fathers's Hearts with generous Woe, / And taught your Mothers' youthful Eyes to flow."[58] By 1759 the behavior modeled by Whaley's Lucretia was understood to be the English norm, to the extent that Southerne's play had to be rendered more dignified to better fit its audience.

Hawkesworth corrected what he considered to be inaccuracies in Southerne's plot, expanding notably the part played by the traitorous slave Hotman. For Hawkesworth, the honorable Oroonoko could not be suffered to strike the first blow. Such act is, according to Hawkesworth, unjustifiable, as "Oroonoko had yet nothing to resent that could justify his taking Arms. . . . This seems, therefore, to be a Fault in his Conduct, which renders him somewhat less worthy both of Reverence and Pity, than if his Misfortunes had arisen from the Fault of another."[59] By Hawkesworth's logic, wrongs, like honor, are an individual matter to be assessed by an informed audience, but slavery, while providing the play's backdrop, has nothing to do with Oroonoko's woes. As Wylie Sypher contends, as the "temper" of the times grew increasingly in opposition to slavery, *Oroonoko* became attached to abolitionism simply by virtue of its featuring a noble African characterized in terms palatable to the tastes and refinement of the age, but neither Hawkesworth's nor Ferriar's 1784 revision actually opposes slavery.[60] These texts participated in a broader system of representation that "tended to reduce black Africans to an enslaved male," a universal and finite set of general truths about all Africans conveniently molded into a singular figure. As Andrew S. Curran further argues, the individual black Africans concurrently introduced in literature and ethnographic texts to challenge such reductions were in turn read by most as "simply exceptions that proved the rule"—a rule by then well anchored in Western minds, according to which (black) Africans were intrinsically different from, and naturally inferior to, (white) Europeans.[61] In such texts the theme of revenge specifically pointed to issues of justice and politics but equally dismissed them to underline their irrelevance as the regrettable norm. They did so as part of reflections on both race and the nation, notably in the wake of Voltaire's writings on these topics.

FRENCH SPARTACUS

The new English versions of *Oroonoko* entered in conversation with France as much as they questioned English slavery. Beyond Laplace's translation, *Oroonoko* provided French literature with narrative staples that would become standard in eighteenth-century "triangular texts": African protagonists of French literature such as Ziméo—the leader of a Jamaican Maroon uprising who, in Jean-François de Saint-Lambert's 1769 eponymous novel, "avenged [his] race and [himself]"—thus tend to be honorable princes tricked into slavery by unscrupulous European traders and involved in tragic and outlandish love stories.[62] The popularity and increasing visibility of these narratives in the second half of the eighteenth century coincided with the broad popular (re)discovery of the figure of Spartacus.

English writers explored Rome's republican history when their own country was in the process of transitioning to parliamentary monarchy. Yet if Rome was a political reference, modern England looked both to its own idealized Saxon past and to biblical Israel for cultural matters. The French had fewer qualms claiming inheritance to Rome as the "open and welcoming center of a universal civilization."[63] Classical references and English influence were equally on display in Voltaire's *Brutus*. Though generally considered one of his minor works, the play had a consequent legacy in French literature, where it inspired many "'anti-tyrannical' performances," including Bernard-Joseph Saurin's *Spartacus*. It might seem somewhat ironic that the most popular of *Brutus*'s stage descendants would celebrate one of the Roman Republic's most formidable foes, but Saurin's tragedy in heroic couplets echoed broader national and pan-European, Enlightenment reflections on freedom, the subject, and the nation. It marked "the birth of the modern icon," that is, the Spartacus we are familiar with to this day. Yet, as Brent D.

Shaw notes, there was little doubt then that Spartacus was "an imaginary character who responded to the demand at the time for a model of just resistance."[64] As such, *Spartacus* itself offers a peculiar mix of elements from *Brutus*, *Oroonoko*, and the Lucretia myth.

The play begins with Spartacus's revolt in full swing, and his mother, Ermengarde, a prisoner of Rome. She stabs herself rather than compromise her honor and sends along with the bloodstained dagger this message: "Bring him this iron, and my supreme law.... Tell him to avenge the Universe, and myself." Spartacus makes the promise but encounters a major obstacle when he falls in love with Emilie, the daughter of the Roman consul Crassus. Needless to say, their love is impossible and dooms both of them and the revolt. The lovers eventually commit suicide, Emilie stabbing herself before handing another bloody dagger to Spartacus, who in turn stabs himself and dies a "free man," invoking political thought when he all but abandoned it in the name of love.[65] Among the singular innovations Saurin brings to an old tale is his focus on the relations between private and public matters. Somewhat oddly for a slave, Saurin's Spartacus is already "domesticated": he has a personal life that his involvement in collective politics jeopardizes, and the play's dynamic fluctuates with his "vacillation between domestic security and political leadership."[66] The contrast drawn between private and public domains crosses at odd angles with another dichotomy fundamental to the play that contrasts nationalist politics and cosmopolitan, human rights ideology. Indeed, the dilemma faced by Spartacus and Emilie is centered on nationality and nationalism: Emilie, a true descendant of Lucretia, is a virtuous woman and Roman. She first fell for Spartacus on witnessing his honorable and heroic behavior in the gladiatorial arena, and her impressions were confirmed when he saved her life. Yet she cannot choose him over her country— nor does she choose Rome over him. They can be together only after his defeat, and in death. Loving a man who is twice a noncitizen—as a barbarian and a slave—has guaranteed her demise.

Spartacus will have either freedom or death, but his mother made clear early on that for the enslaved, death and freedom are indistinguishable, so long as Rome exists. Short of Rome's destruction, the only alternative would be the foundation of a nation: that is to say, following the Roman model that underlay even Spartacus's reflections on universal freedom. This logic pervades the play. Spartacus evokes Roman history in conversation with Crassus's envoy: "What, indeed, was Rome? Who were your ancestors? / A vile band of serfs escaped from their Masters, / Perfidious robbers of women and goods." He is of course alluding to the early days of the kingdom of Rome, when Romulus and Remus surrounded themselves with the outcasts of the Italian peninsula and suffered the scorn of surrounding tribes. The similarities do not end there: Ermengarde's choosing death over dishonor and suicide by stabbing is of course not without evoking Lucretia and the birth of the Roman Republic. Lucretia's oath keepers, elite Roman citizens all, eschewed revenge for politics and raised the Republic of Rome to a standard Spartacus himself admires. Later, speaking to Crassus, Spartacus evokes with wonder Rome's victory over Carthage in the Second Punic War: "In the time of the Scipios . . . , being adopted by Rome would have been honorable." The Rome he now knows—arrogant, bloated with success and corruption—is responsible for his personal ills. Rome's ambition "for which nothing is sacred / Dragged into captivity the son with the mother." Rome has forsaken magnanimity and turned to equating its power with nature: as Messala advances, "woe to the vanquished is the law of the Universe."[67] What heroic idealism might have once characterized Rome has disappeared, replaced by this protosocial Darwinist outlook on the superiority of the Roman nation.

The play makes clear that military success constitutes but a part of Rome's might: it rests more squarely in the national sentiment it modeled, in patria, a cement that connects Romans and forms that "eternal obstacle . . . that invincible wall" strong enough to even separate Emilie from Spartacus.[68] Saurin's play participates in France's evolving national sentiment, initiating a conversation between Catholic universalism and Roman-English nationalism. It exposes the limits in both strains: exclusionary nationalism leads even dignified citizens to arrogance and condescension for other nations and ultimately to condone tyranny. Universalism, though it holds the moral high ground, appears to suffer from its lack of pragmatism. Saurin's Spartacus has no political plan but universal freedom, a term that means everything and, therefore, nothing. In the play citizenship is the paramount force. Spartacus's idealism is as admirable as Rome's tyranny is despicable. But deprived of a political project, idealism is reduced to domestic matters: personal vendettas and suicides, love and family affairs, singular acts that begin and end with individuals. The contrast between Lucretia's tale and Spartacus's is here again telling. Spartacus swears alone to his mother, whereas Brutus led a coalition. No one pragmatically transcends the personal elements of Spartacus's feud; no one turns them into respectable collective politics. His assault on Rome remains ineluctably tied to the personal wrongs he has suffered and his emotional life.

Significantly, Saurin himself saw his Spartacus as a potential model for future monarchs rather than as a hero for the people. Early critics of the play lamented the fact that his Spartacus is a nobleman by birth as both historically inaccurate and theatrically disappointing. "It is far more beautiful to make a name for oneself than to simply carry the name of one's ancestors, however honorably," declared Elie Catherine Fréron, who also mocked Spartacus's desire to fight for the "Happiness of the Universe" as "Encyclopedic lunacy."[69] In the name of aesthetics and theatrical conventions, Fréron makes a case for a meritocratic vision of Spartacus that Duchosal would recognize thirty-four years later as in keeping with revolutionary ideals. Yet it is the friend of the philosophes, Saurin himself, who explained, in the preface to the 1769 edition of the play, his decision to make Spartacus a prince as an effort in actual verisimilitude. However "blessed by nature," a low-born, uneducated Spartacus would naturally also be ferocious, which would make for great theater but fail to serve Saurin's object: "I wanted to portray . . . a man who would be great for being a benefit to mankind rather than a woe." "Historians and Poets," Saurin continues, "have done great harm to humankind" by showing conquerors and ambitious men in too warm a light: "How many young Princes, heated by their readings, seduced by the glimmer of false heroism, have caused desolation and ravages in order to walk in the footsteps of Alexander and Caesar?"[70] With this new model for heroic behavior, Saurin claims he hoped to influence monarchs. His characterization of Spartacus as a nobleman underlines how the play participates in the complex and at times self-contradictory movement by which "French people turned citizen writers . . . open a breach into the edifice of absolutism," remaining beholden to an ancien régime worldview even as it introduces themes that profoundly undermine it.[71] It also makes clear that slavery is here merely understood as a metaphor for French political oppression.

SILENCING SLAVERY

Voltaire praised Saurin's play and, more specifically, the characterization of Spartacus, whose fiery temperament and honorable behavior he found to be "in the English fashion."[72] Love of liberty was increasingly seen as an essential trait of civilization, but it also served to obfuscate how the very idea might contradict France's and England's involvement in the slave trade. In his 1763 entry on "slaves" for the *Dictionnaire philosophique*, Voltaire writes, "Slavery is as ancient as war, and war as human nature," commenting further that slavery in antiquity was a "principle of society." He goes on to present varied examples showing how widespread slavery has been, and remains, in human history. Yet for all the ubiquity and normality of slavery, to revolt against it can be righteous: "Of all wars, that of Spartacus was the more just, and possibly the only one that was ever absolutely so."[73] Although he affects to speak of the historical figure rather than the theatrical representation, Voltaire sees Spartacus through the prism of Saurin's play as a kind of European natural man, speaking the modern language of freedom inspired by English rhetoric and propped up as commentary on the state of French politics. That Voltaire would not take into consideration any of the many American slave revolts he undoubtedly was aware of demonstrates, if need be, that he has only the white world in mind, and France in particular, when he reflects on the struggle for freedom.

Thus those examples of contemporary enslavement Voltaire discusses in some detail in his dictionary entry are forms of serfdom enforced by the French clergy. By contrast, Voltaire mentions the Atlantic slave trade only once, matter-of-factly, as one in many current forms of slavery, noting without comment that "the Pennsylvanians alone have renounced this traffic, which they account flagitious."[74] In *Candide*, the philosophe expressed broad moral outrage for chattel slavery; his overlooking it in an encyclopedic entry dedicated to matters of culture and justice points to the fact that Voltaire had by the 1760s developed the notion that Africans belonged to a different realm of humanity, contra Buffon.[75] For Voltaire, "the most race-oriented thinker of his generation," Africans formed a race—or a species, as the philosophe used the terms interchangeably—distinct from, but also inferior to, whites.[76] By his notions Africans "had barely advanced past the most basic era of human development" and as such sat at a point in the timeline even more primitive than a Spartacus. If he considered that the betterment of French serfs might take centuries, he also thought that "at some point, all people were for centuries what the inhabitants of the southern coasts of Africa . . . are today."[77] Such people might express basic human emotions to which even civilized, sophisticated Europeans could still relate, but they were *physiologically* incapable of processing such advanced notions as politics. Revenge, then, as expressed in more or less exotic heroes onstage, had potentially political meaning only to the extent that it spoke to sophisticated Western audiences. As far as *real* Africans were concerned, such evolution would likely have to wait several centuries.

Still, incapable of political thought as they allegedly were, *real* Africans—increasingly visible, observable, and analyzable as physical bodies in continental Europe, increasingly essential to the West's economic and military machinery—nevertheless practiced revenge. Slave revolts were incessant in the Americas from the introduction of slavery by the Spaniards. Escaped slaves—known as Maroons, from the Spanish *cimarrón*, a term that "originally referred to domestic cattle that had taken to the hills in Hispaniola"—built hidden camps in the mountains of Cuba, known as *palenques*, from the sixteenth century on, and they were found in other Spanish colonies on the South American continent.[78] There existed a dozen of *quilombos*, their Brazilian equivalent; the most formidable one, the "Negro Republic" of Palmares, was home to close to thirty thousand people when it was destroyed by the Portuguese after decades of attempts. As noted by R. K. Kent, the resilience of Palmares suggests that, had it not been destroyed, it may well have been emulated by "a number of independent African states dominating the backlands of eighteenth-century Brazil."[79] There was *marronage* in every single European colony in the Americas and in some cases yielded collective outcomes that even Europeans could understand as political: thus, after close to a century of war between Maroons and English troops in Jamaica, English authorities in 1740 struck an agreement with the Leeward Maroons, led by Cudjoe, by which the latter were allowed to live in relative independence under English supervision. References to these events feature prominently in antislavery writings, as they developed in late eighteenth-century literature on both sides of the Channel, expressed in a language of freedom designed for Europe. Slave leaders of the European stage performed romantic scenes following Western conventions and expectations and conquered European hearts: their real-life counterparts gained no European admirers in showing their military prowess. The victories they obtained were won using tactics adapted to their situations, unlike anything called for in the European art of war. The threat of mass slave revolt was rising in the American colonies, and the literature of colonial powers was finding new ways to temper increasingly racialized notions of national identity and politics in light of the coming storm.

EARLY ABOLITIONIST POETRY

Saurin lamented poets' portrayals of heroes and their influence on young princes, yet these portrayals' ultimate impact on the course of human events may be better measured by the influence they had on other young poets. In the late eighteenth century, authors took to treating the particulars of the Atlantic slave trade more directly and regularly, notably in poetry, and in terms meaning to implicate national sensibility. Thomas Chatterton's three *African Eclogues*—published in the *Court and City Magazine* and the *London Magazine* in 1770—are among the earliest English poems to evoke antislavery scenes and sentiments.[80] The eclogue form originated in antiquity with Virgil's *Eclogues*, a dark elaboration on the ancient Greek bucolic genre. Virgil's poem is "permeated through and through with portrayals of human infelicity, catastrophic loss, and emotional turbulence," reflecting the intense social and political turmoil of the last years of the Roman Republic.[81] A similar spirit, laden with exoticism and musings on culture, animated William Collins's popular *Persian Eclogues* (1742), arguably a more direct influence on Chatterton. The pastoral mode to which the eclogue is related was greatly appreciated in the eighteenth century and participated in broader reflections on culture, civilization, and national definition: the shepherds of eighteenth-century pastorals have educated, sophisticated minds so unlike the rural workers they supposedly portray that they generated a spate of comedic takedowns on the enterprise. At the same time, writers such as Collins sought "new means for an idealized shepherd pastoral that referred to objective conditions."[82] He found such conditions in the East, where, according to contemporary sources, aristocratic shepherds still roamed. These peculiar notions ring with the diachronic, hierarchical views of culture and human history expressed by Voltaire and clarify the purpose of Collins's shepherds as standard by which to measure his own culture.

Englishness, as it appears in Collins's writings, is defined through an exotic prism that invokes colonialism, if it does not directly refer to it. Collins, who presents the text as his translation of Persian poems "received . . . at the Hands of a Merchant," opens his preface by extolling national peculiarities in literature: "It is with the Writings of Mankind, in some Measure, as with their Complexion or their Dress, each Nation hath a Peculiarity in all these, to distinguish it from the rest of the World." If the English style is "naturally Strong and Nervous," the Persian is "rich and figurative," further characterized by "Elegancy and Wildness of Thought," qualities so foreign to the English that surely, finding them displayed in the poem will be sufficient proof of "their Being Original."[83] Collins's effort puts in relief the utter artificiality of national characteristics, yet that is not quite his purpose. The idyllic vision presented in Collins's first eclogue is ruined in the fourth, as Turk and Tartar invaders send the shepherds into flight. When Collins's poem was published, the country was engaged in the War of Jenkins' Ear against Spain, a succession of long indecisive actions and battles around the Caribbean, and would soon be involved in the War of the Austrian Succession on the Continent. According to Carson Bergstrom, the eclogue provides Collins with a vehicle to "convey his concerns about the consequences of political decisions, particularly military ones, upon the public weal," thus echoing not only Virgil's original mood but also commenting on threats—local and global—to England's welfare inseparable from its colonialist ventures.[84]

Chatterton's *African Eclogues* emulate both Virgil's and Collins's somber musings but also operate a drastic shift in focus: where Virgil reflected on social upheaval internal to Rome, and Collins on turmoil in the East, Chatterton portrays "the preying of civilization upon the innocent denizens of paradise."[85] In "Heccar and Gaira: An African Eclogue," Chatterton's African warriors are recovering from a bloody battle with European enslavers, whom they did not manage to stop from abducting their kin, including Gaira's wife and children.[86] His friend Heccar promises eternal war on the enslavers, yet the poem expresses ambivalence toward revenge. Gaira vows to "strew the beaches with the mighty dead" and announces a future of endless retaliation: his weapon "with vengeance shall be never satisfied."[87] With this poem Chatterton introduces the theme of revenge into antislavery poetry as well as the somewhat reluctant approach to it that becomes standard in later antislavery poems. Violent retaliation is at the heart of the text, yet it remains out of it: the warriors' vow never does, and never can, come to fruition. One issue with vengeance, Peter A. French offers, is that it "forges an intermediate causal linkage between the moral quality of an act, its wrongness, and an appropriate penalty."[88] Throughout Western culture, "revenge is morally permissible if the venue of civil redress of serious grievances are blocked," which is undeniably the case here. A central matter in the performance of justifiable, "moral" vengeance is "tailoring the fit," or finding the punishment acceptably matching the wrong. The issue permeates Chatterton's poem, but ultimately he does not address it. Even as the action of European slavers is shown to be morally wrong, stopping short of showing vengeance performed effectively leaves the qualification of this immorality in abeyance. The unnamed culprits in the poem could well be English, engaging in a practice partially responsible for England's rise as world superpower; what form, in the moral equation at work in vengeance, should fit retribution take? The poem does not quite ask this question from its English readers. It reduces the Atlantic slave trade to a private affair, the abduction of Gaira's family. In this framing Gaira's violent response, though understandable, can only be morally tainted. The individual scale chosen by Chatterton not only allows English readers to feel sympathy for Gaira without questioning their own position in his woes; it also throws back the responsibility for moral action on the poem's sole visible actors. Presented with exotic scenes from Africa, English readers can safely retreat into the same position in which we found Whaley's Lucretia: sensible spectators judging for themselves the sincerity and morals of—while ignoring their own role in—the performance at hand. Tellingly, it is as the issue of slavery became a domestic issue that its treatment in literature shifted.

This phenomenon spilled off the stages and pages of English literature and into the streets of England, and there also it attached to the particular fate of one African individual. Lord Mansfield's verdict in the 1772 *Somerset v. Stewart* case made West Indian slavery a national matter: Charles Stewart, a customs officer from Massachusetts, came to London with his slave Somerset. When Somerset refused to return to Boston and a life of bondage, Stewart had him forcibly taken onto a ship. Somerset's English friends alerted the authorities on his behalf and sued for his freedom. Lord Mansfield decided Somerset should go free, a verdict widely interpreted by worried Caribbean planters and hopeful slaves alike as meaning that all slaves would immediately gain freedom upon reaching English soil. This was far from the truth. The gross irony of this notion was noted in a letter by Benjamin Franklin, who saw a "Country which encourages such a detestable Commerce by Laws, for promoting the Guinea Trade, while it piqu'd itself on its Virtue Love of Liberty, and the Equity of its Courts in setting free a single Negro."[89] The Somerset decision further emphasized focus on individual stories possibly influenced by literature in the first place, but which in turn set the tone for antislavery texts. In 1773 Thomas Day and John Bicknell first published *The Dying Negro*, a poem inspired by the true story of a black man who had preferred to commit suicide in London rather than be brought back to the Americas as a slave. The issue of national morals in relation to the slave trade is especially salient in Day and Bicknell's poem, and the way they approach it set standards for antislavery literature. Eschewing Chatterton's tentative approach of the politics of violent retaliation, the authors turn to metaphysics instead.

Day and Bicknell show the dying slave calling to the heavens from the bottom of the ship where he is chained, reminiscing about his love affair, until his tone turns angrier in the last verses: "Thanks, righteous God! — Revenge shall yet be mine; / Your flashing lightning gave the dreadful sign." In this regard Day and Bicknell's poem illustrate a shift otherwise expressed in the text itself by the speaker: this Westernized African also happens to be a Christian and is therefore warranted in expecting divine justice. As such, he upends long-standing interpretations of natural phenomena. Early modern writings routinely analyze weather events and catastrophes as expressions of divine providence. Increased English presence in the West Indies made it difficult for English writers to interpret the destruction wrought by hurricanes on their possessions as God's punishment, when their colonizing enterprise was undertaken in his name. As Peter Hulme notes, hurricanes were therefore considered "less a message from God for his chosen people than an attribute of savagery itself . . . a fact confirmed by its tendency of attacking precisely . . . the marks of civility."[90] Though the Dying Negro speaks from the London docks, he makes it possible to read even West Indian weather as a message from the Christian God, as through him it retains its exotic character. Day and Bicknell's speaker thus calls to God, but also fancies Discord and War rampaging through the West:

> Then, while with horror sick'ning Nature groans,
> And earth and heav'n the monstrous race disowns,—
> Then the stern genius of my native land,
> With delegated vengeance in his hand,
> Shall raging cross the troubled seas, and pour
> The plagues of Hell on yon devoted shore....
> For Afric triumphs!—his avenging rage
> No tears can soften, and no blood assuage....
> Flyswift ye years!—Arise thou glorious morn!
> Thou great avenger of thy race be born![91]

Sitting at the threshold of pagan and Christian culture, Day and Bicknell's speaker summons supernatural figures from both worlds for a cause marked as justifiable by Christian—read English—standards. The news story on which the poets elaborated their poem made clear that Mansfield's decision had changed little for slaves, including those who did make it to England.[92] Nevertheless, it allowed them to hint at a moral divide between metropolitan Englishmen and their colonial counterparts.

Between the first and the second edition of the poem, news of the seditious Boston Tea Party had reached England: "What has *America* to boast?" the authors ask in the dedication added to the second edition. "What are the graces or the virtues which distinguish its inhabitants?... For them the Negro is dragged from his cottage, and his plantane shade.... Yet, such is the inconsistency of mankind! these are the men whose clamours for liberty and independence are heard across the Atlantic Ocean!" Day and Bicknell are in effect turning Franklin's argument about England's hypocrisy against American colonists, criticizing the way they resort to the language of freedom while keeping men in bondage: "It is in Britain alone, that laws are equally favourable to liberty and humanity; it is in Britain the sacred rights of nature have received their most awful ratification."[93] This argument became a staple of early abolitionist literature dedicated to proving that Britain's essential commitment to freedom had not been jeopardized by its war against American colonists.[94] Not without irony, the death of an anonymous slave on the Thames becomes evidence of England's superior morals. The practice of slavery is dismissed as foreign to British character and physically distanced in the same process: it is isolated as an American practice, at a geographic, cultural, and moral remove from Britons. The poem maintains English readers' ability to sympathize with the slave's suffering, shudder with his imprecations, and observe righteously America's impending doom, boosting in the process a paradoxically racialized vision of abolitionism itself by which "to be opposed to slavery was to be proudly white, virtuous, mainland Britons."[95] Day and Bicknell's supernatural, embodied genius of Africa crosses the ocean, his destination unspecified: his vengeance is directed against Europeans at large, but the American colonies seem the likely place where he will strike.

English abolitionist poetry in the wake of Chatterton, Day, and Bicknell favored allegorical genii of Africa in their reflections on morality, vengeance, and slavery. Such a figure appears, for example, in the anonymously written *Jamaica, A Poem* (1777), "clank[ing] his chains, / And damn[ing] the race that robs his native plains," or in the 1788 version of Hugh Mulligan's "The Lovers: An African Eclogue": "Afric's Genius mourn'd an injur'd land, / And wrapt in clouds, her foe's destruction plann'd" and further "sees the wild, the dread tornado driven / By all th'avenging ministers of Heav'n."[96] When they do not invoke the embodied spirit of their land, the enslaved of abolitionist poetry call to pagan gods or the almighty Christian one for the accomplishment of their revenge.

Whether or not to represent slaves performing retaliatory violence was a major dilemma for antislavery poets. Mulligan's two African lovers, Bura and Zelma, escape a slave ship moored off the coast of Africa just as "A warlike chief hath faithful friends prepar'd, / With engines meet to bind the drowsy guard. . . . And free the captives while the tyrants sleep." Unable to join in the fight, they watch as the ship eventually bursts into flames. The lovers support their peers' violence, but they do not partake in it. The apocalyptic collective effort at retaliatory violence is contrasted with, and abandoned for, two idealized "sentimental heroes . . . endowed with all the outward signs of a highly developed sensibility," whose commitment to revenge is wholly verbal.[97] Letting enslaved voices speak of retribution against enslavers ultimately performed by the Most High could also spare and poets accusations of stoking the fires of slave revolt. Speaking of revolt rather than revolting is evidence that one subscribes to a robust but civil and sensible exchange of ideas. The sympathetic and necessarily passive enslaved speaker in Hugh Mulligan's "The Slave: An American Eclogue" makes clear the function revenge is expected to play in the abolitionist rhetoric of sensibility: "Will thy slow vengeance never never fall? / . . . Oh hear a suppliant wretch's last sad prayer! / Dart fiercest rage! Infect the ambient air! / This pallid race, whose hearts are bound in steel, / By dint of suff'ring teach them how to feel."[98] For Mulligan's speaker, only pain—fit retribution for the pain they wrought— could acquaint Europeans with sensibility. But this speaker is the creation of an English poet, addressing English readers from the pages of English publications: the suffering he is referring to is literary but not literal. It is another, elaborate layer of the spectacle of sensibility designed to train model citizens. At the theater the performance of sympathy was part of the overall spectacle—an essential characteristic of the English performative commons. Abolitionist poetry, in which English spectators are embodied in both author and reader, reiterates in print the national and racial dynamics developed around the stage.

EDWARD RUSHTON'S *WEST INDIAN ECLOGUES* IN AMELIORATIONIST TIMES

The cultural context within which abolitionist poetry was conceived imposed nationalistic patterns even on material that challenged nationalistic impulses. A case in point is Edward Rushton, a known journalist and pamphleteer from Liverpool who advocated republican and abolitionist beliefs and agitated for sailors' rights and Irish autonomy.[99] As a young man, he worked as a sailor on slave ships and "resided several years in the West-Indies" before becoming blind from ophthalmia contracted while attending to sick slaves. His experiences profoundly changed him and made him an abolitionist for life.[100] These opinions were first expressed in his 1787 *West Indian Eclogues*—a collection of four poems (three dialogues and one monologue) set in Jamaica and spoken by enslaved Africans abducted from their native land. Undeniable parallels exist between Mulligan's and Rushton's eclogues, notably in their depiction—however abstract—of violence performed by the enslaved.[101] Crucially, Rushton's poem departs from Mulligan's in featuring a speaker who actually performs revenge. Just as important, this new development is, perhaps more than any other abolitionist depiction of slave revenge, rooted in the personal, foreclosing potential political readings of the act.

The first three eclogues, all spoken by Jamaican slaves, describe their abduction in Africa and the extreme brutality they are made to suffer in the West Indies. The poems are bolstered by extensive footnotes referring to a variety of works of natural history as well as testimonies lending credibility to Rushton's accounts of the treatment of slaves. Revenge plays an especially central role in the fourth and final eclogue in the collection: the midnight monologue of Loango, whose wife, Quamva, was "torn from [his] arms by that accursed white," the plantation owner. The poem begins with the elements already raging: The "fierce northern tempest" is hitting the island, and we find Loango "at this dread hour, deep in an orange grove," where he used to meet Quamva. He first calls on "spirits of the air / Who rule the storms" to grant him his wish for revenge and destroy all but his wife. Loango is gradually overtaken by the conviction that Quamva genuinely enjoys the company of the planter. Loango's wish for revenge narrows as he calls for it to "steel his soul" and give him the resolve necessary to kill Quamva, the planter, and himself. "Three, three must fall!" he declares, and fall they do. The poem's last two lines, separated from Loango's monologue by a bold dividing line, announce succinctly, "Then to the place, with frenzy fir'd, he fled / And the next morn beheld the mangled dead!"[102]

Rushton's *Eclogues* were widely and positively reviewed in the press, each journal reading Rushton through the prism of its political stance on slavery. The *Monthly Review* argues that "writers have greatly exaggerated in their account of the *cruelties* exercised towards the Negroes." Yet far from denying the brutality of slavery wholesale, the reviewer declares further that the enslaved must be "held in obedience by *fear* . . . for deterring them from mutiny and revolt, to which they are not a little prone."[103] This point evokes Edward Long's *History of Jamaica* (1774), according to which slave revolts were the reason for planters' "restrictions," rather than the other way around.[104] The *Critical Review*'s assessment of Rushton's poems reverses the *Monthly*'s causal link, finding it "extremely natural" for the enslaved to "[vent] imprecations and [plan] revenge against their oppressors." Planning revenge may have been natural, but it was not rhetorically sound: "The tears and supplications, not the impotent rage and defiance of the wretched, are most likely to melt their persecutors' hearts, if formed, as we trust some of our West-India planters are, of 'penetrable stuff'": here again, the underlying argument centers on the effect the spectacle of slavery might have on English readers.[105] Franca Dellarosa advances that the "irreducibility of Rushton's enslaved Africans to the stock model of the kneeling slave" clashed with the "rhetoric of sensibility" then central to discussions about slavery, and whose echoes can also be heard in the *General Magazine*'s review of Rushton's poems.[106] The reviewer in the *General Magazine* has no concern regarding the accuracy of Rushton's descriptions: "Alas! He tells us, and we have too much reason to believe him, that 'in delineating the following scenes, he has painted from actual observation.'" He challenges readers' ability to feel; what Rushton "describes must be felt in all its force by every reader whose breast is not rendered inhumanly callous by deriving immediate advantage from the most infamous of all human traffick!"[107] The review says little about the poems themselves and entirely avoids discussing Rushton's use of revenge and violence, focusing instead on what in his poem appears to follow mainstream abolitionism's appeal to sensibility.

For the reviewer, only economic profit drawn from slavery could trump the natural sensibility characteristic of Englishmen. A similar notion appears notably in the pamphlets of Anthony Benezet, James Ramsay, Thomas Clarkson, and Granville Sharp, who developed what Philip Gould dubs "commercial jeremiad," a secularized version of the sermon form popularized by Puritan preachers and focused on warning of the terrible consequences that follow a people's breach of their compact with God.[108] Early abolitionists for the most part privileged what they saw as a pragmatic argument for the improvement of the living conditions of the enslaved rather than the impossible demand of complete abolition of slavery. Although this argument generally ignored or downplayed slaves' efforts at fighting against the brutality of slavery, even this early, moderate, and ameliorationist form of antislavery politics developed as a response to the 1760 Jamaican slave uprising known as Tacky's War. Faced with the concrete prospect of violent retaliation, planters pondered ways to save the institution. In the aftermath of Tacky's War, "amelioration became the most favored formula for anti-insurgency" in the minds of supporters and opponents of slavery alike.[109] Ameliorationist authors drew arguments from the writings of the same Edward Long who blamed planters' brutality on slave revolts: they used his view that blacks constituted a separate, inferior species of humankind to justify their call for benevolent husbandry on the part of their superiors. This outlook went hand in hand with the ominous visions of commercial jeremiads and their promises of divine punishment in the form of economic doom. Englishmen were to rise to the responsibilities of their moral and biological superiority or face the wrath of their maker. Abolitionist poetry tapped into similar sentiment, though it favored more direct and elemental forms of destruction. Gradually, poets came to include more specific, graphic examples of the abuse the enslaved met at the hands of their oppressors. Rushton is unique among eighteenth-century abolitionist poets for the way he addresses the issue of rape.

DROIT DU SEIGNEUR IN IMPORTED FRENCH THEATER

Rushton's poem makes use of the expected elemental tropes; yet if Loango falls prey to this particular mode of pathetic fallacy, he quickly turns to even darker thoughts. The storm becomes a concrete cover for him to perform the violent deeds previous abolitionist poems would have modestly eschewed. They come as a response to the kind of abuse other poets also tended to avoid. Such abuse appears in Mulligan's "African Eclogue," where Zelma evokes the specter of rape mostly to emphasize her heroic resistance to it:

"Think how against the tyrant's wiles I strove, / Us'd every art t' evade his lawless love," she enjoins him. Further in the poem, as she describes living on the ship after her abduction, she adds, "Worse than all, to be their passion's slave; / T'avoid such lust I brav'd the dashing wave."[110] Jumping off the ship allowed Zelma to elude rape and, subsequently, death in the ship's explosion. By contrast, Rushton makes the sexual terror wrought on the enslaved the principal reason for the retaliatory violence performed in the poem. In this Rushton ties the eminently politicized treatment of rape in the English theatrical and poetic tradition with a more specific motif that was then all the rage in French literature: droit du seigneur.

Sexual violence at large and Lucretia's story in particular were commonly used in English drama during the revolutionary and Restoration periods, imbued as they were with the political concerns of the day for the rights of subjects and citizens in the face of royal power. In the late seventeenth-century plays, Derek Hughes notes, rape served as "a justification of extreme political action: a means of focusing attention on the supremacy of private rights over tyrannical power," and as such, merged as it was with the story of Lucretia, it constituted an essential element in England's national self-definition. By the mid-eighteenth century, stage rape had become a "self-reproducing theatrical attraction." It came to play a crucial role in national self-making and political change across the Channel, under the French guise of droit du seigneur, or *jus prima noctis*—a lord's right to claim a vassal's bride on her wedding night.[111] There is no evidence that the practice was ever common or widespread, yet French playwrights and philosophers used it as a tool to criticize the privileges of the French aristocracy in the ancien régime.[112] Among the earliest texts to treat *jus prima noctis* in Enlightenment France was *Le droit du seigneur ou l'écueil du sage*, a play by none other than Voltaire, first performed in a truncated form in 1762.[113] The epitome of this genre, M. de Beaumarchais's *Le mariage de Figaro*, was originally written in the late 1770s and accepted for production in 1781, but its material was deemed so shocking it was not performed until 1784, notably after Beaumarchais moved the action of the play from France to nearby Spain. An English adaptation by Thomas Holcroft was performed the following year in London, and in 1786 Mozart created his opera, confirming the broad success met by Beaumarchais's play around Europe.

The "gothic right . . . of sleeping the first night with every bride" hangs like a dark cloud over the heads of sympathetic servants Figaro and his partner, Suzanne, who suffers the unwanted advances of Count Almaviva.[114] Droit du seigneur is the expression of feudal rights at their vilest, as Figaro laments in his famous monologue in the fifth act: "And what, most noble Count, are your claims to distinction, to pompous titles, and immense wealth, of which you are so proud, and which, by accident, you possess?" Nobility is the fruit of chance, not merit; unfair systems breed unfair situations and impunity, which in turn are likely to produce resentment, and worse. Near the end of the play Figaro finds himself in a situation remarkably similar to Loango's. Though Figaro is aware that the count's interest in Suzanne has gone unrequited, a series of quid pro quos have convinced him that Suzanne is now about to meet the count willingly in the middle of the night, in a chestnut grove. Figaro delivers a monologue expressing rage at his utter powerlessness: considering the unbridgeable social gap that separates him from the count, Figaro notes bitterly that Almaviva is "a Lord—and I am—a Man!—Yes, I am a Man, but the nocturnal spells of that enchantress woman, soon shall make me a monster."[115] *Figaro* is a comedy: the situation is defused, the count is tricked into abandoning his plans, and spouses are reunited with their rightful others. All is well that ends well.

In French texts "the *droit du seigneur* is dramatized in narrative primarily in its subversion": droit du seigneur is always foiled, and the lower-class characters obtain victories of sorts over the oppressive nobility.[116] In *Figaro* tyranny is explored with levity: "Dear Sirs, the comedy / We are now judging / Depicts the life—lest we're mistaken / Of the good people in this audience. / When oppressed, they curse and cry; / Writhe and seethe against their wrongs / Still everything ends with a song."[117] If *Figaro* gestures toward social equality, it is achieved onstage through merriment, badinage, and music. Unity is performed in unison, and if there is a social compact at the end of the play, it is one that all—status notwithstanding—ultimately have contributed to achieve. In the process geographic pretenses are abandoned: the play was never about Spaniards after all, but truly about the French. They are the people sitting in the Parisian audience evoked in the play's final song. The lyrics glorify a national spirit that may suffer from censorship but that will also mock censorship in music, in a country where "Twenty kings praised in life / In death will lose their altar / but Voltaire is immortal."[118] Figaro and Suzanne discuss an intimate plight, but it is presented onstage, where the audience is constantly asked to consider its meaning collectively. Some certainly did: French revolutionary leader Georges Danton famously declared, "Figaro killed the nobility."[119]

Figaro's impact across the Channel, where "authors never seemed to take seriously the existence of the *droit*," was much more subdued.[120] Of course, it is unclear whether the French believed in the reality of the droit or saw the truth of the oppression it embodies. Either way, it worked as a metaphor for the outrageous abuses of the ancien régime. By contrast, Edward Rushton knew rape to be a weapon of social and political oppression in Europe, as he makes clear in his famous poems about English colonial oppression in Ireland "Mary le More," "The Maniac," and "Mary's Death."[121] Furthermore, Rushton saw clearly that there was one system in which legal sexual assault—droit du seigneur, in short—not only did exist but was actively practiced by all Europeans alike: American slavery. Feudalism survived in the "blood-sprinkled scythe of oppression" against the Irish and the exploitation of the working class—two of Rushton's topics of choice—but it was alive and well in a horrifyingly absolutist version in Britain's overseas possessions and as likely to inspire revolt there as its literary representation would in France.[122]

Rushton's poem, though it echoes French droit du seigneur scenarios, also bears the unmistakable mark of British ameliorationism. This is especially notable in the way Rushton's poem reverses *Figaro*'s movement from individual tale to communally relevant critique: much like the abolitionist rhetoric of its time, Loango's story stems from and evokes the collective history of slave revolt, but it eschews the notion of black political agency by devolving to the personal.

AMELIORATIONISM AND THE ENGLISH SPIRIT

Loango's monologue in *The West Indian Eclogues* was inspired by an old and allegedly real story. In 1655 English troops sent by Oliver Cromwell as part of his Western Design against Spanish possessions in the Americas invaded the island of Jamaica. During the campaign many among those enslaved by the Spaniards joined the English to fight their more immediate oppressors. Charles Leslie recorded the story of one of them: married with children, he saw his wife taken and abused by a slave owner. The man vowed to take revenge, a project he shared with his wife shortly before revealing to her that "he never could take an Adulteress to his Arms; and therefore, closely embracing her, plunged a poniard to the Heart of the unhappy Creature: Thus, says he, I exert the Right of a Husband." He then joined British ranks and later killed the Spaniard in battle. The unnamed slave was freed and granted land by the English officer and future governor of Jamaica, Edward D'Oyley. His son helped the English fight the French but also "exposed his Life in the Pursuit of the rebellious Negroes," that is, the Maroons who took to the mountains after the island fell into English hands. Performed in the service of England, the nameless, enslaved man's revenge gained status as a feat of war. There could be a life after revenge after all: one could become an exemplary black colonial subject, even a defender of English order. Leslie ends the section with the peculiar argument that the Spaniards lost the island because "where-ever Subjects are oppressed, that Colony or State is nigh to Ruin.... [The Spaniards] fought with the Spirit of Slaves, and not of Freemen ... and the consequence was, when the Enemy appeared, they deserted his Defence, and not Life to oppose the brisk Onsets of that brave Nation who knew the Blessings of Liberty."[123] Not a trace of irony in this comment about the "Spirit of Slaves": this tale of successful slave revolt is no challenge to a vision by which being enslaved by a brave and free nation such as England is, seemingly, already an amelioration.[124] Leslie's nationalist outlook survives in the abolitionist texts inspired by his *New History*, as they offer amelioration-ist warnings to their readers: commentary as much about the immorality of slavery as it is about encouraging Englishmen to act their superior selves.

The pervasive influence of ameliorism can be seen in *The Wrongs of Almoona; or, The African's Revenge*, a long poem in heroic couplets published anonymously a year after Rushton's *Eclogues*; it also draws its inspiration from Leslie's account of the invasion of Jamaica.[125] Here English ships are agents of providence, "a change of fate approach[ing] fast," by which "the worn Slave shall be reveng'd at last." Almoona kills his wife and vows revenge on her Spanish abuser, Alphonso. He speaks to D'Oyley, who, "tho' a soldier," like a true Englishman has a "heart to feel" and demonstrates as much by shedding a tear upon hearing about Almoona's fate. Yet the Englishman imparts on Almoona that revenge will not do: "Compassion guides us," he explains, with immediate effect on Almoona, for whom "savage vengeance is no more desir'd." Almoona finds Alphonso and kills him on the battlefield, forgiving the Spaniard as he breathes his last. He is given freedom and land, to little avail. Almoona delivers a final monologue:

> And if my countrymen must still be brought,
> From their own shores and here like beasts be bought,
> Pray ye! reflect that they are men like you,
> And let humanity be kept in view!
> Add not new rigors to their wretched state,
> Nor let them be the object of your hate.
> Let some compassion o'er their labours smile,
> And comfort cheer them in their weary'd toil.[126]

Walking off the battlefield still reeking of the blood of the Spaniards he and his fellow slaves defeated, Almoona now coyly speaks in ameliorist terms and walks off with no guarantee that the English listened. The passive voice detaches the English from their own involvement in the slave trade, only to renew the equation of humane behavior with Englishness. The poem turns back on itself: Almoona measures his future life by his ruined marriage. He will live within the new English order, but never fully be part of it.[127] His freedom—and, by extension, that of the silent slaves around him—amounts to nothing, crushed as it is under the weight of his personal woes. Simultaneously, the new colonists' involvement in slavery is pushed to the background.

In Rushton's poem mentions of Leslie's account are pushed into footnotes. Nothing in the poem itself explicitly references the circumstances of the original anecdote: Loango's story is placed geographically, but outside of history. Rushton does away with context and utterly abstracts the original story, shrinking the world to a triangle between Loango; his wife, Quamva; and the anonymous "accursed white" who took her away from him. No mention of Spanish rule or the English invasion here: Loango's tale is a claustrophobic close-up. In the enclosed space of the orange grove, he "mourns his absent love" and declaims his plans for revenge to the raging elements under whose cover he intends to act. The climatic motif so typical of abolitionist poetry takes on a slightly different meaning when directly attached to violent retribution. In William Cowper's later ballad "The Negro's Complaint" (1788), for example, when the titular enslaved African enjoins "masters iron-hearted" to ask God "if your knotted scourges, / Matches, blood-extorted screws, / Are the means that duty urges / Agents of his will to use," the response comes in the form of tornadoes ravaging habitations and cultures: "His whirlwinds answer—No."[128] Cowper's titular "Negro" retains the moral high ground: all he asks is for Europeans to "Prove that [they] have human feelings," and what violence is unleashed in the poem is God's alone. Loango does not merely decide to take "wild justice" into his own hands; conflated as it is with the rolling waves and the dark clouds, his revenge is taken out of his hands, naturalized. It is brought squarely into the realm of passion and cannot possibly be mistaken for, or quite understood as, an act of God, nor as a social or political act. Not that the act's social and political dimensions can be avoided: on two occasions Loango calls his wife's abductor and rapist a "tyrant," a pointedly political term Rushton also uses twice in the related footnote evoking Leslie.[129] This term is crucial, as it connects the tale of Loango to the rape of Lucretia.

NO BLACK LUCRETIA IN THE WEST INDIES

Quamva's circumstances are at some level comparable to Lucretia's: both women are assaulted by men in position of power, and to that extent the planter is very similar to Sextus. Both die stabbed because they were raped.

Differences between the two stories are just as important. Lucretia's act of speech, the testimony by which she made her private shame public, provided the original dynamic for a political movement. Even her agency in death flashed the possibility of active female citizenship in Rome, which was technically a fact for noblewomen, but in practice eminently restricted. By contrast, Rushton's Quamva is wholly silent. She has no agency whatsoever: she is an African slave in Jamaica, and the man assaulting her has legal, if not moral, rights over her. Her ordeal would not have registered as *raptus* in Rome, but it does to Loango. We never find out for certain what happened to Quamva: she has not met Loango in their secret grove in three days, and he suspects the "pale-fac'd villain" has kept her from him. Loango knows that "Quamva... the odious rape endures, but not enjoys" and calls on revenge and death; "he bravely falls, who stops a tyrant's breath."[130]

Loango's monologue rings with the vocabulary of Brutus, but its logic follows the Roman path in reverse: while it begins with political overtones and hints of rebellion—Loango calls on the elements to "hurl destruction on each cruel White"—it soon discards them to privilege the personal and wild justice. Loango jumps to conclusions regarding Quamva's agency and desires in terms at first strikingly reminiscent of Figaro: Are not the planter's exterior signs of wealth, his "gaudy cloaths" and "downy bed," strong enough arguments to seduce her? After all, "'Tis said that woman's mind / Still changes like the Hurricane's fierce wind." "Fool that I was," Loango exclaims, "to think... that one so beauteous would endure / My lowly bed, a mat upon the floor," and soon he convinces himself that "she likes the Driver's bed."[131] In the economy of Rushton's poem, Quamva dies so that Loango can "exert the right of the husband" that has been denied him in his station as a slave. In bypassing Quamva's voice, Loango repeats Brutus's appropriation of Lucretia's voice, with a significant difference: Loango's speech has no political consequence. It rouses no outraged crowd to action; within the poem its rhetoric is wholly solipsistic. Unlike the men in the Roman forum who longed for political independence, Loango pines for a pastoral Africa of the mind, where he expects to be transported when he dies after achieving his revenge. Loango's newfound freedom has no political valence; it is the spiritual liberation of death. England is the new Rome, and Roman rule still applies: for the enslaved, death and freedom must remain indistinguishable, so long as Rome exists.

For Dellarosa, the *Eclogues* express "the crucial political assumption underlying Rushton's poetics," a profoundly democratic vision that aims to "give voice to those whose voice is barely—if ever—heard."[132] Loango appropriates Quamva's voice, and in turn his voice is necessarily ventriloquized by Rushton, in a process by which Rushton himself emulates Brutus meta-textually. Rushton takes over Loango's voice to address British citizens—Rushton's peers—in their own language, intending to make them consider the possibility that enslaved Africans may well be men and brothers. Loango's language confirms the same pseudoscientific understandings of race expressed by Rushton in his footnotes, where he notably declares that "the desire of revenge is an impetuous, ruling passion, in the mind of these *African slaves.*" In the words of Beilby Porteus, bishop of Chester, whom Rushton quotes: "Being heathens not only in their hearts, but in their lives, and knowing no distinction between vice and virtue, they give themselves up freely to the grossest immoralities, without being even conscious they are doing wrong."[133] Porteus numbers among early, highly visible advocates of the abolition of the slave trade. He, like other abolitionists, sees little moral difference between the enslaved African and "the fabulously wealthy Caribbean planter that emerged in fact and fiction . . . to represent the West Indian uncouthness, backwardness and degeneracy that inverted the acclaimed standards of English civility and culture." According to Kathleen Wilson, the planter embodied a "'secret, underground Self' of English society, and the projected screen of an imagined West Indian 'national character' was constantly disrupted with recognition as well as disavowal."[134] The suffering of the enslaved played a role in the disavowal of West Indian national character, but recognition in turn contributed to keep sympathy for the enslaved within bounds. "The contradictions inherent in the colonial relation—between British liberty and race slavery—were managed in the metropole, in part, by means of recourse to geographical distance," Dillon tells us.[135] In this reworking of the Roman nation-making myth, distance also separates Rushton's intended audience—a community of sensible, moral Englishmen, dedicated to doing what was best for all humankind—from both the degenerate West Indian planter and the childlike, natural African man. Rushton and English abolitionists could think of Africans as men and brothers but could not go so far as to think that they might be political.

Rushton was unable to imagine black revolt beyond the most epidermic: Loango, the only slave brought to action in the *Eclogues*, is driven by passion and therefore unable to think politically. Much of the abolitionist poetry of his English peers, even as it attacks the slave trade practiced by many English citizens, manages to pet national pride by emphasizing the more intense immorality of others: Americans but also more traditionally Spaniards, and through them all Catholics. Issuing from the quills of Hannah More or William Roscoe, English abolitionism is to slavery as the Reformation is to the "slavish superstition" of Catholicism: Englishmen may be involved in the trade, but Englishmen will eventually put a stop to it.[136] In the meantime they could do justice to their national values by treating the enslaved with the humanity allegedly typical of the British. Rushton defines the planter's tyranny in exclusively personal terms that echo ameliorist arguments: soothed by the proximity of his betrothed, Loango might have endured it forever. Treated with a modicum of decency, perhaps blackmailed with love, slaves might well make do with their lot. But it was decidedly impolitic to go after their wives. Rushton's variations on droit du seigneur testify to the problematic stance of white abolitionist writers in the late eighteenth century. Rushton used the motif of rape to summon the sympathy of his white, British readers for the black enslaved population of Great Britain's West Indian colonies. He relied on a system of representation in which the female body had traditionally come to stand as a metaphor for the body politic, and its violation a pretext to set terms for ethnic and national belonging. This motif traditionally applied to free citizens rather than slaves. In attempting to extend it to people whom neither he nor his readers considered able to rule themselves, Rushton exposed the difficulty for an early abolitionism steeped in English nationalism to adequately address the issues raised by Atlantic slavery.

By contrast, French authors, from Voltaire to Raynal, were simultaneously engaged in reflection on the meaning of the French nation and on its position in the world. An essential part of this reflection concerned the form the government of the French nation should take. During the Seven Years' War, French thinkers reluctantly agreed that English superiority was beholden to an unflinching patriotism based on a profound belief in the singularity of English virtue. Simultaneously, the catastrophe of the war triggered "remarkable patriotic zeal" in the French public and efforts to define what made the French as a people.[137] Such efforts, resting as they did on appeals to popular mobilization, also fueled reflections on better ways to represent and perform the nation and its spirit, imagined as generous and fair. Throughout the last third of the eighteenth century, as plays increasingly attacked the unfairness of the ancien régime, Saurin's Spartacus came to embody this spirit, so by the beginning of the French Revolution in the summer of 1789 it was counted among the texts considered to have favored the movement. The portrayal of enslaved Africans played a peculiar but crucial part in these profound cultural and social changes. The black avenger served both as a dark mirror and a foil to European nationalism, but the figure also served to obfuscate and diminish increasingly sophisticated attempts at political autonomy among communities of the African diaspora in the Americas. France's obsession with nationalism in the late eighteenth century and the Revolution made it difficult to ignore the political import—both for French people and for the Africans they enslaved—of the black avenger figure, even as its potential to obfuscate black agency and politics remained intact. The enslavement of Spartacus, read as a metaphor in the metropolitan context, would regain a drastically literal meaning as the enslaved population of the colony of Saint-Domingue rose up in arms in 1791.

CHAPTER 3

A TALE OF TWO AVENGERS

*The Haitian Revolution and the
Racial Politics of Novelty*

RACE AND LITERACY

National sentiment in ancien régime France developed in part around a pantheon of Frenchmen beholden to the heroes and model republican citizens of antiquity as well as to Renaissance courtly literature and its engagement with the place of personal virtue and honor within aristocratic society. While it "helped teach French elites to see their nation as a single, homogenous country," the virtual pantheon instrumentalized by the ancien régime also provided material for a critique of the fundamental logic of that régime's existence: throughout its development, the body of national heroes encompassed people of *all* social stations, a variety that reflected badly on the feudal system, where birth mattered more than deeds. During the revolution, works began to circulate that criticized "the current monarch's failure to live up to the standards of greatness" set by national models of heroism.[1] In turn, the leaders rising in the French West Indian colony of Saint-Domingue challenged many of the assumptions built into France's growing heroic nationalist iconography.

In 1791 the enslaved population of Saint-Domingue rose up in arms for its own sake, setting the colony on course for a revolution that would push France to abolish slavery, see Spain and Great Britain attempt and fail to subdue republican and enslaved armies, and eventually witness the insurgent army defeat a formidable expedition sent by Napoleon Bonaparte to reestablish slavery. Haitian independence was officially proclaimed on January 1, 1804, in a document signed by the commander in chief of the indigenous army, Jean-Jacques Dessalines, and Haiti's main officers. It first appeared in Europe two months later, at about the time when Dessalines, now Haiti's governor general, ordered French civilians rounded up and killed. The massacres paled by comparison to the atrocities perpetrated by the French in Saint-Domingue mere months before. More crucially, they also paled by contrast: Dessalines's victims were exclusively white. News of the killings appeared in American newspapers a few weeks after they began and were soon confirmed by the Haitian government in a proclamation that circulated first on the island and then around the Atlantic world. Though he nominally addressed it to "the inhabitants of Haiti," Dessalines undoubtedly had a much broader intended audience when he unapologetically declared, "Yes, I have saved my country; I have avenged America."[2] With this phrase, Dessalines took on the double mantle of redeemer of his nation and founder of its country. This black avenger had succeeded and founded a black nation in America, and he now crowned himself the nation's original hero, in a transparent effort at replacing his immediate predecessor at the head of the island: the late governor and general Toussaint Louverture.

Dessalines's effort was not exactly successful. To this day it generally is not the victorious Jean-Jacques Dessalines but instead the defeated Toussaint Louverture whom writers and commentators designate as the revolution's hero. Born a slave in the mid-1740s, Louverture was emancipated when the revolution began in 1791 and joined the movement early on, rising quickly through the ranks of the rebel army. By 1800 he had authored the island's first constitution, and he ruled the colony alone, in virtual autonomy from France. This was too much for the quintessential Romantic great man of history, Consul for Life Napoleon Bonaparte, who late in 1801 sent a massive expedition headed by Gen. Charles Leclerc to subdue the revolutionaries and reestablish slavery on the island. The French captured Louverture and shipped him to France, but they could not conquer the island. In November 1803 the majority of French troops surrendered, some crossing the land border into Spanish Santo Domingo. Louverture never saw its triumph: he died in the French Alps in April 1803.

Many so-called great men of history did not achieve their goals, and even Napoleon Bonaparte died defeated, "a nameless thing," exiled on a speck of an island in the South Atlantic.[3] Yet in his tragic death in defeat and captivity, Louverture paradoxically achieved exactly the destiny the West at large and France in particular had in mind for him when he was dubbed the "black Spartacus," after a popular figure of the French Enlightenment. Abbé Raynal's *Histoire philosophique et politique des établissements et du commerce des Européens dans les deux Indes*—a lengthy study of European colonization written by a small army of writers under Raynal's name—was first published in 1770 and regularly republished in the following decades. From the first edition, the treatise contained a passage critical of slavery.[4] The passage was drastically expanded in the 1774 second edition, the first to be translated into English as *A Philosophical and Political History of the Settlements and Trade of the Europeans in the East and West Indies* (1776) — notably with this famous paragraph strongly reminiscent of Thomas Day and John Bicknell's *The Dying Negro*: "Where is this great man to be found, whom nature, perhaps, owes to the honour of the human species? Where is this new Spartacus, who will not find a Crassus? Then will the *black code* be no more; and the *white code* will be a dreadful one, if the conqueror only regards the right of reprisals."[5]

The last French edition of the text (1780) featured an even longer discussion of the wrongs of slavery that eschewed evocations of Spartacus for references to a passage from another best seller, a fantasy novel by Louis-Sébastien Mercier titled *L'An 2440, rêve s'il en fût jamais* (1770). What French Enlightenment thought it owed to English political thought could not be portrayed more symbolically than in the novel's opening. Its Parisian protagonist, after an earnest conversation about political freedom with an "old Englishman," falls asleep only to wake up to a vision of future, free France in the year 2440. Strolling through a hall of statues portraying the atrocities wrought on humanity by the nations, the protagonist happens on a statue of "the Avenger of the New World," who led slaves into a massive uprising against "all their tyrants; French, Spanish, English, Dutch, and Portuguese" and wiped out European power across the Americas. The man of 2440 goes on to explain that since the revolution, the unnamed avenger has become the new world's "titular deity . . . the exterminating angel to whom God resigned his sword of justice."[6]

Denis Diderot borrowed freely from Mercier, and Mercier in turn borrowed back: a second edition of his novel published in 1786 hints at *Histoire philosophique* with its mention of "a Spartacus on the banks of the Gambia."[7] Raynal's and Mercier's black Spartacus was an informed abstraction; applied to the events of the Haitian Revolution after 1791, it forced them into a profoundly racist frame of interpretation. Scholars have highlighted the general connection between Raynal, Mercier, and this characterization of Louverture on many occasions, especially in the past two decades. Yet the minutiae of the process by which Louverture's contemporaries came to attach him to one of the most famous texts of their generation have been ignored for the better part of two centuries. This, I contend, is very much a function of the dynamic that reshaped Louverture into a literary figure. The phrase "black Spartacus" connects by way of the French Enlightenment the Americas and a line of racial representation that constantly rewrites and rediscovers canonical texts. This chapter follows the chain of documents in which the phrase appeared and circulated and replaces it within its political context. The mythologization of Louverture was a painstaking, deliberate process meant to translate and reduce the complex politics of Saint-Domingue into simplified, convenient, and profoundly inadequate racialized language for an Atlantic readership.

THE POLITICS OF LITERACY

Literacy in colonial Saint-Domingue society was an ostentatious sign of socioracial belonging and status in the slaveholding world—quite literally one of the master's tools. Those among the formerly enslaved who mastered it used it warily, in full awareness that their words—like themselves—might be turned against them, overwhelmed, kidnapped again.[8] In the complex context of a Creole, slaveholding colony, in the aftermath of the United States' successful bid for independence from the English metropole and in the throes of the French Revolution, racism and nationalism were inseparable. To an extent difficult to accurately measure, they were also a function of one's access to literacy and its technologies—an access eminently dependent on race and class. The colony rested on a socioracial hierarchy that posited an absolute divide between whites and blacks even as it necessarily took into account the unavoidable reality of interracial mixing. Martinican-born lawyer and writer Médéric Louis Elie Moreau de Saint-Méry infamously produced a taxonomy meant to account for all color- and blood-part combinations produced by interracial mixing.[9] Among these categories the term *mulâtres* (mulattoes) designated those with equal mathematical degrees of whiteness and blackness; by the end of the eighteenth century the term was used interchangeably with *gens de couleur*, a broad class term designating free people of African descent.[10] At the heart of this linguistic instability, French writing framed and organized the material existence of Caribbean bodies, and literacy defined the very meaning of one's own skin. These racial categories, the policing required to maintain them, and the literature they inspired circulated to the metropole and influenced understandings of Frenchness.[11]

Beginning in the late 1760s and riding on the "new focus on French whiteness" in continental France, administrators introduced increasingly strict racial laws meant to separate locals into supposedly hermetic racial categories.[12] The reflection on the meaning of the French nation that animated the last years of the ancien régime thus led to a flurry of legal decisions concerning the status on metropolitan soil of slaves in particular and people of African descent in general. French authorities inaugurated a "new classification system that they hoped would regulate the boundaries between France and its colonies: the policing of race." West Indian planters were concerned with the possibility that, upon being brought to France, their enslaved servants would gain freedom, and administrators worried about the threat of miscegenation embodied by black presence in France. The creation of the Police des Noirs in 1777, whose language "prescrib[ed] actions based on skin color alone, rather than slave status," was the culmination of this trend.[13] The new institution suggested a fundamental opposition between blackness and Frenchness and turned into law a binary separation inspired by colonial prejudice rather than colonial reality. This, in turn, exacerbated white supremacy in the West Indies.

Literature and law developed together to stigmatize gens de couleur and blame them for interracial relations increasingly considered immoral—and therefore titillating—while simultaneously exonerating the free white men involved in these unions.[14] If the color line was meant to be seen as an absolute divide, finding oneself riding this line was eminently problematic. The pseudoscience of the day saw the "problem" of race mixing as one for which nature had a solution: polygenists such as Edward Long thought that unions between mulattoes were increasingly infertile, a theory shared notably by Moreau de Saint-Méry.[15] This calculus resonated with romantic, Herderian Volksgeist, implying as it did that nations could reach their most natural and productive state by avoiding admixture. The division between white and nonwhite widened further in the eighteenth century, fueling among island whites the idea that they constituted a "unified French colonial community." Enforced racial division extended to the Americas the reflections on national spirit and essence that agitated the metropole. Racism and nationalism mingled in French and colonial legal texts, helping create the circumstances in which the Haitian Revolution occurred. John Garrigus finds a direct correlation between increased legal restrictions against gens de couleur of the late eighteenth century and the first revolutionary stirrings among the wealthy gens de couleur of the southern region, beginning with the writings of gens de couleur activist Julien Raimond and first culminating in Vincent Ogé's rebellion on his return from revolutionary Paris in 1790.[16] The racialization of French and colonial legislation developed alongside increasingly racist notions expressed in, and influenced by, the literature that helped form Saint-Domingue's racialized audience in the first place.

What Marlene Daut calls the "Enlightenment literacy narrative" of the Haitian Revolution—the notion that Saint-Domingue revolutionaries in general and Louverture in particular "could have been inspired to revolt by reading Raynal or other works of philosophy"—stems from a historical outlook beholden to notions of nation and race issued from European pseudoscientific writings and historiography discussed in the previous chapter.[17] The great man theory of history—the notion notably popularized by Thomas Carlyle in the nineteenth century, that "the History of the world is but the Biography of great men"—crossed with the increasingly popular fiction of race yielded narrative frames specific to Saint-Domingue.[18] The literacy narrative focuses on West Indian agents accessing European writing, but, simultaneously, it is also the product of Europeans writing these agents into literate being. As it appeared to connect Louverture to antiquity, the phrase "black Spartacus" also retroactively colored Rome and all that touched it. Plutarch tried to recuperate the Thracian gladiator for Western civilization; by adding the qualifier "black," this new phrase defined him as white *by default* and *in contrast* with his black contemporary peers. Under the pretense of praise, the phrase suggests and supports racial divide.[19] Mercier's and Raynal's warnings contained an abstract curse against the mysterious figure they described. New Rome should be wary that a new Spartacus should rise, but the original Spartacus, however bold, honorable, and justified, disappeared in defeat. Mercier may have depicted and supported—initially, at least—the victory of his fictional Spartacus, but the figure still carried the name of a leader vanquished in battle, and Mercier's entire novel was as much prediction as warning.[20] With the Enlightenment narrative, and with two centuries' hindsight, the curse seemed like it was extended to Louverture, whose death in captivity months before the victory of his peers has struck many as quasi-theatrical.[21]

Such semantic weight makes it is easy to overlook that the phrase was applied to the general when he was a living, active political figure. Doris Garraway proposes that in producing letters, pamphlets, and other written material, "revolutionary leaders such as Toussaint Louverture and Jean-Jacques Dessalines sought to disprove the thesis of black barbarity and to emulate the trappings of state needed to claim both sovereignty and civilizational equality with other nations."[22] The tale of the black Spartacus shows how the principal figures in one among the innumerable instances of political intrigue that make up what we call the Haitian Revolution often used raced language *precisely* for its power to obfuscate politics. Both because they were virtually unable to avoid using the terminology of race and because that terminology could serve their immediate political goals, people of color living in colonial society channeled the literary tradition of black avenger figures, in the process giving it renewed life and meaning. Deborah Jenson dubs Louverture a "spin doctor" who used the rhetoric of the French Revolution to "sell" the Haitian Revolution. She places him "in the ranks of the French or francophone pre-Romantics . . . who graft subjectivity and *citoyenneté* together" and shows how his famously illiterate successor Dessalines followed in his footsteps.[23] Toussaint Louverture and Jean-Jacques Dessalines made drastically different use of the black avenger figure at the heart of the Enlightenment narrative of the revolution. Toussaint Louverture was the black Spartacus, but it would fall to his former subordinate Jean-Jacques Dessalines to become the avenger of the Americas, a role he would take in earnest, for better and for worse. But first, behold a man transformed into a trope.

BUILDING THE BLACK SPARTACUS

Toussaint was born around 1745 on the Bréda plantation in Saint-Domingue, where he was enslaved before he began living as a free man of color sometime in the 1770s.[24] That same decade in continental France, Etienne Magneaud Bizefranc de Laveaux, second son of an old aristocratic family, entered into a military career in the royal French army, rising quickly through the ranks in the early years of the revolution. Even as a new member of Saint-Domingue's free-colored population, Toussaint continued to work for wages on the Bréda plantation, and for a short time (1779–1781) managed a small coffee plantation, complete with a dozen enslaved laborers he rented from his son-in-law. Among them was a young man by the name of Jean-Jacques, whom the world would soon know by the name of his last owner, Dessalines.[25] While the future emperor toiled in the fields, the rich planter of color Vincent Ogé was in Paris, witnessing firsthand the early stages of the French Revolution. There he met with members of the Société des Amis des Noirs, a group founded the year before by the Anglophile lawyer Jacques Pierre Brissot on the model of the English Society for Effecting the Abolition of the Slave Trade, founded in 1787. The *société*'s debt to the English organization was obvious in its principal activity: the translation of English abolitionist publications. The social elitism of the société and the efficient work of the Club Massiac—a lobbying group founded by the planter lobby in August 1789 expressly to oppose the société's influence among members of the newly constituted legislative body of the Assemblée Nationale—made this English connection a public liability. But much about the société was uniquely French: its avowed goal of obtaining the immediate abolition of slavery, for example, was more radical than the ameliorist aims of its English counterpart. Its stance was also much more radical than that of Julien Raimond's, a wealthy planter of color from Saint-Domingue who, since his arrival in the metropole in 1784, had been attempting to convince French authorities and absentee planters of the necessity to grant gens de couleur civil rights. They owned slaves like their white fellow planters and logically sought their support, both Ogé and Raimond notably meeting with representatives of

Club Massiac. Their arguments fell on deaf ears: white planters "saw no reason to chip away at racial categories."[26]

Société member and prominent revolutionary Abbé Grégoire published *Mémoire en faveur des gens de couleur ou sang-mêlés de St.-Domingue* (1789) in support of the bid for full citizenship put forth by Vincent Ogé and Julien Raimond to the Assemblée Nationale. After providing a detailed list of the humiliations and injustices faced by gens de couleur in Saint-Domingue, Grégoire defends their valor and potential as full-fledged French citizens, arguing that "they are a sure support in the struggle against slave insurrection":

> A secret fire smolders in all of Europe and forebodes a coming revolution, that Potentates could and should make calm and soft. Yes, the cry of liberty resounds in both Worlds, and there is need only of an Othello, a Padréjean, to awaken in the souls of Negroes the sentiment of their inalienable rights. Seeing then that the mixed bloods cannot protect them against their despots, they may turn their irons against all, a sudden explosion will drop their chains; and who among us will dare condemn them, if he imagined himself in their place?[27]

Grégoire's take on Raynal's motif was certainly informed by the knowledge and experience of Raimond, who provided the evidence of the abuse gens de couleur had to suffer in Saint-Domingue cited by Grégoire throughout the pamphlet. Although Grégoire's disquisitions on the coming slave insurrection went much further than Raimond would have liked, his point was seemingly only to bolster Raimond's claim.[28] Granting citizenship to gens de couleur would ensure their service in preventing a slave insurrection.[29] We can see that the literary and more specifically theatrical roots of the black avenger trope remained crucial, even in a pamphlet with political ramifications. Grégoire makes the fictional Moor of Venice and the real-life leader of an unsuccessful West Indian slave revolt equal in the promise of black military leadership. Neither Othello nor Padréjean delivered on the goods of a lasting black polity, and therefore they are considered brothers in a theatrical tradition of black avengers. Wittingly or not, in perpetuating this tradition Grégoire was also performing an exorcism of sorts that allowed for a preemptive framing of slave revolt, were it to ever succeed. Prophesied by a French author in a French publication, the coming revolution—or, in any case, its narrative—might well be controlled the same way.

Within this literature-inflected frame, the coming black nation was primed to take on the same characteristics as a stage production, teasing the audience with this most uncommon, most terrifying of theatrical thrills: a successful theatrical villain. It would enact the feverish dreams expressed by generations of vindictive stage Moors. Following their imprecations, slaves would revolt and take back what was stolen from them and then go even further. One should imagine that prospect was terrifying enough: if, like their stage predecessors, Raynal's and Mercier's black avengers find their basis in historical precedent, the future they announce does not go very far beyond the abstract notion of an America controlled by blacks. The force of these visions is all in their potentiality, in the nagging suggestion that, contrary to all their predecessors, these black avengers might pull it off and execute all their threats. Stepping in where the allegedly unsophisticated, uncivilized African could not deliver, French authors imagined a black nation from the outside, for white readers. Now with revolution brewing in the Caribbean, the European-designed figure of the black avenger was about to meet actual black Americans.

Ogé returned from France in October thinking that the new laws of the republic made propertied gens de couleur full-fledged citizens, but he misjudged the depth of colonial racism. Incensed at Saint-Domingue governor Philippe François Rouxel de Blanchelande's refusal to grant civil rights to his peers, he led a few hundred gens de couleur in rebellion against the government. The uprising was crushed, and Ogé was captured and gruesomely executed in Cap Français in February 1791. He had promised he would not "rouse the plantations," but after his execution, as violent conflict between the white and free-colored factions spread throughout the colony, both sides took to drafting the enslaved to fight for them, promising freedom as a recompense. Simultaneously, increasingly numerous groups of slaves rose up in arms around the island, claiming to fight for king and freedom.[30] On August 14, 1791, the mythical beginning of the slave revolution took place, with the voodoo ceremony at Bwa Kayiman followed by a campaign of systematic destruction of the sugar plantations in the Plaine du Cap a week later.[31]

In September 1792 Laveaux first arrived on the island at the head of a regiment sent to support republican commissioners—Léger-Félicité Sonthonax, Etienne Polverel, and Jean-Antoine Ailhaud—in enforcing the decree of April 4, 1792, specifically granting equal civil rights to gens de couleur. Sonthonax and the newly arrived troops faced the hostility of local white inhabitants and colonial authorities, and Sonthonax owed his life to the protection of gens de couleur troops during an assault led by white militias in December 1792.[32] By then the colony was torn by widespread civil war between whites and gens de couleur and slave uprisings unofficially supported by the Spanish colony of Santo Domingo.[33] Toussaint and Dessalines were among those who joined Spanish forces, under the leadership of Jean-François and Biassou. Having to face slave armies, the Spanish, and soon British troops in 1793, Sonthonax took the radical decision to abolish slavery outright in the colony on August 24, 1793. Toussaint Louverture joined French forces in May 1794, after news arrived from the metropole that the French Republic had in turn voted to abolish slavery. New terms entered local vocabulary: gens de couleur were now also *anciens libres*, those who had been free before the decree, and they were now joined in freedom by *nouveaux libres*, the formerly enslaved formally freed by the new law of the republic. Commander in chief of republican forces on the island and governor general since October 1793, Laveaux finally met Louverture face to face in August 1794, the two of them now officers of the same army. They showed each other respect and admiration and developed a close relationship that proved central notably in the Affair of 30 Ventôse Year IV (March 20, 1796).[34]

Sonthonax's often brash behavior and taste for intrigue gradually alienated him from gens de couleur; Laveaux continued in his footsteps. During his tenure as governor, Laveaux, a white, metropolitan officer at the head of republican regiments increasingly reliant on gens de couleur and *nouveaux libres* soldiers successful in the field, made enemies of many of his former supporters, and his authority waned significantly after 1794. Historians have portrayed his rule alternatively as naive or downright tyrannical; in any case, by early 1796 he was being challenged by local officers who enjoyed a level of support from their troops and from the population that the metropolitan Laveaux never did entertain. Along with Louverture, André Rigaud, and Louis-Jacques Bauvais, Jean-Louis Villatte was the highest ranking native officer on the island. He was popular with the inhabitants of Le Cap, whose heroic defense against the Spanish and English he had organized. It was in part to express frustration at Laveaux's mismanagement that, on 30 Ventôse, Villatte led a group of officers that captured, beat, and threw in jail the governor, his civil administrator Henry Perroud, and others, with the approval of the municipality.[35] In the chaos that ensued, Laveaux and his companions likely owed their lives to the intervention of Toussaint Louverture.

THE MAN OF RAYNAL'S PROPHECY

On April 1, 1796, General Laveaux named Toussaint Louverture his lieutenant governor as a reward for saving his life. No person of African descent had ever risen to such a position in a colony that, a mere five years earlier, still had not allowed gens de couleur to participate in administration and politics. Legend has it that on this occasion Laveaux first dubbed Toussaint Louverture "black Spartacus, the man of Raynal's prophecy." If, as Srinivas Aravamudan asserts, in the Age of Revolution "readers are heroes, and writers are gods," this moment represents Louverture's baptism into French Enlightenment.[36]

The population of color of Saint-Domingue, free or enslaved, could well have been familiar with Raynal's text, firsthand or secondhand: according to Thomas Prosper Gragnon-Lacoste, "European negrophiles smuggled [Raynal's book] into America."[37] A play performed in Le Cap in 1787 apparently borrowed material from Raynal.[38] Yet it bears noting that hints of affinities between Raynal's figure and Louverture's textual persona appeared as soon as Louverture wrote himself into the record. Thus, in a letter written on the day Sonthonax abolished slavery on the island on August 29, 1793, Louverture had declared in terms reminiscent of Raynal, "Brothers and friends. I am Toussaint Louverture; my name is perhaps known to you. I have undertaken vengeance for my race."[39] By 1799 this precocious connection could be accounted for: an anonymous "citizen recently arrived from Saint Domingue" asserted in *Le Moniteur Universel*, the official organ of the French government, that Louverture had been aware of Raynal even before the revolution. He had procured, the author claimed, a copy of his book, "returning incessantly" to "that page where Raynal appears to announce the liberator meant to tear off the shackles of much of humanity."[40] The article further claims that Louverture later sent money to a "European philanthropist" to subscribe to French newspapers and keep abreast of developments on the continent. That Louverture saw himself in Raynal's so-called prophecy is only part of what is at stake here. If reading Raynal opened Louverture's eyes to the word of the French, his subsequent transatlantic engagement with the continental public sphere was but the practice of the secular faith, culminating in the moment when, through Laveaux's ministrations, Louverture accepted Raynal—and beyond him the French Enlightenment project—as his personal savior. In subsequent years, authors as hostile as the French publicist Louis Dubroca or as sympathetic as the British writer Marcus Rainsford would repeat the claim that Louverture had read Raynal, until, by the 1820s, it had become a staple of Haitian historiography.[41] It has been repeatedly used ever since as a colorful and usually unquestioned image, a convenient link between the French and the Haitian Revolutions. Aravamudan voiced reasonable doubts about the veracity of the tale but also asserted, "Haitian national memory and historiography has persistently relied on Toussaint's apocryphal self-recognition.... If Toussaint never really read the black Spartacus passage, Haitian historiography would have needed to invent an equivalent incident." No Haitian historian was referenced in the making of this claim, but Louverture's act of reading certainly served Aravamudan's need for an example for his theory of colonial "cultural and political deformation" of European discourse through counterreading.[42]

The circuit Aravamudan describes, even as it acknowledges that the empire can strike back, remains desperately Eurocentric. It follows Benedict Andersons's ideas regarding the importance of print in building the modern nation, a community of readers partaking in the national text formed where "fiction seeps quietly and continuously into reality, creating that remarkable confidence of community and anonymity which is the hallmark of modern nations."[43] Aravamudan, following a line of argument described by David Scott, marvels at the way "the rebel slaves appropriated the modern concepts and institutions they found around them and creatively turned them to their own purposes." But in presenting Louverture's *reading* of Raynal as a heroic act of resistance, Aravamudan fails to consider Louverture's stance. The general was not just a reader. He was also a writer himself—the author of memoirs, hundreds of letters, and of Saint-Domingue's first constitution: a statesman in the Western mold, not simply by a romantic feat of self-making, but also, as David Scott argues, because Haitian revolutionaries' appropriation of European modernity "was not a prior choice they made as preconstituted subjects waking up in the middle of a world they found objectionable and in need of change; it was a choice partly constructed through its conceptual and ideological apparatuses."[44] To read and write in an eighteenth-century colonial context was necessary to do, and participate in, Western politics, the only option viable in these circumstances.

Deborah Jenson sees Louverture's influence on the 1799 *Moniteur* article and evidence of his effort at "counter-balanc[ing] the subversive aspects of his pursuit of political autonomy . . . by 'spinning' the Haitian Revolution for an Enlightenment audience."[45] This analysis provides a welcome alternative to the usual assumption that Louverture was a passive receptacle for Raynal's wisdom. But, contrary to Jenson's claim, *Le Moniteur* was not the first French print source to evoke Louverture's alleged reading of Raynal: the honor goes to a polemic pamphlet by a certain "Mandar-Argeaut" (an "enigmatic signature" with which the author meant to protect himself against the potential retaliation of republican commissioner Léger-Félicité Sonthonax) written in 1797 in the wake of the Affair of 30 Ventôse.[46] That the claim that Louverture had read Raynal was originally made in commentary about Laveaux's April 1 speech is all the more important here for demonstrating that it in fact constituted an eminently political appeal to revolutionary cultural references, made with a keen sense of what it would evoke for the metropolitan French audiences it was addressing.

The ceremony on April 1, 1796, marked a turning point in the balance of power on the island soon recognized as such by observers. For Louis Dubroca, an early French chronicler of the Haitian Revolution hostile to Louverture, writing in 1802, it made Toussaint Louverture the "arbiter of the fate of the colony."[47] Pamphile de Lacroix, a white Saint-Domingue planter who served as an officer in the English army during the occupation, wrote in 1819 that this declaration had been "the coup de grace that killed the authority of the metropole in Saint-Domingue. One can date to this day the end of the credit granted to whites and the birth of power among blacks."[48] This event became part of a narrative frame for the Haitian Revolution that Daut calls the "mulatto/a vengeance narrative." Its similarity with the black vengeance plot should come as no surprise, as both are products of racial pseudoscience. The "mulatto/a vengeance narrative" evokes "ideas of savagery precisely because they suggest that people of color, regardless of any genealogical connection to 'whiteness,' would never be able to rid themselves of the 'original stain of their barbarity.'"[49] The model spread in late eighteenth-century culture explains the Haitian Revolution as the parricidal revenge of mixed-race children; Daut's examples show the early development of characters that would yield the tragic mulatto, in plots that put front and center the plight of people who can neither be fully white nor black.

Tales of Vincent Ogé's failed uprising bear much resemblance to the Oroonoko plot: incensed at the injustice dealt his socioracial class in the colonial order, the unfortunate Ogé led a failed revolt against the colonial order only to be captured, broken on the wheel, and dismembered in public. Ogé's tragic end soon became fodder for antislavery activists in France and beyond.[50] Of course, differences here are significant—or so we have grown to think: Ogé refused to involve the enslaved in a citizenship struggle he fought for gens de couleur alone. His effort came about at a time when socioracial definitions were quickly congealing and in a system whose wealth was predicated on slave labor. Though fully aware of his own African lineage, Ogé considered himself and his fellow gens de couleur a community separate from both Europeans and Africans. As free people of color, they were quintessentially Americans, close to the northern neighbors who a decade earlier had gained their civil rights from Great Britain without parting with slavery. Later gens de couleur leaders such as André Rigaud, though they did not abandon his color prejudice, would show more pragmatism in allying with free and formerly enslaved blacks. Ogé, however, wanted nothing to do with them. Revolutionary pragmatism made gens de couleur and the enslaved allies, but the original rift between the two groups was used efficiently and early by white planters.

Thus white planters routinely claimed that black slaves themselves scorned mulattoes. In November 1789, an anonymous text—likely produced by white planters in an effort to discredit Ogé's and Raimond's efforts in Paris—was published in *Le Moniteur*, titled "Réclamation des nègres libres, colons américains [Complaint of the free Negroes, American colonists]."[51] It argued that "the negro comes from a pure blood; the mulatto instead comes from mixed blood; he is composed of black and white, a bastard species. From this truth, it is as evident that the negro is above the mulatto as pure gold is above mixed gold."[52] Grégoire ridiculed the notion in his *Mémoire*, to which in turn an anonymous "inhabitant of the colonies" responded:

> This color prejudice, it has to be said, is not even white men's alone. The free negro is scorned by the enslaved quarteroon. Lower than him by law, but closer to his master by skin color, he feels superior to him. . . . Thus a kind of pride, increasing as hue recedes, tends to invigorate this prejudice that is the hidden spring in the colonial machine. It can be *softened* but not *annihilated*; time, with its blunt file, can destroy its most vulgar aspects, but if the spring is cut, the entire machine will noisily come down.[53]

In this light, mixed-race people are exclusively characterized by their difference from "pure" black and "pure" whites and alternatively criticized for their proximity to either hermetic group. Ogé's fate was undoubtedly as horrible as Toussaint Louverture's, but in a world of representation increasingly keen on tracing uncrossable racial lines, Ogé lacked the "racial purity" necessary to see his story mythicized as that of a black avenger. By the time Saint-Domingue gens de couleur rallied the French Republic en masse, even accepting, however reluctantly, complete emancipation, there was a new candidate for the position of black avenger and reasons for all parties involved to minimize what the two gens de couleur—for such was indeed Louverture's status when the revolution began—had in common.

Of course, contrary to Ogé, Louverture had been enslaved for thirty years of his life, and he could summon this experience to sway those revolutionaries with a similar background. This appears to be the rationale that pushed Laveaux to name him lieutenant governor: "I understood that I would succeed in asserting the trust given me by the blacks only by choosing as collaborator a man of a different color. . . . I chose to reward the brave, the faithful *Toussaint Louverture*."[54] There is no doubt that Laveaux rewarded Louverture: whether or not he also called him "that Negro, that Spartacus foretold by Raynal, whose destiny is to avenge the wrongs committed on his race" on this occasion is much less clear.[55] Exploring the documentary trail of this generally unquestioned claim exposes its cultural and political stakes and reveals it as a deliberate, calculated rhetorical move meant to frame the colony's political feuds in simplified, convenient, and profoundly inadequate racialized discourse. In subsequent communications on the affair, Laveaux, Perroud, and Louverture deceptively portrayed Villatte's action as a bid to install so-called mulatto power by striking at white republican representatives, ultimately to undermine the freedom of black laborers. Reality, as often, was much more complex: most of Villatte's troops were dark-skinned *nouveaux libres*, and the gens de couleur officers Laveaux and Louverture accused more or less overtly to be behind Villatte's coup—Rigaud foremost among them—never attempted to support his action.[56] Portraying the Affair of 30 Ventôse as a mulatto coup attempt would nevertheless prove crucial in Louverture's own bid to power.

THE ARCHIVAL TRAIL

Laveaux's speech dubbing Louverture the "black Spartacus" is regularly "quoted" in history books, yet no copy of the alleged speech exists. In his own report to the French Conseil des Cinq-Cents published on 1 Floreal year V (April 20, 1797), Laveaux makes no mention of even having delivered a speech on the occasion.[57] Yet by then the phrase had already begun to circulate: the earliest instance of a text comparing Louverture to Raynal's black Spartacus in relation to the coup attempt of 30 Ventôse was most likely Henry Perroud's letter to the plenipotentiary minister and the French consul in the United States, dated 10 Germinal year IV (March 30, 1796), one day prior to Laveaux's speech. In it, Perroud declares somewhat cryptically about 30 Ventôse: "As a well-prepared carnage was about to take place, the valorous Toussaint Louverture demonstrated such character, such prudence and activity, that one is forced to recognize in him this great Man, announced by a sublime political author, to be born one day for the happiness of his Brethren and the salvation of his country."[58] Whatever doubts there might be that the "great Man" and "sublime political author" are the black Spartacus and Raynal are cleared up by Perroud's report to the Ministry of the Navy and the Colonies, dated 26 Germinal year IV (April 15, 1796), in which he elaborates in similar fashion:

> The most pernicious seduction was used to deceive the credulity of some Africans in the garrison; they were primed for murder, being told that chains were being unloaded from ships in order to return them to slavery! . . . Fright-

ened by this, these men rise; weapons in hand, they run; threaten; forcibly enter the Republic's stores; open the dressers; break barrels of flour and salted meat; take over our positions; aim their weapons at the Governor, myself, and the other whites; and would have given the signal of death, if the valorous Toussaint Louverture, this African genius designated by a great Philosopher as the savior of his country, had not rushed over, saber in hand, to repress these ferocious satellites, unworthy of the name of soldiers.[59]

Laveaux and Perroud reserved references to Raynal for a revolutionary French audience they knew to be familiar with, and generally admiring of, Raynal's text.[60] The way Perroud evokes Raynal without naming him hints at a reference so familiar no name is necessary, a discreet nod to people in the know. These documents also strongly suggest that it was Perroud, rather than Laveaux, who first dubbed Louverture "the man of Raynal's prophecy," prior to Laveaux's speech.

Perroud's text was designed to sway those potentially hostile French readers in diverse positions of power in the republican apparel of state to whom he and Laveaux had to answer. Perroud's and Laveaux's way out of trouble was predicated on exacerbating and naturalizing their woes. By the time the two French officials published a letter to reassure "the merchants and captains of the continent of America, and the Danish islands," their narrative described abuse at the hands of a "horde of factious people and intriguers," and praised "Toussaint Louverture, this man, without his equal." Racial dog whistles are subtle here: the letter never nominally mentions mulattoes or gens de couleur but instead announces that "a horrible proscription extending to all the white people was already pronounced in all the quarters of the colony.... When on a sudden, the true people ..., the true Republicans, the African cultivators, were struck with the horror of that outrage and hastened to join in mass, in arms, in order to take off our fetters."[61] Laveaux's and Perroud's coalescing narrative would rest on an exclusively racial reading of the conflict. In this and the coming communications by the two men, the Affair of 30 Ventôse is a demonstration of mulatto deviousness in a plan to destroy whites and fool blacks to assert mulatto supremacy on the island.

In official communications sent to republican authorities in the hopes of counteracting Laveaux's and Perroud's narratives, their opponents on the island argued that Laveaux had in fact been planning the extermination of gens de couleur. Notably, Villatte and his co-conspirators, writing from the jail in Bayonne, where they were deported after 30 Ventôse, repeatedly mention a little-known, chilling episode, when Sonthonax apparently commissioned Laveaux to draft "proscriptive plans... to exterminate every man of color until the last."[62] François-Frédéric Cotterel, who discusses this same plan in another publication, argues that it was the fruit of a Machiavellian maneuver by which Sonthonax hoped to consolidate the support of gens de couleur by pretending he had in fact thwarted Laveaux's plan.[63] Daut marvels at how routinely the idea of "exterminating the entire population of 'mulattoes,' free people of color, and eventually all 'negroes'" is alluded to in the literary history of the Haitian Revolution," notably pointing to Rigaud's mention of "a faction that tends to want the destruction of all the citizens of color in Saint Domingue."[64] Rigaud is referring to none other than Commissioner Sonthonax, once the friend of people of color, but by then "declaring [against them] a war as cruel as it is unjust."[65] In this war he apparently hoped to recruit *nouveaux libres* to his side. Sonthonax was rumored to have told formerly enslaved leader Dieudonné as he designated him commander in the Western region in 1794, "Do not forget that as long as you will see men of color among your troops, you will not be free."[66] Republican agents Sonthonax, Laveaux, and Perroud expressed hostility against allies challenging their authority and against political enemies in very much the same naturalizing rhetoric of "monstrous hybridity" invented and employed by slavery apologists and planters, which presented mulattoes' alleged hatred of whites and scorn for blacks as a natural consequence of their being racially mixed.[67] In letters and publications in the mid- to late-1790s, they increasingly fail to distinguish between the generally concrete reasons behind their feuds and the blatantly erroneous but convenient notion that these feuds opposed them exclusively to gens de couleur, often naturalized as mulattoes.

Pierre-François Barbault-Royer's 1797 letter to denounce the actions of Sonthonax, Laveaux, and Perroud to the Directoire further discusses the Raynal reference. As a former Jacobin and aide-de-camp to Julien Raimond, Barbault-Royer might have shared much of his opponents' politics. Yet he also meant to defend his soci"racial class as well the economic interests of planters, white or colored, against the threat represented by Sonthonax and other "white levellers." Whereas in their descriptions of the situation in the colony Sonthonax and his supporters portrayed an alliance of black laborers with white revolutionaries against traitorous white planters and devious gens de couleur, Barbault-Royer presents Saint-Domingue's poor whites as Sonthonax's foot soldiers, responsible for tricking gullible blacks into fighting gens de couleur. He further writes that in "his proclamations distributed around the island and transported beyond the continent, Laveaux calls Toussaint Louverture *the man predicted by abbé Raynal*."[68] French author François-Frédéric Cotterel soon after published several texts to challenge the legality of Laveaux and Sonthonax's 1796 election as representatives for

Saint-Domingue and attack their handling of affairs in the colony.[69] The letter notably meant to contradict portrayals of the Affair of 30 Ventôse as a racialized, gens de couleur coup attempt, a notion created by Sonthonax, Laveaux, and Perroud in "their relentlessness in hunting down men of color."[70]

In another publication, a paragraph-by-paragraph, acerbic riposte to Perroud's memoir, Cotterel returned to his antagonist's use of Raynal:

> When the illustrious Raynal predicted a savior for Africa, he was far from believing that you would prevail on him to advocate a brigand who, after being degraded by a long time in slavery in America, supposedly became its scourge, by way of assassination, devastation, and arson, to which he has incessantly resorted while fighting against the homeland of Breda, his former master, until the time when, as recompense for his important services, Governor Laveaux put him at the head of Republican troops and associated him to his government.[71]

Laveaux's and Perroud's intent in using a passage known by whites for its dreary foreboding could appear somewhat puzzling, as nineteenth-century Haitian historian Beaubrun Ardouin once noted.[72] Indeed, Raynal promised merciless race vengeance and utter doom for white planters in the Americas, an apocalyptic vision that ill-matched the events at hand and offered little positive prospect for whites, including the revolutionary agents. But the reference itself apparently mattered more than its contents: Perroud clearly does not include himself or French revolutionaries in the ranks of white enemies of a figure that remained aloof and quasi-fictional for the metropolitan audience he addressed but laden with political and moral righteousness of the kind endorsed by the French Republic.

Perroud superimposes Raynal's black avenger as it was seen by sympathetic European radicals—an avenging angel with whose radical righteousness they aligned, if only theoretically—on a local situation much too complex to match the original image's absolute division between white planters and black slaves. Quoting Raynal, Perroud presents Laveaux—and encourages like-minded people to see themselves too—as savvy readers and spectators, capable of recognizing in Toussaint Louverture the performance of the role popularized by Raynal. As the 1799 *Moniteur* article about Louverture later would, Perroud retroactively makes Laveaux's speech into a performative act by which the representative of the French Republic designates in Toussaint Louverture the fulfillment of a well-known prophecy of the republican canon.[73] This act rests on confirming rather than contradicting the increasingly racialized—and increasingly white—vision of Frenchness that had begun to develop in the preceding decades. The textual apparatus around Laveaux's alleged speech makes racial division part of the official language of the republic and proposes the idea that blacks and whites have more in common together than either have with mulattoes. Simplifying the complex socioracial reality of Saint-Domingue's politics allows Perroud to mobilize Raynal's threatening prophecy to serve the officials' goals and reclaim *cultural* agency over political events that had in effect escaped their control.

This is not to say that Louverture's political enemies were devoid of racial prejudice: Cotterel evokes time and again Louverture's slave past and his blackness in the same breath as he reminisces about Louverture fighting on the Spanish side against France, the significant material gains he obtained in the revolution, and other unpalatable, but undeniable, aspects of the general's life.[74] André Rigaud declared on several occasions that he was not "made to obey a Negro, and it was a monstrosity to see whites and gens de couleur under the authority of a formerly enslaved negro."[75] Louverture does not fit the part of Raynal's avenger, because Raynal's avenger is the abstraction of the righteous struggle for freedom that any true lover of liberty can identify with. Louverture, a man of flesh and blood, a political man—for good or bad—cannot possibly be his incarnation. The importance of the comparison is here revealed in its utter literariness: reproduced and circulated as it was around the Atlantic world, it became the center of a discussion over the revolution in general and Toussaint in particular as Western productions, in all the theatrical sense of the word.

CLASS STRUGGLE

In the rhetoric of the French Revolution, virtue and patriotism are one and the same. The parties involved in the Affair of 30 Ventôse and the related strife that would eventually lead to the War of Knives in 1799 all wielded the same rhetoric, each presenting himself as more virtuous and patriotic than the opponent. The black avenger image became crucial to the political polemic surrounding the affair because it was an incredibly efficient means to take control of the narrative. All parties involved resorted to racialized simplifications to defend their interests. It bears noting that Louverture's plans were virtually indistinguishable from those of fellow gens de couleur, however lighter their skin tone or whiter their background: though he criticized Rigaud's autocratic behavior in the south, in the north Louverture implemented similar rules to reorganize the plantation system with free but coerced labor and to profit from it. They disagreed on what treatment white planters should receive: early motives for his feud with Rigaud thus concerned Louverture's leniency toward those white planters who had collaborated with the English invader. Whereas Rigaud had forcibly exiled them from the south or worse, Louverture forgave them and maintained them in their possessions, against the Directoire's orders.[76] When Louverture set out to take control of the colony on his own, his self-identification with Raynal extended Perroud's and Laveaux's schemes. His personal interests were those of his class—*anciens libres*—and depended on the manual labor of *nouveaux libres*, whom he addressed as equals in print but treated much differently in fact.

There is no clearer evidence of this discrepancy than the brutal repression of the laborers' revolt in 1801: having reduced all opposition thanks to the indefectible support of *nouveaux libres* troops, Louverture was, by 1800, sole ruler on the entire island and bent on jumpstarting sugar production. To that effect, he organized his state to enforce drastic work rules in line with those designed by Sonthonax that were meant to force laborers back on plantations. Article 17 of his 1801 constitution called for "the introduction of cultivators," a euphemistic hint that Louverture intended to buy more African slaves to replenish the island's workforce. The strictures of Louverture's agrarian militarism led to revolts in the large northern plantations, where laborers massacred hundreds of white planters in October 1801. In the aftermath Louverture arrested and executed a group of officers designated as co-conspirators, foremost among them his own nephew and radical republican general Moyse. The black Spartacus had become a black Brutus beholden to the reason of state.[77]

Scholars disagree on the extent to which Louverture prepared to cut ties with France with his constitution or gain an extensive degree of autonomy. Either way, Napoleon's outrage and his reaction were imbued with racial prejudice and blinded him to the political pragmatism that would make him realize a decade too late that other arrangements might have been possible.[78] Louverture himself had likely underestimated how racial rhetoric could trump realpolitik. He had found readier ears in the no less racist Anglophone Atlantic.

The identification of Louverture and the black Spartacus circulated around the Atlantic world, and its reception varied depending on audience and circumstances. Thus, the third English translation of Mercier's novel departs in one important detail from previous renditions of the black avenger passage: "It was the figure of an AMERICAN raised upon a pedestal; his head was bare, his eyes expressed a haughty courage, his attitude was noble and commanding. . . . He has dissolved the chains of his countrymen. Unnumbered slaves, oppressed under the most odious slavery, seemed only to wait his signal to become so many heroes."[79] Formerly translated directly from the French as "the figure of a negro," the statue of the black avenger was now turned into a metaphor for America. This altered translation, published in 1797 at the height of England's involvement in Saint-Domingue, provides a striking illustration of the ways in which British anxiety regarding slave emancipation literally translated into the erasure of the slaves' political agency, even in fiction.

ENGLISH TOUSSAINT

As Toussaint Louverture gained a certain amount of recognition in England in the late 1790s, a story began circulating assigning his legendary wit and wisdom in no small part to his good master's will. The *Annual Register* for the year 1798 explains that "while young, he was sent by his master, merchant of St. Domingo, into France, to learn the language and acquire other accomplishments, which might render him useful in business."[80] A different tale, this one published after Louverture's deportation to France, advanced that "it has been said, we believe upon good authority, that [Louverture] could neither write nor read. . . . His principal counsellors were two white persons, a priest and a military officer; and of their abilities the fairest testimony is the conduct of their pupil."[81] Most of these stories—though not all—appeared after Louverture was captured and sent to die in a French dungeon. They were written at a time when his fate was all but guaranteed to follow the tragic, unsuccessful outcome of the black avengers of fiction. As Toussaint sat in chains in the Fort de Joux, stories often contrasted his magnanimity with the extreme violence of the conflict. It was proof of his extraordinary character, a follower of European values, which set him apart from his savage, bloodthirsty people.

The link between Louverture and Western literature became even more transparent after his death. In 1805 a review of Marcus Rainsford's *An Historical Account of the Black Empire of Hayti* declares without citing sources that "Toussaint was fond of theatrical declamation, and especially of Saurin's *Spartacus*." The reviewer continued,

> As some poets copy their characters from nature, so some natures copy their characters from the poet. The feeling and loftiness manifested on all occasions by Toussaint seem to place him in that category. It appears, however, that one Pascal . . . and an Italian ecclesiastic named Marini were among the literary coadjutors of Toussaint, and drew up his proclamations and constitutions of government. The Moses is oftener of essential importance than the Joshua of a revolution; because he is less replaceable.[82]

The implications of tying Toussaint Louverture to American avenger figures born of European minds could not be clearer: modeled after a Western European literary creation, Toussaint can be portrayed as the puppet of three European éminences grises, made responsible for all his official pronouncements. Toussaint's notoriously prolific correspondence is attributed to European handlers, and his stature as the leader of slaves who revolted subsumed to European clairvoyance.[83] The rumor both exposes and exacerbates the implications of the Enlightenment narrative: in the face of undeniable greatness, this story assigns it to European influence, not unlike the way in which Plutarch tied Spartacus's valor to his alleged Greekness, and Behn emphasized Oroonoko's French education. In both news stories Louverture's political savvy is presented in terms of debt: Louverture is an impressive head of state, but he can only express these skills intelligibly thanks to European social capital. He is a product of Western literary culture and therefore worthy of interest at least, and most surely of patronization.

Great Britain had a political stake in portraying Louverture positively following the withdrawal of its troops from the island in 1798 and its secret agreement with the island's governor. British accounts regarding Toussaint written between 1798 and 1802 made him into a benevolent, monarch-like figure. Many noted Toussaint's royal African extraction.[84] These claims participated in taking Toussaint out of the realm of politics and into that of British literature. William Earle's best-selling novel *Obi; or, Three-Fingered Jack*, William Burdett's *Life and Exploits of Mansong*, and John Fawcett's pantomime *Songs, Duets, and Choruses*, all based on real-life Maroon Jamaican slave Jack Mansong and published or performed in 1800, were then the most recent incarnations of the black avenger in England.[85] Fawcett's pantomime offers a complacent view of West Indian slavery, inviting "its audience to sympathize with the loyal slaves but to vilify . . . Jack."[86] Earle's Mansong, in the more sophisticated black avenger mold, is of royal African stock, the son of parents treacherously captured in Africa, sold to slave traders, and deported to Jamaica. His father, Makro, dies on the Middle Passage, whipped to death for rebellious behavior, but not before enjoining his wife to teach their unborn son "how to hate the European race." Jack's mother, Amri, raises him to become "the avenger of Makro's wrongs . . . , the saviour of our country! the abolisher of the slave trade."[87] Though offered as an expression of African defiance, the words clearly evoke Raynal and a broader network of Western intertextual appropriation.

Mansong is the son of Oroonoko as much as he is Makro's. So much is emphasized throughout the novel: grown to become as extraordinary as announced, Jack attempts to rouse the slaves into revolt with a speech utterly reminiscent of Oroonoko's. Like his predecessor, Jack is ultimately unsuccessful: the "affrighted negroes" flee at first sight of British soldiers, at which point Jack decides to "seek the woods alone," loathing the slaves "more than [his] enemies, under whose whip [they] would rather die than by one exertion shake off the thing [they] hate."[88] Collective slave revolt, ever the fear of British proprietors in the West Indies, is evacuated early. A failed revolutionary, Jack turns lone highwayman and dies a tragic hero, hunted down and eventually killed by the same Maroon Quashee, who in an earlier encounter deprived him of two fingers.

As Aravamudan notes, "The story of Jack's individual heroism and failure is founded on the suppression of a more complex story, of collective rebellion by many participants whose identities remain unknown."[89] This suppression is achieved in part through idealization. Jack is constantly shown as unique among blacks for his physical might, intelligence, and royal extraction; "had he shone in a higher sphere, would have proved as bright a luminary as ever graced the Roman annals, or ever boldly asserted the rights of a Briton."[90] The passage echoes a *London Gazette* article of December 1798, which boldly proclaims the independence of Saint-Domingue and, providing the obligatory paraphrase of Raynal, states that "[Toussaint Louverture] is a negro born to vindicate the claims of this species and to show that the character of men is independent of exterior colour.... Every Liberal Briton will feel proud that this country brought about the happy revolution."[91] As soon as Great Britain withdrew from the island, British news began representing Louverture not only as a virtual British ally but also as an honorary Briton, in the literary tradition of the heroic slave.

That the advent of independent Haiti did little to diminish the equation of Louverture to the black avenger is perhaps a testimony to the efficacy of the literary pattern. It also reveals the position occupied by Saint-Domingue in Great Britain's own brand of national self-questioning. Saint-Domingue was a formidable test for the newly formed French nation in terms of race and moral principles. British uses of the black avenger figure in relation to Saint-Domingue helped set Great Britain apart from France. Michael Tomko argues that certain abolitionist poems used the topic of slavery to reflect on British anti-Catholic and anti-Irish oppression, which war with the French Republic had only exacerbated.[92] Late in 1796 a first French naval expedition failed to invade Ireland in support of Wolf Tone's United Irishmen. British authorities responded to the attempt with utter and relentless brutality. The violence failed to bend the United Irishmen's spirit: in May 1798 they rose up in arms and were later joined by a second, smaller French expedition. Again, British repression of the rebels was merciless, and tales of atrocities circulated widely. Focusing on Saint-Domingue redirected British public attention toward a conflict that no longer directly involved the country and connected notions of immorality and atrocity to French perpetrators and black victims. The character of Toussaint provided a figure on which both the British and the Irish, specifically Catholics, might agree. In that regard, the way Toussaint's faith is regularly alluded to in British letters is exemplary. Toussaint is praised for being a "devout man and sincere disciple of Christ," "found faithful in the great duties to which it pleased God to call him." The fact that he is a Catholic is rarely raised by mostly Protestant British writers at a time when anti-Catholic resentment was high and Catholics were still barred from public office. In his 1803 book *Buonaparte in the West Indies; or, The History of Toussaint Louverture, the African Hero*, abolitionist James Stephen mentions Toussaint's Catholicism to better discard it: "He was a Roman Catholic, it is true, but he knew no better faith."[93] Yet Toussaint's faith is opposed to the French's alleged lack thereof, and his being defined as a Christian situates him by implication on the British side.

Stephen published the book anonymously "soon after the recommencement of the war with France [in 1802], with a view chiefly to its probable influence on the minds of the lower classes of the English readers," whose feelings he hoped to rouse "against [Napoleon,] that dangerous enemy of their country, as a monster of perfidy, cruelty, and baseness."[94] As noted in an October 1803 review, two other goals of the book were to "elevate the negro character in the estimation of Europeans" and "to excite a prejudice against the slave-trade." These aims were dismissed in most reviews and chastised when mentioned at all: "As to the slave-trade, the author deals in abuse solely, without deigning to employ an argument on the subject, which, in no case, is justifiable; but in a question, in which not a difference of opinion subsists, between men equally enlightened, and equally honourable, particularly indecorous and reprehensible."[95] With the righteousness of a man living in a country apparently set on doing away with the slave trade, Stephen asserts that "every well-informed man knows already" about "the dreadful effects of West India slavery upon the minds, both of the master and the slave." Stephen's stellar portrait of "the pious and humane" Toussaint regularly contrasts examples of French barbarity with the civilized (re)actions of the British: mentioning a meeting between Gen. Thomas Maitland and Toussaint, Stephen explains that Maitland was so trusting of Louverture that he "did not scruple to go to him with only two or three attendants," even though the two sides had but recently been at war. "The French," Stephen adds, with understated outrage no doubt born of British sincerity, "are an odd people, and their words never mean the same thing that meet the ear."[96]

French barbarity is contrasted with the alleged natural barbarity of blacks, only to reinforce the idea of British humanity. The rise of French nationalism during the Seven Years' War rested in part on contrasting French "martyrs" fallen to Englishmen portrayed as barbarians, an essentializing gesture that bolstered a fledgling sense of Frenchness by suggesting that "the English, despite their membership in the white race and in a common European civilization, in fact were fundamentally alien," guilty among many other crimes listed by French representative Bertrand Barère, of "corrupting the humanity of savages" in America. Barère noted with bitterness that in the early days of the French Revolution, the credulousness of representatives had drawn them to the British constitutional model. Now freed from the nefarious influence of Britain, France looked on its neighbor with the same hatred republican Rome had for Carthage.[97] Similarly, Stephen insists that "the only savages in St Domingo . . . were savages with white faces." Stephen's goals are most transparent when he addresses the circumstances of the British invasion of Saint-Domingue in 1794; the sole justification he gives is that the local white planters had intrigued and invited Great Britain to invade the island. Stephen avoids any other mention of British presence on the island, under the pretext that it is a topic "upon which an Englishman cannot like to enlarge." Yet he assures his reader that "there is nothing in the conduct of our brave soldiers in that field, but what does them honour, yet I chuse [sic] to be silent as to that unhappy attempt, and shall only say, that Toussaint through the whole of the long contest with our army, acted so as to win the admiration of his enemies as well as the praise of his ungrateful country."[98] A telling ellipse: in Stephen's otherwise scathing pamphlet, all that is left of the nearly four-year-long British expedition is glory on the battlefield, along with that of "our hero," Toussaint Louverture. The British are idealized and identified by correspondence not to their European *frères ennemis*, the French, nor to the slaves who revolted, but to a figure of ideal moral purity in the person of Toussaint Louverture. British people could recognize themselves in Toussaint, against the French, as in a distorting mirror.

Toussaint's persona and image, reconstructed as they were in the British context, were propped up for the United Kingdom to reflect on as an alternative to republican, pre-imperial France and Napoleon Bonaparte. France had provided new and dangerous notions of freedom, democracy, and nation that had inspired discussion and action throughout Europe. Republican France had even hit very close to home with the failed attempt at the invasion of Ireland in 1798. In revealing France's own moral shortcomings, Toussaint could also improve the United Kingdom's own reflection. As shown by the rave reviews Stephen's book received when it was released, the timing for its publication was impeccable. With Toussaint dead, France at war again, and Britain helping the insurrection in Saint-Domingue, the ambivalence over the island's affairs could be evaded by focusing on Toussaint, whose pristine character sublimated the issue of his skin color and the bigger question of slavery. Formerly a "brigand," the leader of a slave rebellion, he became a symbol of valor and righteousness in the face of French villainy. Toussaint's politics in real life had been a source of constant worry for British powers; in death, he could be—and was—turned into a powerful symbol that both exorcised the threat of slave revolt and countered the hero-effect of Napoleon. Toussaint was reduced to a literary character, a tragic hero, the better to serve British interests.

In 1805 former Third West India Regiment officer Marcus Rainsford published *An Historical Account of the Black Empire of Hayti*, one of the earliest European studies of the Haitian Revolution, and an expanded version of a personal account of the author's adventures on the island originally published in 1802.[99] Rainsford's is a peculiar text, part history, part personal narrative, part news roundup, interspersed with graphic illustrations, among which one of the most ubiquitous visual portraits of Toussaint Louverture to this day.[100] Yet the most peculiar aspect of Rainsford's book may be the terms in which he expresses his admiration of Louverture and of the Haitian Revolution. *An Historical Account* floats on the rising tide of the great man theory of history. Rainsford cannot help but recognize the achievement of Haitians at large, but he does so through praise of the admirable Louverture, the hero who comes to define his nation almost in spite of itself.

Marcus Rainsford's life bears the marks of Great Britain's continuing debate over national self-definition in the border regions of the empire at the end of the eighteenth century. Born into an Anglo-Irish family of renown, he fought in an Irish volunteer regiment in the American Revolution, was stationed in Jamaica for a few years, and fought on the Continent before becoming a recruiting officer in the Third West India Regiment, a unit created for Great Britain's West Indian campaign and meant to be manned with black soldiers. Rainsford was a witness to the Second Maroon War in Jamaica when he sailed to the West Indies in 1795 in the expedition dedicated to taking Saint-Domingue. In the last days of British presence on the island, he went to shore and passed as an American sailor, living among the population for a short while before he was arrested and condemned to death as a spy. He apparently owed his life only to Louverture's direct intervention. The general graced him and allowed him to sail back to England.

Earlier in his life Rainsford had dabbled in poetry, publishing a long epic poem on the Glorious Revolution. Similar intentions animate Rainsford's *Historical Account*: it is a national epic disguised as a history book.[101] Rainsford bestows on Haiti the highest honor he could fathom: he measures it against English national standards and does not find it wanting. Discussing Dessalines's defense of Fort Crête-à-Pierrot against Leclerc's troops, Rainsford declares, "The fortress which they occupied had been regularly built by the English during their possession of this part of the island, and the defence of it was truly English." Recognizing the achievements of Haiti becomes a matter of respecting English—and therefore, civilized—values:

> It has frequently been the fate of striking events, and particularly those which have altered the condition of mankind, to be denied that consideration by their cotemporaries [*sic*], which they obtain from the veneration of posterity. . . .
>
> It will scarcely be credited in another age, that philosophers heard unmoved, of the ascertainment of a brilliant fact, hitherto unknown, or confined to the vague knowledge of those whose experience is not admitted within the pale of historical truth. It will not be believed, that enlightened Europe calmly witnessed its contrasted brilliancy with actions which, like the opaque view of night, for a sullen hour obscured the dazzling splendour.[102]

Rainsford projects himself into the future, from whence he looks back to his own book's pioneering status. With this peculiar time twist, he all but designates himself the European discoverer of independent Haiti's greatness. Rainsford confirms Raynal's prophecy: indeed, much of Rainsford's telling of the revolution rests on characterizing Louverture as the hero necessary for a national narrative deemed worthy of English approval.

Rainsford operates a distinction between Louverture's allegedly moral statesmanship—portrayed as dignified and English in spirit—and revenge, an understandable but ultimately inexcusable and savage behavior. This dichotomy clearly owes something to late eighteenth-century abolitionist poetry; it now becomes a means to control the portrayal of events of the Haitian Revolution. Rainsford's Louverture thus is a consumed head of state, a diplomat, a paragon of rational thought and action: "His government does not appear to have been sullied by the influence of any ruling passion." Toussaint in his wisdom is wary of such passionate course of action as "wasteful vengeance." In Rainsford's account "the great, the good, the pious and benevolent Toussaint Louverture" is consecrated as a tragic hero, "greater in his fall than his enemies in their assumed power." Dead, Louverture could be recognized as an extraordinary head of state at no cost and enter the pantheon of enlightened rulers: "His principles, when becoming an actor in the revolution of his country, were as pure and legitimate, as those which actuated the great founders of liberty in any former age or clime."[103]

Rainsford grants Louverture the nobility of the literary Spartacus, but he foists onto Jean-Jacques Dessalines characteristics traditionally attached to black stage villains, even as he appears to admire him. His book contributes to contrasting Louverture, now canonized as the providential, measured, rational—in one word, British—statesman and Dessalines, who was already paradoxically equated with the French for his brutality. Indeed, events of the revolution unbefitting the precepts of British civilization are presented as the result of surrendering to the passion of "public vengeance," not unlike the French themselves allegedly had during the Terror.[104] It falls to Dessalines to be the merciless, and this time victorious, black avenger. Consider how Rainsford describes the "Affair of Acul," a particularly bloody episode of the war against the French, in which, upon finding out about the massacre of thousands of Haitian prisoners by Rochambeau, Dessalines

> when acquainted with the case although the maxim of the benevolent Toussaint, not to retaliate, had been hitherto followed up, could no longer forbear; he instantly caused a number of gibbets to be formed, selected the officers whom he had taken, and supplying the deficiency with privates, had them tied up in every direction by break of day, in sight of the French camp, who dared not to interfere. . . . Such was the retaliation produced by this sanguinary measure; a retaliation, the justice of which, however it is lamented, cannot be called in question.[105]

Rainsford's last sentence testifies to the paradoxical stance of his text: Dessalines's revenge is undeniably just, but it is wild justice. Louverture's alleged magnanimity is enhanced in the contrast and explains the status he reaches in Rainsford's account. Rainsford's Louverture is the extraordinary figure Cotterel refused to see; Dessalines, unable to refrain from an understandable urge for revenge, fails the test of extraordinariness. In revenge he is equal to the French, whereas Louverture was able to transcend such base behavior. The national epic demands a hero above the common people: the black avenger of literature can exist only in the absence of historical fact. Dead, Louverture and his actions are canonized—and Anglicized—by contrast with the living Dessalines. By the time Rainsford's book was published in 1805, the concept of black vengeance had coalesced around the massacre of the white colonists ordered and carried out by Dessalines throughout the early months of his tenure at the head of the new country. Rainsford's characterization of Haiti's first head of state was therefore in part inspired by the terms of Dessalines's own self-fashioning. These terms meant to emphasize the rupture with France and as such always ran the risk of being used against the emperor of Haiti.

Upon independence at the turn of 1804, Haiti had been ravaged by ten years of war. French troops remained on the Spanish side of the island, dangerously close. In such dire circumstances, the support of a consequent military power was of the essence. This meant either Great Britain or the United States, and this meant playing the game of diplomacy and following its conventions.

A POLITICS AND A DIPLOMACY

Discussing Dessalines's letters brings us back to the issue of literacy: contrary to Louverture, by all accounts Dessalines was illiterate and able only to sign his own name. This fact has led some scholars to conclude that Dessalines's letters, his proclamations, his Constitution of 1805, all signed in his name and in the name of his secretaries, were therefore never fully *his*. We assume that these amanuenses—for the most part sons of older free stock and educated in France, cognizant in the ways of Western writing—necessarily refined the raw material provided by the emperor and his successor, Gen. Henry Christophe, whose illiteracy is equally proverbial. Thus, Chris Bongie, as he focuses on the stylistic idiosyncrasies of Dessalines's secretary, Juste Chanlatte, traces his contribution from more literary and individual endeavors of his own to official communications he helped produce on behalf of Dessalines and later Christophe.[106] It goes without saying that literacy matters in letter writing. But by too definitely equating literacy with textual production, we run the risk of diminishing the role of formerly enslaved heads of state in crafting texts produced in their name. While with Jean Fouchard we can recognize how "along with *marronage*," literacy constituted for many of the enslaved "their first flight from the colonial night, their first escape into paths of Liberty," we must also keep in mind that the discourse of literacy is tied to understandings of knowledge and education profoundly influenced by race prejudice and predicated on downplaying contributions beyond the scribal.[107] As a military commander, Dessalines routinely devised strategy, gave orders, formed queries, many of which were eventually transcribed and circulated in letter form. His authorship in such cases can hardly be questioned, even as we know for a fact he did not inscribe the words themselves. As Jenson has argued about longer, more sophisticated texts signed in Dessalines's name, "Formal education in Western alphabetic literacy and putting pen to paper were not the conditions for Dessalines's authorial role, but rather the shared characteristics and ambitions of a corpus of work produced under his direction by secretaries and military colleagues and issued in his name."[108] What sound did Dessalines make when he dictated words to Chanlatte? Can we still hear this sound on the page?

The matter of literacy plays a central role in scholarly assessments of the figures of the Haitian Revolution, in part—though not simply—because said assessments develop around the written and print record. This may seem self-evident, but the doubts that come with matters of literacy are enhanced in singular ways in discussions of the Haitian Revolution. Literacy, then and now, is social and racial. Some of the enslaved were literate—even though every effort was made by colonial authorities to keep them away from "the primer"—and among revolutionaries the literate were mostly *anciens libres*. The risk is to reproduce in analysis the racist systems that pervade the intellectual and material record by essentializing literacy as a character trait rather than a mere tool. Studying the rhetoric of Dessalines's official documents, Deborah Jenson attempts to balance out Chanlatte's European-inflected flair with Dessalines's unlettered, "African character": not only are those texts replete with metaphors, but Dessalines himself could well have been their actual author. Jenson concludes her piece with a puzzling epiphany: "Recent neuroscience on right hemispheric poetic activation tells us that *poetry is absolutely not the prerogative of the educated*." Is it necessary to underline that culture exists outside of the text that is not, that cannot, be fully accounted for and registered in the print records of the Western world? Earlier in her article, Jenson notes that "in modern Western history, poetry has been the provenance of the literate, the poet with quill or pen, connected to literary salons and schools and manifestoes."[109] Those working-class writers whom Robert Southey called the "uneducated poets," the unlettered poets of oral tradition of the world, the griots forced into the Americas in the Atlantic slave trade, to mention but a few, might beg to differ.[110] Or they might underline in these lines evidence of a struggle to part with the very assumption one affects to debunk: namely, that some prior, formal Western education was necessary for Dessalines to engage in the highest levels of diplomacy, international politics, and state making.

We must keep in mind that formal, Western education and politics are not intrinsically related and that our belief—conscious or not—to the contrary is in many ways a product of this and many other Enlightenment narratives of historical events. Literacy is a tool one may or may not have access to; it is also a tool one may or may not decide to use. In certain circumstances avoiding the traditional record is a strategy. As Jessica A. Krug provocatively proposes in her discussion of stateless Maroons around the Atlantic world, it may well be that such communities "chose to eschew writing and forms of oral history and tradition that reinforce hierarchy," in full awareness of the ways in which writing and the print archive could act as tools of hegemony.[111] Avoiding the record, Maroons could address their peers in fugitive terms and modes beneath the awareness of the literate world, "on the lower frequencies," as it were.[112] By the same token it is obviously to engage the West outside and in terms Westerners might understand that Dessalines chose to use the written record, but we would do well not to think the medium more sophisticated than the man. Fully aware of the strictures in which Western cultural frames kept them, yet engaged in a state project necessarily contingent to those frames, Haiti's early leaders maintained the nation in print. Haiti's founders had to make sure that, having won the military war, they might also gain advantage in—if not win—the cultural peace. Such peace at the dawn of the nineteenth century was always going to involve the same print culture and conventions of writing and rhetoric against which they had to struggle, so they put their "hostage" to work. In state matters there certainly was "no outside-text": to try and make the *unthinkable* independent state of Haiti thinkable in the concert of nations, it had to become *literally* thinkable, that is, thinkable as text.[113]

In 1805 the independent state of Haiti was in newspapers the world around, but it did not exist in those papers that mattered most: official statements by governments that would have recognized its existence. In such circumstances Haiti had few alternatives: it could speak to itself and its citizens in a variety of modes, but to engage foreign authorities it obviously had to speak in the language of diplomacy, collaboration, trade, exchange, threat, danger—registers inflected not by fact and action so much as literature and culture. A man like Dessalines, grown in the heart of the Western slave factory before becoming an officer in the French army, would have known Western conventions of expression and representation, whether he liked them or not. The issue facing him as the head of Haiti was how to convey information convincingly.

The atrocities of slavery exist only to those who suffer them. For the rest there is representation, the game of sensibility and empathy, the pornography of pain.[114] No wonder that in such circumstances one might prefer the concrete business of state making to the spectacle of moral values, real and affected. This spectacle was the domain of Great Britain, the nation that, a mere decade prior to abolishing the slave trade, had fought to maintain slavery on the same Haitian officers now lavishing praise on their European ally. While with Chris Bongie we can wonder whether it is possible to ever recover "more imaginative and emotionally honest uses of language" under the artifice of utilitarian, diplomatic writing, we can also consider closely the strictures within which the writers of independent Haiti worked.[115] Dessalines, of course, had been enslaved, made into an object. But in 1805 he now spoke and wrote as one who had made himself into a sovereign, and he made the West register the process, willy-nilly, as it was reported, performed, and circulated through the expected channels. Jenson has studied closely what she calls Dessalines's "poetics/politics of violence," reading his communications in the context of later postcolonial theory and in the context of his "determined outreach to an American media sphere."[116] Of course, Dessalines's texts must also be read in the context of his British diplomacy, as a defiant and playful engagement with a tradition of representation of black agency—or lack thereof—notably expressed in early British abolitionist poetry. Dessalines and his secretaries for diplomatic leverage channeled the fear of a black nation coursing through the very language of their international interlocutors: this language also provided the material of his international infamy.

In the early months of Haiti's independence, Great Britain tried to secure advantageous terms for a trade and military agreement without giving Haiti official recognition. As Haiti's privileged interlocutor and military ally, Great Britain already had a strong commercial foothold on the island, and British traders were present in all of the country's main ports. The U.S. government, fearing Great Britain might obtain a trade monopoly with Haiti, pondered official trade agreements of its own. Great Britain had no immediate plans to recognize Haiti as an independent nation. Rather than an envoy or ambassador of the British government, it was Gen. George Nugent, governor of Jamaica, who led discussions with Dessalines.

Dessalines could not afford losing the support of Great Britain, but he also needed to assert Haiti's autonomy. The tenuousness of his position appears in the language he uses in correspondence with Nugent, concerning the "renewal of the convention between the island of Jamaica and Haiti such as it existed under the government of general Toussaint": "General Toussaint treated with the British Government as a subject or delegate of the French government.... I, sole leader of my country, treat on behalf of all my fellow citizens and need account for my actions to no power, nor do I wait for the permission of any government in order to subscribe to accommodations or treaties."[117] Haiti was under the immediate threat of French troops that remained on the Spanish side of Hispaniola, and he had no navy to speak of. But he also knew he could not give an inch of Haiti's autonomy to Great Britain. Dessalines had plans of his own.

ACTING THE VILLAIN

If Louverture's identification with Raynal's black Spartacus was in part an effort at placating European audiences familiar with Raynal, after independence Dessalines's evocation of the figure was meant strictly to terrify. He systematically put vengeance at the heart of his political decisions. Thus, in an early declaration presenting his resolve in dealing with "every man who has dishonored human nature, by prostituting himself with enthusiasm to the vile offices of informers and executioners," Dessalines vows that "nothing shall ever turn our vengeance from those murderers who have delighted to bathe themselves in the blood of the innocent children of Hayti."[118] In document after document Dessalines made sure to define Haiti as the black nation of Europe's nightmares. The process that he channeled and exacerbated was the language of righteous public vengeance that "had been the foundation of the juridical legitimacy of the revolutionary movement" in France under Jacobin rule but that by 1805 had become "intolerable" around Europe and even in France. Sophie Wahnich argues that the much maligned Terror was a profoundly political effort on the part of France's representatives at appropriating the expression of the people's vengeance. Taking charge of "public vengeance" — that is, common rather than personal politics, in short — also demonstrated the democratic legitimacy of a new form of government confronted to enemies abroad and in its midst. The Terror was "a process welded to a regime of popular sovereignty in which the object was to conquer tyranny or die for liberty."[119] The same can arguably be said of the massacre of the whites in the opening months of Dessalines's tenure, a time when the spectacle of popular vengeance served to perform the unbreakable bond between a formerly enslaved people and its newly formed state, by way of the drama-inflected black avenger tradition.

Dessalines's self-identification with the avenger of the Americas in his official proclamations proves a willful, self-aware, and eminently sarcastic intertextual gesture. The April 28, 1804, proclamation following the massacre of the whites at times reads like a pastiche of Raynal's and Mercier's texts.[120] Here Dessalines reverses Raynal's famous question: "Where is that vile Haitian, so unworthy of his regeneration, who thinks he has not accomplished the decrees of the Eternal, by exterminating these blood-thirsty tigers?" The inversion is a striking performance of the rhetoric of righteous revolutionary vengeance described by Wahnich. What individual scruples might prevent a singular Haitian from participating in acts of public vengeance instantly expels him from the collective entity that is the nation. But the nation is immediately subsumed in the person of its leader. Further in the text Dessalines riffs on other abolitionist motifs, summoning a gigantic spirit of the country:

> Let that nation come who may be mad and daring enough to attack me. Already at its approach the irritated genius of Hayti, rising out of the bosom of the ocean appears; his menacing aspect throws the waves into commotion, excites tempests, and with his mighty hand disperses ships; or dashes them in pieces; to his formidable voice the laws of nature pay obedience; diseases, plagues, famine, conflagration, poison, are his constant attendants. But why calculate on the assistance of the climate and the elements? Have I forgotten that I command a people of no common cast, brought up in adversity, whose audacious daring frowns at obstacles and increases by dangers?

Dessalines echoes the elemental trope so familiar to abolitionist poets only to dismiss it. An army general has no need to call on the heavens; it is the elements that must be compared to his troops, rather than the reverse. He takes over the characteristics of the avenger as villain, leaving to his predecessor, Toussaint Louverture, the role of the tragic, and unsuccessful, hero. Dessalines admits so much when in the same document he declares, "Somewhat unlike him who has preceded me, the Ex-general Toussaint Louverture, I have been faithful to the promise I made to you, when I took up arms against tyranny, and whilst the last spark of life remains in me I will keep my oath. 'Never again shall a colonist, or an European, set his foot upon this territory with the title of master or proprietor.' This resolution shall henceforward form the fundamental basis of our constitution."[121] The black avenger of Western literary tradition was either unsuccessful or an abstract warning. By winning the war Dessalines had effectively turned Raynal's and Mercier's abstract warnings to planters into their walking nightmare, putting aside the tragic avenger in the Oroonoko vein and reconnecting with the ruthlessness of the black villains of revenge tragedy. He could write with obvious pride, "My name has become a horror to all friends of slavery, or despots; and tyrants only pronounce it, cursing the day that gave me birth" and dub himself "avenger and deliverer of his fellow citizens" in the Constitution of 1805.

Taking on the characteristics of the stage villain had some benefits: following victory over the French, who had the strongest army in the Western world, Dessalines and his troops appeared decidedly fearsome, the reservations of some notwithstanding.[122] Although French troops remained in the

Spanish half of the island in Santo Domingo until they were expelled by the local population allied with the British in 1809, Napoleon never attempted to retake Saint-Domingue. The dictator would later admit that he had been wrong not to leave the administration of the island to Louverture, calling it "the greatest error that in all my government I ever committed."[123] With the circulation of Dessalines's texts came the circulation of planters' fear, as well as slave action, real and imagined: uprisings around the Caribbean basin were blamed on Saint-Domingue throughout the 1790s and continued to be well into the nineteenth century. Haitian influence on those uprisings was generally indirect at best; bent on striking economic agreements with England and the United States, Louverture had shown his good will by helping sabotage a French republican plot aimed at starting a slave revolt in Jamaica. Later Dessalines and his successors, when they overtly supported revolutionary movements in the Americas, kept to those led by Creole planters rather than their servants.[124] Yet official action, or lack thereof, counted for only part of the threat the revolution represented to the slaveholding world.

The violence of the French Revolution already had a deep impact on American politics, and "Jacobins" became a common insult used against Thomas Jefferson and his followers. The Haitian Revolution hit much closer and literally spilled onto American shores, with Saint-Domingue exiles settling in cities all along the eastern seaboard. Rumors that the Jacobins had plans to foster slave rebellions in the United States came to a head with the slave revolt scare in Charleston, North Carolina, in 1793.[125] In 1795 and 1796 several revolts were thwarted in Spanish Louisiana that were, rightly or wrongly, similarly blamed on the dangerous example of Saint-Domingue.[126] Finally, Jacobin and Saint Dominguan influences were very much at the center of discussions that followed the aborted 1800 Richmond uprising known as Gabriel's Rebellion.[127] The alleged involvement of two Frenchmen in the revolt was enough evidence to suggest that the French were behind an effort very similar to the plan thwarted by Louverture in Jamaica. Mentioning early rumors of an organized slave uprising to Vice President Thomas Jefferson, Virginia governor James Monroe wrote, "The scenes which are acted at St. Domingo must produce an effect on all the people of colour in this and the States south of us, especially our slaves, and it is our duty to be on guard to prevent any mischief resulting from it."[128] That planters around the Americas trembled at the possibility of another Saint-Domingue is undeniable; news of the revolution circulated through print but also by word of mouth, coming from the Saint-Domingue enslaved, free-colored, and white exiles that spread throughout the Americas. Michael Drexler and Ed White make the argument that "following its dissemination throughout the U.S. in the fall of 1801, Toussaint's Constitution became the most widely read piece of literature authored by an African American."[129] Worse than a successful slave revolution, Haiti offered the entire slaveholding world the terrifying prospect of a black nation in the Americas.

Dessalines's proclamations circulated around the Americas and were deemed instrumental in starting several slave uprisings, in particular in the United States. They were notably reproduced freely in southern newspapers, and it is indeed unlikely that they failed to reach the black eyes and ears they contributed to conceptualize.[130] Indeed, article 14 of his constitution made Haiti the global home of blackness: "All acception of colour among the children of one and the same family, of whom the chief magistrate is the father, being necessarily to cease, the Haytians shall hence forward be known only by the generic appellation of Blacks."[131] In this effort, Dessalines's argument is strikingly reminiscent of Ottobah Cugoano's in his *Thoughts and Sentiments on the Evil and Wicked Traffic of Slavery and Commerce of the Human Species*, in which the self-professed "black man" defined his community as "brethren and countrymen in complexion."[132] Article 13 also made clear that even those phenotypically white people naturalized as Haitians would be considered black. The effort at curing the wounds inflicted by the socioracial civil wars that overlapped the revolution and the War of Independence is fairly transparent. It was also ultimately unsuccessful, as later developments proved. But in the meantime, here was a bold attempt at lighting a beacon beyond the confines of white Western thoughts.

Speaking in the language of freedom is a gambit. The birth of Haiti might have brought its population out of the realm of European fiction and into that of international politics, did the two not overlap so thoroughly. The black avenger trope, if it allows for the recognition of extraordinary black individuals, simultaneously does work to maintain the racist assumptions of the day. Dessalines's efforts at appropriating the device did little to challenge its most problematic aspect: the black avenger myth is a racialized version of the great man theory of history. Upon declaring himself emperor of Haiti, despite pressure from his foremost officers, Dessalines refused to create a Haitian nobility, stating, "I alone am noble."[133] This unmistakable declaration of uniqueness kept him within the confines of a tradition the revolution had threatened to explode: the dreaded, unthinkable black nation looming large in Mercier's text could immediately be cut to size as its revolutionary, collective potential took second seat to Dessalines's personal ambition and the coming elitist state apparatus. Dessalines's subversion of the black avenger trope also confirmed its cultural relevance and contributed

The Negro revenged.

Vol. I. P. 376.

H. Fuseli R.A. pinx.t   Raimbach sculp.t

Hark! he answers—Wild tornadoes,
   Strewing yonder sea with wrecks,
Wasting towns, plantations, meadows,
   Are the voice, with which he speaks.

Pub. by J. Johnson, London March 1 1807.

"The Negro Revenged" (1807), after a painting by Henry Fuseli,
in William Cowper's *Poems* (1808). © The Trustees of the British Museum.

to its perpetuation as a valid representational frame for the Haitian Revolution. Henry Fuseli's engraving "The Negro Revenged" demonstrates this in striking fashion (fig. 1). The image was first published in the 1808 edition of William Cowper's *Poems*, purportedly as an illustration for those lines in "The Negro's Complaint" portraying natural catastrophe as God's answer to slavery. Yet designed as it was two decades after the poem's first publication and in the aftermath of the English abolition of the slave trade and the Haitian Revolution, the engraving is more commentary than illustration. The image shows a black man and his lighter-skinned companion hugging and cheering from a cliff the destruction of a ship down below, with a cloaked figure, possibly their child, sitting behind them. It may not be too bold to see an indirect reference to the success of the Haitian Revolution in Fuseli's granting the lone voice of Cowper's poem a companion and child. It also channels decades-old elemental tropes: the engraving's title all but assigns the destruction to the man himself, lending in the process a supernatural quality to the proceedings. Fuseli's "Negro" is not so much an individual as it is the same scary but familiar type channeled by Dessalines himself. Both Dessalines and his opponents found something in preserving the black avenger figure: a singular image of racial purity, which served both outsider racist and Haitian nationalist purposes.

CHAPTER 4

FEAR OF A BLACK AMERICA

Literary Racial Uprisings in the Antebellum United States

Could the United States avoid a black revolution? The question underlay conversations between the republic's founders when they gathered to design its foundational documents and discuss the place slavery should occupy in the new country. Thomas Jefferson infamously expressed in his *Notes on the State of Virginia* the view that peaceful coexistence between whites and blacks in the United States would never be possible. Short of deporting all black people, "deep rooted prejudices entertained by the whites; ten thousand recollections, by the blacks, of the injuries they have sustained . . . , will divide us into parties, and produce convulsions which will probably never end but in the extermination of the one or the other race."[1] Notwithstanding the justifications for racism and slavery he then proceeds to list, Jefferson's anxieties suggest his awareness of the profoundly immoral character of slavery. Abolition is impossible because it would confirm this truth of this immorality, and what vengeance might freedom bring on the former slaveholders? The issue of slavery grew to occupy a central position in national debates at the time of the Haitian Revolution and in its aftermath: the influx of Saint Dominguan refugees brought physical evidence of the revolution into the United States, and "no event more clearly laid bare the contradiction between republican principles and slavery than the Haitian Revolution."[2] To the bodily presence of Saint-Domingue exiles was added the overwhelming textual presence of the revolution: documents by and about the Haitian revolutionaries floated freely into the United States during and long after the conflict, carrying with them threats of slave insurrection and race war intimately tied to the notion and possibility of black literacy. In antebellum American politics, abolitionists and proslavery advocates alike constantly presented the antislavery struggle in and around the United States through a Haitian prism. The specter of the Haitian Revolution hovered over U.S.

gothic romance, where it served as "short hand for impending violence," but also as a worrisome reminder that increasingly extreme white national sentiment in the United States might have to count, and possibly contend with, its black equivalent.[3] The Haitian Revolution was proof of black worth or evidence of black savagery, a blueprint of what to expect—fear, or hope, for the future, depending on the audience it reached. As it developed and maintained itself in the neighboring Haitian Republic, the notion of a black citizenry increasingly became anathema in national public discourse in the United States. In the run-up to the Civil War, the Haitian Revolution was an entire grammar in U.S. American public discourse, bracketed by two polar opposite narratives of the revolution, the "horrific Haitian Revolution" and the "heroic Haitian Revolution," and endless combinations in between.[4] This spectrum also provided filters through which to discuss black collective agency in the United States—many of which lay the black avenger narrative over factual revolts.

Thwarted slave uprisings on American soil in the early nineteenth century—Gabriel's Rebellion in 1800 Virginia, the 1811 German Coast Uprising, Denmark Vesey's in 1822 North Carolina, and Nat Turner's Virginian uprising in 1831—kept alive the fear of a black nation in a country increasingly defined as a white Canaan, a "herrenvolk Republic."[5] These revolts all bore the mark of Haitian influence, real or imagined. During and after the Haitian Revolution, Saint-Domingue revolutionaries—literate or not—showed they knew how to use the Atlantic world's print networks. Stories about and by them circulated on three continents and made a very concrete case for the correlation between literacy and revolution implied in the Enlightenment literacy narrative. The narrative became part of a rhetorical arsenal used to both address and circumscribe matters of black political agency in the United States. The leaders of the aforementioned U.S. uprisings were all literate, which allowed commentators to highlight connections between literacy, extraordinary individuals, and black political agency under the sign of the Haitian Revolution. South Carolina governor Thomas Bennett thus argued that Monday Gell, one of Denmark Vesey's co-conspirators, had "attained an extraordinary and dangerous influences over his fellows" thanks to his ability to "read and write with facility." It allowed him to read and circulate "seditious pamphlets" but also to write President Jean-Pierre Boyer for help.[6] Similarly, soon after Turner's revolt, a newspaper account reprinted throughout the country presented Turner as a "fanatic preacher . . . who had been taught how to read and write."[7] In the bloody immediate aftermath of the revolt, authorities scrambled to design new rules to outlaw literacy in the enslaved black population of Virginia. The story of Turner's quasi-magical learning of the alphabet makes clear that his wonted extraordinariness—portrayed in Thomas R. Gray's *Confessions of Nat Turner* and in contemporary news as relying strongly on the superstition and gullibility of the slaves around him—was in the broader American culture inseparable from literacy.[8] The role assigned to literacy in American conceptualizations of black revolt and freedom implies that in the United States, one must be familiar with narrative conventions to become free. The American black avenger would be a reader.

This notion also carried singular weight among free African Americans: the rising black public sphere in the nineteenth century, organized as it was around such social institutions as churches and Masonic halls, also rested on print culture. Sermons and speeches were published as pamphlets; African American–owned newspapers were created that provided spaces for black voices to express themselves. Tied though they were to white Western views of black agency, black avenger narratives held undeniable appeal for a class whose values were overall fairly similar to those of their white counterparts. This chapter looks at the crucial position occupied by the black avenger trope in American reflections on black political agency in the aftermath of the Haitian Revolution and before the U.S. Civil War. In that period the black avenger trope and the Enlightenment literacy narrative of the revolution became virtually interchangeable. In the American context, and most notably as free African Americans such as David Walker were concerned, it also allowed for the development of a discourse in which literacy itself served as symbol or code word for freedom and the struggle to obtain it.

The Haitian model of the black Spartacus came to occupy a prominent position in American discussions of slavery. U.S. black avenger narratives also developed singular variations on the Lucretia narrative. In 1808 the U.S. formally abolished the slave trade. Although the international trade continued to thrive illegally, the institution officially became a domestic one, relying on the production of enslaved bodies within the continental United States.[9] Thus the ban confirmed systematic rape as a crucial element of the institution of slavery. Not by chance, proslavery opposition to the rising U.S. abolitionist movement in the 1830s focused on voluntary race mixing as evidence of the destructive nature of the movement. Lucretia figures thus appear simultaneously in both pro- and antislavery literature. As antislavery activism grew increasingly radical on the eve of the Civil War, such prominent American voices as Harriet Beecher Stowe, Frederick Douglass, and Martin R. Delany offered their own American black avengers, in efforts to draw from, and model after, the well-known literary pattern, a uniquely American vision of black political agency.

A "black print counterpublic" developed in late eighteenth-century United States, notably in a series of publications written and financed by African American authors who engaged previous texts by black authors such as Phillis Wheatley or Sons of Africa Ottobah Cugoano and Olaudah Equiano but who owed nothing to white sponsors.[10] Thanks to these texts, a "corporate consciousness" rose among the free, literate black communities of the United States, predicated on the "very notion of blackness as a group condition covering diverse African peoples."[11] The appropriation of a notion of race first issued within the regime of slavery follows the same logic on display in independent Haiti's declarations: taking over the means of self-definition was a demonstration of agency, however conceptual.

This effort spread through networks of churches—such as Richard Allen's African Methodist Episcopal Church, with its services reserved to "our African brethren and the descendents of the African race"—or the black Prince Hall Freemasonry lodges that defined themselves in no small part by their relation to text literacy and print. African Americans used "collective venues to claim, secure, and enact for themselves the civil rights that whites under the auspices of racial privilege assumed, understood, and enjoyed as the natural provenance of the individual."[12] The Naturalization Act of 1790 and its subsequent iterations equated citizenship and whiteness, allowing only "any Alien being a free white person" to become a U.S. citizen. Some northern states offered local citizenship to propertied African Americans, but black civic life was restrained and grew only more so as local exceptions dwindled throughout the first half of the nineteenth century. By the 1820s the assault on black civil rights was widespread: the so-called Black Laws implemented in Ohio in 1807 to make black immigration into the state as difficult as possible served as a model for surrounding states to pass similar legislature so that "by 1840, some 93 per cent of the northern free black population lived in states which completely or practically excluded them from the right to vote."[13] In a country increasingly defined along racial lines, such legal decisions normalized the alienation of all people of color, including those who were free, from the national body.[14] The black counterpublic offered the closest thing to civic life, then, and print seemed a venue that allowed for a semblance of participation in national debates. In effect, the values of the black print counterpublic flipped the individualistic values of the white American Republic upside down as a matter of survival. Text provided a sense of political community to those free inhabitants denied citizen status. Print also made black voices available to broader national circles at any time, in any place.

In a country whose freedom discourse found its rhetorical roots in Protestant politics and exegesis, it should come as no surprise that African American notions of literacy should be closely related to religious sentiment. African American activists in the eighteenth and nineteenth centuries couched their arguments in biblical rhetoric, focusing on sections referencing more or less overtly black-skinned people but also identifying their plight as enslaved people in the Americas to that of biblical Hebrews in Egypt. This correlation never was simple or clear-cut: "Black Americans wanted to be the children of Pharaoh as well as children of Israel," connected to the glory and might of the ancient civilization but also to Judeo-Christian culture, values, and beliefs.[15] Early nineteenth-century visions of black redemption rested on the expected rise of a black messiah: a chosen, extraordinary—if not aristocratic—redeemer.[16] As Simon Rawidowicz reminds us, the etymology of the term makes clear that angry redeemers always lurk behind meek messiahs.[17] To navigate the demands of social life with and within a hostile, white supremacist society, African American authors and thinkers considering means of political and social redress and representation simultaneously engaged with the Christian rhetoric of messianism and with the black avenger trope, a global grammar for black agency indelibly marked by the Haitian Revolution.

On June 24, 1797, speaking to the African Masonic Lodge of Boston, Massachusetts, founder Prince Hall had these words to share: "My brethren, let us remember what a dark day it was with our African brethren six years ago, in the French West-Indies . . . : but blessed be God, the scene is changed; they now confess that God hath no respect of persons, and therefore receive them as their friends, and treat them as brothers. Thus doth Ethiopia begin to stretch forth her hand, from a sink of slavery to freedom and equality." While on the one hand African American notables such as Hall remained cautious and encouraged their peers to "kiss the rod and be still, and see the works of the Lord," on the other hand they also suggested with clarity that divine will was also expressed in the revolution in Saint-Domingue, which should be an inspiration to the black population of the United States, free and enslaved.[18] In the 1820s the U.S. black counterpublic could boast the first newspaper owned, written, and distributed by African Americans, John Russwurm and Samuel Cornish's the *Freedom's Journal*. It was directly related to the most significant abolitionist pamphlet of the early nineteenth century: David Walker's *An Appeal to the Coloured Citizens of the World, but in Particular, and Very Expressly, to Those of the United States of America* (1829).

David Walker, North Carolina–born son of a free mother and an enslaved father, agent and sometimes writer for the *Freedom's Journal*, lived for a time in Charleston and Philadelphia—two hubs for the Saint-Domingue diaspora—before settling in Boston in the 1820s. His *Appeal* is a radical rebuke of Thomas Jefferson's racist theories that also doubles as a political plan for black emancipation in the United States. As a member of Charleston's African Methodist Episcopal Church, Walker was acquainted early with American movements for black liberation and may even have been involved in Denmark Vesey's plot.[19] Yet his explosive, religiously inflected call to arms appears to engage at a more global scale with Son of Africa Ottobah Cugoano's 1787 *Thoughts and Sentiments on the Evil and Wicked Traffic of Slavery and Commerce of the Human Species*.[20]

Walker makes his case for the Americanness of people of African descent by way of the jeremiad, a rhetorical form especially popular in the United States, where, according to Wilson J. Moses, it developed a distinctly black variation that allowed for a "verbal outlet for hostilities" and a "means of demonstrating loyalty—both to the principles of egalitarian liberalism and to the Anglo-Christian code of values."[21] The black jeremiad expresses "complete acceptance of and incorporation into the national cultural norm of millennial faith in America's promise," while simultaneously declaring "black nationalist faith in the missionary destiny of the African." For Walker, African Americans constitute "a chosen people *within* a chosen people" yet his pamphlet addresses "*two* American chosen peoples—black and white—whose millennial destinies, while distinct, are also inextricably entwined," simultaneously pointing to the paradox of black life: within America yet separate from it.[22] Presenting the African diaspora in the Americas as one people, Walker lets the idea of a black nation that could potentially spread beyond, or ignore, the United States' fluctuating borders—with all the threat such a notion packed in the years following the Haitian Revolution—weigh in the balance, even as he harshly criticizes colonization projects.[23]

Walker presents his white readers with two choices: "You may do your best to keep us in wretchedness and misery, to enrich you and your children, but God will deliver us from under you. And wo, wo, will be to you if we have to obtain our freedom by fighting. Throw away your fears and prejudices then, and enlighten us and treat us like men, and we will like you more than we do now hate you, and tell us now no more about colonization, for America is as much our country, as it is yours." Walker dangles the prospect of race war, but he also echoes ameliorist arguments with the claim that to reach a peaceful solution, whites should "enlighten"—that is, educate—people of color. If white Americans do not help, black Americans will take their destiny in their own hands and educate for independence rather than coexistence: "Our sufferings will come to an end, in spite of all the Americans this side of eternity. Then we will want all the learning and talents amongst ourselves, and perhaps more, to govern ourselves.—'Every dog must have its day,' the American's is coming to an end."[24] Throughout his text Walker also calls for blacks to educate themselves, as a necessary step toward racial autonomy and power. If Walker insists that he hopes he and his brethren will gain American citizenship rather than seek a separate state, he also makes clear that the time for patience is over. Education and literacy are essential to the formation of citizenship—either in collaboration or in struggle, in which case they double as weapons.

Walker had expressed his ideas about education and literacy in the pages of the *Freedom's Journal* before. The April 25, 1828, issue thus reported on one of his speeches:

> Mr. *David Walker* . . . stated largely the disadvantages the people of Colour labour under, by the neglect of literature—and concluded by saying, that the very derision, violence and oppression, with which we as a part of the community are treated by a benevolent and Christian people, ought to stimulate us to the greatest exertion for the acquirement both of literature and of property, for although we may complain of the almost inhospitality with which we are treated; yet if we continue to slumber on and take our ease, our wheel of reformation will progress but slowly.[25]

Throughout the *Appeal* Walker demonstrates his own literacy and education, notably by rooting his call for action in religious and historical exegesis, presenting scripture supporting his view of armed struggle as a God-ordained mission. Walker also shows his knowledge of history and operates in the process a fundamental reversal: he eschews white Rome for colored Carthage and "that mighty son of Africa, HANNIBAL, one of the greatest generals of antiquity, who defeated and cut off so many thousands of the white Romans or murderers." This becomes proof of the necessity of black union but also a subtle reminder of the precedence of African civilization: "Had Carthage been well united and had given him good support, he would have carried that cruel and barbarous city by storm." Only thanks to literacy and education could Walker find out that white Romans once were barbarians to Africans, a well-recorded fact routinely obfuscated in popular culture. To spread knowledge and the means of obtaining it is the mission on which Walker sends his black readers: "Men of colour . . . I call upon you therefore to cast your eyes upon the wretchedness of your brethren, and to do your utmost to enlighten them—*go to work and enlighten your brethren!*—Let the Lord see you doing what you can to rescue them and yourselves from degradation." National redemption comes through access to text. In terms carrying double references to religion and politics, Walker asks that his readers, "all coloured men, women and children of every nation, language and tongue under heaven, will try to procure a copy of this Appeal and read it, or get some one to read it to them, for it is designed more particularly for them."[26] Literacy replicates citizens of a black American nation in the making.

Walker sets missionary goals for his black nation of readers in terms evocative of, and in drastic contrast with, those of the American Colonization Society, the organization founded with support from pro- and antislavery white businessmen and politicians to create a colony in western Africa for free black Americans. For the leadership of the ACS, the increase of free people of color in the United States was a serious issue: "This description of persons are not and cannot be, either useful or happy among us; and . . . there should be a separation." The ACS bought land and started settlement in West Africa with plans for free people of color to "diffuse their light and gradually dispel the darkness which has so long enshrouded that continent."[27] By the late 1820s many in the African American community opposed the ACS's scheme, not least among them contributors to the *Freedom's Journal.*[28] Only a "traitor to his brethren" would consider leaving for Africa, Walker declares in his *Appeal*, quoting the *Freedom's Journal's* Samuel Cornish.[29] Walker recycles the rhetoric of black settler colonialism of the ACS, but he does not dream of Africa: he envisages this civilizing mission for the "internal colony" constituted by black Americans, strongly implying that it needs a territory.[30] He regularly addresses his potential white audience in the second person, as "you Americans," acknowledging in the process that his local black audience does not have national status.[31] Yet "America is more our country, than it is the whites—we have enriched it with our *blood and tears*," Walker declares, claiming America's ownership for those who physically toiled to build it.[32]

This incendiary rhetoric—the nerve of claiming homestead rights for America's black inhabitants—was not lost on slaveholders, whom Walker designated as "the Lord's enemies."[33] His pamphlet gained notoriety around the United States following its discovery in Georgia in December 1829. Hysteria about the potential influence of the text among the states' black population soon spread. Mere months earlier, fires had consumed portions of Augusta and Savannah, Georgia, that were believed to have been set by slaves, and another apparent conspiracy had been discovered in the state in the spring of 1829. Within weeks the pamphlet was appearing in Virginia, North and South Carolina, and Louisiana, everywhere bolstering fears already stoked by recent instances of slave agitation.[34] Alluding in the pamphlet to the numerous people of color in these very states, Walker argues that, properly equipped, he "would put [them] against every white person on the whole continent of America" and adds with foresight "the whites know this too, which make them quake and tremble."[35] The prospect of a continent-wide black uprising evokes the half-century-old visions of Raynal, with the added measure of threat provided by the existence of the free, independent nation of Haiti in the Caribbean basin.

Following the suicide of King Henry I in 1820, the country was reunified under President Boyer and accepted to pay an exorbitant tribute to France in return for diplomatic recognition and the end of French claims on the island. Great Britain, basking in the moral superiority of the 1807 abolition of the slave trade, dealt with Haiti through agents and navy officers and would grant the country official recognition in 1833, only when Great Britain abolished slavery. The United States, though it traded with the Haitian Republic, also actively blocked its access to the concert of nations, a slight exacerbated by the comparatively favorable relation the United States entertained with the nations born of Creole revolution in South America. In spite of this hostility, a portion of the African American community, aware that the Haitian Constitution allowed for African American emigration, chose to make the trip. Supported by Rev. Richard Allen of the African Methodist Episcopal Church, the abolitionist Benjamin Lundy, and later by the African Colonization Society agent Loring Dewey, African Americans first moved in numbers to Haiti in the 1820s, with dire results.[36] Haiti retained a unique aura among African Americans that would fluctuate in the first half of the century as the United States' imperialist expansion, driven by the southern plantocracy, increasingly looked threatening to the Caribbean nation.[37]

Walker presents Haiti as a refuge for African Americans, and its people as "our brethren, the Haytians, who, according to their word, are bound to protect and comfort us," but he ranks it second to Great Britain.[38] Earlier that year African Americans forcibly expelled from Cincinnati had found refuge in the British colony, an event Walker alludes to indirectly.[39] Religion also played a part: Walker laments that the West Indian nation is "plagued with that scourge of nations, the Catholic religion; but I hope and pray God that she may rid herself of it, and adopt in its stead the Protestant faith."[40] In this, the vision of global blackness expressed by Walker shows itself to be profoundly American. U.S. blacks could teach their Haitian brethren the better religious ways of Protestantism. They could also learn from Haitian political successes and failures and *do better*. Walker refers somewhat cryptically to the Haitian Revolution as the latest in a long history of warnings against racial disunion:

> O my suffering brethren! remember the divisions and consequent sufferings of *Carthage* and of *Hayti*. Read the history particularly of Hayti, and see how they were butchered by the whites, and do you take warning. The person whom God shall give you, give him your support and let him go his length, and behold in him the salvation of your God. God will indeed, deliver you through him from your deplorable and wretched condition under the Christians of America. I charge you this day before my God to lay no obstacle in his way, but let him go.[41]

What episode of the revolution Walker is alluding to here is not so clear, but the passage's biblical inflections unmistakably suggest a Moses-like figure that we can surmise is Toussaint, the God-ordained national redeemer. Recognizing such a figure is presented as a matter of biblical and historical literacy: one must read in order to *see*. For a person of African descent in the 1820s, *seeing* is knowing what to make of Haiti and its tutelary figure, Toussaint Louverture, and what potential equivalent he might have in the United States.

Two years after the publication of Walker's *Appeal*, in August 1831, Nat Turner, a literate slave who preached in plantations in Southampton County, Virginia, led a rebellion that left over fifty white people dead. The short-lived uprising, the deadliest of its kind in the United States, was crushed by local authorities, and in its aftermath hundreds or more African Americans were massacred in the region. "The specter of Haiti" lurked over the proceedings, and the link from Walker to Turner seemed an evidence to many in the South and beyond, the aforementioned passage appearing as prophetic as Raynal once did.[42] The panic that seized Virginia in the wake of Turner's revolt, characterized notably by increasingly drastic regulations against black education, appeared to confirm the correlation Walker himself drew between literacy and slave revolt. Yet it also revealed how, after the Haitian Revolution, the black avenger trope merged almost fully with the Enlightenment literacy narrative, to the point that the narrative construct itself was understood as a kind of metonym for the actions and politics at play in actual slave revolts. Elements of this simplification appear in Walker's text, weaponized; they appear, in significantly different terms, also in the works of white American abolitionists in the aftermath of Turner's revolt.

Proslavery agitation in the North took a distinctly radical turn in the 1830s, in the wake of the spread of so-called Black Laws, meant to block the influx of black Americans into midwestern states, and whose influence spread eastward, inspiring racist legislation and practices in New England. The creation of the American Anti-Slavery Society in 1833 was also met with brutal reaction. At the height of the society's activity, proslavery mobs from Boston to Saint Louis routinely attacked abolitionists newspapers and destroyed their presses. The midwestern territories of Ohio, Illinois, and Missouri were the theater of brutal confrontations between hordes of "gentlemen of property and standing" with economic interests in the South and abolitionists, whose organizational successes appeared to "threaten to disrupt the polity and to transfer the leadership to the 'wrong' groups in society."[43] Other mobs made up mostly of skilled white workers assaulted African Americans on the suspicion that they were unfair job competitors. Thus, in April 1836 a mob attacked the black section of Cincinnati, Ohio, killing several people and destroying houses. In July a proslavery mob attacked the black neighborhood again and descended on the office of James G. Birney's newspaper, the *Cincinnati Weekly and Abolitionist*, destroying the printing press and driving Birney out of town. This son of the southern aristocracy had become something of a national sensation when he resigned from the vice-presidential position in the American Colonization Society, to which he had just been elected, denouncing the society's goals and actions in a letter reproduced throughout the country's newspapers.[44] "The violent and almost murderous opposition" he faced in his home state of Kentucky followed him across the river into the free state of Ohio.[45] Proslavery mobs often killed, as in the infamous 1837 murder of abolitionist journalist Elijah Lovejoy—"first American Martyr to THE FREEDOM OF THE PRESS, AND THE FREEDOM OF THE SLAVE"— in Alton, Illinois.[46]

Supporters of slavery justified their routine use of physical violence with rhetoric that systematically presented abolitionist rhetoric as a form of violence. An article in the *Charleston Courier* thus defined abolitionists as "misguided fanatics who, in the reckless prosecution of their views of false philanthropy, would apply the torch to our dwellings, and the knife to our throats," effortlessly equating opposition to slavery and slaughter. For the author, "any attempt ... to direct public sentiment against this institution ... is justly to be regarded as an act of hostility towards the South, such as in a foreign people would be a justifiable cause of war."[47] Much of the debate over abolitionism similarly blurred the distinction between words and deeds. Abolitionists' writings were shown to carry in words the seeds of Haitian-like atrocities, this conceit justifying in turn the brutality of proslavery mobs as fit retaliation and self-defense. Antislavery activists beholden to the Enlightenment narrative occupied uneasy ground: they meant to claim black political agency, if not as a product of their action, at least as a phenomenon that they could, and should be allowed to, control textually, for fear it might devolve in Haitian-like horror. In the process they promoted righteous variations on the black avenger narrative.

Not long after the attack on Birney, William Ellery Channing, the nationally renowned spiritual leader of the Universal Unitarian Church and a recent convert to moderate abolitionism, wrote an open letter to Birney that was published as a pamphlet and reprinted in newspapers around the country. Addressing the favored excuse of proslavery mobs that abolitionists and their writings "[stirred] up insurrection at the South," Channing relativizes it in the following terms:

> The truth is that any exposition of Slavery, no matter from whom it may come, may chance to favor revolt. It may chance to fall into the hand of a fanatic, who may think himself summoned by Heaven to remove violently this great wrong; or it may happen to reach the hut of some intelligent daring slave, who may think himself called to be the avenger of his race. All things are possible. . . . The truth is that the great danger to the slaveholder comes from slavery itself, from the silent innovations of time, from political conflicts and convulsions, and not from the writings of strangers.[48]

For decades, most U.S. abolitionists did not voice support violent action and vehemently denied any causal relation between their texts and slave revolts. Channing awkwardly attempts to downplay the influence of written "exposition[s] of Slavery"— Raynal or, say, the Bible—on anonymous examples that are transparent references to Nat Turner, the "fanatic" whose actions had terrified the South a mere five years earlier, and Toussaint Louverture, Raynal's "avenger of his race." His task is complicated by the fact that he fairly clearly subscribes to the notion that Turner and Louverture are indeed beholden to liberal print culture, that what makes them extraordinary is the literacy, thanks to which they held sway over wretched masses of slaves who revolted.

Channing's letter engages with a broadly Western, post-Haiti approach to matters of black political agency. The political fact of Haiti could not be denied, yet its unthinkability perdured, maintained in the sense of wonder, of perpetual novelty attached to evocations of the event. In the aftermath of the Haitian Revolution, white commentators the world around reworked the black avenger trope and Enlightenment narrative in what can be termed a discovery mode: if white authors did not reveal the greatness of black leaders and commit these revelations to print, these extraordinary men might forever be passed over. In these texts black political agency as embodied in black heroes becomes beholden to white literate gatekeepers. Further underlying the discovery mode is the notion developed in texts, studied in previous chapters, according to which black leaders' peers were unworthy of a form of greatness considered the property of white people. The discovery mode takes for granted absolute racial distinction between blacks and whites; it also demands that the cultural production of blacks be crassly ignored. Marcus Rainsford presented himself as the "discoverer" of Haiti in his *Historical Account*, even though he was well aware that the new nation of Haiti was already producing its own historical texts: indeed, he knew that one of Dessalines's secretaries had written a "History of St. Domingo" as early as 1804.[49] Yet he and other white apologists for Louverture after him routinely begin their accounts by insisting on the pioneering character of their study. The discovery mode almost naturally spread from texts strictly about the Haitian Revolution to texts more broadly addressing the issue of slavery. Channing's reference to the race avenger trope makes clear how familiar it was in American discourse and how easily it could be used to transform discussions about black agency into discussions about white writing.

The fact of black writing was to Rainsford and those who came after him less useful than the more dramatic, if inaccurate, claim to its absence. Asserting this absence intensified the sympathetic character of abolitionist writers' endeavor: black-skinned people not having produced worthy writers, and light-skinned blacks being perpetually presented as ideologically suspect, the task of singing the praise of the black race hero naturally fell to white allies. English and American abolitionists alone could give the Haitian Revolution its unbiased due, portray it without passion, coolly and rationally separate the admirable from the despicable, the horror from the glory. English Unitarian minister John Relly Beard could thus argue in the introduction to *The Life of Toussaint L'Ouverture* (1853), that his effort was both necessary and unique: "The blacks have no authors; their cause, consequently, has not yet been pleaded. In the authorities we possess on the subject, either French or mulatto interests, for the most part, predominate."[50] Beard dismisses the many texts published by Haitian authors throughout the half century since independence, many of which were widely discussed in European and American publications.[51] He roots his claim to innovation in what Marlene Daut calls a "colorized understanding of Haitian history," the racist notion that mulatto writers' racial interests render them incapable of accurately assessing the dark-skinned Toussaint. According to Beard, the Haitian historian Joseph Saint-Rémy is not black enough for his 1850 *Vie de Toussaint-L'Ouverture* to do justice to the "First of the Blacks."

Saint-Rémy indeed assesses critically what he sees as Louverture's rhetorical effort to turn the War of Knives into a race war against mulattoes. His Toussaint is no saint, but he is no devil either: Saint-Rémy calls Toussaint "the hero who has graced my race" and gives as heroic a portrayal of the general as Beard. More of a problem for Beard's own rhetorical purposes is Saint-Rémy's own version of the discovery trope: noting that Louverture "did not have a national Plutarch and lives on only in the heart of pious islanders," he accepts the task and becomes "the writer who approaches virgin territory, who is the first to compile and gather documents that no other hand has touched, who opens a path no one else has attempted to open."[52] These words suggest how a certain extent of the discovery mode might simply belong to the epic, the genre of reference for historians. Yet, tied as it is to the profoundly racial thinking of the age, the discovery mode necessarily takes on racial meaning: in the mid-nineteenth century, even written by whites, the epic of Haiti was the epic of the black race, and it posed a problem for the West at large and specifically for France and the United States. Saint-Rémy presents Louverture as an "immense figure, who belongs to all races and ages," a man "whose high intelligence and genius proved that in giving human skin white or black coloration, God only meant to vary his works, and not establish hierarchy and dependence," making his biography of the "black Spartacus" an intervention in French race politics, at a time when theories of racial hierarchy, though they no longer coalesced around slavery, were nevertheless gaining ground.

Beard, by contrast, was hoping to influence public opinion in the United States at a time when the national debate on slavery was reaching a boiling point. The Fugitive Slave Act of 1850 had made it illegal to assist escaped slaves even in the states of the Union that did not practice slavery. In 1854 the Kansas-Nebraska Act would lead to an open war between pro- and antislavery supporters attempting to gain demographic superiority in the Kansas territory and thus secure it as a slaveholding or free state. Haitian-authored histories of the revolution were too nuanced, too specific for a text Beard envisaged as a textual weapon in the looming war. For his purpose Beard needed an absolute black hero. He says as much when introducing Toussaint in a passage that, of course, evokes Raynal: "The appearance of a hero of negro blood was ardently to be wished, as affording the best proof of negro capability.... The presentiment found expression in the words of the philosophic Abbé Raynal, who, in some sort, predicted that a vindicator of negro wrongs would ere long arise out of the bosom of the negro race. That prediction had its fulfillment in Toussaint L'Ouverture." To the long excerpt of Raynal that follows in Beard's text is appended this footnote: "Some parts which breathe too much the spirit of revenge have been softened or omitted in the translation." Beard's subscription to the Enlightenment literacy narrative is tempered by the imperatives of his brand of abolitionism: his Toussaint must appear to be driven by righteousness rather than resentment. For Beard, revenge and passion are the prerogative of the mulatto, whom he describes as proud, mean, physically strong, and rash, "ever prepared, if not panting, for revenge." He supports what Daut calls the "mulatto/a vengeance narrative," echoing Laveaux and offering a counterpoint to Saint-Rémy's mulatto history with a "black history" written by a white Englishman. As the line between nineteenth-century English-language treatments of Toussaint, the Enlightenment literacy narrative could not be stated more clearly. Beard's Louverture is necessarily racially pure and aristocratic: "We wish emphatically to mark the fact that he was wholly without white blood. . . . Though of negro extraction, Toussaint, if we may believe family traditions, was not of common origin. His great grandfather is reported to have been an African king."[53] The text illustrates the rhetorical contortions necessary to fit the facts of the Haitian Revolution to a black avenger figure meant to simultaneously act as an ethical model, a reassuring example of racial purity set against the dangerous and rhetorically problematic—in a U.S. context—free people of color, and yet retain an acceptable level of threat.

Ironically, Beard's book was republished in the United States in 1863 in an edition expanded to include an English-language translation of Louverture's autobiographical sketch originally published in Saint-Rémy's *Vie de Toussaint-L'Ouverture*. Two years into the Civil War, the American publication of Beard's book carried extra political weight: it was published by James Redpath, the Scottish American abolitionist, a friend of John Brown's and an agent of the Haitian government in the United States. In the new preface Redpath asserts that "it is but justice to say, that, although 'the blacks have no authors,' they have found in Dr. Beard not a friend only, but an able and zealous partisan," who, like English and American abolitionists, has "adopted the negro standard" of Haitian history, recognizing Louverture as "Hayti's hero, 'Great, ill-requited chief.'"[54] Redpath advances that there is a different Haitian history for each of the three racial castes, yet he does not address the paradox that the "negro standard" allegedly adopted by Beard seems drawn entirely from sources written by white authors. What transpires from Redpath's comments is that histories of the revolution by Haitian authors, here dismissed as "yellow history" (David Nicholls's infamous "mulatto legend"), were not adapted to the specific use American abolitionists wanted to make of Haitian history in the fraught moment when this book was published, at the height of the Civil War.[55] The United States needed a pristine, righteous, and martial black hero in history and fiction, a representation of black agency that would not trigger white racial anxieties. Many among white abolitionist writers addressed the issue by proposing a black hero as controllable as a textual creation, portraying his inevitable literacy not as a tool for liberation so much as evidence of white influence.

Such limitations are exposed in Wendell Phillips's famous lecture on Toussaint Louverture, performed for several years before it was published in Redpath's *Pine and Palm* in 1861. The avowed goal of Wendell Phillips's lecture was to convince white audiences that "the Negro race is entitled, judged by the facts of history, to a place close by the side of the Saxon."[56] The racial hierarchy underlying this vision was paramount in his time and exposes the importance of the hero as genius of the race. Unsurprisingly and in full discovery mode, Phillips portrays the historical record as exclusively white: Louverture "has left hardly one written line," and "all the materials for his biography are from the lips of his enemies."[57] Louverture's legacy—or lack thereof—is first and foremost a textual matter; as such, it is treated as a white property.

The black historians, biographers, and thinkers ignored time and again by white abolitionists, well aware of this proprietary outlook, emphasized the importance of *appropriating* the archive for their own purposes. The appropriation of the black avenger trope became a conscious element in this program, nowhere more obviously than in Martin R. Delany's serial novel *Blake*.

BLAKE, AMERICAN AVENGER

Literacy profoundly impacted Delany's life: born in 1812 to an enslaved father and free mother in Virginia, he had to flee to Pennsylvania with his siblings and mother because she had taught them how to read and write— then a crime in the state of Virginia.[58] He went on to become a barber and a practicing physician, gaining acceptance into Harvard Medicine School and attending for a few weeks before irate white students demanded he and two other black students be expelled. Delany became one of the foremost black voices in the land, notably by way of the *Mystery*, the newspaper he founded and edited from 1843 to 1847, at which point he began coediting the *North Star* with Frederick Douglass and traveling around the country on lecture tours and journalistic assignments. His 1852 treatise *The Condition, Eleva-*

tion, Emigration, and Destiny of the Colored People of the United States argued that blacks should leave the United States and found their own country in Central America, the West Indies, or Africa.[59] By the late 1850s Delany had grown convinced that Africa should be the destination. Delany's articles circulated widely in the African American press, notably in the pages of the *Weekly Anglo-African*.

The first section of *Blake* had been published in the *Anglo-African Magazine* in 1859; the *Weekly Anglo-African* run started over from the beginning on November 23, 1861, and the novel's last recovered chapters were published in the April 26, 1862, issue. The novel is in conversation with contemporary efforts by fellow abolitionists—Frederick Douglass's *The Heroic Slave* (1853) and Harriet Beecher Stowe's *Dred* (1856)—and also resonated deeply with David Walker's *Appeal*.[60] *Blake*'s protagonist follows in Walker's footsteps "in the Southern and Western sections of this country," taking to organizing where his forebear had "traveled and observed nearly the whole of those things."[61] In turn, the idea of an organized black uprising throughout the U.S. South and the West Indies developed in Delany's novel also had connections with, if not roots in, Haiti. Yet the island nation goes almost unmentioned in the novel. Katy Chiles studied the "relative silence on Haiti in the novel," explaining it by "the change of focus in Delany's emigration politics in the late 1850s." Chiles also demonstrates that as "text within a text," *Blake* was engaging Haiti on the very pages of the *Anglo-African*.[62]

One story in particular generated a spate of articles and letters: an enthusiastic group of African American emigrants from New Haven, Connecticut, left to settle in Haiti in August 1861. The experiment soon turned sour: the local population was hostile to the Americans, with whom they could not communicate and who knew nothing of local agriculture or customs. Illness struck the group and many died.[63] When the emigrants attempted to return to the United States, they found that the Haitian government, which had paid for their passage, required them to stay for at least three years. The problems faced by the New Haven colonists were routinely discussed in the pages of the *Weekly Anglo-African*, which also gave a regular tribune to Mary Ann Shad Cary's vitriolic critique of Haitian schemes.[64] On November 16, 1861, the *Anglo-African* announced the forthcoming first installment of *Blake*. On the front page, and amid columns full of reports from the front lines of the Civil War, a letter from Boston announced that "two anti-Haytian meetings" had recently been held, at which participants—including a returnee from the New Haven colony—asserted that Redpath was in fact selling African Americans "to the Haytian government for three years at thirty dollars per head."[65] That an African American newspaper would repeat words so evocative of slavery in relation to Haiti suggests how negatively the country was seen in some quarters.

At that point in time Delany was an ardent supporter of African emigration. In 1859 Delany had spent months in Liberia securing an agreement with local leaders for an African American settlement. Upon his return he gave lectures presenting this plan. Delany's African scheme undoubtedly influenced his fiction writing. Jerome McGann speculates that the novel's missing final chapters may well have featured the protagonists migrating to Africa.[66] For Delany Haiti paled in comparison to Liberia as a destination, but in *Blake* Delany nevertheless engaged Haiti as a narrative. It is arguably because Haiti and the very idea of black revolution seemed inseparable in U.S. print culture that Delany so adamantly disconnected them in *Blake*. In its incarnation as a cultural object produced at the crossroads of historical fact, racial representation, and nationalistic fantasies, Haiti weighed heavily on the notion of black revolution, as did the looming figure of Toussaint Louverture: increasingly summoned in abolitionist rhetoric, the revolution's charismatic leader and martyr was both an example and an impediment for proponents of black autonomy in the United States. Haiti's own national mythology was equally problematic. In April 1861 the *Anglo-African* had published a letter written by Haitian readers addressing the question, "Slavery in America: How Can It Be Abolished?" Their response contained this notable passage: "As Haytians, having constantly present in our imagination the remembrance of 1804, the dawning of our national existence, we are astonished that a Spartacus more fortunate than John Brown, has not yet arisen from the very midst of the slaves of the South, showing them the reality and its triumph."[67] *Blake*, albeit fictionally, seemingly offered just such a figure. Yet in strategically avoiding Haiti in *Blake*, Delany defined his novel as a cultural intervention, a new narrative of black agency offering an alternative to the story of the Haitian Revolution, a renovated literary model for a coming nation of black readers.

Henry Blake is a skilled slave on the Franks plantation in Natchez, Mississippi. As he is away running their errands, the Franks sell his wife, Maggie, to friends of theirs on their way to Cuba. Upon finding out, Blake leaves the plantation to go after her. He travels throughout the southern states, meeting secretly with select slaves in plantations to impart his "plan for a general insurrection of the slaves in every state, and the successful overthrow of slavery!" After an attempt at insurrection in New Orleans fails, Blake accompanies Maggie's family members to safety in Canada. He then makes the trip to Cuba, where he finds Maggie and manages to buy her freedom. The Caribbean island becomes the new headquarters for his scheme. Blake—who it turns out was born and raised in Cuba—forms an alliance with people of color of all social backgrounds to undertake "war—war upon the whites." The novel, as we know it, ends with a scene heavy with foreboding, as Gofer Gondolier, a member of the executive committee of the uprising dubbed the Grand Council, steps out into the streets of Havana, "to spread among the blacks an authentic statement of the outrage: 'Woe be unto those devils of whites, I say!'"[68]

Popular works of the early American canon built the United States as the natural home of an "American race" defined against Europeans, Native Americans, and Africans long before Justice Roger Brooke Taney's decision in the *Dred Scott* Supreme Court case of 1857 equated citizenship with whiteness.[69] By contrast, Delany put his projects squarely under the seal of blackness: as he could not be recognized a U.S. citizen, he dedicated his efforts to black people and the "nation within the nation" they constituted on U.S. soil.[70] In this sense *Blake* constituted a response in kind to Taney, a "literary intervention in American jurisprudence."[71] For Taney the United States was a nation where might makes right, and white supremacy could be defined as natural law because whites held power. *Blake* appears to upend Taney's statement, proposing Cuba as the potential geographic base for a black counterpart to the white United States. Critics have lamented the novel for merely adapting the "ideology of the racializing nation-state" to a black American nation.[72] What other frames Delany might have had at hand at a time when even his closest white allies took for granted the idea of a hierarchy of races is unclear. In *The Condition, Elevation, Emigration, and Destiny*, Delany stated that nationhood was a necessary step for the rights of blacks around the world to be recognized: "The claims of no people, according to established policy and usage, are respected by any nation, until they are presented in a national capacity."[73] Basing his conclusions of observations of the world in general and the U.S. herrenvolk republic in particular, Delany argued that race was a strictly political matter, the means by which "one political population dominated others as an internal colony," and black Americans would face oppression as long as they did not launch their own settler-colony project.[74] His positions evolved drastically throughout his life; *Blake* itself only partially illustrates his opinion. *Blake* is obviously not a strict political program; rather, it is a fictional exercise with wider political pretensions. Delany's novel was an intervention into historical writing and an exercise in black (i.e., political) writing, in which the "transnational shift enables Delany's narration of a black historical experience that does not refer ultimately to white revolutionary ideology."[75]

What classical nationalism is displayed in *Blake* matches what Tommie Shelby calls "defensive and rhetorical posture": it is a retort built with rhetorical weapons designed and used in the real world by the proslavery party and delivered on paper.[76] Delany is not only writing an alternative history or "black militant near-future fiction"; he is writing for the national library of a nation to come.[77] *Blake* follows David Walker in a tradition of self-referential black literary activism that aims at building the nation on readers plied with textual frames designed to help them imagine their new community.

FLIPPING THE SCRIPT

David Walker invoked in the same breath the prospect of slave revolution and an educational mission, knowing that "for colored people to acquire learning in this country, makes tyrants quake and tremble on their sandy foundation."[78] The foundations were in part built on narrative quicksand, as Louverture and Dessalines both demonstrated in striking—albeit limited— fashion: defined as it was by white Western conventions, literacy could never fully be separated from white Western interests. In *Blake* this notion attaches more specifically to white influence over grand narratives. The grandest of these narratives addressed in *Blake* is undoubtedly revolution. It is at the core of the novel but also evinces strong ambivalence. For Jerome McGann, "In *Blake* the very word 'insurrection' becomes slowly glossed as a white word drawn out of white history. . . . When blacks look at the past, white culture and history encourage them to see it in a white perspective."[79] McGann's remark points to *Blake* as a literary experiment: if black action could be hijacked by white voices and turned into white textual property, could this dynamic be in turn altered? With *Blake* Delany attempts to revert the dynamic of white narrative appropriation of black agency by retaking narrative control over scenarios of black revolt rooted in white supremacist literature.

This effort at flipping the script of white cultural appropriation of black agency notably finds expression in the second part of the novel, where fiction appears to confirm the fears expressed by slaveholders in the Americas and beyond regarding the future of Cuba. Henry Blake's plan for black revolution involves recruiting slaves around the southern states, sailing to Africa and Cuba, and using connections in all those places to organize a movement for the independence of Cuba as a new black republic. The broad possibility of a black revolution in Cuba, if not this specific scenario, was evoked constantly in U.S. American public discourse, perhaps rightly so: during several months in 1812, groups of rebellious slaves attacked and burned plantations to the ground until the capture of the conspiracy's leader, free black and militia commander José Aponte.[80] For years afterward rumors of slave rebellions backed by the free black population regularly agitated Cuba. Several conspiracies were thwarted in the following decades, the most famous being the 1844 Escalera conspiracy, in which thousands, allegedly led by the poet Plácido, plotted to overthrow white rule in Cuba. It remains unclear to this day how real the plot was, but thousands of blacks, slave and free, suffered in the subsequent island-wide repression. These attempts had a tremendous effect on the white population in Cuba, and the shock waves reached U.S. shores.

Beginning in the mid-1840s southern interests well settled in Cuba pushed for the annexation of Cuba, by purchase or by force. The threat of an independent, black Cuba was often dangled to justify the enterprise. Spain rejected successive monetary offers from Presidents James K. Polk and Franklin Pierce, and between 1849 and 1851 the Cuban filibuster Narciso Lopez, backed by southern money and men, unsuccessfully attempted to invade the island on several occasions.[81] In 1853 the appointment as captain general of Cuba of Juan de la Pezuela, a notorious opponent to slavery, only bolstered the fears of planters on Cuban and U.S. shores. Their influence on U.S. politics is clear in the "Ostend Manifesto," a dispatch to President Pierce in which U.S. diplomats James Buchanan, John Mason, and Pierre Soulé present the annexation of the island as a matter of national—and, hence, racial—security: "We should, however, be recreant to our duty, be unworthy of our gallant forefathers, and commit base treason against our posterity, should we permit Cuba to be Africanized and become a second St. Domingo, with all its attendant horrors to the white race, and suffer the flames to extend to our own neighboring shores, seriously to endanger or actually to consume the fair fabric of our Union."[82] The terminology of white supremacy made systematic use of a lexicon of black agency attached to depictions of the Haitian Revolution. Aponte was rumored to have asked the Haitian government for support in his endeavor.[83] Some of the slaves involved in the uprising had been soldiers with Jean François, once Toussaint's commanding officer in the service of the Spanish Crown.[84] Similar rumors pervaded reports about the Escalera conspiracy, whose purported leader, the poet Plácido, appears in *Blake* as Blake's uncle. The linking of Cuba and Haiti performed in the "Ostend Manifesto" was a Pan-American phenomenon: when Cuba found itself at "moments of revolutionary change, the image of Haiti would reappear, metaphorically revealing how racial divisions continued to structure Cuban society."[85] Yet evocations of Haiti served paradoxically to maintain the "unthinkability" of black revolution.[86] While the simple notion of black citizenship was the true "horrors to the white race," Soulé and others would argue that independent Haiti was a failed state and in this way evidence that there was nothing to be expected from black political agency but ruin. Jeffory Clymer reads *Blake* as a response to the "Ostend Manifesto," in which Delany "reproduces terminology of the Ostend Manifesto as he shows how white violence breeds black revolution."[87] Delany offers to respond, beyond the manifesto itself, to a tradition of white narrative framing of black political agency. He enjoins his readers to entertain the "horrific Haitian Revolution" not as historical truth but as a narrative construct that can be edited into a counternarrative.[88] *Blake* asks if a white disaster can be turned into a foundational black myth.

HAITI'S BLACK AURA

During the meeting of the Grand Council, Blake declares that "the like of tonight's gathering, save in a neighboring island years before any of us had an existence, in this region is without a parallel."[89] He had no need to name Haiti, the only nation born of a slave revolution, long a terrifying symbol of potentiality throughout the slaveholding countries of the American hemisphere. Yet, while the Haitian Revolution marked spirits around the world, Haiti's most direct involvement in international revolution was not on the side of another black American community, but with the South American Creole revolution of Simón Bolívar. El Libertador started his first two campaigns from President Alexandre Pétion's Republic of Haiti, backed by Haitian money and armed with Haitian weapons. A decade later President Bolívar of Great Colombia presented his project for an independent federation of South American countries as a guarantee against "that horrific monster which has devoured the island of Santo Domingo," showing as little gratitude for the nation that had made his success possible as he showed himself beholden to the Haitian disaster narrative.[90]

This telling of the Haitian Revolution also held sway over mainstream public discourse in the United States. The black nation of Haiti was a white defeat and therefore a step back in civilizational progress. This vision indirectly referred to the performative declaration of race unity in the Haitian Constitution of 1805, which made the fiction of race a reality to the rare benefit of people of color. This declaration of unity represented as much of a threat to the slaveholding United States as the reality of Haiti itself: words travel better than armies. Yet it worked in a different register within a Haiti now conceptually bereft of white people: the gesture was also designed to smooth over the complex dynamics of political and racial strife among the different socioethnic groups on the island. New disputes were born after independence that owed both to the old socioracial order and to the inequities brought by the new order. After Dessalines's assassination, the country split between his two principal rivals, Henry Christophe to the north and Alexandre Pétion to the south. They wrote their own constitutions, each toning down the radicalism of Dessalines's and expressing a more conciliatory stance toward European powers and whiteness, now defined as intrinsically foreign.[91]

Statesmen in the early Haitian period mobilized the language of racial unity but also wielded the language of racial difference when and where it was useful to their designs. King Henry Christophe thus followed in Louverture's footsteps to present himself as the leader of dark-skinned Haitians and *nouveaux libres* to better accuse his rival, the light-skinned Pétion, of conniving with the French. Pétion's successor, the Francophile Jean-Pierre Boyer, ruled over unified Haiti from 1820 to 1843 and accepted to pay a tribute to France in exchange for the recognition of Haiti's independence. He was eventually ousted by an insurrection led by the foremost members of his own party in 1843. What followed were a few years of utter political instability, during which the social elite ran the country by putting dark-skinned puppet presidents at the head of the country to placate the black masses. The *politique de doublure* paid lip service to national unity and maintained the elite's hold on the country "under cover of blackness" understood as synonymous with low class.[92] Successive Haitian heads of state, members of the elite or controlled by them, focused on keeping their entourage, the people, and the Spanish side of the island under control, with little success, as palace revolutions followed popular uprisings. Haitian might, once so feared by slaveholders around the hemisphere, was kept within the bounds of the island, directed inward—against Haitians and Dominicans—and a perpetual subject to racialized interpretation abroad.

Repeated Haitian attempts at annexing the eastern side of the island were "sometimes perceived abroad as a campaign to exterminate the white race."[93] This vision of things conveniently played into the narrative framework by then well installed in Western public discourse. Continuing factional strife on the island was used abroad as evidence in condescending judgments of the revolution and of black people in general. Colorism on the island cannot be ignored, but the notion that skin tone explains Haitian politics has been and remains an easy shortcut out of complex situations. It notably played an essential part in French reports on Faustin Soulouque, a general elected president of Haiti in 1847 only to proclaim himself emperor in 1849. Soon events in France put the "grotesque dignity" of Soulouque's court in perspective.[94] "Europe was laughing at the other continent, her eyes on Haiti, when she saw this white Soulouque appear," Victor Hugo notes with no shortage of disdain, mentioning further how Parisian crowds met the troops involved in Louis-Napoléon Bonaparte's coup with outraged cries of "down with Soulouque!"[95] Karl Marx had in mind only the two revolutions of 1789 and 1848 and the two Napoleons when he famously declared that "great historic facts and personages recur twice . . . once as tragedy, and again as farce."[96] Yet twice also the head of the independent state of Haiti had declared himself emperor before a Bonaparte followed suit. As Joan (Colin) Dayan notes, no amount of racialist scorn could erase "the reciprocal dependencies, the uncanny resemblances" between the two nations thereby revealed; but they could be painted over with an old brush.[97] It was used in drastic fashion in *The Inequality of Human Races* (*Essai sur l'Inégalité des races* [1853–1855]), where Arthur de Gobineau used the example of Haiti to underline what he saw as profound differences between "pure blacks" and mulattoes: only thanks to the "European blood" coursing through the veins of mulattoes, who "tend, like all hybrids, to identify themselves with the more creditable of the races to which they belong," had Haiti remained slightly civilized. Haiti had proven as "depraved, brutal, and savage" as Africa, and "the history of Hayti, of democratic Hayti . . . [was] merely a long series of massacres; massacres of mulattoes by negroes, or negroes by mulattoes."[98] Gobineau's hysterical vision of Haitian history did not challenge prior, possibly more sensible, narratives: it swallowed them whole with a racial logic all the more efficient that it appeared to appeal to science.

In a striking parallel, in international public discourse increasingly influenced by scientific racist interpretations such as Gobineau's, Haiti's political troubles boiled down to "Africanization," which also threatened Cuba. In *Negroes and Negro "Slavery": The First an Inferior Race, the Latter Its Normal Condition* (1861)—a work of rabid racism defending the polygenist view according to which whites and blacks were separate species—John H. Van Evrie thus asserted that in the absence of "control and guidance of the superior race," blacks revert to "their native Africanism"; he also used Haiti as an example. "Haiti's commitment to unified blackness was a rhetorical bounty for the staunchest opponents of emancipation, though they painstakingly attempted to empty it of all political content. Echoing Gobineau, Van Evrie asserted that the massacre of the whites under Dessalines had been but the expression of "negro instinct under those unnatural circumstances": naturally driven to fear, blacks had been "forced or betrayed into resistance" by "mongrel leaders."[99] By the 1860s Haiti was still rhetorically used as the perfect bogeyman for proslavery rhetoric, a figure of speech that could simultaneously embody racial terror and, when laced with colorism backed by pseudoscience, ridicule the notion of black political revolution.

In the early days of the Civil War, Haitian military force no longer seemed like it could protect Haiti against Western encroachment or violence. The country had become an easy target for gunboat diplomacy, a specific and shameful instance of which the *Anglo-African* reported on extensively and mercilessly: in the summer of 1861, not long after Spain regained control over the Dominican Republic, Spanish warships appeared in the Port-au-Prince harbor. Their officers claimed the Spanish flag had been trampled by Haitians at the border with Santo Domingo and demanded that Haitian authorities salute the Spanish flag and pay a tribute to repay the original insult.[100] To the outrage of many in and outside of Haiti, the Haitian government agreed to these humiliating demands. In the first issue of the *Anglo-African* featuring *Blake*, an article noted with no uncertain scorn that Fabre Geffrard, Haiti's "heroic President" had not raised a finger after getting "'kicked and cuffed' by Spain" and further wondered if after retaking Santo Domingo, Spain might not "take it in her head to finish the meal" and take over Haiti in turn.[101] This sentiment is echoed indirectly in the novel, when during a meeting of the Grand Council, Madame Montego asks a candid question: "'What aid may we expect from Hayti—she is independent?" Plácido didactically replies, "'Hayti is a noble self-emancipated nation, but not able to aid us, excepting to give such of us shelter, as might find it necessary or convenient to go there'."[102] Geffrard's campaign calling on U.S. blacks to rejoin "the common country of the black race" was already terminally undermined.[103]

It bears noting that while Delany was relatively measured in his critique of Haiti per se, he did not hold back in his judgment of James Redpath: "Neither do I regard or believe Mr. Redpath, the Haytian Government Agent, nor any other white man, competent to judge and decide upon the destiny of the colored people or the fitness of any place for the bettering of their condition, any more than I should be a Frenchman to direct the destiny of Englishmen."[104] For Delany, Geffrard's choice of Redpath as agent represented his and his country's inability to truly overcome color prejudice and deliver on its foundational promise of a country for and by black people. Such disappointment in Haiti's race politics appears indirectly in *Blake*, notably in the protagonist himself.

Indeed, Henry Blake's personal history evokes Haitian history and the intricacies of its race politics: he is a free black Creole by birth, and he expresses throughout the novel an elitist vision of the black race seemingly typical of his class. His conspiracy relies on a fraternity of worthy, educated black readers, most of them pragmatically chosen among the wealthy. He is wary of slaves, whose lack of education and spine may jeopardize the project, unless they are initiated into his Masonic-inspired "secret," an obvious reference to rites to which both Walker and Delany were privy as Masons.[105] The secret can be accessed through the literacy denied the enslaved and accessible to freemen: it is the power of interpretation, hermeneutics. Whoever masters it enters a masonry of readers and interpreters of history that exists in spite of the hostility of white proslavery advocates and the problematic stance of white abolitionists. With *Blake* Delany set out to wrestle with the Atlantic tradition of the black avenger and produce a new hero to write over Toussaint and his predecessors, real or imagined. He is a repetition with a difference of the literary black avenger, in which Delany attempts to deal with the white Western tradition of the black avenger, but also with American abolitionist versions of the trope. Walker enjoined African American readers to become "missionaries of nationalism": Delany's Blake has heard the call and goes about his mission within the plot and metatextually, as *Blake* itself is a tool to decipher history.[106]

COVERING THE OROONOKO TRADITION

In the Anglo-Saxon "race myth" delineated by Laura Doyle, freedom is the birthright of Saxons, untamable in England and abroad. Much of the myth's power seems connected to storytelling as a form of (hostile) takeover. Doyle argues further that the centrality of this scenario to Atlantic culture meant that "African American writers must adopt the *race* plot of freedom," and, as a result, "Afro-Atlantic counternarratives at once resist and embrace the racial order of Atlantic modernity."[107] *Oroonoko* shows that in modern nations, reading is also necessarily writing and interpreting, the same logic defended by Walker and Delany. The appropriation of Oroonoko's experience by Behn's narrator is a historical cover-up, a (re)writing of history necessary to the expression of English national sentiment in an imperial context. The racial logic underlying this phenomenon had by the nineteenth century become the foundation for modern nation making, making freedom as race plot an international norm. But this plot cannot be transferred wholesale to fit the situation of black people in the United States, for paradoxically, the standardization of the one-drop rule complicated even further already problematic purity narratives. As a "race myth," *Oroonoko* speaks only to white readers; for black readers, it is more readily a black avenger plot, and this is what Delany set to rewrite in *Blake*. His goal is to reappropriate the black hero and rewrite his story so that it serves as a founding myth of blackness rather than whiteness. He does this by echoing, altering, and repurposing aspects of *Oroonoko*, most prominent among them the scene of the Middle Passage.

Oroonoko and his retinue are taken on board a slave ship by a regular at the prince's court, a British captain "very well known to Oroonoko, with whom he had traffick'd for slaves." Seemingly returning Oroonoko's hospitality, the captain offers to let the prince and his entourage visit his ship. But he has them seized and put in chains and then takes off for the American coast. Outraged at being thus humiliated, Oroonoko starts a hunger strike, in which his entourage soon joins him. The captain coaxes him into eating again, after assuring him that "he should be freed as soon as they came to land."[108] Left to roam free on the ship, Oroonoko gives his word that he will not try to take control of it and convinces his devoted followers not to attempt anything. Upon landing in Suriname, the captain sells them all immediately into slavery. Blake's first encounter with a slave ship also occurred under the sign of deception: as a young man, the freeborn Blake—then known as Henrico Blacus—decided to join the crew of what he thought was a Spanish man-of-war. Blake seems even more clueless than Oroonoko, but just as self-righteous: upon finding out the ship's true nature as a slaver, he voices an "expression of dissatisfaction at being deceived."[109] This is enough to irritate the ship captain, who in retaliation sells Blacus as a slave on their return to the Americas.

Blake's outrage does not seem directed so much against the slave trade as against the lie he fell for. After all, his father is a wealthy Cuban tobacco trader, more than likely to have used slave labor. Not unlike Prince Oroonoko, Blake has to experience the abasement of slavery to understand and oppose it. Yet it is not until Blake's wife, Maggie, is taken away from him that he decides to begin his campaign against slavery. Upon finding out his wife's fate, Blake declares to her master, Col. Stephen Franks, "I'm not your slave, nor never was and you know it! And but for my wife and her people, I never would have stayed with you till now." In this again, he is reminiscent of Oroonoko, who organizes a slave uprising only when he comes to the realization that, as slaves, his wife and unborn child are under constant threat from their masters. Blake gets his political education in the heart of the slave trade. These similarities are signposts erected in the text to better emphasize how it departs from *Oroonoko*. In Aphra Behn's novella the African prince dies of overestimating the moral conscience of everyone around him and of believing that the heroic code of honor he lives by has any sway in the Americas. Henry Blake is not so naive: the initial treachery that occasioned his enslavement is lesson enough for him. When Blake sets out against the peculiar institution, he does so armed with his own plot and with the conviction that success will demand organized, collective action. This is made clear in Blake's second trip on a slave ship, one he very purposefully chooses to undertake.

His goal in joining the slaver's crew is to "tak[e] her in mid-ocean as a prize for ourselves, as we must have a vessel at our command before we make a strike." Once on the African coast, he will negotiate with Krumen leaders. Blake somehow knows them well and expects to "obtain as many [men] as I wish, who will make a powerful force in carrying out my scheme on the vessel."[110] The atmosphere on the crossing to Africa is heavy with wariness and foreboding, as the white captains quickly become suspicious of Blake.

In Africa Blake disappears during several days while the ship fills with its human cargo, but it is unclear what he does during this time, beyond spying on the local slave factor. On the way back from Africa, a British patrol chases the slave ship, and the captains order black crew members to throw overboard six hundred of the "dead, dying and damaged" slaves, as Blake "looked on without an evidence of emotion." Later in the passage, the slaves, led by the native chief Mendi, a "fine specimen of a man," manage to procure weapons during a tempest and seem ready to take over the ship. A puzzling scene then follows in which the two American captains catch glimpses of Mendi and his fellow slaves up in arms in the hold and discuss the best way to contain the upcoming mutiny, as thunder and lightning shake the vessel. The weather then clears, and the ship arrives in Cuba. "Blake during the entire troubles was strangely passive to occurring events below," seemingly because of the suspicion under which he was throughout the journey. But what of his original plan to take over the ship and what of the slaves in the hold armed with billhooks and sugar knives? We learn only that "the most restless spirits among the captive were disposed of as soon as possible," and what echoes of eighteenth-century abolitionist poetry could be found in the scene—the traditional association of storms and hurricanes with divine justice and slave revolt—melt as the ship reaches American shores.[111]

The episode dangles the possibility of an outcome similar to that of Frederick Douglass's 1853 novel, *The Heroic Slave*, a fictionalized account of the adventures of Madison Washington, a real-life African American slave who took over a slave ship to escape to freedom. This may well be the main point to this curious passage: to distinguish this story from Douglass's and show it to be one of willful, thought-out collective salvation rather than individual safety. Rather than sail for the English islands like Washington and his anonymous followers, Blake chooses to wait and organize instead for a massive strike. Blake sees his mission as directed against the transnational commercial institution of slavery. A ship mutiny alone would achieve little. The slaves who revolted are more useful on land than on sea: once back on Cuban shores, Blake decides to spread the news that the slaves were rebellious, thus bringing down their price, making it possible for him and his allies in Cuba to buy them all. Blake seemingly adapted his plan to the circumstances, abandoning the idea of taking over the ship to privilege the recruitment of manpower in Africa. This particular aspect is crucial to define the originality of *Blake* within black avenger tradition. The mutiny was a red herring meant to fool even the novel's readers. Blake's ultimate plan is more complex.

Throughout the novel Blake recycles the motto of the subservient parents of his wife, which he had seemingly rejected early on: "Stand still and see the salvation." For Jerome McGann, what happens—and does not happen—on the ship is evidence of Delany's profoundly religious vision for the future of African Americans. The storm is the act of a "providential God," ensuring that the mutiny fails so that Blake and his companions fulfill their ordained destiny, which is to eventually sail across the ocean and "establish a black city on an African hill."[112] However convincing, McGann's theory only partially accounts for the way in which Blake turns words of Christian passivity into a code for revolutionary strategy, an order to the organized slaves around the hemisphere to wait for the signal to begin a continent-wide uprising. It clashes drastically with Blake's cold, pragmatic behavior during the Middle Passage.

THE FREEMASONRY OF THE RACE

Strength, efficiency, and pragmatism are arguably more crucial values for the collective Blake works at building than Christian values—how else could one justify helping to drown hundreds of people on the Middle Passage?[113] Blake is no infallible great man of history: he cultivates networks and organizes groups. This sustained dedication to the collective marks a crucial turn away from black avenger tradition. Earlier in the novel Blake declares to a companion, "I'll do anything not morally wrong, to gain our freedom."[114] Blake's behavior on the slave ship suggests that pragmatism colors his morals. We find out that prior to the crossing, he had made contact with Mendi and Abyssa, military and spiritual leaders among the newly enslaved Africans. They later appear again as members of the Grand Council. The would-be mutineers become the shock troops of an organized revolution. The cost of Blake's strategy is chilling: six hundred people die to ensure that the remaining four hundred or so make it to Cuba to become soldiers for the black revolution. The design of the plan and its execution signal a crucial departure from the classic black avenger tale, in which the righteous leader finds, when action is needed, that his followers have abandoned him. Blake is pragmatic and calculating: in engaging with the "economics of slavery," he performs a staple of African American literature, the awareness that "black expressive wholeness" demands a negotiation with the economic reality of slavery.[115] Later, with his scheme to drop the price of the African slaves, Blake demonstrates his profound understanding of the slave system and simultaneously transcends it.

Blake's actions on the ship were a test of wills, and in the process he found in Mendi and Abyssa strong delegates, officers in his cause in the Grand Council, a collective body aiming at collective liberation. *Blake* purposefully departs from the black avenger tradition by offering a collection of heroes instead of a single figure, a dynamic that develops throughout the novel. Even before forming the council, as he travels the United States, Blake encounters the Maroons of the Seven Heads, a group of venerable high conjurors leading the Maroons of the Dismal Swamp, counting in their ranks Gamby Gholar, a former companion of Nat Turner, who has been hiding in the swamp since the rebellion, close to thirty years earlier. The Swamp Maroons are portrayed as old, superstitious, and unreliable storytellers. They try—in vain—one of their tricks on Blake, attempting to scare him with a "large sluggish, lazily moving serpent," which Blake instantly identifies as "so entirely tame and petted that it wagged its tail."[116] Among other such apparently comical behavior, they claim outlandish connections to the Revolutionary War or, rather, "de Molution wah," and, when prodded by Blake, assert that General Gabriel, the leader of the 1800 Prosser slave rebellion, also took part in it. As noted by Andy Doolen, in their incorrect historical references, the high conjurers suggest an alternative, illiterate historiography that reinscribes the largely obfuscated black participation in the revolution: "In prayer, prophesy, and song, another version of the Revolutionary War is being narrated, this one not linked to the Founding Fathers or their documents."[117] The conjurers' oral history substitutes a line of black heroes for the fathers of American independence and emphasizes the fact that the former are still working at completing the quest for freedom the latter did not bother to finish. Though he looks down on their practices, Blake seeks and obtains the Seven Heads' approval because their spiritual clout "makes the more ignorant slaves have greater confidence in, and more respect for, their headmen and leaders." The high conjurors' uneducated revisionist history of the American Revolution burns with the fire necessary to Blake's movement. Significantly, the chapter describing his encounter with them also discusses the "Brown Society," "an organized association of mulattos, created by the influence of the whites, for the purpose of preventing pure-blooded Negroes from entering the social circle, or holding intercourse with them."[118] Blake's encounter with one of the society's members almost results in his arrest—they have integrated color prejudice. By contrast, the high conjurors may be easy to ridicule, but their commitment to black revolution is undeniable. Literacy alone is not sufficient; what is needed is a nation of readers and interpreters.

Colorism harms African Americans the same way it harms Haitians, but Blake's nationalist cadre, the Grand Council, borrows the best of the Haitian Revolution: it represents the "African race" that "includes the mixed as well as the pure bloods."[119] Members of the council can be found among "the fairest complexion among the quadroons, who were classed as white," but they are also "fine looking mulatto officers" and wealthy blacks; some are planters or merchants, soldiers, artists, artisans, and slaves. All social and ethnic groups that form unified blackness are represented. The Grand Council is an unelected representative body, a synecdoche for a black race understood as a political choice rather than mere biological accident. Its collection of extraordinary leaders provides a fictional answer to the reductive individualism of the black avenger figure. Pride in one's blackness is the cement of the movement, which exorcises color prejudice through practice. Blake's own scorn for illiterate slaves disappears when he initiates them into his plan. Initiation grants them a status more important than social belonging. The secret society in which future rebels and members of the Grand Council are initiated is the black race considered as a political choice.

GENDER IDEALS

In his discussion of the influence of Freemasonry over the "black masculine ideal," Maurice Wallace is reluctant to emphasize Masonic overtones in *Blake*. Wallace sees a more striking example of Masonic influence in forms of self-fashioning used by Delany during the Civil War. Reflecting on Delany's famous portrait in U.S. Army uniform, Wallace sees in it a sign of his turn from "Constitutional cipher and political nonconformist to disciplinary individual and 'model' citizen . . . extraordinary in one sense, 'typical' in another."[120] Significantly, the visual line Wallace draws between Delany and Marcus Garvey extends back to Toussaint Louverture and, more specifically, to the famous portrait from Marcus Rainsford's *Historical Account*.[121] Delany made himself out to look the part of an "American Toussaint," adapting the mythified version of the Haitian leader to serve the purposes of Civil War and African American liberatory politics. Yet Blake can indeed be seen as a literary "model of black masculine perfectibility," the typical member of an African American community in the making: not an idealized individual but indeed an idealized community. This notion is echoed in the title of the novel, itself a crucial and profoundly new contribution of Delany's novel to the black avenger canon, which suggests that one can choose either Blake *or* the Huts of America as the hero of the novel, as they are meant to perpetually stand in one for the other. Delany's pragmatism during the Civil War does not contradict his effort in *Blake* so much as confirm his goal: to recover Haitian history but also to dress it in African American vestments.

Black Freemasonry was a crucial essential element in the governance of independent Haiti and in the fashioning of Haitian masculinity, of which Delany himself was a recipient. The independent state apparatus was inseparable from the army, many of whose officers had, even before the revolution, been members of Haiti's numerous Masonic lodges. Haitian thinkers in turn merged the "masculinist discourse of military republicanism and the paternalistic discourse of Freemasonry in their writing on nationhood," thoroughly limiting the presence of women in portrayals of the nation in the process.[122] Female characterizations of Haiti as "mother of African liberty" channeled the same Greco-Roman model that inspired textual and visual national representations such as France's Marianne, Great Britain's Britannia, or the United States' Lady Columbia: motherly figures all, expecting that their sons do their manly duty in defending them.[123] The infantilizing rhetoric from European powers depicting Haitians as political children "insidiously shaped Haitian self-representation, distorted the gender order, and demanded a virile model of citizenship" that ignored women's actual contributions to promote patriarchal imagery recognizable to all Western audiences.[124] Can the metaphors of the white West be separated from its values and prejudices? In *Blake* we see Delany attempt to adapt the Lucretia myth to African American circumstances.

The event that sets Blake on his journey to revolution is the sale of his wife, Maggie. The circumstances of this sale recycle elements of abolitionist rhetoric discussed in chapter 2: Colonel Franks, Maggie's owner, means to sell her because "Maggie was true to her womanhood, and loyal to her mistress" and rejected Franks's sexual advances.[125] Much as in Rushton's poems, rape serves as a symbol of slavery's assault on the West's supposed Christian, patriarchal values. The layer added by the revelation that Franks is Maggie's father makes clear what rhetorical purpose the element serves: slavery makes a mockery of the sacred institution of patriarchy, marriage. Delany hints at how Henry might react to rape in his question to Maggie's parents: "Has she disgraced herself?" Her virtue is paramount, and one shudders to think what Henry might do differently had she indeed "disgraced herself." Not to fear: Maggie is not just true to her womanhood; she is the embodiment of "true womanhood"—even after her deportation to Cuba, she managed to thwart sexual assault, at great physical cost to herself. Her lecherous master, unable to rape her, beat her mercilessly instead. Thanks to Cuban laws allowing slaves to buy their freedom, Blake redeems Maggie with money, once again underlining economics as slavery's only morals. But, significantly, Maggie provides the moral foundation on which the future nation will build.

As much is made clear in Blake's words to Maggie: "As God lives, I will avenge your wrongs; and not until they let us alone—cease to steal away our people from their native country and oppress us in their own—will I let them alone.... Our whole race among them must be brought to this determination, and then, and not til then, will they fear and respect us." Blake begins his sentence with the personal ("*I* will avenge *your* wrongs") only to slip into the collective (if the first "us" may be referring to Blake and Maggie, it soon turns to "our people"). The abuse inflicted on Maggie by her former masters originally pushed Blake to act; once he is reunited with his wife, his struggle continues, but it is no longer personal. Action has become a matter of "political arithmetic": "Whatever liberty is worth to the whites, it is worth to the blacks; therefore, whatever it cost the whites to obtain it, the black would be willing and ready to pay, if they desire it."[126] Delany's vision is staunchly masculinist; the emphasis in black abolitionist writing on portraying sexuality "primarily as a vector of white male domination and violation of black women" participates in a politics resting, among other things, on erasing those experiences that do not fit the mold of true womanhood and middle-class respectability.[127] In Maggie, however, Delany offers the first developed black answer to the Lucretia figure. Rome's Lucretia was a citizen threatened with defilement from below—by Tarquin's slave—and ultimately violated by the prince himself. She is defined as a body against (male) political tyranny and by contrast to the flesh of the "not-quite-humans" below her, and on the stage of this body the republic is staged.[128] Could a nation rise from mere flesh, and on what terms?

Maggie is like Lucretia in that she is assaulted, but she somehow manages to eschew rape and, more important, she stays alive. In her, Delany adapts patriarchal values to the singular circumstances of enslavement: that Maggie would have managed to resist sexual assault so long in these circumstances is virtually impossible. But Maggie is a character in the foundational myth of a black American nation. In Delany's eminently patriarchal view, the imagined, future black nation springs out of Maggie's experience of abjection and *survival*. Out of the "hieroglyphics of the flesh," which Hortense Spillers discerns in the wounds visible on the flesh of the enslaved, this future nation writes the body out of which black citizenship might rise. In one problematic movement, *Blake* recognizes "the heritage of the *mother*" Spillers considers so specific to African American culture and simultaneously harnesses it to a project of black nation building rooted in patriarchal values.[129]

Blake, as we know it, ends before the announced general uprising. Be that as it may, the novel builds a sense of unstoppable communal black agency. The final scene in "American Tyranny—Oppression of the Negroes," the last recovered chapter of the novel, deserves close attention: a white American savagely beats Ambrosina, the daughter of Montego, one of the conspirators. A conversation ensues between the men and women present in the Montego house. To the dismay of Ambrosina's mother and her friend Madame Barbosa, who urge caution, Ambrosina states, "I wish I was a man, I'd lay the city in ashes this night" and further challenges the resolve of the men around her: "If our men do not decide on something in our favor, they will soon be called to look upon us in a state of concubinage; for such treatment as this will force every weak-minded woman to place herself under the care of those who are able to protect them from personal abuse." This sally pointedly evokes the words of Lucretia killing herself for fear that less virtuous women might think she had consented to Tarquin's assault. Yet Ambrosina's intermediary status grants her words profoundly different valance. Ambrosina is no slave; as a free woman of color in Cuba, she thought herself above this kind of treatment, but Americans have brought absolute racial difference along with them: no black woman is safe from an order that sees them as mere flesh. Demoted to fleshly status in this brutal assault, Ambrosina understands and explains how rational a choice concubinage is for women put in this position. She restates Lucretia's challenge to Roman men. Concubinage also is an assault on patriarchal order; will they stand by and do nothing? In a final statement she declares that she will destroy herself first rather than jeopardize her honor, an argument that finishes to convince her mother and the men around her. The page closes with Gondolier rushing out to "spread among the blacks an authentic statement of the outrage."[130]

Blake offers a political vision that is also the revision of a popular scenario. Here the "African race" is a black Pan-American project: it designates Cuba, the heart of the Americas, as the future homeland of the coming nation. The African Americans described in *Blake* are connected to the Haitians, but they will form a distinct nation, a "better" one, no doubt wiser for learning from Haiti's mistakes, building on a carefully constructed literary image of itself. Of the many ways in which Western powers worked to silence the Haitian Revolution, the black avenger trope is perhaps the most widely circulated and the most subtly undermining. Though always located at the heart of collective movements, black avenger narratives are tales of individual greatness, and as such work against the wide movements they, often sympathetically, portray. Delany's *Blake* must be read within and against that literary tradition, as a commentary on the ways in which it contributed to impose a deforming lens over historical occurrences of black revolution. *Blake* offers an illuminated black avenger narrative, aware of its narrative lineage and proactive in its attempt to appropriate the trope. Delany explodes the trope, summoning its many elements to revise them all in turn. At a time of profound hopelessness for U.S. blacks, Delany's *Blake* and its coalition of black avengers built a new narrative of black revolt, one that revived the sense of black political agency once imparted by the Haitian Revolution by writing it over, and writing over it.

Delany imagines a black nation drawing from all cultural sources, one able to construct a foundational myth blending "all the usages of civilized life" with the experience of all of civilized life's horrors.[131] The future black nation will be the jewel of human civilization, Delany asserts boldly. It will be unapologetically black, though this notion, drawing as it claimed to do on a transnational diaspora, was irremediably rooted in a vision centered on U.S. American understandings of blackness.

CHAPTER 5

AMERICAN HERO

The Black Avenger in the Age of U.S. Empire

If the Reconstruction period carried promise for the integration of African Americans into the body politic, with African Americans being elected into political office throughout the Reconstructed South, these developments did not come easy: as soon as the last shots of the Civil War had been fired, white supremacists constituted terrorist groups—the Ku Klux Klan, Knights of the White Camelia, the Red Shirts, to name but a few—whose goal was to oppose so-called "Negro domination." The "military arm of the Democratic Party" led military-style attacks against African American people in their homes and on their way to the polls and against elected officials of local and federal government and, in some cases, against police forces.[1] Under the Grant administration, between 1869 and 1877, the United States saw meaningful advances for the African American community, with the securing of the Fifteenth Amendment, the Ku Klux Klan Act, and the Civil Rights Act of 1875. These advances were brutally rescinded with the election of Ulysses Grant's successor, Rutherford B. Hayes, who in return for electoral victory agreed to pull federal troops stationed in the southern states. In the following two decades, Jim Crow took hold of the former Confederate states, effectively leaving the field open for white supremacists, who rolled back civil rights gains throughout the South over the next two decades. As *Dred Scott* had defined the state of racial relations in the antebellum period, another Supreme Court decision would embody Jim Crow: *Plessy v. Ferguson* (1896) infamously decided that "equal, but separate, accommodations for the white and colored races . . . are not in conflict with the provisions either of the Thirteenth Amendment or the Fourteenth Amendment of the Constitution of the United States."[2] Along with terror at the polls, African Americans, with the normalization of lynching, increasingly had to face terror on the streets and in their homes.

The brutal reassertion of white supremacy in the South occasioned distinct reactions among African Americans: the number of exiles to Liberia was at its highest during the two decades following the end of the Civil War. Some African Americans moved out West, notably in the Exoduster migration of 1879, in which thousands of southern blacks went to Kansas seeking for a chance to create the modicum of autonomy white supremacists were stripping from them in the postbellum Union.[3] Yet another reaction was the choice of many African American men to join the U.S. Army. So-called Buffalo Soldiers—members of four all-black cavalry regiments formed in 1866—served on the front lines of the United States' imperial wars, notably in the expansion into Native American lands in the West, where some hoped that "their willingness to dispossess and exterminate American Indians would persuade Whites to grant African Americans the privilege of citizenship."[4] Already in these circumstances the African American men involved had to face the contradictions of their positions and duties: on the volatile border region with Mexico, "they found themselves both required to fight and to defend the Mexican other along the Texas border . . . identifying with and disavowing sympathies with these other ethnic groups."[5] The popular revolt against Spanish rule in Cuba started in 1895 found strong support among African Americans who saw it as "a black man's war" and advocated for American intervention in support of the freedom fighters. African American leaders such as Booker T. Washington clamored for African Americans to be included, presenting the War of 1898 as an opportunity to demonstrate black men's patriotism and worth to American whites.[6] Other religious leaders saw U.S. military encroachment in Cuba, Puerto Rico, and the Philippines as a civilizing effort akin to their own missions around the West Indies and beyond.[7]

The irony of doing the white republic's dirty work abroad at a time when African Americans were disenfranchised and lynching was the domestic rule was not lost on all: in 1906, reflecting on Jim Crow law in Georgia, African Methodist Episcopal Church bishop Henry McNeal Turner—who had organized a black regiment during the Civil War and served as the U.S. Army's first black chaplain—declared "I used to love what I thought was the grand old flag . . . but to the Negro in the country, the American flag is a dirty and contemptible rag." Summoned to explain himself, Turner added, "I did say that there was not a star in the flag that the Negro could claim, or that recognized his civil liberty and unconditional manhood more than if it was a dirty rag. I was talking to colored men, not white men."[8] By contrast to this assessment and in the face of dire circumstances, a variety of African American voices asserted the possibility and even the development of black manhood in the segregationist United States, aligning with the "quest for manhood" promoted in earnest since the 1890s throughout American culture, perhaps most visibly by former president Theodore Roosevelt.[9] Some, like lawyer, political operative, and writer Robert Lewis Waring, did this in novel form: in *As We See It* (1910), he penned the graphic, sensationalist account of a black man's revenge on the white rapists of his mother and sister. Waring's clarion call to black manhood did not simply echo the American obsession with masculinity; it also held a mirror to the southern rape narrative bandied by white supremacists in courts, newspapers, and literature to defend lynching and white terror, according to which black men were naturally driven to raping white women.[10] What if the "black brute" of the southern rape narrative were white? We would get a story as old as the Black Atlantic.

Waring's is chronologically the last of three novels published by African American authors at the turn of the century offering variations on the black avenger theme. In profoundly different ways, Sutton E. Griggs's *Imperium in Imperio: A Study of the Negro Race Problem* (1899), Charles Chesnutt's *The Marrow of Tradition* (1901), and Waring's *As We See It* illustrate how important the motif was in American culture at large, at a time Kenneth Warren provocatively designates as the birth of African American literature. If, before the Civil War, there were for the most part "Negroes who were writers . . . [then] the necessity of confronting the constraints of the segregation era" in turn dictated the formation of a literature dedicated to the race.[11] African Americans had once legally been noncitizens; they were now in the untenable position of being legal citizens and factually much less. According to Warren, the impetus that created African American literature is the same that pushed African American elites to work for black uplift within white supremacist institutions and to define themselves by, and against, American standards shaped in the crucible of the cult of masculinity, racial pseudo-science, social Darwinism, and imperialism. In these texts authors expressed this dynamic in a language of agency increasingly stripped of political valence—until all that remained was a grammar of power more than compatible with racist oppression.

NO COUNTRY FOR BLACK MEN

In 1867 Hinton Rowan Helper published *Nojoque: A Question for a Continent* (1867). This was his third book and the first since *The Impending Crisis of the South: How to Meet It* (1857), which had made the North Carolinian famous around the country; his book was called "one of the best-selling abolitionist works of nonfiction, rivaled only by the novel *Uncle Tom's Cabin* in terms of its national impact."[12] In *The Impending Crisis* he defended the abolition of slavery, not out of "special friendliness or sympathy for the blacks" but with the elevation of poor white southerners in mind. Helper designated the southern slaveholding oligarchy as the bane of the South for perpetuating the immoral practice of slavery but also for using it to fool poor whites into acting against their better economic and political interests. Helper called for the abolition of slavery by July 4, 1876, with compensation to the formerly enslaved; the entire black population of the United States would then be shipped to Liberia.[13]

A decade later Helper still had the welfare of white men in mind, but in the aftermath of the Civil War, his vision had somewhat changed. In the opening lines of his preface to *Nojoque*, Helper admitted, "Were I to state here, categorically and frankly, that the primary object of this work is to write the negro out of America, and that the secondary object is to write him . . . out of existence, God's simple truth would be told." Helper, as always, had a plan: to accelerate what he saw as the path of all nonwhite people toward natural extinction, there should be "an absolute and eternal separation of the races." The end goal was to send all black people "and all other effete and dingy-hued races" to any land south of the Mexican border: this would be one in a long line of forced migrations and massacres in human history, among which he listed the expulsion of the Tarquins from Rome and Dessalines's massacre of the whites in 1804. Helper reprised the centennial of the Declaration of Independence as a deadline to purge the republic of all people of color but admitted that this might happen in stages or that the transportation to Africa of millions might not be feasible, so he pondered alternatives. All nonwhites currently residing in the United States might "be colonized in a State or Territory by themselves, in Texas or Arizona for instance, and there, under suitable regulations, required to remain strictly within the limits assigned them."[14] Ever magnanimous, Helper would allow for the establishment of a temporary black colony within the United States. Eventually, they would go extinct, and the white race would take its rightful dominion over the entire Earth.

Helper's book has long embarrassed historians, but the theories developed in *Nojoque* were in some obvious ways in direct continuation of his seemingly more palatable antebellum effort: in both books Helper made clear he saw no place for people of African descent in the United States, but in this regard he was not alone. President Abraham Lincoln, long a proponent of separation and black resettlement, was on the eve of Emancipation still considering ways of transporting the entire U.S. population of color into Texas, and, more generally speaking, "the lure of a geographical partitioning of the races comfortably survived both emancipation and the Union victory at Appomatox."[15] If by the 1890s projects of black resettlement more routinely considered Liberia as a destination, the idea of a mass migration of African Americans into Texas was explored in earnest by Texas-born minister, pamphleteer, novelist, and activist Sutton Griggs in his first novel. *Imperium in Imperio* is routinely described as a black nationalist novel, based on its general plot. The title of the novel, itself evocative of Delany's definition of the African American community as a nation within a nation, is in the economy of the novel both a diagnosis and the source of elaborate plans on the part of the novel's protagonists. The novel proposes to imagine what black autonomy might mean in the post–*Plessy v. Ferguson* era, offering variations on traditional elements of the black avenger trope that illuminate its place in American culture at large.

IMPERIUM IN IMPERIO

Imperium in Imperio's opening address "To the Public," signed in Griggs's name, designates the text as written and given to him by a Berl Trout, former secretary of state of the imperium. Griggs vouches for the veracity of Trout's claims, going as far as asserting his ability to present "indisputable proofs" to whoever might call Trout a liar.[16] Griggs's address is reminiscent of the authorizing apparatus typical of antebellum slave narratives; in this case, it simultaneously serves a politics of respectability: Griggs symbolically put his reputation in the balance as a young deacon at the First Baptist Church of Berkley, Virginia.[17] Trout mysteriously presents himself in his "Dying Declaration" as both a traitor to his race and a patriot—to humankind, to whom he delivers this "revelation." His is the tale of two friends: the poor, dark-skinned Belton Piedmont and the wealthy, light-skinned Bernard Belgrave, and it follows their separate comings-of-age. They reunite in the Imperium, an African American conspiracy dedicated to securing "protection for their lives and the full enjoyment of all rights and privileges due American citizens." The Imperium is a parallel black United States: it has a government, an elected Congress, a standing army, and competing plans for the future of black people in and outside of the United States. In the novel's climax Belton and Bernard clash in a debate to decide the Imperium's course of action: Belton's moderate plan focuses on demonstrating the worth of African Americans to the entire nation; Bernard means to forcibly take over Texas and secede from the Union. Bernard imposes his vision, to Belton's dismay—he considers it treason against the United States. Belton resigns from the Imperium, a decision punishable by death. He accepts his fate and is executed, "the last of that peculiar type of Negro heroes that could so fondly kiss the smiting hand."[18] Berl Trout, the novel's intradiegetic author, fears that Bernard's intransigence will lead to catastrophe.

Griggs's novel functions more as a warning than a program: though it evokes *Blake* in many aspects, it is also very much written in counterpoint to it. In presenting the plights of Bernard, who chooses race over country; Belton, who chooses country over race; and Berl Trout, who chooses humanity and spares white America, Griggs reflects on themes approached by David Scott in his study of Haitian revolutionary historiography, *Conscripts of Modernity*. Griggs's characters do not make choices so much as they are "conscripted" into narratives. This might seem self-evident for a work of fiction, but the narratives in question had an undeniable hold on the public discourse of his time. In *Imperium in Imperio* Griggs strives to give voice to the many different opinions animating the African American community regarding their future in the United States. Both Belton and Bernard at times defend positions Griggs himself may have agreed with, and if we judge him by his career as a minister, political activist, and Democratic operative, we may be right to say that his personal opinions "tend to echo Belton more than Bernard."[19] Yet Griggs also critiques black conservatism; as Stephen Knadler shows, *Imperium in Imperio* also debunks in Belton the figure of "Citizen Tom"—the naturally loyal and subservient African American man turned ideal U.S. soldier—a representation of black sentimental patriotism notably promoted by the likes of Booker T. Washington.[20] While this critique develops mostly around the character of Belton, I am especially interested in Griggs's critical engagement with the black avenger tradition, which he rightly portrays as equally crucial to issues of black agency and nationhood in his time.

The Imperium was founded "in the early days of the American Republic" by an unnamed black scientist reminiscent of Benjamin Banneker, who used his wealth to build a secret society whose "first object was to endeavor to secure for the free negroes all the rights and privileges of men, according to the teachings of Thomas Jefferson. Its other object was to secure the freedom of the enslaved negroes the world over." After the Civil War the Imperium trained teachers to teach newly freed African Americans the true meaning of freedom. African Americans launched a number of secret societies after the Civil War. Faced with unchallenged white supremacist terror after the Reconstruction, the imperium federated them all. Each society added a shared final degree of initiation: "The last degree was nothing more nor less than a compact government exercising all the functions of a nation."[21]

The Imperium is quite literally the "freemasonry of the race" developed in *Blake* and invoked a decade later by James Weldon Johnson: simultaneously the safe space in which black men reveal the side of themselves they hide from white people, and the achievement of their education in the ways of the West into political agency and autonomy. Whereas *Blake*'s was a transnational black Freemasonry aiming at the constitution of a federating black nation in the Americas, the imperium first strives for the constitution of a black nation within the United States—or excised from it, if need be.

The novel's invocation of Jefferson says much about the difference between the visions developed in Griggs's novel and that expressed by Benjamin Banneker, or by David Walker some seventy years earlier: where the latter was taking Jefferson to task over his contradictions, the former takes them in stride, defending the "doctrine of equality as taught by Thomas Jefferson."[22] African Americans must prove themselves worthy of white democratic values rather than point to the system's inherent contradictions. The Imperium means to realize the promise of the American Revolution for African Americans, and then for blacks everywhere, replacing Haiti as the epitome of black power and becoming the global black power the island nation failed to truly become. The Imperium is a peculiar embodiment of the Jeffersonian democratic ideal. Here the nation is completely inseparable from its state apparatus: the intellectual, commercial, and political elite of the race also conveniently provides its political representatives. They represent the people, but it seems clear that only secret society members can elect and be elected, and to become a member one has to give proof of his worth to the community. The Imperium is a clear emanation of the theory W. E. B. Du Bois described a few years later in "The Talented Tenth": in his paean to the "exceptional men" whom he designated as future saviors of the race, Du Bois particularly extolled the virtues of teachers, "group-leaders of the Negro people," without whom the country at large might "suffer the evil consequences of a headless misguided rabble."[23] Belton the teacher embodies precisely this combination of measure and pedagogy. No wonder that the showdown between the moderate Belton and the radical Bernard comes down to an oratory duel.

Wealthy, Ivy League–educated Bernard proves worthy of the secret only when he successfully defends Belton's life in the Supreme Court. Before then he and his mother's "relation to the Anglo-Saxon race had not been clearly understood," preventing his initiation into the secret. This is one of the ways in which Griggs broaches the issue of skin color and lineage and how they impact black nationalism. If Bernard's comparatively easy and comfortable upbringing and his close relations to white supremacy—however benevolent—made the Imperium doubt his blackness, he eventually proves to be the most radical of the Imperium's representatives, advocating for a violent secession from the United States. When the Imperium gathers to decide on a course of action, Bernard—now president of the Imperium—delivers an address that further clarifies this relation. In his opening lines he pits the call to war against Spain against the murder of a black postmaster (member of the Imperium) and his family by a white mob. The episode was inspired by the real assassination of Postmaster Frazier Baker and his baby girl in Lake City, South Carolina, in 1898, which occurred a week after USS Maine sunk in Havana harbor, precipitating the chain of events that would lead to U.S. intervention in Cuba. Bernard enjoins the imperium to consider "what shall be our attitude, present and future, to this Anglo-Saxon race" and prefaces proceedings with a chilling survey of past and present wrongs suffered by African Americans. Following Bernard, Imperium members present different proposals: an aged representative advocates integration and is copiously jeered; a younger one defends emigration to Africa, an idea well received though judged impracticable; a third one's description of the horrors suffered by African Americans brings the crowd to a frenzy. With the assembly ready to vote for war, Belton stands to deliver "one of the most remarkable feats of oratory known to history."[24]

He wants to reveal the existence of the Imperium to the broader U.S. public and allow members of the secret order to prove themselves to white Americans. Were this effort to fail to impress, the Imperium could organize a lawful takeover of the state of Texas: mass emigration of African Americans to one of the last southern states to permit blacks to vote would guarantee demographic, and therefore electoral, superiority. African Americans would soon control the state and fulfill their "destiny as a separate and distinct race in the United States of America." Belton proposes to secure a territory for African Americans—effectively constituting the community into a black settler colony within the United States—by lawful means and resort to violence only in self-defense if provoked, thus demonstrating to "the Anglo-Saxon that we have arrived at the stage of development as a people, where we prefer to die in honor rather than live in disgrace."[25] As noted by John Cullen Gruesser, Griggs's fictional plan appears outlandish in our day and age, but it echoes "the many actual and proposed movements of blacks to and from Texas" still routinely discussed at the turn of the century.[26] Belton's plan takes the racial logic brought into jurisprudence by *Plessy v. Ferguson* at its word and transposes it to the nation's geopolitics: "Equal and separate accommodations" should apply to territorial and political matters. It is a measure of what separates Belton and Bernard that the latter presents his own scheme not in debate but only to the highest-ranking members of the Congress, whom he tricks into supporting it. His plan involves secretly buying land around Texas's borders to fortify it, infiltrating the U.S. Navy, and helping the U.S. black population move into and take over Texas and Louisiana. The latter would be given to enemies of the United States, while Texas in the hands of the Imperium would secede from the Union, giving "the Negro an empire of his own."[27] Belton refuses to agree to what he sees as treason and resigns his position in the Imperium, a decision he pays for with his life. As patriotic as Belton sees himself, both his and Bernard's plans stem from the same understanding that blacks constitute a distinct internal colony in the white supremacist United States perfectly compatible with its values and references.

Indeed, Bernard's plan, though it puts little stock in white Americans' honesty and virtue, still relies—not unlike Belton's—on understandings of manliness, worth, and might borrowed from the white supremacist United States. Its focus on the U.S. Navy evokes the paramount role it had recently taken in U.S. military strategy, notably in the buildup to the annexation of Hawaii and in the Spanish-American War.[28] In turn, this plot point reprises conversations in the African American community regarding the role it should play in the United States' colonial endeavors in the late 1890s. Participating in the War of 1898 was a point of pride for many who saw it as evidence and demonstration of black masculinity and its worthiness to the U.S. national project, echoing Martin R. Delany's engagement with the politics of military masculinity during the Civil War. Bernard's initial contrast in his speech between, on the one hand, the call to go fight in Cuba and "carry the cup of liberty to a people perishing for its healing draught" and on the other hand the ignominy of lynch law at home reduces options to two choices presented as exclusive. Throughout his writings Griggs makes such provocative use of binaries, which he just as often debunks in the same movement. Here, he proposes both the peculiar combination of subservience and manliness of Citizen Tom as magnified in Belton and fiery and unforgiving revenge as personified by Bernard. Neither, he tells us, will do.

This binary structure also seemingly recycles narrative patterns developed around the Haitian Revolution, discussed in previous chapters. There is much about Belton and Bernard that evoke racialized narrative patterns inherited from the Haitian Revolution. The feud opposing Belton to Bernard treads narrative paths blazed by representations of the struggle between the dark-skinned, formerly enslaved Louverture and the light-skinned, freeborn son of a wealthy white planter, André Rigaud, and a spate of subsequent retellings. It bears noting that Haiti is never as much as mentioned in any of Griggs's publications, which I see as a measure of the growing irrelevance of the Haitian example to African Americans. Four decades after *Blake*, Griggs no longer has to write over Haiti: narrative patterns inherited from representations of the revolution have seamlessly merged into U.S. racial grammar. Griggs makes use of these patterns and simultaneously questions them.

REVENGE NATION

Griggs was aware of the state of racial science in his day and reflected on its most recent developments; that many of these theories were rooted in systemic racism contributes greatly to some of *Imperium in Imperio*'s seeming contradictions and arguably to the difficulty that critics have faced in attempting to assess the political tenor of its message.[29] Focusing on the novel's treatment of elements of the black avenger narrative reveals how, at the turn of the century, American variations of the black avenger trope had become inseparable from the racist politics that had long undergirded it.

After hearing the war speech uttered before Belton's, Bernard "swore a terrible oath to avenge the wrongs of his people," but he was set on this course earlier. Bernard had a comparatively easy life: he grew up in ease alone with his light-skinned mother. His white father, a senator, did not live with them for fear of ruining his reputation but supported them, paid Bernard's tuition at Harvard, and helped him settle in Virginia to become a lawyer, "scale the high wall of prejudice," and eventually get elected in Congress. Bernard was the most famous man of color in the country when tragedy hit hard: in response to his marriage proposal, his partner, Viola, committed suicide. She found herself unable to marry a mixed-race man, as her readings convinced her "that the intermingling of the races in sexual relationship was sapping the vitality of the Negro race and, in fact, was slowly but surely exterminating the race," as she declares in her death note to Bernard. The text that inspires Viola to commit suicide, *White Supremacy and Negro Subordination* (1867), is John H. Van Evrie's *Negroes and Negro "Slavery": The First an Inferior Race, the Latter Its Normal Condition* (1861), retitled and refurbished with a new preface commenting on postbellum circumstances. Like Long and Médéric Louis Elie Moreau de Saint-Méry before him, Van Evrie "demonstrates" that mulattoes become infertile in the fourth generation, which goes to show that interracial sexual relations are unnatural. Viola, convinced by the theory, further asks of Bernard that he "dedicate [his] soul to the work of separating the white and colored races." Stepping out of Viola's room, he declares, "The races, whose union has been fraught with every curse known to earth and hell, must separate. Viola demands it and I obey."[30] The would-be founder of a nation swears his oath over the dead body of his virginal bride.

At the turn of the twentieth century, the "myth of mulatto demise" remained widely considered a scientific truth.[31] It is unclear to what extent Griggs himself subscribed to the notion that races should not mix, but judging by the hints of sarcasm that pepper his later work, *Wisdom's Call* (1911), he likely took it with a grain of salt. In a section on "The Preservation of the Races," he evokes the theory of Thomas Huxley, according to which humans were originally white, blackness being a natural adaptation to new surroundings. Griggs follows up with this question: "Can, and will this same nature which took a white race, and through the process of the years, converted it into one wholly black, now take this black race and change it back to white?" Such a movement would not happen naturally, but white supremacy in the South seems the kind of situation when nature "may feel inclined to step in and recast the race to meet the conditions encountered in a color-hating land." Griggs further asks if blacks are not allowed to thrive, can they be faulted for seeking light-skinned companions to literally blend into the white race? Ominously and mischievously, he summons the visions of "an army of persons whose ranks are being recruited every day ready for the word of command to disappear into the white race carrying their Negro blood with them."[32] Griggs presents this idea as a logical conclusion drawn from racial science, announcing two decades in advance George Schuyler's satirical novel of mass race transition *Black No More* (1931).

In *Imperium* Griggs shows what impact racial science and the canard of racial purity might have among African Americans: Viola sacrifices her life and love for the preservation of the black race, ironically pushing a mixed-race man to become the foremost proponent of the theory and seemingly confirming in the process other elements of Van Evrie's theory that inform the novel's plot. Indeed, Van Evrie presents freedom as a natural characteristic of the white race; such a thing as "negro insurrection . . . is simply nonsensical," as blacks could not possibly seek something outside of their nature unprompted. Taking the unavoidable example of the Haitian Revolution, Van Evrie asserts that mulattoes in fact caused the uprising by tricking "terror-stricken blacks" into acts contrary to their submissive nature. After Viola's death and his oath, Bernard, as the Imperium's president, proves conniving and tyrannical, notably when he bullies the Imperium into accepting his plan. In the final pages of the novel he is the most dangerous, destructive force facing the world, "a man to be feared," and bent on wreaking revenge on whites—in short, a mulatto after Van Evrie's description.[33]

Or is he? Bernard's acts in the last sections of the novel are hardly in keeping with his former self: they are clearly shown to be the result of grief brought about by Viola's death—and, by extension, by racist pseudoscience.

The cliché of the evil mulatto bandied by the likes of Van Evrie is a self-fulfilling prophecy of sorts here, the outcome of white supremacist terror rather than its justification: a logical conclusion rather than a natural phenomenon. This element of the plot in turn points to the crucial role played by women in narratives of racial order.

LIKE A WOMAN

In his effort to undermine black agency, Van Evrie addresses the topic of rape during the Haitian Revolution: "There are no authenticated instances of the violation of white females," he declares, as such an assault would go against the nature of the "typical, pure-blooded negro," who "driven on by his fears and dread of the master race, would only seek its extermination, never the indulgence to *him* of such unnatural propensities." Only "hybrids and mongrels" could commit such a heinous act. Van Evrie makes clear the connection—narrative and symbolic—he finds between political agency and rape, and although he does not extend his logic to "pure-blooded" blacks, he announces the "equation of political rights and black manhood" that would characterize white supremacist discourse in the Reconstruction South.[34] As he wrote during the Civil War and in its immediate aftermath, his goal was mainly to challenge the very notion of black political agency broadly understood. He does so by indirectly evoking the moment preceding Tarquin's rape of Lucretia, when the prince threatened to spread the rumor of a dalliance with a slave. Van Evrie's dismissal of the occurrence of rape in the Haitian Revolution asserts just as surely as Lucretia's story that slaves—or for Van Evrie, blacks as natural slaves—are less than human, tools in the hands of their masters. The purpose and effect of pseudoscientific naturalization of slaves' alleged passivity is clear: it is meant to deny the Haitian Revolution as politics. It makes the uprising an expression of natural urges controlled in the shadows by the wicked minds of mulattoes. In accepting Van Evrie's theories, Viola becomes a tool for their propagation: in suicide, she becomes the black Lucretia necessary for an essentialist black, patriarchal nation serving as an extension of white supremacy. A paragon of virtue, she erases the stain of whiteness even before it can pollute her. That Bernard is the sole oath taker next to her body shows clearly the dead end to which Griggs dooms this endeavor. Griggs questions not only the influence of scientific racism among the African American intelligentsia but also, more specifically, how it permeates seemingly radical scenarios of black revenge.

The theme of revenge is also important in Belton's characterization, where again Griggs goes against immediate expectations: the racial and social hostility Belton meets repeatedly in the novel pushes him close to resorting to revenge early on, but he learns from an educator—the head of the university where he studies—that revenge is an "unholy passion," following which Belton vows to hold as a "cardinal principle of his life . . . to allow God to avenge all his wrongs."[35] Still, Belton defends a position significantly different from that of a Booker T. Washington: irreproachable African Americans are warranted in defending themselves from harm. Belton is no avenger, and if he is a revolutionary it is expressly in the American tradition of Jefferson and Patrick Henry, both of whom he references. Yet much like Bernard's love story tests his involvement in high-sphere respectability politics and upends his life, extraordinary circumstances test Belton's commitment to nonviolence: here also, they put women at the heart of the race issue.

In his tribulations throughout the novel, Belton strives to live without compromising his integrity. He is respectful but outspoken, which at one point leads him to be barred from teaching and to lose his job at the post office in Richmond, Virginia. Looking for a job to contribute to his household as a newlywed, Belton finds that opportunities for educated African American men are few. Other men in the same predicament "grew to hate the flag that would float in an undisturbed manner over such a condition of affairs. . . . They began to think of rebelling against it and would wish for some foreign power to come in and bury it in the dirt." Worried by the growing antinational sentiment among his peers, Belton decides to "find out just what view the white people were taking of the Negro and of the existing conditions." Possibly to hide his identity, Belton decides to perform his investigation as a woman: he goes to New York and comes back in drag, unbeknownst to all but his wife, and secures a position as a nurse for an elderly white man. Belton discovers that white people know nothing about African American life or public opinion, have no interest in finding out more, and have no sense of the intensity of civil rights activism in the community. But Belton finds out more than he was looking for: young white men hold a "poor opinion of the virtue of colored women." They sexually harass him, attempting to kiss him, but also offering trips, carriage rides, and money. Belton gains a reputation as a prude for rejecting their advances and extolling the virtue of black women. A group of white men decide to "satisfy themselves at all hazards," and they kidnap and overpower him. "After that eventful night Belton did no more nursing": though they do not recognize him, the assailants figure out that he is a man. Belton manages to escape town and comes back as his masculine self, amid general "excitement over the male nurse."[36]

Finnie D. Coleman calls Piedmont's cross-dressing episode "one of the most overlooked passages in Black literature," even as he himself says little about it: he puzzlingly sees the scene as an effort to counter the "emasculating effects of White supremacy" in its reversal of the "scopophilic gaze of contemporary fiction."[37] White supremacist groups used sexual violence as a means of terrorizing African Americans and whites in their intimate or political proximity, a practice as horrifyingly common as it was seldom discussed.[38] But Griggs's story focuses on an arguably even less discussed type of sexual terror, as indeed his elision of the details of Belton's "eventful night" suggests strongly that Belton was raped by the group of white men. Griggs's narrative silence exposes "the denials necessary for the African American reader to redirect the fear and humiliation inherent in a culture of rape and lynching into Belton's nostalgic loyalty."[39] Further yet, I would argue that the scene allows for an in-depth look into the politics of masculinity attached to black avenger stories and nationalist myths. At one level Griggs's narrative scheme appears to be designed to symbolically bypass possible reservations concerning the reliability of female witnesses' testimonies about their abuse at the hands of white men. The witness will be a man, unimpeded by womanly emotions. Yet Belton is not made privy to the experience of women so much as he discovers a woman-like experience of abjection. Discussing the reaction of young white men to Belton's repeated rejections, Griggs writes, "He seemed so hard to reach, that they began to doubt his sex."[40] The notion that "black women either welcomed [white men] or had no moral purity to defend" was widespread in the postbellum era, and working in white households carried well-known "sexual risks."[41] Touching on issues of sexuality and oppression also opens up a door to the place of queer identities in an era and place defined by avowed subscription to conservative, Victorian ideals of true womanhood on the one hand and the rise of exclusive, binary notions of manhood on the other.

Griggs rends a tear in the backdrop of masculinity that his readers to this day tend to take for granted. The "quest for manhood" of the 1890s was essentially a white, middle-class endeavor undertaken in reaction to increased female independence and a sense of anxiety regarding white Anglo-Saxon men's own gender status in the face of immigrant and working-class masculinity. At the time when Griggs published his novel, "hetero-homosexual binarism" did not hold absolute sway over U.S. society, and mattered more in some sections of the population than others: "The most visible gay world of the early twentieth century . . . was a working-class world, centered in African-American and Irish and Italian immigrant neighborhoods and along the city's busy waterfront, and drawing on the social forms of working-class culture." In this world the essential masculine dichotomy was not between the heterosexual and the homosexual but instead between the "fairy" —

"defined as much by his 'womanlike' character of 'effeminacy' as his solicitation of male partners"—and the "normal man," who, though he might respond to such solicitation, "was not considered abnormal . . . as long as he
abided by masculine gender conventions." George Chauncey helps clarify
the unspoken quid pro quo in this scene, which rests on what appears to
be a complete lack of overlap between Belton's beliefs and intentions and
those of the young white men around him.[42] Belton believes that working as
a maid will allow him to find out the true thoughts of whites about blacks, as
they open up and confide in their domestic servants. Beholden as he is to respectability politics borrowed wholesale from the white middle class, he also
appears to assume that he only has to declare his virtue to keep men at bay.

True thoughts are revealed, indeed, if not to Belton, at least to readers:
as a black man, he can have no access whatsoever to the white middle-class
order, not even as regards masculinity and gender—vexed topics, to be sure,
but those one might expect to signify cross-racially. Belton's naive approach
is shot through with casual misogyny—he appears convinced that women
are assaulted only because they do not state their refusal in clear enough
terms. The description of Belton in drag as a "healthy, handsome, robust colored girl, with features rather large for a woman but attractive just the same"
also appears to justify the men's interest in him.[43] Yet for all their harassing
him, the men decide to assault him only after they begin questioning "his
sex." Belton's gender matters little here: the white men see his rejections as
enticements, and his disguise—which they apparently recognize as such—
as solicitation. They attack him with no qualms, and the next day spread the
news about the cross-dressing nurse all around town. Belton's civilized effort
at understanding hostile individuals, approaching the race issue by means of
sympathy, ends in violation, with Belton's physical integrity jeopardized. In
the elided night of the assault, Belton's identity is negated and his body "ungendered," reduced to flesh. Hortense Spillers's comment that "the ungendered female . . . might be invaded/raided by another *woman* or man" applies here to the ungendered male, a diagnosis confirmed in a later episode,
when a doctor organizes Belton's lynching for the sole purpose of dissecting
this "fine specimen of physical manhood."[44] Southern whites are defined by
their boundless voracity for black flesh, in pursuit of which they renege on
their alleged moral values. What transpires in the litany of horrors faced by
Belton is that no amount of compromise can in fact provide shelter for African Americans under the U.S. flag.

Yet Belton refuses this conclusion. He remains attached to the white supremacist, middle-class, masculinist values that confirm the silencing of his

previous experience and reassert a vision of masculinity at odds with the reality around him. After he comes back to Richmond as a man, he is still unable to find work, a situation made worse by the fact that his wife, Antoinette, is pregnant and not working either. She delivers more than just a baby: when Belton comes to see the newborn, the child seems to be white. Horrified, Belton runs away, convinced that his failure to provide for her pushed her to seek concubinage with a white man. He symbolically kills his wife, laying her "to rest in a grave in the very center of his heart."[45] Near the end of the novel we find out that Belton was wrong: his son's skin darkened with time, as babies' skins are wont to do. The entire community shunned Antoinette until the "magic of skin color" proved her innocence; the entire time she remained silent, the image of dignity and a portrait of the "illegitimacy" of motherhood carried over from slavery into post-Emancipation African American life.[46] For Belton as for Bernard, commitment to the race comes at the cost of meaningful relationships ruined by race-centric thinking. The Imperium as expressed through the two protagonists is an impasse, where politics hinges on the death—real and symbolic—of black women and leads nowhere.

As subversive as the Imperium may seem, it only blackens the patterns of white America. Ultimately, neither Belton nor Bernard can escape those influences. Belton Piedmont survives assault, violation, and even apparent death, but these experiences leave him "imprint[ed] with the signs of the white body and mastery," which, according to David Kramer, explains his "final decision to remain loyal to white America."[47] Belton represents the "spirit of conservatism in the Negro race," which Griggs saw as a necessary and natural counterweight to progressive movements. For Griggs, imbalance threatens the fabric of society and so does unmatched white supremacist terror, in terms expressed by Berl Trout in the novel's closing lines: in making black conservatism untenable, white supremacy paves the way for forms of black radicalism unattached to the United States. The novel ends with Trout's pathetic plea for "all mankind" to help African Americans "secure those rights for which they organized the Imperium." This plea is followed by a warning that testifies to Trout's ambivalence about his own actions: he did not trust Bernard, but he still sees the Imperium as stemming from "love of liberty," and he predicts it will be replaced by a more powerful organization.[48] The final line of the novel—"When will all races and classes of men learn that men made in the image of God will not be the slaves of another image?"—finishes to demonstrate that Trout's betrayal of the imperium solves nothing. It returns the reader to the status quo, the "no-man's zone" into which African Americans are forced as they try to reconcile the "two warring ideals in one body" that W. E. B. Du Bois famously evoked in *Souls of Black Folk*.[49]

THE MARROW OF TRADITION

In the South the ripples of the national "quest for manhood" crossed with the interests of the plantocracy, and the broader white supremacist networks merged into a wave of rape paranoia.[50] The notion that black men were roaming the South, empowered by civil rights gains and the Republican Party to seek sexual intercourse with unwilling white women became a ubiquitous narrative, infecting local politics, but also national and international culture. If in 1867 Van Evrie and others could still portray dark-skinned black men as naturally subservient, white supremacist tactics in the post-Reconstruction era called for a more extreme and threatening view of race. The figure of the "black beast" central to the southern rape narrative evoked at some level the black villain of revenge drama, but he might be better characterized as Tarquin and his slave merged into one: in the fantasy circulated in the literature and iconography of southern Redemption, every southern white woman became a pretend Lucretia. Groaning under the yoke of Republican-abetted "Negro domination," southern white men were so many Brutuses and Collatinuses, and each fancied rape an occasion to overthrow tyranny and establish a republic. This narrative notably fed the racist nightmares developed in the literature of Thomas Nelson Page and Thomas Dixon, instant mythifications of southern Redemption that recast white supremacist violence as righteous revolution. It effectively "suppressed dissent among African Americans and simultaneously reinforced white women's dependence," strengthening symbolic ties—however negative—between the two populations and further ostracizing black women.[51] But the narrative had first been perfected in media and propaganda campaigns built simultaneously to the campaigns of white terror. Its structure was as old as Rome and obfuscated black avenger narratives now inseparable from the very notion of black political engagement.

This narrative notably undergirded the attack on the African American community of Wilmington, North Carolina, that same year. Municipal elections had brought a biracial alliance of Republicans and Populists at the head of this majority black town. The Democratic Party ran a white supremacy campaign, claiming that a fusionist victory would usher in "Negro domination." The cartoons of Norman Ethre Jennett, published alongside incendiary articles in the local white press throughout the campaign, played a crucial role in whipping up racist frenzy by dangling the threat of miscegenation and rape condoned and encouraged by Republicans, goading white men into acting in the defense of white women and for their own honor.[52] The Democratic Party won the state in a landslide. Still, the presence of African Americans in civil-service positions led Wilmington Red Shirts and other white supremacist groups to rampage through the city. They first burned down the offices of the only black newspaper in the state. Its editor, Alexander Manly, had previously published an editorial debunking white southern myths regarding interracial relations. Weapons in hand, the white mob then forced the municipal government to resign their positions, killing between a dozen and two hundred people.[53]

The Wilmington coup, evoked in *Imperium in Imperio*, provided Charles Chesnutt with material for his second novel, *The Marrow of Tradition* (1901). It follows a cast of characters, including Dr. William Miller, an African American physician returning to the fictional southern city of Wellington to open a black hospital. His wife, Janet, is the colored, illegitimate half-sister of Olivia Carteret, wife to Maj. Philip Carteret, leader of the town's white elite and owner of the white newspaper, through which he agitates for white supremacy. The overlapping personal stories of the characters collide around the coup, which wreaks tragedy and havoc. Chesnutt offers a dim and seemingly hopeless vision of black life in the South. The novel focuses on "the twin axes of sexual conduct that link the antebellum and postbellum worlds": the history and presence of miscegenation in the fabric of southern society and the southern obsession with rape.[54] Sandra Gunning argues that *The Marrow of Tradition* also takes for granted the "inevitability of racial union," making an argument for the necessity of cross-racial, class-based alliances to improve the South. Yet Chesnutt's "inescapable adherence to the values of a male heroism built upon a certain pattern of female silencing" presents readers with an ironic dilemma: this critique of white supremacy relies on "racialized and gendered discursive patterns shared by white supremacist fiction."[55] The black avenger trope provides a compelling angle into the vexed semantic networks evoked by Gunning: indeed, it shows how the dilemma in Chesnutt's novel has in part to do with the limited narrative and conceptual structures by which the very notion of black political agency could be expressed at the turn of the century.

The African American characters in Chesnutt's novel embody different outlooks in the face of white supremacist terror. In counterpoint to the conciliatory, middle-class Dr. Miller, Chesnutt presents a variation on the black avenger trope in the character of Josh Green, a "black giant" with a "reputation for absolute fearlessness." Green first appears in the novel as an anonymous black man riding secretly on the train to Wellington. Dr. Miller espies Green jumping from the train to get a drink as it is stopped at a water station. Miller notices Green cast a "glance of intense ferocity . . . suggest[ing] a concentrated hatred almost uncanny in its murderousness" at Capt. George McBane, a despicable white man who embodies "the aggressive, offensive element among the white people of the New South." Green is a working-class man: his body is his tool and his weapon, as he symbolically demonstrates by fighting "one er dem dagoes" on the docks. Dr. Miller's doesn't condone Green's recklessness and warns him against the potential repercussions of his actions. But Green has plans: he already knows he will die "in a quarrel wid a w'ite man . . . an' fu'thermo', he 's gwine ter die at the same time, er a little befo'." The white man is George McBane, who killed Green's father in a Ku Klux Klan raid that also made Green's mother lose her mind. Green was ten and "seen de whole thing, an' it wuz branded on my mem'ry, suh, like a red-hot iron bran's de skin."[56] Green lives to kill McBane, and only the fact that he must care for his mother stops him from enacting revenge immediately.

Gunning notes how in the novel black female characters are "only barely visible as virtuous figureheads": Green's mother, in a significant departure from black avenger commonplaces, barely factors as that.[57] The familiar pattern of violation and death for women is absent here, and although Green's mother was harmed by white supremacy, it was only indirectly. McBane killed her husband, a father, a figure forcibly erased in the slave system. The cultural legacy of this erasure in the African American community and how it has contributed to the abjection of African American women seeps through in this scene: the perpetuation of "*father-lacking*" is squarely assigned to a physical agent of white supremacy, and its immediate result is to make the African American mother wholly inadequate. Josh Green's mother—"Silly Milly," as children call her—"for twenty years . . . walked the earth as a child, as the result of one night's terror."[58] Racial terrorism has inverted the natural filiation scheme, making Josh his mother's keeper. Her death near the end of the novel frees him to fight McBane and his thugs but also confirms Green's own insight about his endeavor: it is a nihilistic declaration, a kind of suicide wholly turned toward the past, with no horizon beyond evening scores.

Dr. Miller ponders Green's dedication to revenge in terms that reprise racist clichés: "Negroes were not a vindictive people. If swayed by passion or emotion, they sometimes gave way to gusts of rage, these were of brief duration." He nevertheless finds in his commitment signs of a fledgling political consciousness: "Here was a negro who could remember an injury. . . . When his race reached the point where they would resent a wrong, there was hope that they might soon attain the stage where they would try, and, if need be, die, to defend a right." But Miller, from the heights of his educated, middle-class position, cannot condone violence: he recognizes and welcomes a familiar pattern but also knows to dismiss it. As he tells himself,

> McBane was probably deserving of any evil fate which might befall him; but such a revenge would do no good, would right no wrong; while every such crime, committed by a colored man, would be imputed to the race, which was already staggering under a load of obloquy because, in the eyes of a prejudiced and undiscriminating public, it must answer as a whole for the offenses of each separate individual. To die in defense of the right was heroic. To kill another for revenge was pitifully human and weak: "Vengeance is mine, I will repay," saith the Lord.[59]

Miller echoes the legalistic bend already witnessed in Griggs's novel: self-defense is the only situation in which killing is acceptable. That white supremacist terror routinely made a constant mockery of the law does not enter Miller's reflection: his is the politics of respectability typical of his class, laced with Christian values. Miller's political arithmetic, like Belton Piedmont's in *Imperium in Imperio*, marks a turn from Delany's treatment. Whereas Delany showed indecision and passivity as symptoms of slaves' lack of education, both Griggs and Chesnutt portray violence at large and vindictive violence in particular as symptoms of emotional immaturity and lack of education. One best serves the race by being a model individual. In the antebellum era the righteous avenger could be portrayed as an example for the community; in Jim Crow America educated African Americans worried that the suffering of the many may be blotted out by the actions of the one.

Much has been said about the logic and motives behind lynchings: in the *Red Record* Ida B. Wells-Barnett already pointed to the fact that rape narratives and even the specter of "Negro domination" usually covered much simpler and pettier matters: a majority of lynchings targeted African Americans whose successes—financial, political, or even sexual—or defiance irked their white neighbors.[60] Under Jim Crow any hint of individual "bad behavior" counted against the race at large. This is the trick of white supremacist terror: it flips upside down the tactic of exemplarity so dear to abolitionist and African American activists. Whereas the extraordinary African—the reader, the writer, the artist, and so on—was put on display as evidence of the entire race's potential for excellence, now every lynching victim was retroactively made into an extraordinary threat to white womanhood and, by extension, to civilization. The terrible impact of this flip lies in the way it manages to break down organized, widespread campaigns of racial terror into individual instances of revenge, while simultaneously involving the entire race in each isolated case.

Similar forces are at work in *The Marrow of Tradition*. White supremacist terror in the novel develops from a media campaign built with very concrete goals in mind: the small group of white supremacists running the show from Carteret's office act mostly out of personal greed. Carteret attacks the town's black newspaper at least partly out of outrage at seeing a black man competing with him. Destroying newspaper offices and presses has long been a specialty of the white supremacist and proslavery movements in the United States, a transparent attempt at controlling the means of production of the story. But southern propaganda in *The Marrow of Tradition* comes in other forms: when northern entrepreneurs and their wives visit the town, "the ladies were much interested in the study of social conditions, and especially in the negro problem," and soon find themselves led by southern guides who provide them with the official storyline and make sure they not meet anybody or see anything that might contradict the South as presented by its tourism-dedicated denizens. The crowning event in this improvised tour is a "genuine negro cakewalk." On this occasion "degenerate aristocrat" Tom Delamere—in blackface and in clothes taken from his grandfather's servant Sandy—wins the cake, no one realizing his true nature.[61]

Significantly, even Sandy misrecognizes himself in Delamere's mimicry. The comical scene shows a passably drunk Sandy following Delamere—who is wearing Sandy's clothes—in the middle of the night. Sandy thinks he is seeing a haunt, a ghostly version of himself. He puzzles at the vision in the following terms: "'Ef dat 's me gwine 'long in front,' mused Sandy, in vinous perplexity, 'den who is dis behin' here? Dere ain' but one er me, an' my ha'nt would n' leave my body 'tel I wuz dead.'"[62] As argued by John Mac Kilgore, in this scene "Sandy realizes that he doesn't have a self apart from racial performance, indeed, that he's a void subject haunted by his own representation. Thus, the answer to Sandy's sphinx-like riddle . . . is that 'I' would be nowhere. Only the place or role of Sandy exists."[63] Further yet: Delamere's disguise spells Sandy's death, and the force of prejudice makes his own version of himself the least likely to matter in the eyes of the white public. Indeed, later in the novel the consequences of misrecognition become dire: Sandy is accused of a murder Tom Delamere committed in blackface, while wearing Sandy's clothes. Delamere frames Sandy by giving him some of the victim's belongings, but, more important, Sandy is condemned by the newspaper campaign immediately launched against him. He is miraculously saved from the lynch mob gathering outside his cell by the intercession of the elder Delamere. Chesnutt suggests the scale of the collective downfall of this story:

> Nothing further was ever done about the case; but though the crime went unpunished, it carried evil in its train. As we have seen, the charge against Campbell had been made against the whole colored race. All over the United States the Associated Press had flashed the report of another dastardly outrage by a burly black brute,—all black brutes it seems are burly,—and of the impending lynching with its prospective horrors. This news, being highly sensational in its character, had been displayed in large black type on the front pages of the daily papers.[64]

For David Garland, the "public torture lynchings" typical of the turn of the century were "collective performances that involved a set of formal conventions and recognizable roles. . . . Lynchers sought to represent their violent acts as collective rituals rather than private actions." Lynchers were performing a kind of "morality play" and adopted "the ritual forms of public executions."[65] These were also the conventions of scapegoating rituals whose fundamental purpose they perverted.

According to René Girard, the essential function of the sacrifice is "to quell violence within the community and to prevent conflicts from erupting"—it is a means to thwart the impulse to revenge brought about by social conflict. To achieve this goal, the choice of a victim is crucial. Indeed, to suppress the impulse to retaliate, "we must divert that impulse, therefore, toward the sacrificial victim, the creature we can strike down without fear of reprisal, since he lacks a champion." Girard tells us that outcasts high (kings) or low (slaves) are equally adequate as sacrificial victims.[66] Although lynchings symbolically represent African Americans as powerful, tyrannical foes, natural threats against white womanhood, they necessarily both promote and rest on the understanding that African Americans are such outcasts. Their purpose is to remind blacks of their status as sacrifice fodder, pariahs within white society, and make clear that racial boundaries are also impenetrable national borders. In ancient societies slaves were scapegoat material but also potential citizens: southern public torture lynchings declared that full citizenship was foreclosed to African Americans.

The political character of lynching is paradoxically demonstrated in its very process, its recourse to the outdated savagery of human sacrifice, which suggests the intensity of white southern anxiety at the prospect of black political agency. Garland notes that the official rhetoric of these lynchings, as expressed in the newspapers that called for them or in the speeches that later defended them, justified the executions as forms of justice. The victims were always accused of having committed a heinous crime demanding an equally heinous retribution. In the process lynchers asserted much more. They reinforced racial order, and the presence of the crowd gave the proceedings a semblance of respectability: "The crowd converted an act of private justice into a public act. It *politicized* it, converting its significance from an act of unlawful violence into a law of its own."[67] In turn, making the protection of white women central to the rhetoric of lynching makes clear the intrinsically political nature of the act. Discussing the dynamics of white supremacist rape narratives, Gunning notes, "The white female is merely transformed into essentially a figurative space where white men can slay the black beast to protect their racial integrity."[68] This use of the female body as a stage should seem familiar: in Livy, Lucretia's violation is the pretext for revenge and revolution, her suicide the sacrifice that purifies it, and her body the stage on which the republic is performed into existence.

The self-victimization so typical of postbellum white supremacist rhetoric channels the rhetoric of Anglo-Saxon insurgency. The public torture lynchings that peaked in the 1890s make racial terror a performance of Anglo-Saxon citizenship. In the herrenvolk republic African Americans may be nominal citizens, but symbolically they remain slaves. Southern lynchings recycle the myth of the birth of the Roman Republic and turn it into a masquerade revolution: each rape—real or imagined—is the occasion for a new performance of the men's oath over the violated female body, the rehearsal of grievances against the tyrant, and he and the "old order"—alleged "Negro domination" in this case—are overthrown in a mass movement that overwhelms institutions and authorities. This perverted ritual, far from keeping the risk of cyclical violence at bay, ultimately welcomes it.

Kilgore argues that "mob violence, as a form of mass lynching, publicizes itself as a circus, a new kind of racist 'poetry' that General Belmont and Major Carteret, who foment the riot, wish to write," but this "poetry" has in fact a long history both as ritual and as literary production, as it were, and the tradition it invokes centers on the reduction of collective, political dynamics to the individual.[69] Miller recognizes this dynamic and its potential for complete destruction in the mirrored characters of Green and McBane. The apocalypse at the hospital is the only possible outcome for their antagonistic, vindictive relation, and it leaves both men dead. Yet Miller proves unable to fully eschew the logic that underlies the black avenger narrative pattern. When trying to convince Green not to intervene to stop Sandy's lynching, Miller offered that the only available solution was to find a decent white man; "one good white man, if he choose, may stem the flood long enough to give justice a chance."[70] What alternative Miller promotes in the novel relies on transposing similar patterns away from race and into class as marker of belonging. Traditional black avengers were always aristocrats: it is a sign of Chesnutt's distaste for violent action that he makes his avenger a dialect-speaking stevedore whom he equates across the racial divide with McBane, a poor white–turned–nouveau riche and arguably the novel's most unredeemably loathsome character. In *The Marrow of Tradition* "the only possible alliance must be between the white elite . . . and the light-skinned black elite," an alliance rooted in common class interests and set in contrast with working-class mobs, defined by their gullibility, rage, and tendency to spread chaos.[71]

Though he shows the responsibility of the white elite in provoking the mob to violence, Chesnutt also suggests that only the elites have the smarts and the economic reasons to pull the South out of racial strife and that this solution can come only out of nonviolent action. The final scene of the novel sees Olivia Carteret beg Dr. Miller for help with her ailing son. Earlier her husband had tried to convince Miller, to no avail: Miller's own son died in the coup fomented by Carteret, and the major finds himself feeling "involuntary admiration for a man who held in his hands the power of life and death, and could use it, with strict justice, to avenge his own wrongs."[72] Carteret finds that Miller, as an educated black man and skilled physician, holds individual power over him that his political schemes cannot appropriate. This is a dreary consolation, and it does not last: Olivia Carteret visits Miller's house to try and convince him. Miller makes her ask Janet, who is still grieving the death of their own son killed during the coup. Carteret admits that Janet is her half-sister, and Janet allows William to go help, "that you may know that a woman may be foully wronged, and yet may have a heart to feel, even for one who has injured her." The novel ends as Miller walks into the Carteret house. The American nation we glimpse in these final moments recognizes, if reluctantly, its multiracial character and the fact that the individuals— rather than the communities—that make it up are irrevocably tied together, even by blood. Chesnutt takes issue with the violent hero, shown as an agent of division, but the vision of alliance he proposes "occurs at the expense of women": Janet and Olivia are mirror, cross-racial symbols of virtue whose suffering serves principally to foster "male resurrection."[73] Still, his novel did very poorly both critically and commercially when it was published, proving no match for the sweeping wave of masculinism taking hold of the nation on the eve of the twentieth century.

Robert Jewett and John Sheldon Lawrence see *Birth of a Nation* (1915), D. W. Griffith's film adaptation of Thomas Dixon's *The Clansman* (1905), as a "classic statement" of "the myth of an innocent public afflicted by evil foes" that bring the innocents to use "heroic violence" to save themselves. Dixon's "Klan cycle," three best-selling novels published in the early twentieth century, demonstrated the nationwide popularity of the southern rape narrative. For Jewett and Lawrence, Dixon's vision of the Klan as a gathering of white southern heroes was "decisively shaped by cowboy Westerns in the last third of the nineteenth century."[74] Yet these two distinct versions of the white avenger in fact developed in parallel, tapping into a variety of precedents and inspiring later forms. Thus the "avenger detective" of 1890s dime novels preceded and inspired in some regards Dixon's romanticized vision of the Ku Klux Klan as anonymous defenders of moral order and "American vigilante hero type[s]."[75] In turn, Dixon's Grand Wizard Ben Cameron—in his moral stand for principles, his secret identity, and his commitment to deliver justice in the face of the state apparatus—is a clear ancestor of the 1930s superhero. Chris Gavaler's convincing argument addresses only indirectly a crucial difference between Dixon's Klansmen and superheroes: not unlike cowboys, superheroes may at times join groups, but they are essentially loners. Dixon, though he focuses on the leader of the Ku Klux Klan, still makes clear that the Klan is an organization counting thousands of members and dedicated to overthrowing what it presents as the majority "Negro rule." This connection suggests one important way in which, as literary and cultural figures, the Klansman and the cowboy are also in conversation with the black avenger that preceded and informs both of them.

In 1895 Owen Wister contributed his own stone to the edifice of Western mythology with "The Evolution of the Cow-Puncher." Following in the footsteps of Western historians and mythmakers Theodore Roosevelt and Frederick Jackson Turner, Wister's *Harper's* article offered a portrait of the cowboy as a modern knight, "nothing but the same Saxon of different environments, the nobleman in London and the nobleman in Texas." In Wister's peculiar outlook, the cowboy is like the heroes of Arthurian legend defined by a code of honor. He is not just the embodiment of the Anglo-Saxon's natural thirst for freedom; he also expresses the conquering spirit at work in westward expansion. That same spirit, Wister strongly hints, breathes in the U.S. imperial turn. Wister's cowboy is not simply a type; he is a bulwark of racial purity in the rising tide of "encroaching alien vermin that turn our cities to Babels and our citizenship to a hybrid farce." Yet by 1895, a mere five years after the official closing of the frontier, Wister already lamented the disappearance of "this latest outcropping of the Saxon ... dispersed ... as all wild animals must inevitably be dispersed," receding in the path of progress. Wister's portrayal of the Western hero is characterized by ambivalence toward modernity, its urban, industrial, technological trappings and its influence on the demographics of the United States. Though he claims that his cowboy "has never made a good citizen, but a good soldier," Wister unmistakably posits him as a model for the ideal American man.[76]

On his "quest for manhood," the eastern Ivy Leaguer minted a hero that spoke both to his learning and to a yearning for physical toughness to counteract the hints of effeminacy assigned to the well-educated, upper middle class. The result, with its roots in aristocratic European values as assumed as its celebration of brawn, evokes the figure of the southern gentleman of plantation literature as much as the noble savage of the Enlightenment. Wister's cowboy is a brazen construct influenced by his author's background and ideology. His maternal grandfather was Pierce Butler, absentee owner of plantations in the Georgia Sea Islands, about which his wife, actor Frances Anne Kemble, wrote her *Journal of a Residence on a Georgian Plantation in 1838–1839*. Wister himself held a romantic view of the Old South and profoundly racist views dressed in the pretense of realism and historical accuracy.[77] The West, as described in the works of Wister and his contemporaries, is not a geographic place so much as a concept, "a condition of displacement" whose "region was the mind."[78] Modern United States may not have been worthy of the purity of the cowboy, but he would become its most recognizable icon, notably through the fiction of Owen Wister and his first best seller, *The Virginian* (1902).

The novel was "among the most popular in American literary history" and introduced narrative patterns and plot developments on which the Western genre relies to this day.[79] Its protagonist, the eponymous Virginian, left the southern state for Wyoming, where he became a ranch hand for Judge Henry, whom the novel's easterner narrator comes to meet at the beginning of the novel. Upon meeting him, the narrator recognizes in the Virginian a truth at first belied by the cowboy's demeanor: in spite of his poor upbringing and his workingman status, the Virginian is a true gentleman. This realization brings about another epiphany: "The creature we call a GENTLEMAN lies deep in the hearts of thousands that are born without chance to muster the outward graces of the type."[80] The Virginian is one of possibly many poor southern whites revealed as natural aristocrats in the crucible of the West. At a time when the Populist movement—which Wister agonized over repeatedly—was mobilizing the same population to fight for their collective welfare against upper-class, Democratic rule in the South, Wister's natural aristocrat is first and foremost an individual who in the Western context can and must follow his personal moral code with minimal interference from the artifices of modern society.

Out West "fundamental principles of honor and the will of the community transcend responsibilities to the official agencies of the government and the codified, written law." These values are routinely tested in the vagaries of cowboy life, but also more fundamentally by the Virginian's budding relationship with Molly Wood, a teacher from Vermont who represents the Western progress of civilization. As such, she and women in general are "a threat to the code . . . , harbingers of law and order."[81] The terms of the Virginian's relationship with Wood are exposed when, in the course of his adventures, Wister's hero lynches cattle rustlers—including an acquaintance of his—to Molly's horror. When she asks Judge Henry, the Virginian's employer, if he condones lynching, he responds, "Of burning Southern negroes in public, no. Of hanging Wyoming cattle thieves in private, yes. You perceive there's a difference, don't you?" According to the (not innocently titled) judge, there is a difference in principle: the former, in its use of torture and reliance on spectacle, proves the South to be "semi-barbarous"; the latter, in its relative sobriety, proves "that Wyoming is determined to become civilized." Judge Henry sees Western lynching as an expression of justice in a place where organized justice has no actual sway, a land that lies beyond the pale of civilization: "When your ordinary citizen . . . sees that he has placed justice in a dead hand, he must take justice back into his own hands," the judge continues, defining vigilantism as the "fundamental assertion of self-governing men."[82] He speaks as a white man, from the assumption that black victims of southern lynchings were indeed criminals. But from an African American point of view, situations were reversed: at the time when the novel takes place—between 1874 and 1890—while the Old South was a lawless land, the unincorporated West was full of promise for African Americans, offering what Stephen Knadler calls an "accommodated citizenship . . . a polycultural political identity in which the black citizen tentatively belongs to numerous overlapping groups and to multiple sites of democratic participation and action."[83] In these circumstances the cowboy hero developed by Wister's and other contemporary writers' texts had the appeal that his values of nobility, honor, and manliness, presented as they were as Saxon racial characteristics, also appeared to offer the chance that one could be assessed and valued for one's individual worth. The same logic runs here that underlay black avenger narratives prior to the Haitian Revolution: nobility could exist deep in any and all hearts. If that were indeed the case, then Western-style revenge was equally warranted for cowboys or African Americans in situations of lawlessness.

"THIS NEGRO IS A WHITE MAN"

The treatment of black avenger figures in mainstream American literature bears the mark of broader national trends in African American cultural politics. At the turn of the century, powerless in the face of Jim Crow, many in the African American elite focused instead on education and economic development, building in the process rhetoric that allowed for the combination of race pride and patriotism. Robert Lewis Waring was a product of the African American middle class, son of a minister and civil servant. He served for a time as a police officer in Washington, D.C., and as a lawyer later in New York City, but he also campaigned for the Democratic Party in the 1912 elections, at a time when many in the African American community were reconsidering their allegiance to the Republican Party.[84] Waring expresses his views on American society and the role African Americans play in the book's opening pages, through imagery and text. They say much about the contortions necessary to defend a black conservative stance in a white supremacist state and how returning to the white, antipolitical roots of the black avenger trope could serve such purposes.

On the photo that graces the opening pages of *As We See It*, Robert Lewis Waring sits in an armchair, wearing a crisp pencil-stripe suit and a tie, reading a sheaf of papers held with both hands in front of him (fig. 2). Sitting on the chair's arm with her hand on his shoulder is a seemingly younger woman; pristine in her dress and white apron, she leans onto the balding, middle-aged lawyer-turned-novelist to read with him. She is his niece, it turns out, although nothing on the page indicates it: the photograph's only caption is the author's name, "Robert Lewis Waring."[85] They are reading the proofs of the very novel in which readers find them, forever frozen in the act. *As We See It*: the photograph seems an illustration of the title it faces, and for the time it takes to turn a page, a reader might think this is who "We" are, young and old, man and woman, middle-class, educated African Americans immortalized in a moment of a semidomestic demonstration of respectability. The following page tells us in capital letters that this book is dedicated "TO THOSE NEGRO MEN WHO DARE DEFEND THE WOMANHOOD OF THEIR RACE," confirming the anonymous position women hold in relation to this

"Robert Lewis Waring." HD US 10727.9,
Houghton Library, Harvard University.

text. Though necessary to the novel's dedicatees, they are prop to, more than part of, their group; they form a concept essential to a definition of black citizenship molded in the age-old Roman frame and revised in the white supremacist American Republic. What Waring retained of the black avenger tradition had by 1910 wholly blended into the fabric of American culture.[86]

Waring's *As We See It* is in many aspects a variation on what Robert Jewett and John Sheldon Lawrence call the "American monomyth," a narrative that "begins and ends in Eden.... A disruption of harmony occurs, and must be eliminated by the superhero, before the Edenic condition can be re-established in a happy ending."[87] Waring's novel shows that the "frontier vigilante," if it did not influence Dixon's Klan cycle, certainly contributed to building a black literary response to the white supremacist mythology it did so much to contribute to. The vision of black masculinity and citizenship offered in the process nevertheless bore the unmistakable marks of an absolutist form of racial thinking that eschewed the "black hybrid cosmopolitanism" characteristic of many recorded working-class black experiences of the frontier, in favor of a racial elitist individualism paradoxically more in tune with white supremacy.[88]

The novel takes place in 1876, the year of the centennial of the Declaration of Independence. It opens up on two old men sitting on the front porch of an Alabama plantation house: one is "Abe Overley, black," the fifth by this name to serve the other, "Abe Overley, white," fifth by this name. Their respective sons, unsurprisingly both called Abe as well, are considering going to college. Waring enjoys onomastic play: the Overleys, as their name announces somewhat unsubtly, have been distinct but inseparable for generations. Much like Chesnutt's Janet Miller and Olivia Carteret, they are what Katja Kanzler—after Samira Kawash—calls "interracial twins . . . characters whose parties 'actually,' ostensibly belong to different 'races,' yet whom the text presents as . . . similar in their appearance."[89] Indeed, "both are about six feet tall, one is very white, with curly chestnut hair. . . . The other is as black as the first boy is white; six feet, good features, with curly black hair," though in their case similarity is much deeper than the skin. They are "both of the royal blood, the kind that never knows a friend but as a friend." The first white Overley struck an agreement with the first of the black Overleys after buying him at a slave auction: he would never whip him, and in turn Abe would become his faithful righthand man. The two Overleys are "nature's noblemen," fair and honorable men of their word, and the Overley plantation is the original Eden of this American tale, a pastoral, idyllic place where whites and blacks live in harmony.[90] This Eden is threatened by Nick Lashum, a "cracker" who used to work as the overseer on the Overley plantation and made a fortune profiting off the Civil War. The war left the Overleys almost ruined, and to save their possessions they've had to borrow money from Lashum, whose secret dream is to take over the Overley plantation.

The two young Abes go to college to Oberlin, where black Abe (white Abe is from then on called Malcolm) shows impervious dignity in clashes with hostile white students, among whom is Lashum's son, Buck. There they meet other men "of royal blood" from Japan, China, Persia, and the West Indies—aristocrats of color whom Lashum and his young American friends try in vain to ostracize—but also white Europeans, Yankees, and southern aristocrats puzzled by the poor southerners' prejudices. Abe and Malcolm meet young women—Miss Donewell and Miss Watson—who could also be sisters, "but for the color of their skins."[91] They form another set of interracial twins, united by class, upbringing, and middle-class values. Lashum and his friends try on several occasions to get Abe in trouble, to no avail. Horror strikes when Abe finds out that Buck, recently dismissed from Oberlin after attempting to stain Abe's reputation through treachery, went home to Alabama and assaulted Abe's mother and sister in retaliation. Driven by the desire to avenge his humiliation and encouraged by his father's mistress, Black Sue, Lashum led a party of young men to the black Overley residence and whipped both women to death. The men are arrested, tried, and freed, as no Alabama jury would sentence white men for attacking black people.

Upon hearing the news, Abe transforms into the "very incarnation of the avenging demon." Impervious to all appeals to reason, Abe the avenging demon sets out in pursuit of the culprits, hunts them down one by one, and kills them, leaving by each body a piece of the horse trace with which they originally committed their crime. His revenge evokes classic revenge tragedy by way of the Western, and he is ready to live by the convention that an avenger, once his deed is done, will live—if at all—on the outskirts of society: "I shall then be an outcast, a homeless wanderer, an outlaw, maybe, with my hand raised against mankind and a price upon my head."[92] For Jerry Bryant, in revenge Abe "casts off a humanity that was transcendentally precious to blacks."[93] Yet in the process he also demonstrates, as argued by his professor Dr. Finley, the extent of his integration to, and literacy in, white society: "He has been educated, developed . . . up to the point that has been reached by our civilization, where men take the lives of one another in revenge for the lives of their kindred or for wrongs perpetrated upon their women." The professor contrasts young black men who reason like Abe to the God-fearing "old type," whom he believes are now a minority. Speaking of Abe, Finley adds, "This Negro is a white man, in the sense that his ambitions and desires for the good things of this world are identical with yours."[94] There, then, is the secret to Abe's success: a form of passing deeper than the skin. As a white man, Abe gains status as subject and individual. Individuals can resort to revenge in the face of systemic injustice; his is the ancestral justice of *lex talionis*, not the savagery of the lynch mob. It is precisely because Abe takes pains not to see the political dimension of his mother's and sister's murder, because he makes the political personal, that he is considered an honorable man. The Shakespearean accents of Abe's call to revenge invoke a model that predates, and indeed ignores, the racialization of the figure in the modern era. It bypasses Spartacus as well, whose connection to slavery is wholly irrelevant to Waring's purpose. This black avenger is a white avenger.

No doom befalls Abe once he avenges his mother and sister by killing every man involved in their death. His fiancée, Nancy, absolves him; they get married, and Abe is allowed to finish his studies at Oberlin. Peace comes back to Eden: the Overley plantation is saved from the Lashums by a coalition of southern gentry, and Abe buys a plantation of his own in Louisiana, where his family can finally—and rather improbably—live happily ever after. The Overleys, black and white, bear the same name because they are of the same world: natural aristocrats, the pinnacle of American democracy. According to Owen Wister: "It was through the Declaration of Independence that we Americans acknowledged the ETERNAL INEQUALITY of man. . . . Let the best man win! That is America's word. That is true democracy. And true democracy and true aristocracy are one and the same thing."[95] In delivering righteous vengeance, Abe proves a "white man." Indeed, as he declares in a conversation with an Italian worker with apparent anarchist leanings who suggests he start an indiscriminate bombing campaign against white people in his county, "This is not a question of race with me." The Italian man is not convinced by Abe's praise of righteous revenge as a pillar of civilization: "You say civilizationa. Thata for biga mana, not for poor mana and blacka mana. No. Civilizationa no gooda." Subsequent lines describe how the Italian man in question eventually married into one of the oldest families in Alabama, the narrator noting dryly, "It is to be hoped that Amato 'absorbed' the American idea to the point where he could understand the meaning of our civilization. At this writing, we do not understand the American civilization."[96] Yet the episode makes clear that the missing link in Overley's logic is precisely that which he thinks is not relevant: race.

Except for Abe Overley's family members, the most notable black character is Black Sue. She is one of the black concubines ubiquitous in the literature of the Jim Crow South, but where similar characters—Bertrand's mother in *Imperium in Imperio*, for example—were generally tragic mothers in African American texts, Waring portrays Sue without any sympathy. Black Sue has been Nick Lashum's mistress since before the Civil War—together they have "several doubtful looking children of variegated colors" roundly despised by black people as well as white. Every bit his accomplice, she is an evil and venal woman involved in most of his bad deeds and more: she is the one who suggests to Buck Lashum that he flog the Overley women, denying all responsibility afterward. Contempt drips from every passage concerning her, as when she is described as a "vulture swooping down on a carcass of carrion" when she grabs a coin held out by Lashum. It is fairly clear that Waring means to demonstrate that natural aristocracy and natural lowliness alike can be found among whites and blacks. Yet if anyone can supposedly be noble, despicable people like Lashum or Sue all hail strictly from the lower classes, and the narrator will not let readers forget it: on the same page, Sue's behavior is described as typical of "the Negro women among her class" and of "Negroes of this class."[97] Waring ultimately portrays differences between the honorable and the despicable as social absolutes, not unlike alleged racial differences but strictly hinging on personal responsibility.

Race is dismissed time and again as a valid prism for interpreting anything. The words Dr. Finley addresses to his colleagues illustrate the matter plainly: "This 'exceptional Negro' is the one under discussion, not the race to which he belongs."[98] After he is given a job by a rich Jewish man impressed by his work ethic and studiousness, Abe can afford returning to college, where he finds two Japanese men he had first met while at Oberlin who attempt to convince him to work for Japan. The Empire of Japan had risen in the 1890s to become the United States' main rival in the Pacific. The rationale for the American annexation of Hawaii was in part dictated by the need the U.S. government and military felt to check Japan's influence. In 1905 the Japanese Empire had stunned the Western world by defeating Russia in the Russo-Japanese War, a conflict fought over imperial influence over China and the Korean Peninsula. The ripples of the victory were felt especially strongly by African Americans, who hailed it as a demonstration that white racial superiority was a fable. W. E. B. Du Bois saw in the Japanese triumph a harbinger of "the awakening of the brown and black races," in which he hoped to see African Americans play a constructive part.[99] In the racist, anti-Japanese backlash that followed notably in California, African Americans tended to take the side of Asians, to the extent that "concerned whites" wrote the government about alleged "Japanese collusion with American blacks."[100] This plotline appears to directly address the rumor; Abe's two Japanese acquaintances, having already commissioned three other black students, approach him to recruit him into the Imperial Navy. The envoys evoke Abe's mother in hopes of kindling hatred for the United States in him, arguing that "he has no reason to love nor fight for a flag that was no protection to him."[101] It is a measure of the reputation of Japan among African Americans that Abe gives himself time to ponder the question and speak about it to his wife, Nancy.

Abe eventually refuses, as in the middle of explaining his woes to his wife he suddenly exclaims, "Nancy, my mother appeared to me in my thoughts. She held the Stars and Stripes proudly above her head while her other hand was extended to me. My mother wills that I shall defend the flag of my country."[102] Abe's martyred mother, killed by agents of American white supremacy, becomes a black Lady Columbia. Whereas the female image of the nation had been used in white supremacist propaganda to convince the white masses to go out and vote in preparation of the Wilmington coup, Waring uses it here to convince his hero. Manhood can only be proven in the face of the nation by the ability to defend women. Waring shares this gendered vision of the nation with white supremacist authors, much like he shares the patriarchal code that justifies the lynching myth.[103] Her suffering is sublimated, and Overley is redeemed into the Edenic American nation when he refuses to follow the Japanese. They are surprised by his reaction, having never considered that "a Negro's heart was governed by the same honorable impulses that other men's are . . . in short, that a Negro is a Man."[104] The essence of Waring's logic is on full display in this sentence: his avenger speaks and acts only for himself, and if he is meaningful for the race at large, it is in his personal financial and moral success and in his allegiance to country—however racist and hostile—rather than in recognition of racial belonging.

Much like Dr. Finley, Abe systematically rejects the relevance of race, and there is no hint in the novel that such a thing as a black community exists in the novel. Family units are introduced, whose worth is measured by the way they are organized. Abe's wife, Nancy, thus represents the new virtuous black woman; though known for her "passive Christian spirit," she surprises Abe with her wholehearted support for his revenge and even suggests a pragmatic plan that would let him reach personal success and avenge his mother and daughter. When, following this conversation, Abe asks Nancy's father for her hand, the old man asks, "Would you give *your* daughter to a murderer . . . ?" to which Abe responds, "Mr. Watson, should your daughter Nancy be foully murdered—lynched—what would you do?" No answer is forthcoming, the silence both an indictment of the "old Negro" and a show of masculinity that is not without evoking elements of the pro-lynching propaganda of the time. Instances of white terror in the novel are boiled down to personal conflict that themselves are tests of masculinity, the measure by which black and white characters are assessed. Nancy, though she contributes witty repartees and appears headstrong throughout the novel, systematically undercuts herself; she concludes each of her interventions by deferring to her father or to Abe, after she marries him. The novel's final lines celebrate a woman's love, faith, and tenderness and give us a vision of claustrophobic domesticity with the Overleys and their son kneeling in prayer, Abe whispering in Nancy's ear, "God grant, Nancy, that he loves you as I loved my mother."[105] Considering that Abe's mother features in the novel exclusively as a victim of lynching and that his love for her is demonstrated strictly in his bloody revenge, this final note is somewhat chilling. In the end, Waring's Overleys are revealed for what they are: a veneer of would-be colorblind respectability and domesticity so thin it cannot but reveal the latent horror of a social system resting on gender and racial oppression.

Jewett and Lawrence evoke how the American monomyth tends to dissolve all complexity through "mythic massage . . . a process of assuring spectators that the gap between myth and reality can be bridged," by which "complex social problems are solved with a single gesture; tangled human relations are sorted out and resolved; evil is eliminated with a single heroic stroke."[106] Waring is a dedicated practitioner of the technique. He gestures toward the collective reality of white supremacist terror in the South only to reduce it to an individual matter, the story of the individual nobility of a black man connected to a racial community through ambition and class. Indeed, Waring speaks to and for his peers, not all black people, not even all black men, but specifically those he thinks will recognize themselves in Abe. They are "the educated Negroes, those of cultured families of the third and fourth generations," a new aristocracy Waring believes has been kept out of the pages of American literature in favor of the lowbrow "Jim Crow Nigger," in tacit support of "the 'Jim Crow law' industry." For Waring, books about the post-Reconstruction U.S. South usually avoid telling this truth: paradoxically, while the postbellum "'crackers' of the South" remained proudly illiterate, incestuous, and idle, segregation allowed for the rise of industrious, well-to-do, educated blacks, a new aristocracy. The "Negro's" progress is unstoppable: soon he will be "a man, thoroughly trained, a true American, ready and willing, as he has ever been, to fight and die for the flag that now protects him—NOT."[107] Though Waring's address is defiant, it invokes the meritocratic mythology of the American dream. African Americans, though they have been forcibly kept down, have nevertheless managed to partake in it. The United States can be the black man's country if he, individually, adopts its values. Eschewing race thinking but not the reality of race, Waring proposes a vision of reality that wholly absorbs and accepts the negation of black collective agency that always undergirded the black avenger trope. Waring's aristocracy is only a group in that it is a collection of individuals with similar backgrounds, means, and goals. Abe is the harbinger of things to come, the first of a new wave of black Americans that will normalize the "extraordinary." He is the black avenger redeemed: the "Negro" as white man.

CONCLUSION

Black Avengers of America
in Hollywood, 2018

This is a story about the stories men tell one another.

The island, this "original Garden of Eden," has long been inhabited, but when men tell the tale, they always first discover it. It is a place of rapturous beauty, but there is trouble in paradise: the island's "virgin fertility" falls into the hands of a "master . . . [of] unsurpassable cruelty." This "tyrant" rapes the land, massacres locals, and imports slaves, influencing in the process the "whole of Western civilization."[1] This original wrong dooms Eden: in all the violence wrought on the island, none came to right this original wrong, no oath to make the martyred land the foundation of civilization.

Thus begins the story of Haiti as told in a 1903 speech by future NAACP field secretary William Pickens, then a student at Yale. No Brutus stands up to the European Tarquins here: there are only "mulattoes" who launch "the most bloody, cruel and vindictive struggle of history," after catching the "intractable spirit of liberty from the mother country." That unnamed "mother country" of spirit is faraway, Enlightened France; Hispaniola is for the tortured flesh. Pickens speaks in the halls of white supremacy, and it shows. He speaks of Toussaint Louverture, whose kindness to his former master's family is deemed a form of fidelity similar to that showed by "the American slave, who lay like a watchful mastiff on the doorsteps of the absent confederate soldier." Things could have been so good: but Louverture failed, and he was replaced by Dessalines, the "first black emperor" whose name Pickens cannot find it in himself to pronounce. Imagine a Rome where Spartacus has won. Former slaves do not build a republic over an outraged woman's body; they build it on a pile of the former oppressors' dead, and thus, "having destroyed every trace and hope of internal civilization," are apparently doomed not to enter the concert of nations. The United States could teach Haitians what black American men like him purported to have learned during the

Reconstruction: "that the savage and the child to rise to higher things must feel the power of a stronger hand." Pickens demands an American intervention, employing to that effect the vocabulary of a rapist: "All weak sentimentalism must be dismissed. The letter of humanity should be violated for the sake of the spirit. The subjugation of the island would be an act of kindness."[2] There is a right way to do this, and it begins with rape.

Pickens must have sounded convincing: with this speech, he became the first African American to win the prestigious Ten Eyck prize for oratory. The text was circulated broadly around the country, and African American voices rose to sternly rebuke him.[3] But Pickens also found supporters. Evangelist N. L. Musgrove contacted him from rural Kentucky, where he had recently settled to found one in a purported national network of lodges of the "Sons of Freedom," a brotherhood of "true members of the Afro-American race." Musgrove read about Pickens and decided he had found in the college student the extraordinary leader his black nation-building organization needed. In full awareness that "a true union between the Afro-American and the Anglo-Saxon peoples of America" was impossible "and that the future welfare of both would be best conserved by a friendly, but none the less irrevocable separation as regards national existence," Musgrove advocated the annexation of Haiti, "whose sovereignty might be bought or wrested from revolutionary and unworthy hands—or other countries contiguous."[4] Building on Pickens's speech, Musgrove floated the idea of a segregated, black version of U.S. imperialism.

The details of Musgrove's scheme were listed in many articles published around the country. Lodges would contribute money to the treasurer in Alabama, the money serving notably to secure one or two warships and organize black troops to take over Haiti and organize a new form of government, "republican in its formation . . . yet to be administered as a gigantic corporation, of which all members of the society are to be stockholders." The United States would likely condone the invasion of Haiti, as "the blacks there, being usurpers themselves, have no moral or legal claims to the country which the Afro-Americans or anybody else need necessarily respect."[5] Can Musgrove have meant to echo the wording of the *Dred Scott* decision? In any case, the implication was clear: as African Americans were to white Americans in 1857, so Haitians were to African Americans in 1903, on the eve of the centennial of their independence. The evangelist used the rhetoric of white supremacy to challenge the legitimacy of a revolution that had created the first independent black nation in the Americas. Musgrove's plan provided a sorry end point to a century of white resentment and cultural retaliation by turning against Haiti a declaration of black insurgency and independence. In his outlandish scenario, Musgrove squarely replaces the black republic and its legend with a plot for a black settler colony shaped by, and palatable to, the white supremacist United States. The term "usurpers" exposed the old literary undercurrent in Musgrove's plan, with its evocation of undeserving rulers (the barbaric Haitians, having wrested the country from Europe) and of the heroes who challenge them (African Americans, champions of Western civilization), coming to set things right. The plan invoked all the elements of black avenger narratives of old; like them, though it spoke in the accents of black politics, it seemed dedicated mostly to the white audience implied in the venues in which Musgrove's plan appeared: Lexington, Kentucky's *Morning Herald*; Cleveland's *Plain Dealer*; the *Washington Post*, all marveling at the prospect that such a familiarly novel spectacle as "Government for the Negro, by the Negro" might unfold under the West's watchful eyes.[6]

A decade later, in July 1915, pretexting the volatile political situation on the island warranted the armed defense of U.S. interests, marines landed in Port-au-Prince and took control of the Haitian capital and its governing institutions. The African American press—notably W. E. B. Du Bois in *The Crisis*—was quick to criticize U.S. encroachment on Haiti and the litany of abuses the population soon had to suffer from occupying troops. Calls for a withdrawal of the United States were left unheeded.[7] Although somewhat reserved in their support for the invasion, more moderate African American figures such as Booker T. Washington could not but see the invasion as the work of (Western) civilization—its righteous revenge. African American outlook on the occupation took a drastic turn in the aftermath of the Red Summer of 1919, when cities around the United States erupted in racist violence, and white mobs—sometimes including police officers—chased African Americans in the streets of Charleston, Memphis, Chicago, Philadelphia, Baltimore, and even in the country's capital. The plight of the Haitians, forced into quasi slavery, assaulted, tortured, raped, and killed in their own land by the same white Americans now setting African American neighborhoods on fire suddenly felt increasingly close; "the spirit of the times made Haiti an important issue to blacks," and newspapers, but also organizations such as the NAACP, took up the cause of Haiti.[8] Support for Haiti led to renewed interest in its history and most notably in the heroic figures of its revolution. Louverture, Dessalines, and Christophe informed the living, active figure of Jamaican-born, Harlem-based political activist Marcus Garvey. Ridiculed by black and white intelligentsia alike, Garvey and his message of international black autonomy nevertheless found an audience: thousands of members around the world joined his United Negro Improvement Association, and the organization's newspaper, *Negro World*, had a broad international readership. Garvey wielded a rhetoric of national redemption whose historical roots he made quite clear: "Africa must be redeemed, and all of us pledge our manhood, our wealth and our blood to this sacred cause. Yes, the Negroes of the world have found . . . a Toussant L'Overture [*sic*], and he will be announced to the world when the time comes."[9] Emulating the Haitian hero in appearance and intent, Garvey once more revised the trope by which black agency defines itself in the West as a tale of extraordinary manhood, redemption, and blood.

The story goes on. Not a decade has gone by in the twentieth and twenty-first centuries that did not see a revisitation of the black avenger trope. There is no "ancient taboo" against black avengers: they systematically sprout as a paradoxical cultural rampart against that bogeyman of old, the terrifying prospect that is collective black political agency. When voices claim that black lives matter, demand that the names of the victims of white supremacy be said and their stories told, and expect new iterations of the same old *story*: soon an extraordinary black man will rise from the mass of his peers to lead a mass movement that will unavoidably fail.

I open this book with Quentin Tarantino's *Django Unchained*; I conclude it with two more recent film iterations of the black avenger trope: Nate Parker's *The Birth of a Nation* (2016) and Ryan Coogler's *Black Panther* (2018), the former a retelling of Nat Turner's revolt, the latter an adaptation of the Marvel comic book about the superhero king of a fictional, hypertechnological African country. Parker's Turner evokes Jesus Christ, notably in the heavy-handed execution scene, but for most of the film he is a modern-day black Spartacus, enlightened avenger ushering in an American age where extraordinary, singular black males have their day. Coogler's film—though centered on an actual Avenger (the superhero team, that is)—reintroduces the black avenger as an American supervillain whose "monstrous hybridity" threatens an international racial order, where blackness and whiteness are equal but must remain separate.

The principal source of information on Turner's revolt, *The Confessions of Nat Turner* (1831), taken down by Thomas R. Gray, set the standards by which Turner has generally been represented: a smart, literate, well-treated, skilled slave and "complete fanatic," who explained that he had received instructions for the uprising from God. Gray was not satisfied: Turner and his companions died "without revealing any thing at all satisfactory, as to the motives which governed them, or the means by which they expected to accomplish their object."[10] What personal information Turner offered Gray says precious little about himself, some about his parents.

It says nothing about his wife.

Gray does not mention her in *The Confessions of Nat Turner*, but he had written of her before, when the authorities, still looking for Nat Turner, tortured her into confessing that Nat had been considering insurrection for years and into relinquishing to them some of Turner's private documents.[11] Some historians speculate from this information that her name was Cherry, "a slave belonging to Mr. Reese," and that she and Turner may have had a son together, a theory Nate Parker adopts in his film.[12] In 1831 reporters did not care: "Before the trials in Jerusalem were over, curiosity about this woman either faded, as if her identity had been merely of passing interest, or was suppressed for reasons never explained."[13] Thirty years after the revolt, Boston abolitionist and John Brown supporter Thomas Higginson had peculiar words to address the matter of Turner's wife: "By day or by night, her husband had no more power to protect her than the man who lies bound upon a plundered vessel's deck has power to protect his wife on board the pirate schooner disappearing in the horizon. She may be well treated, she may be outraged; it is in the powerlessness that the agony lies."[14] The well-meaning Higginson turns the torture of Cherry into Nat's ordeal; the lash is a metaphor for rape, and rape a symbol of the unmanning of Turner before it is an atrocity visited on Cherry. As if to temper Higginson's allusions, David F. Allmendinger Jr. warns, "Nat Turner said nothing in 1831 to indicate that a separation from a wife and child had provoked him to rebellion, nothing to suggest a merely personal grievance fueled by sentiments about family. . . . Gray settled for an easier, stock explanation of motives, one that rested on the confession and involved the chief insurgent's fanaticism."[15] Allmendinger himself cannot completely discard the idea that the assault on his family may be what decided Turner; maybe his revolt was his revenge, a remembering after emasculation. Things would be much simpler that way.

And so things appear to be in Nate Parker's film: Nat is tasked with preaching to slaves in plantations all around, and at first he advocates submission. After patrollers brutally assault Cherry in Nat's absence, the tenor of his sermons changes drastically—the vengeful God of the Old Testament rises. The death of his grandmother Bridget finally pushes Parker's Nat to prepare for revolt. Bridget is Nat's last direct link to Africa; with that connection gone, Turner can fully become American. Céleste-Marie Bernier, reflecting on Cherry and more generally on "the erasure of enslaved female bodies," notes how "black female heroism has been a casualty not only of white dominant archives but also of revisionist attempts to commemorate black male exceptionalism."[16] Parker's film is one such attempt; in making Cherry's ordeal but a bit part of Turner's consciousness, it shows the birth not of the black American nation of white Western nightmares but of a dreamed United

States of male opportunity. In the last scene of the film, a black child, witness to Turner's execution, morphs into a grown man fighting in an African American military unit during the Civil War. Nate Parker's film is an inverted paean to respectability politics and assimilation. As in Waring's *As We See It*, by avenging his woman's honor, bleeding for the U.S. flag, and weaving himself into the violent fabric of this country's imaginary, any outstanding black man will earn the manly right—or so does the film strongly suggest—to claim a seat at the citizen's table.

The seat did not materialize; still a corpus of African American black avenger texts stretching from Waring to Parker insists on suggesting that this seat was gloriously earned, as if another tale of extraordinary black masculinity might finally do it, as if one day the *right* Spartacus might be summoned that would make a difference. Seeping as it did by way of African American contributions into African diasporic debates throughout the twentieth century, this U.S.-centered spirit has become a seemingly unavoidable element in global discussions of blackness. As I write this, Ryan Coogler's cinematic adaptation of Marvel Comics' African superhero, *Black Panther* (2018), has become the most commercially successful superhero film in history and is well on its way to breaking other records. With its quasi all-black cast, *Black Panther* met demands for black representation and simultaneously reminded those who might not have known that black sells. Black Panther's novelty has been a selling point ever since the character first appeared in comic-book form in July 1966 as a new character in the successful *Fantastic Four* comic-book series. T'Challa, prince of Wakanda, is initially driven by righteous revenge: he has spent much of his life preparing for the return of his father's assassin, the evil Klaw. T'Challa defeats him and, like most superheroes, transcends his initial motives to dedicate his life to fighting injustice and crime. T'Challa might be mistaken for a black avenger in the Atlantic mold but for one essential difference: his country, Wakanda, has somehow managed to eschew the Atlantic slave trade and colonialism, two defining traumas of collective, global black experience. Wakanda and its hero king wear a mask of Atlantic blackness but do not, cannot, quite embody it.

The black avenger in *Black Panther* is T'Challa's foe and cousin, Erik "Killmonger" Stevens. Erik's father, Prince N'Jobu, is a secret agent for Wakanda living undercover in an Oakland, California, project in 1992 with his American son, whom he tells stories of faraway Wakanda. There he is confronted with the systemic racism faced by people of African descent in the United States and the West at large. As a result, N'Jobu decides to forswear Wakanda's splendid isolation; instead of keeping to his mission of observation, he decides to tackle the problem of racism, weapons in hand. His plan for a black uprising is thwarted by none other than his own brother, T'Chaka, who kills N'Jobu and leaves Erik behind. Erik grows to become an extraordinary black man: a brilliant student and graduate from MIT, he decides to join the special forces and later on the CIA, excelling in killing foreign leaders and overthrowing governments—training he later reveals to have followed to achieve his father's plans of global black liberation. Like Dan Freeman, the protagonist of Sam Greenlee's 1969 novel of black revolution *The Spook Who Sat by the Door*, Killmonger wants to turn the master's tools against the master's house. This and other references to revolutionary variations in the black avenger tradition pepper the film. Visual hints to the Black Panther Party flash in N'Jobu's apartment—the famous photo of Huey Newton holding gun and spear, an Emory Williams poster—tie the historical party's carefully designed political program and initiatives to N'Jobu's and Killmonger's cartoonish plans. With Wakanda as headquarters (he manages to wrest the crown from T'Challa after winning in ritual hand-to-hand combat), Killmonger means to support the wretched of the earth in a world insurrection that will lead the hidden country to become a global empire. This is the coming of the Black Code that Abbé Raynal warned against, the horrible prospect of a black nation that would behave the way white nations have. This is not what the Black Panthers had in mind, but it matters not: in twenty-first-century popular culture, their political legacy is forever tainted by their willingness to defend themselves, and all that surfaces here is Killmonger's unstoppable black rage. Killmonger cannot be allowed to be too sympathetic: he can ask the right questions but cannot possibly provide the right answers. His invocation of collective agency is but a fig leaf on what truly drives him: individual pain and ambition, the sorrow and anger of the cultural orphan. Killmonger is a patchwork of the black avengers that came before him: if his life history and master plan evoke American avengers, as a prince deprived of his birthright, he also hearkens back to the villains of revenge drama and, like one, dies stabbed in the side by his own kin, after proving that the mass movement he fostered was but an extension of his all-consuming personal ambition.

The curtailed pathos of Killmonger's death is tempered by the understanding that there is no other option for a "monstrous hybrid" like him. Not by chance is it the moment when he delivers his, and possibly the film's, best line: a spear stuck in his side, watching the only Wakandan sunset he will ever see, Killmonger chooses to die rather than be judged and likely imprisoned by the Wakandans. He tells T'Challa, "Bury me in the ocean with my ancestors who jumped from the ships, 'cause they knew death was better than bondage." The reference to the Middle Passage indirectly evokes that side of his family nobody talks about: his mother's. She is neither shown nor named; for all accounts and purposes, she serves as a mere womb, a way for N'Jobu to clone himself into a leaner, meaner version. Women in *Black Panther* stand out for their intelligence and strength. The king's sister, Shuri, is a genius scientist and inventor; his praetorian guard, the Dora Milaje, is composed exclusively of women; and interactions at the court suggest that, in Wakanda, gender equality is taken for granted. There are no Lucretias there. By contrast, the complete erasure of the mother in a black American context is especially jarring. Hortense Spillers demonstrates the importance of *partus sequitur ventrem*—the central principle of American slavery by which the condition of the enslaved mother is bestowed to her children, a gross anathema in patriarchal societies—to the black condition in the Americas. In this context "the African-American woman, the mother, the daughter, becomes historically the powerful and shadowy evocation of a cultural synthesis long evaporated—the law of the Mother—only and precisely because legal enslavement removed the African-American male not so much from sight as from mimetic view as a partner in the prevailing social fiction of the Father's name, the Father's law." In the system of slavery, black fathers were forcibly removed, but black women were ungendered, turned into slavemakers, their motherhood denied "at the very same time that it becomes the founding term of a human and social enactment." It is Spillers's argument that rather than seek to achieve patriarchal and gendered relations traditionally foreclosed to them, "it is the heritage of the mother that the African-American male must regain as an aspect of his own personhood—the power of 'yes' to the 'female' within."[17] Measure that exhortation against Killmonger's final moment: even where he appears to renounce his father's fairy tale, he still chooses the alleged purity of a defiant death over the defiance of black American life, honoring ancestors and ignoring his mother. Full personhood will have to wait.

In this partial genealogy of the black avenger trope, I have tried to suggest how certain narrative patterns are so engrained in our sense of history that they seem to erase what lies beyond their frame. It is a function of the black avenger narrative that we see the hero and imagine away the pedestal of ungendered flesh on which he stands. It is never too late to listen: for all that they rely on structures and arguments designed in fear of black agency, black avenger narratives also necessarily maintain black politics as a topic of conversation. There has never been any incompatibility between the visual celebration of blackness and the narrative undermining of black politics. Still, *Black Panther*, for all the gaping cracks in its narrative structure, can bring us back to grounded, earthly daydreams. Stepping out of the fairy tale and back into this other world, I caught myself dreaming of a different, unsung Pan-Africa, which connects African shepherds and black American city teens, not as extras, not as chorus to the protagonist, but as an international collective, scorning states, parties, and nations — the hushed network of those who walk so they don't have to bow. Call them a Black Panther Party; call them Kisama, like the early modern fugitives who, fleeing the oppression of African monarchs and European slave traders alike, decided that the collectives they would build would eschew the repeating patterns of power. In her 2018 book *Fugitive Modernities*, Jessica A. Krug proposes, "Instead of searching for narratives to explain the accretion of power, we can begin to listen to the fragmented ideologies that underwrote what we all too often dismiss as mere survival."[18] These ideologies tell tales that need neither heroes nor kings.

NOTES

PRELUDE

1. Alexander Weheliye defines the order of Man as "the western configuration of the human as synonymous with the heteromasculine, white, propertied, and liberal subject that renders all those who do not conform to these characteristics as exploitable nonhumans, literal legal no-bodies." *Habeas Viscus*, 135.

2. Brownmiller, *Against Our Will*, 387.

3. Livy, *History of Rome*, 1.58.5, 10

4. Diana C. Moses, "Livy's Lucretia," 50; Livy, *History of Rome*, 1.8.5–6.

5. Diana C. Moses, "Livy's Lucretia," 46, 47–49.

6. Fantham, "*Stuprum*," 118.

7. Ibid., 115–116.

8. Belsey, "Tarquin Dispossessed," 315, 318.

9. French, *Virtues of Vengeance*, 225.

10. Plutarch, "Crassus," 339.

11. Appian, *Civil Wars*, bk. 1, 225.

12. Florus, *Epitome of Roman History*, 243.

13. Aristotle, *Nicomachean Ethics*, 1133a.

14. Plutarch, "Crassus," 337.

15. Aristotle, *Aristotle's Politics*, 1255a.

16. See Price, *Maroon Societies*.

INTRODUCTION

1. A. O. Scott, "Black, the White."

2. Jewett and Lawrence, *American Monomyth*, xii.

3. Raynal, *Philosophical and Political History*, 466. This translation comes from the first English edition of Raynal's work.

4. Doyle, *Freedom's Empire*, 202, 2.

5. Weheliye, *Habeas Viscus*.

6. Lorde, "Master's Tools Will Never Dismantle."

7. Shaw, *Spartacus and the Slave Wars*, 18.

8. See Lemieux, "*Django Unchained*"; and Obenson, "I've Read Tarantino's 'Django Unchained.'"

9. Doyle, *Freedom's Empire*, 6.

10. See Cawelti, *Adventure, Mystery, and Romance*. Regarding black nationalism in the mid-1970s, see Simanga, *Amiri Baraka and the Congress*.

11. See Rojas, *From Black Power to Black Studies*; Ibram H. Rogers, *Black Campus Movement*; and Biondi, *Black Revolution on Campus*.

12. Starke, *Black Portraiture in American Fiction*, 225.

13. Bernier, *Characters of Blood*, 5.

14. Waters, *Racism on the Victorian Stage*.

15. Dillon, *New World Drama*, 33.

16. Gibbs, *Performing the Temple of Liberty*, 7.

17. Edwards, *Practice of Diaspora*, 14.

18. A. O. Scott, "Black, the White."

19. Trouillot, *Silencing the Past*, 96.

20. Aldon L. Nielsen, personal conversation, 2009, Pennsylvania State University, State College.

CHAPTER I. STILLBIRTH OF A NATION

1. See Turner, "'Romance' and the Novel"; Zurcher, "Serious Extravagance"; McKeon, *Origins of the English Novel*; Spengemann, "Earliest American Novel."

2. See Katherine M. Rogers, "Fact and Fiction"; and Lipking, "Confusing Matters."

3. Ferguson, "*Oroonoko*." See also Doyle's argument that Behn channels the typically post–English Revolution style of the secret history in *Oroonoko*: Doyle, *Freedom's Empire*, 100.

4. See Ferguson, "*Oroonoko*."

5. Aravamudan *Tropicopolitans*, 34.

6. Rose-Millar, *Witchcraft, the Devil, and Emotions*, 73.

7. Ferguson, "*Oroonoko*," 356.

8. Behn, *Oroonoko*, 25.

9. Doyle, *Freedom's Empire*, 9.

10. Aercke, "Theatrical Background in English Novels"; Fowler, "Dramatic and Narrative Techniques."

11. Fludernik, *Towards a "Natural" Narratology*, 130–131.

12. René Girard, *Violence and the Sacred*, 22.

13. Burnett, *Revenge in Attic and Later Tragedy*, 64.

14. See Bowers, *Elizabethan Revenge Tragedy*, 184; on Christianity and stage revenge, see also French, *Virtues of Vengeance*, 32.

15. Woodbridge, *English Revenge Drama*, 12.

16. Shakespeare, *Tragedy of Titus Andronicus*, 1.1.107–108.

17. On Xeque, see Asín, *Vida de Don Felipe*.

18. Shakespeare, *Tragedy of Titus Andronicus*, 5.3.204–207.

19. Bowers, *Elizabethan Revenge Tragedy*, 29, 129–130.

20. Dollimore, *Radical Tragedy*, 191–198.

21. Bartels, *Speaking of the Moor*, 18.

22. Habib, *Black Lives*, 7. See also Fryer, *Staying Power*.

23. Habib, *Black Lives*, 119; Bartels, *Speaking of the Moor*, 116.

24. Habib, *Black Lives*, 268–270.

25. [Dekker], *Lust's Dominion*, 5.5.3584–3586, 5.6.3713–3714 (hereafter cited in text).

26. Thorndike, *Tragedy*, 200–201.

27. Barthelemy, *Black Face, Maligned Race*, 105.

28. Hughes, *Versions of Blackness*, xxi.

29. Bartels, *Speaking of the Moor*, 118–119.

30. Regarding the argument about the play's revision, see Ayres, "Revision of *Lust's Dominion*."

31. Clare, *Drama of the English Republic*.

32. William Davenant to John Thurloe, 1656, cited in Clare, *Drama of the English Republic*, 30, 7.

33. Julián Juderías, qtd. in Powell, *Tree of Hate*, 11.

34. Mignolo, "Afterword," 322.

35. Jean Howard, qtd. in Vaughan, *Performing Blackness on English Stages*, 55.

36. Barthelemy, *Black Face, Maligned Race*, 107.

37. Vaughan, *Performing Blackness on English Stages*, 2, 4.

38. See Casellas, "Enemy Within."

39. Woodbridge, *English Revenge Drama*, 51.

40. Bartels, *Speaking of the Moor*, 136–137.

41. Vaughan, *Performing Blackness on English Stages*, 56.

42. Bartels, *Speaking of the Moor*, 136.

43. Vaughan, *Performing Blackness on English Stages*, 54.

44. See, for example, John Milton on hereditary monarchy: "To say, as is usual, the King hath as good right to his Crown and dignitie, as any man to his inheritance, is to make the Subject no better then the Kings slave, his chattell, or his possession that may be bought and sould." *Tenure of Kings and Magistrates*, 12. See also Doyle, *Freedom's Empire*.

45. Shaw argues, "In the vast span of time before the mid-eighteenth century, no one cared about Spartacus or even mentioned him as an especially important historical character. He merited nothing more than perfunctory notices in the standard histories of Rome." While Shaw's chronology is qualitatively accurate, the earlier paragraph significantly tempers his assessment. *Spartacus and the Slave Wars*, 19.

46. Tomlinson, "Restoration English History Plays," 561.

47. See Lynch, *Roger Boyle*.

48. See, notably, Laura Brown, "Romance of Empire."

49. Artabanes's name, one could argue, is to La Calprenède's Artaban (*Cleopatra*) as Oroonoko is to La Calprenède's Oroondates (*Cassandra*).

50. [Boyle], *Parthenissa*, bk. 3, pp. 89, 269.

51. Morgan, *Rise of the Novel*, 35.

52. [Boyle], *Parthenissa*, 85.

53. Aristotle, *Aristotle's Politics*, 1.1255a.

54. See Pagden, *Fall of Natural Man*.

55. [Boyle], *Parthenissa*, 86.

56. Ibid., 87.

57. Plutarch, "Crassus," 337.

58. See Craton, *Testing the Chains*, 67–71. See also Patterson, "Slavery and Slave Revolts."

59. By 1650 England had population settlements in many Caribbean islands (Saint Kitts, Barbados, Nevis, and the Bahamas, notably) and along the eastern seaboard in North America.

60. The Earl of Shaftesbury was one of the lords protector of the American colony of Carolina. He had shares in a plantation in Barbados, in the Royal African Company, and in a slave ship, the *Rose*. See Spurr, "Shaftesbury and the Seventeenth Century."

61. In 1681 the Earl of Shaftesbury led a parliamentary coalition that came to be known as the Whigs. Its goal was to oppose the potential accession of James, Duke of York, to the throne. James was a known Catholic and close ally to Louis XIV, and many feared that his reign would spell disaster for English Protestants. James became king in 1685. The long political battle between James II's supporters and their opponents eventually led to the Glorious Revolution in 1688 and James's ouster and his replacement by the "Protestant Defender" Dutch stadtholder, William of Orange.

62. Locke, *Two Treatises on Government*, 2.8.85.

63. Ibid., 2.3.17.

64. Farr, "Locke, Natural Law."

65. MacPherson, *Political Theory of Possessive Individualism*, 269.

66. See Ashcraft, *Revolutionary Politics*, 200–205; Farr, "So Vile and Miserable"; Hersch, "On James Farr's 'So Vile.'"

67. Hughes, *Versions of Blackness*, xviii.

68. Thorndike, *Tragedy*, 201.

69. Behn, *Abdelazer*, 1.1.39 (hereafter cited in text); Thomas, "This Thing of Darkness," 27.

70. Hughes, *Theatre of Aphra Behn*, 64.

71. Barthelemy, *Black Face, Maligned Race*, 116.

72. Hughes, *Theatre of Aphra Behn*, 60–61.

73. Thomas, "This Thing of Darkness," 22.

74. Hughes, *Theatre of Aphra Behn*, 61.

75. Rymer, *Tragedies of the Last Age*, 37.

76. Dryden, "Heads of an Answer," 191, 188–189.

77. Barthelemy, *Black Face, Maligned Race*, 112.

78. Zarrack says, "swear to advance me; / And by yo'n setting sun, this hand, and this / Shall rid you of a tyrant." [Dekker], *Lust's Dominion*, 5.5.

79. Beach, "Global Slavery," 425, 424.

80. Behn, *Oroonoko*, 7, 8.

81. Todd, *Secret Life of Aphra Behn*, 434.

82. Behn, *Oroonoko*, 9; Hughes, *Theatre of Aphra Behn*, 56.

83. Campbell, *Wonder and Science*, 262.

84. Figlerowicz, "Frightful Spectacles," 322.

85. Behn, *Oroonoko*, 19.

86. Poitevin, "Inventing Whiteness," 69.

87. Behn, *Oroonoko*, 13.

88. Vaughan, *Performing Blackness on English Stages*, 15.

89. Figlerowicz, "Frightful Spectacles," 333.

90. Behn, *Oroonoko*, 36, 40.

91. Ibid., 32.

92. Behn, *Oroonoko*, 30.

93. Andrade, "White Skin, Black Masks," 202.

94. [Castiglione], *Courtyer*, 23 (C. iii).

95. Jennifer Richards, "Assumed Simplicity and the Critique," 461.

96. Ibid., 482.

97. Andrade, "White Skin, Black Masks," 198.

98. Behn, *Oroonoko*, 27, 26.

99. Ibid., 32, 33, 34.

100. Ibid., 41, 42.

101. Turner, "'Romance' and the Novel," 67.

102. Behn, *Oroonoko*, 32, 33.

103. The first hint at the role of justice in the afterlife is brought up by Oroonoko's grandfather, who tells him that "death, that common revenger of all injuries, would soon even the account between him and a feeble old man." This somewhat Christian-sounding argument, which appears to go counter to Oroonoko's own religious beliefs, should remind us that the narrative about Oroonoko's past is clearly presented as a secondhand performance by Behn's narrator.

104. Behn, *Oroonoko*, 60, 61, 65.

105. See Doyle, *Freedom's Empire*, 113–114.

106. See Turner, "'Romance' and the Novel," 76n44.

107. Behn, *Oroonoko*, 52. Note that here the narrator does not account for her knowledge of the speech's contents, although in other instances when she reports on a scene she could not have witnessed firsthand, she usually indicates her source.

108. Doyle, *Freedom's Empire*, 199.

109. Lee, *Lucius Junius Brutus*, 19–20.

110. Behn, *Oroonoko*, 53–54, 56.

111. Ibid., 63.

112. Laura Brown, "Romance of Empire," 40.

113. Behn, *Oroonoko*, 60.

114. Thompson, *Performing Race and Torture*, 73, 69.

115. Behn, *Oroonoko*, 59, 64.

116. Ibid., 36.

117. Andrade, "White Skin, Black Masks."

118. René Girard, *Violence and the Sacred*, 79–80.

119. Hughes, *Versions of Blackness*, xiv.

120. René Girard, *Violence and the Sacred*, 65, 77, 40.

CHAPTER 2. GENII OF THE NATIONS

1. Whaley, "On a Young Lady's Weeping," in Whaley, *Collection of Poems*, 92–93.

2. See Sypher, *Guinea's Captive Kings*, 116; Oldfield, "Eighteenth Century Background"; and Kowaleski-Wallace, *British Slave Trade*, 186.

3. Waters, *Racism on the Victorian Stage*, 15.

4. Southerne, *Oroonoko*, 5.4.

5. See Tissier, *Les spectacles à Paris*.

6. "Une tragédie médiocre. . . . Quel prestige a pu produire un tel enthousiasme? Comment se fait-il qu'un drame, reçu froidement il y a près de quarante ans, obtient aujourd'hui tant de suffrages?" [Duchosal], "Reprise de *Spartacus*," 81. Unless otherwise noted, all translations are my own.

7. "Ces autorités célèbres en imposèrent à la multitude. . . . [Ils] avaient publié que *Spartacus* étoit un *ouvrage estimable*, et tous les hommes superficiels, les ignorans, les sots, les enthousiastes répétèrent et répètent encore: *Spartacus est un ouvrage estimable*." "Observations sur le Spartacus," 101.

8. Seeber, "Oroonoko in France"; Hoffmann, *Le Nègre romantique*.

9. Colley, *Britons*, 46.

10. See Hill, "Norman Yoke."

11. According to Eustace Budgell, Boyle wrote the poem expressly for the king, who kept the only known copy. How Budgell, who was born in 1686, would have been privy to its contents is a mystery. *Memoirs of the Lives*, 91–92.

12. "Genius of True English-Men."

13. Colley, *Britons*, 5.

14. Gerald Newman, *Rise of English Nationalism*, 139.

15. Bell, *Cult of the Nation*, 95.

16. Gerald Newman, *Rise of English Nationalism*, 127.

17. Roach, *Cities of the Dead*, 153.

18. Dillon, *New World Drama*, 3, 4.

19. Wilson, *Island Race*, 4; Roach, *Cities of the Dead*, 155.

20. [Wharton], *True Briton*, 1.

21. Markley, "Sentimentality as Performance."

22. Halttunen, "Humanitarianism and the Pornography," 332.

23. Montesquieu, *Persian Letters*, letter CI.

24. Montesquieu, *Montesquieu's Considerations in the Causes*, 173.

25. Gerald Newman, *Rise of English Nationalism*, 46. About the transition from Anglophilia to Anglomania, see Dziembowski, *Un nouveau patriotisme français*, 29–34.

26. Russell, *Voltaire, Dryden and Heroic Tragedy*, 38.

27. Voltaire, "Discourse on Tragedy," 200.

28. See Hughes, "Rape on the Restoration Stage."

29. Airey, "Lucrece Narratives," 115.

30. Voltaire, "Discourse on Tragedy," 200.

31. Lee's play was also seen as a commentary on the deep strife that followed the Popish Plot in England. The play was censored after a few representations in 1681, but it is difficult to read it as a Whig take on the events: Lee's Brutus is presented simultaneously as a ruthless opportunist who does not hesitate to fake visions to impress and influence the mob and—once in power—as an intransigent republican extremist, who orders the execution of his son even as the Senate makes clear it does not require it. See Loftis, introd. to *Lucius Junius Brutus*; Hayne, "All Language Then Is Vile"; and Airey, "Lucrece Narratives."

32. Voltaire, "Letter to Lyttleton," qtd. in John Churchton Collins, *Bolingbroke*, 240.

33. Voltaire, *Brutus*, 307.

34. Lee, *Lucius Junius Brutus*, 12.

35. Bell, *Cult of the Nation*, 41, 48, 47.

36. "L'Anglais . . . dépend peu de l'Opinion, et dans la Conversation il préfère le plaisir de dire la Vérité, à celui de dire des choses obligeantes aux gens à qui il parle. . . . Le François compte pour beaucoup l'Opinion des autres, et il cherche d'en donner une bonne de soi, aussi bien que de render les autres contens d'eux-mêmes; de là viennent tant de Douceurs, tant de Choses flateuses qu'il dit dans la Conversation. . . . L'Angleterre est un païs de Liberté et d'Impunité: Chacun y est ce qu'il a envie d'être, et de la viennent, sans doute, tant de Caractères extraordinairesl tant de Héros en mal comme en bien, qu'on voit parmi les Anglois. C'est aussi ce qui leur donne une certaine Liberté de Pensées et de Sentimens, qui ne contribue pas peu au Bon Sens qui se trouve chez eux, qui s'y trouve assez generalement, pour mettre quelque différence entre cette Nation et la plûpart des autres." [Muralt], *Lettres sur les Anglois*, 340–341.

37. First developed in Herder, *Auch eine Philosophie*.

38. "Que la Nature soit si bien imitée que l'Art ne paroisse point, qu'on oublie le Poëte. . . . Le Poëte s'y fait toujours entendre par dessus l'Acteur . . . il détrompe le Spectateur à tout moment par ses pensées recherchées, et l'oblige malgré lui à s'apercevoir qu'il assiste à une Comédie." "On diroit qu'ils sont accoutumez [*sic*] à faire un jeu de l'Honnêteté et de la Vertu, et qu'ils ne la croient en sa place que sur le Theatre." "Dès là son plus grand soin est de plaire à la foule." [Muralt], *Lettres sur les Anglois*, 42–43, 60, 39. Voltaire himself would recognize as much in a private letter to Lord Lyttelton, in which he argued, "Your nation two hundred years since is used to a wild scene, to a crowd of tumultuous events to an emphatical poetry mixed with low and comical expressions. . . . And give me leave to say that the taste of your politest countrymen differs not much in point of tragedy from the taste of the mob at beargardens." "Letter to Lyttleton," qtd. in John Churchton Collins, *Bolingbroke*, 240.

39. "J'y ai vû tenailler un homme en croix pendant une demi heure. Il me semble que les Poëtes qui ont le vrai Genie, et qui sçavent émouvoir, ne doivent pas avoir recours à des tenailles." [Muralt], *Lettres sur les Anglois*, 59.

40. On the role of torture in the play, see Thompson, "When Race Is Colored."

41. Dziembowski, *Un nouveau patriotisme français*, 22; "Les Auteurs Anglois de toute espèce manquent toujours de goût." [Le Blanc], *Lettres d'un François*, 246.

42. "Il est vrai qu'avec ce défaut on trouve dans les pièces des bons auteurs un

puissant intérêt, qui résulte de la fidélité avec laquelle la Nature y est peinte. . . . Cette Tragédie cependant ne seroit pas soufferte sur notre Théâtre, à cause du bas Comique dont elle est bigarrée. . . . L'Auteur y a peint des traits les plus touchans et les plus forts, la première de toutes les vertus; et disons-le à l'honneur des Anglois, celle qui caractérise le plus leur Nation, l'humanité." [Le Blanc], *Lettres d'un François*, 263.

43. Dillon, *New World Drama*, 37, 49, 36, 39.

44. "Oronoko a plû à Londres, habillé à l'Angloise: Pour plaire à Paris, j'ai crû qu'il lui falloit un habit François." [Laplace], *Oronoko*, viii. I refer to the protagonist in Laplace's adaptation as Oronoko.

45. Hoffmann, *Le Nègre romantique*, 59.

46. Christopher L. Miller, *French Atlantic Triangle*, 104.

47. Ibid., 14.

48. "Laisse vivre ce cruel. . . . Qu'il sçache, qu'on peut être esclave, et être vertueux!" [Laplace], *Oronoko*, 64.

49. "On en arrive à la conclusion absurde que Laplace a fait d'Imoinda à la fois une Blanche et une Négresse, c'est-à-dire en fin de compte ni l'une ni l'autre." Hoffmann, *Le Nègre romantique*, 61.

50. "Exemple admirable d'amour et de reconnaissance, pour le sang de son bienfaicteur! Qu'on juge combine Oronoko y fut sensible!" Hoffmann, *Le Nègre romantique*, 15.

51. Seeber, "Oroonoko in France."

52. "La pièce historique la plus populaire du dix-huitième siècle." Brenner, *L'Histoire nationale*, 251.

53. Dziembowski, *Un nouveau patriotisme français*, 477, 91. On Britishness, see Colley, *Britons*.

54. Andrew S. Curran, *Anatomy of Blackness*, 141, 12. On Buffon, see chapter 2, "Sameness and Science, 1730–1750."

55. Bell, *Cult of the Nation*, 45, 47, 86–87. 56. [Hawkesworth], *Oroonoko*, v.

57. Gerald Newman, *Rise of English Nationalism*, 117.

58. [Hawkesworth], *Oroonoko*.

59. Gerald Newman, *Rise of English Nationalism*, viii.

60. Sypher, *Guinea's Captive Kings*, 121.

61. Andrew S. Curran, *Anatomy of Blackness*, 10.

62. "J'ai vengé ma race et moi." Saint-Lambert, *Ziméo*, 235.

63. Bell, *Cult of the Nation*, 95.

64. Shaw, "Spartacus before Marx," 11, 12.

65. "Porte à mon fils ce fer et ma suprême loi. / Albin, dis-lui, qu'il venge et l'Univers et moi." "Il vécut avec gloire, et meurt en homme libre." Saurin, *Spartacus*, 1.3, 5.8.

66. Futrell, "Seeing Red," 84.

67. "Qu'étoit Rome en effet? Qui furent vos ancêtres? / Un vil ramas de cerfs échappés à leurs maîtres, / De femmes et de biens, perfidies ravisseurs." "Du tems des Scipions . . . j'aurois pû l'accepter; / Rome étoit digne alors qu'on s'en fit adopter." "Quoi! Son ambition, à qui rien n'est sacré / Traîne en captivité le fils avec la mere. . . . La loi de l'Univers: c'est malheur aux vaincus." Saurin, *Spartacus*, 3.3, 4.3, 3.4.

68. "Cet obstacle éternel que mon pays t'oppose, / Cet invincible mur qu'il éleve entre nous." Saurin, *Spartacus*, 2.4.

69. "Il est bien plus beau de se créer un nom que de porter, quand ce seroit avec honneur, celui de ses ayeux." "Qu'est-ce qu'un homme qui veut faire le Bonheur de l'Univers? . . . Un délire Encyclopédique." [Fréron], "Lettre VII," 162, 163. Somewhat unaccountably, Saurin makes Spartacus the son of Arioviste or, in some editions, of Argétorix, both historical Germanic chiefs, rather than a Thracian. One contemporary French critic took exception to this characterization: "Il n'en eût pas plus coûté . . . de placer le lieu de sa naissance dans quelque partie des Gaules, et sur tout de ne point charger un Gaulois (*Noricus*, lieutenant de *Spartacus*, et Chef des Gaulois Insubriens) du rolle [*sic*] infâme de traître. Ce sont de petits égards qu'il convient d'avoir pour sa Nation; il est rare qu'elle n'en soit pas reconnoissante." "It would not have cost more . . . to locate his birthplace in some part of Gaul, or not to weigh a Gaul (Noricus, Spartacus's lieutenant and chief of the Insubrian Gauls) with the despicable role of the traitor. One must show such consideration for one's nation; it rarely fails to be grateful in return." La Porte, "Lettre XI," 242.

70. "Quelqu'avantagé de la nature que je le suppose." "Je voulois tracer le portrait . . . d'un homme, en un mot, qui fût grand pour le bien des hommes, et non pour leur Malheur." "Combien de jeunes Princes, échauffés par leur lecture, et séduits par l'éclat d'un faux héroïsme, ont cause de désolation et ravage, pour marcher sur les pas des Alexandre et des César?" Saurin, preface to *Spartacus*, xiii–xiv.

71. Dziembowski, *Un nouveau patriotisme français*, 496.

72. "À l'anglaise"; Voltaire, "A M. Saurin," 73.

73. Voltaire, *Philosophical Dictionary from the French*, 104–105.

74. Ibid., 107.

75. Voltaire notably wrote, "None but the blind can doubt that the whites, the negroes, the Albinoes, the Hottentots, the Laplanders, the Chinese, the Americans, are races entirely different." *Philosophy of History*, 5.

76. Andrew S. Curran, *Anatomy of Blackness*, 14.

77. Voltaire, *Essai sur les moeurs*, qtd. in Andrew S. Curran, *Anatomy of Blackness*, 147.

78. Price, *Maroon Societies*, 1n.

79. Kent, "Palmares," 187.

80. See Carey, "Stronger Muse."

81. Davis, introd. to *Virgil's Eclogues*, ix.

82. Eversole, "Collins and the End," 20.

83. William Collins, preface to *Persian Eclogues*.

84. Bergstrom, "Form and the Pleasures," 240.

85. Stuart Curran, *Poetic Form and British Romanticism*, 96.

86. Chatterton, "Heccar and Gaira." See also Dellarosa, *Talking Revolution*, 143–150.

87. Chatterton, "Heccar and Gaira," 58.

88. French, *Virtues of Vengeance*, 80.

89. Franklin, "From Benjamin Franklin."

90. Hulme, *Colonial Encounters*, 99–100.

91. [Day and Bicknell], *Dying Negro*, 23–24.

92. On said news story, see Walvin, *England, Slaves and Freedom*, 41–43.

93. [Day and Bicknell], *Dying Negro*, vii–viii.

94. See Colley, *Britons*, 354–355; Gibbs, *Performing the Temple of Liberty*, 57–59.

95. Gibbs, *Performing the Temple of Liberty*, 65.

96. "Jamaica," 332; [Mulligan], "Lovers," 23.

97. Carey, *British Abolitionism and the Rhetoric*, 74.

98. [Mulligan], "Slave," 6.

99. On Rushton's life, see Dellarosa, *Talking Revolution*, 5–14.

100. "Advertisement," in [Rushton], *West-Indian Eclogues*.

101. See Dellarosa, *Talking Revolution*, 156–157.

102. [Rushton], *West-Indian Eclogues*, 20, 21, 24.

103. "Art. VII. *West-Indian Eclogues*."

104. Long, *History of Jamaica*, 2:442–444.

105. "West-Indian Eclogues," *Critical Review*, 435.

106. Dellarosa, *Talking Revolution*, 169. On the rhetoric of sensibility, see Carey, *British Abolitionism and the Rhetoric*.

107. "West Indian Eclogues," *General Magazine and Impartial Review*, 200.

108. Gould, *Barbaric Traffic*, 13–14.

109. Fergus, *Revolutionary Emancipation*, 38.

110. [Mulligan], "Lovers," 199, 200.

111. Hughes, "Rape on the Restoration Stage," 233, 235.

112. See Litvack, *Le droit du seigneur*.

113. Boussuge, "La présentation.

114. This line is from Thomas Holcroft's adaptation of Beaumarchais: *Follies of a Day*, 2–3.

115. Beaumarchais, *Follies of a Day*, 92.

116. Doniger, *Bedtrick*, 274.

117. The final act of Beaumarchais's play ends with a song, all characters taking a turn. The singing is left out of Holcroft's adaptation, including the play's famous last lines: "Or Messieurs la Comédie, / Que l'on juge en cet instant, / Sauf erreur, nous peint la vie / Du bon people qui l'entend. / Qu'on l'opprime; il peste, il crie; / Il s'agite en cent façons; / Tout finit par des chansons." Beaumarchais, *La folle journée*, 223.

118. "De vingt Rois que l'on encense, / Le trépas brise l'autel; / Et Voltaire est immortel." Beaumarchais, *La folle journée*, 222.

119. Georges Danton, qtd. in Litvack, *Le droit du seigneur*, 52.

120. Ibid., 35.

121. "Mary le More," "The Maniac," and "Mary's Death," in Rushton, *Poems*, 52–55, 56–59, 60–63.

122. Rushton, "Mary's Death," in Rushton, *Poems*, 61.

123. Leslie, *New History of Jamaica*, 73, 78–79.

124. See Fergus, *Revolutionary Emancipation*, 38–41.

125. *Wrongs of Almoona*. In *Peter Newby* Malone identifies Peter Newby as the author.

126. *Wrongs of Almoona*, 2, 44, 49, 51, 65.

127. See Tomko, "Abolition Poetry, National Identity," 39, 38.

128. William Cowper, "The Negro's Complaint," in Cowper, *Poems*, 373–376. Commissioned by the Society for Effecting the Abolition of the Slave Trade, the poem was widely distributed and even put to music. See Cowper, *Poems of William Cowper*, 283.

129. [Rushton], *West-Indian Eclogues*: "A short time before that invasion the tyrant, his master, had barbarously torn her from him"; "having observed his cruel tyrant in the Spanish line, he flew to the place here he fought" (30–31, note *s*).

130. [Rushton], *West-Indian Eclogues*, 20–21.

131. Ibid., 20–22.

132. Dellarosa, *Talking Revolution*, 156.

133. [Rushton], *West-Indian Eclogues*, 31–32, note *x*.

134. Wilson, *Island Race*, 130.

135. Dillon, *New World Drama*, 131.

136. See Tomko, "Abolition Poetry, National Identity."

137. Dziembowski, *Un nouveau patriotisme français*, 9.

CHAPTER 3. A TALE OF TWO AVENGERS

1. Bell, *Cult of the Nation*, 132, 125.

2. [Dessalines], "Proclamation," 193.

3. [Byron], *Ode to Napoleon Buonaparte*, l.3.

4. Jean-Joseph Pechméja wrote the section on slavery in the first edition of Raynal. Following a dispute with Raynal, he did not participate in later editions of the book, but his words remained, and other writers—notably Denis Diderot—added considerably to them in the second edition. On the topic, see Bénot, "Diderot, Pechméja, Raynal et l'anticolonialisme"; and Goggi, "Diderot-Raynal."

5. Raynal, *Philosophical and Political History*, 466.

6. Mercier, *Memoirs*, 171, 172.

7. See Marcellesi, "Louis-Sébastien Mercier," 253.

8. I am borrowing Jenson's concept of "kidnapped narratives": "the liminal category of texts by empowered speakers in contexts of communicative suppression, including not only the deposed leader [Louverture] in his dungeon, but Dessalines proclaiming sovereignty in a slave-holding international domain." *Beyond the Slave Narrative*, 31.

9. Moreau de Saint-Méry, *Description*, 68–99.

10. In the section of his book dedicated to *affranchis* (freedmen), Moreau de Saint-Méry declares them "more universally known as *Gens-de-couleur* or *Sang-mêlés* (mixed bloods), though the latter denomination, taken literally, also designates enslaved negroes"; by Moreau's own insane taxonomy, they were black by 2 out of 128 total degrees (*Description*, 68). Yet *mulâtre*, rather than *sang-mêlé*, is the term used interchangeably with *gens de couleur* and *affranchi* in the texts of the Haitian Revolution. I use *mulatto* to emphasize racial status and *gens de couleur* to designate more generally freeborn and freed people of African ancestry during the ancien régime. After the abolition of slavery by the French Republic on February 4, 1794, the terms

anciens libres and *nouveaux libres* were used to designate those whose legal free status predated or followed the abolition. Saint-Domingue's complex racial laws distinguished between free mixed people and free blacks with no Europeans in their family line, and the prejudice carried over into the colored and black populations. Gen. André Rigaud himself repeatedly writes of *"gens de couleur* and free Negroes," himself equating the first category with people of mixed racial ancestry exclusively (*Mémoire du général de brigade*, 3). While I use these terms in reference to texts and periods in which they were used, I share Marlene Daut's opinion that taking this terminology for granted perpetuates the racializing narrative "that had the ultimate effect of subordinating the Haitian Revolution to the French and American Revolutions." *Tropics of Haiti*, 5.

11. On the influence of Creole literature on notions of Frenchness in the revolutionary era, see, notably, Reid, *Families in Jeopardy*.

12. Garrigus, *Before Haiti*, 159.

13. Peabody, *There Are No Slaves*, 137, 106.

14. See Garraway, *Libertine Colony*, especially 195–239.

15. Long, *History of Jamaica*, 2:335. On Moreau de Saint-Méry's views on the alleged infertility of mixed-race people, see also Garraway, *Libertine Colony*, 268–272.

16. Garrigus, *Before Haiti*, 169–170.

17. Daut, *Tropics of Haiti*, 51.

18. Carlyle, *On Heroes*, 47.

19. See, for example, Hunnings, "Spartacus in Nineteenth-Century England."

20. On the evolution of Mercier's position on black revolution, see Marcellesi, "Louis-Sébastien Mercier."

21. For discussions of the "tragedy" of the Haitian Revolution, see James, *Black Jacobins*; David Scott, *Conscripts of Modernity*, and, more recently, Glick, *Black Radical Tragic*.

22. Garraway, "Print, Publics, and the Scene," 82.

23. Jenson, *Beyond the Slave Narrative*, 70.

24. As Philippe Girard notes, lack of official evidence suggests that Louverture "was never formally freed in the manner required by law." *Toussaint Louverture*, 55.

25. See Cauna, "De Bréda à Cormier," in Cauna, *Toussaint Louverture, le grand précurseur*, 107–114; and Cauna, "Dessalines esclave de Toussaint?"

26. Garrigus, *Before Haiti*, 236.

27. "Un feu secret couve dans l'Europe entière, et présage une révolution prochaine, que les Potentats pourroient et devroient render calme et douce. Oui, le cri de la liberté retentit dans les deux Mondes, il ne faut qu'un Othello, qu'un Padrejan, pour réveiller dans l'âme des Nègres le sentiment de leurs inaliénables droits. Voyant alors que les sang-mêlés ne peuvent les protéger contre leurs despotes, ils tourneront peut-être leurs fers contre tous, une explosion soudaine fera soudain tomber leurs chaînes; et qui de nous osera les condamner, s'il se suppose à leur place?" Grégoire, *Mémoire en faveur des gens*, 34. Padréjean was a leader of an ill-fated 1679 slave revolt in Saint-Domingue.

28. Garrigus, *Before Haiti*, 241–242.

29. Grégoire, *Mémoire en faveur des gens*, 38.

30. See Dubois, *Avengers of the New World*, 135–137, 105–106.

31. The story of the ceremony at Bwa Kayiman is the mother of all anecdotes of the Haitian Revolution. See Geggus's investigation of that anecdote in "Bois Caïman Ceremony."

32. Rigaud, *Mémoire du général de brigade*, 16; Popkin, *You Are All Free*, 113–120.

33. See Philippe Girard, *Toussaint Louverture*, 132–134. See Gainot, "Le général Laveaux."

34. A few years Laveaux's senior, Toussaint affectionately referred to him as his father (*mon père*).

35. Henry Perroud was an agent for a Bordeaux trading house in Saint-Domingue. Mandar-Argeaut claims he participated in persecutions against people of color in Port-de-Paix in 1791. [Mandar-Argeaut], *Quelques éclaircissemens*, 10. It bears noting that, according to Haitian historian Beaubrun Ardouin, Villatte was black. He was also, like Louverture, an *ancien libre*, that is, he did not owe his freedom to the 1794 abolition of slavery.

36. Aravamudan, *Tropicopolitans*, 292.

37. Gragnon-Lacoste, *Toussaint Louverture*, 19.

38. See Fouchard, *Le théâtre à Saint Domingue*, 251. For discussions of theater in Saint-Domingue, see Dayan, *Haiti, History, and the Gods*; and Camier and Dubois, "Voltaire et Zaïre," 40–41.

39. The letter is known as the "Proclamation of Camp Turel." See Dubois, *Avengers of the New World*, 176.

40. "Il avait souvent les yeux sur cette page où Raynal parait annoncer le libérateur qui devait arracher à ses fers une grande portion de l'espèce humaine. Il revenait sans cesse à cette prédiction dont il était si frappé." [Voici, sur Toussaint].

41. Dubroca, *Life of Toussaint Louverture*; Rainsford, *Historical Account*. Pamphile de Lacroix, a veteran of the Leclerc campaign, published an account of the speech in his *Mémoires pour servir*. As Marlene Daut notes, Lacroix's book "did more to inflect understandings of the Haitian Revolution than any other written work until that of C. L. R. James." *Tropics of Haiti*, 55.

42. Aravamudan, *Tropicopolitans*, 301–302, 15.

43. Anderson, *Imagined Communities*, 36.

44. David Scott, *Conscripts of Modernity*, 114, 115.

45. Jenson, *Beyond the Slave Narrative*, 49. In *Haitian Revolutionary Studies* Geggus also discusses this source and its possible accuracy.

46. For the claim, see [Mandar-Argeaut], *Quelques éclaircissemens*, 18.

47. Dubroca, *Life of Toussaint Louverture*, 17.

48. Lacroix, *Mémoires pour servir*, 309.

49. Daut, *Tropics of Haiti*, 82.

50. See Cleves, *Reign of Terror in America*.

51. "Réclamation des nègres libres." On the alleged authorship of the text, see Brette, "Les gens de couleur libres," 397–398.

52. "Le nègre est issue d'un sang pur; le mulâtre, au contraire, est issu d'un sang mélange; c'est un compose du noir et du blanc, c'est une espece abâtardie. D'après

cette vérité, il est aussi evident que le nègre est au-dessus du mulâtre, qu'il l'est que l'or pur est au-dessus de l'or mélange." *"Réclamation des nègres libres,"* 22.

53. "Ce préjugé de la couleur, il faut le dire, n'est pas même celui des Blancs seuls. Le Nègre libre est regardé avec mépris par le Quarteron esclave. Au-dessous de lui par la loi, mais plus près de son maître par la couleur, il se croit supérieur à lui. . . . Ainsi, une sorte de fierté qui s'accroît à mesure que la nuance s'affoiblit, tend à donner une nouvelle force à se préjugé qui est le ressort caché de la machine coloniale. Il peut être *adouci*, mais non pas *anéanti*; le temps peut, avec sa lime sourde, détruire ce qu'il a de grossier, mais si on le coupe, la machine se brisera avec fracas." [PUCPDDLM], *Observations d'un habitant*, 21–22.

54. "Je compris que je ne réusssirais à bien affermir la confiance que m'avaient accordée les noirs, qu'en m'adjoignant en effet un homme d'une autre couleur. . . . Je pris donc mon parti, et fit reconnaître pour adjoint au general gouverneur, le brave, le fidèle, *Toussaint Louverture*." [Laveaux], *Saint Domingue*, 90.

55. "Ce noir, ce Spartacus prédit par Raynal, dont la destinée était de venger les outrages faits à sa race." Dubroca, *Life of Toussaint Louverture*, 17.

56. See, notably, Raimond: "Les hommes de couleur et tous les citoyens blancs et noirs de la partie du Nord." The people of color and all the white and black citizens in the Northern region, bitter against Laveaux, held Villatte's party dear, and a great many of them followed him." *Rapport de Julien Raimond*, 2.

57. [Laveaux], *Saint Domingue*, 90.

58. "En cette occasion, au moment d'un carnage bien préparé, le valeureux Toussaint Louverture a démontré une telle force de caractère, de prudence et d'activité, que l'on est force de reconnaître en lui ce grand Homme annoncé par un sublime Auteur politique, devoir naître un jour pour le Bonheur de ses Frères et le salut de son pays." [Perroud], *L'Ordonnateur de Saint Domingue*, n6.

59. "La seduction la plus perfide fut employee pour tromper la facile crédulité de quelques Africains de la garnison; on les travaillait au meurtre en leur disant qu'on venait de débarquer des boucants de chaînes pour les echaîner et les remettre dans l'esclavage! . . . A cet effroi, ces hommes, les armes à la main, se soulèvent, marchent, courent, menacent, forcent les portes des magasins de la République, ouvrent les armoires, défoncent les barils de farine et de salaison, s'emparent des postes, mettent le Gouverneur, moi et les Blancs, plusieurs fois en joue, et allaient donner le signal de la mort, si le valeureux Toussait Louverture, ce génie africain, indiqué par un grand Auteur philosophe, comme devant être le sauveur de son pays, n'était accouru, le sabre à la main, pour réprimer ces farouches satellites, indignes du nom de soldat." [Perroud], *Précis des derniers troubles*, 15. The memoir reached France on the same ship in which Villatte was exiled. See Gainot, "Le général Laveaux." Beaubrun Ardouin argues that Perroud's text was backdated and actually written shortly before the ship departed Saint-Domingue. Ardouin, *Études sur l'histoire d'Haïti*, 3:200–201.

60. Americans were also familiar with Raynal's text, which one can find quoted and mentioned in U.S. news, but in the slaveholding context of the United States, audiences likely did not appreciate the reference quite the same way.

61. Laveaux and Perroud, "To the United States," 3.

62. "Qu'on suive les plans proscripteurs de *Laveaux*... qu'ils exterminent jusqu'au dernier homme de couleur." *Correspondance des déportés*, 3.

63. Cotterel, *Esquisse historique*, 38n1.

64. Daut, *Tropics of Haiti*, 101; Rigaud, *Mémoire du général de brigade*, iii–iv.

65. "Ce même homme leur déclare aujourd'hui une guerre aussi cruelle qu'elle est injuste." Rigaud, *Mémoire du général de brigade*, iii.

66. "N'oublie pas que tant que tu verras des hommes de couleur parmi les tiens, tu ne seras pas libre." Ardouin, *Études sur l'histoire d'Haïti*, 2:459.

67. Daut, *Tropics of Haiti*, 58–59.

68. "Dans ses proclamations répandues dans toute l'île et transportées au-delà du continent, Laveaux appellee Toussaint-l'Ouverture, *l'homme prédit par l'abbé Raynal*." Barbault-Royer, *Du gouvernement de Saint Domingue*, 49.

69. Cotterel, *Santhonax et Laveaux repoussés*; Cotterel, *Le Gouvernement de Saint Domingue*.

70. "Leur acharnement à poursuivre les hommes de couleur." Cotterel, *Esquisse historique*, viii.

71. "Lorsque l'illustre Raynal prédît un sauveur de l'afrique [*sic*], il était loin de croire que vous en prévaudriez pour préconiser un brigand qui, après avoir été avili par un long esclavage, en amérique [*sic*], en serait devenu le fléau, par les assassinats, la devastation et l'incendie, auxquels il n'a cessé de se livrer en combatant la patrie de *Breda*, son ancient maître, jusqu'au moment où, pour prix de ses importans services, le gouverneur *Laveaux*, le mît à la tête des troupes républicaines, et l'associa à son gouvernement." Cotterel, *Le Gouvernement de Saint Domingue*, 131.

72. See Ardouin, *Études sur l'histoire d'Haïti*, 3:147–148.

73. ["Voici, sur Toussaint."]

74. See Cotterel, *Le Gouvernement de Saint Domingue*, 33, 131–133.

75. "Pas fait pour obéir à un Noir, que c'etait une monstruosité de voir les Blancs et les hommes de couleur soumis à l'autorité d'un nègre jadis esclave." André Rigaud, letter dated 8 Vendémiaire Year VIII (September 30, 1798), qtd. in Cauna, *Toussaint Louverture, le grand précurseur*, 207.

76. See de Cauna, *Toussaint Louverture, le grand précurseur*, 216.

77. According to Bell, series of plays celebrating Brutus-like dedication to the *patrie* were produced during the Terror. *Cult of the Nation*, 157.

78. Napoleon infamously declared to his biographer, "I have to reproach myself with the attempt made upon the colony during the consulship. The design of reducing it by force was a great error. I ought to have been satisfied with governing it through the medium of Toussaint." Even then, he had to downplay Louverture's achievements, claiming that he was "chiefly guided by an officer of engineers or artillery." Las Cases, *Life, Exile, and Conversations*, 2:170, 171.

79. Mercier, *Astræa's Return*, 193.

80. "Toussaint Louverture," 249; a similar piece was published in the *Caledonian Mercury*, April 1, 1802.

81. "Chap. XI," 372.

82. "Art IV," 225–226.

83. As shown by Jenson, the trend of attributing Louverture's writings to white

authors started early: "Yet the mediation bridging Toussaint's speech acts and the polished French texts that represent him to us of course leaves open the possibility that his secretaries were responsible for some of the content as well as the form of his formal communications. This is precisely the claim made by Jules Michelet's young wife, Athenaïs Mialaret, whose father allegedly had served as Toussaint's secretary during the Revolution. . . . It indicates the vulnerability of Toussaint's verbal legacy to appropriation. It furthermore suggests that Romantic writers may have seen Toussaint as a Romantic character written by history, speaking lines that they would like to have articulated for him." *Beyond the Slave Narrative*, 66–67.

84. Toussaint's son Isaac claimed that Toussaint's father "was a prince . . . the son of an Arada king" and that other Arada slaves on the plantation "recognized him as their prince" (Dubois, *Avengers of the New World*, 171). James says that Toussaint's father was "the son of a petty chieftain in Africa" (*Black Jacobins*, 19). Historian Ralph Korngold, in his *Citizen Toussaint*, argued that Toussaint's father was really Pierre Baptiste, the Haitian slave usually credited with educating Toussaint and considered his godfather. See also Cauna, *Toussaint Louverture et l'indépendance*, 259–263.

85. Earle, *Obi*.

86. Botkin, "Revising the Colonial Caribbean," 496.

87. Earle, *Obi*, 90, 95.

88. Ibid., 111.

89. Aravamudan, introd. to *Obi*, 14.

90. Earle, *Obi*, 68.

91. Qtd. in James, *Black Jacobins*, 227.

92. Tomko, "Abolition Poetry, National Identity."

93. [Stephen], *Buonaparte in the West Indies*, pt. 1, pp. 2–3.

94. Advertisement for the 1814 edition of this work, published as Stephens, *History of Toussaint Louverture*, vii.

95. "Buonaparte in the West Indies."

96. [Stephen], *Buonaparte in the West Indies*, pt. 1, pp. 4, 9; pt. 2, p. 13.

97. Barère, *Rapport sur les crimes*, 18, 14.

98. [Stephen], *Buonaparte in the West Indies*, pt. 1, pp. 9, 13.

99. For publication details, see Youngquist and Pierrot, introd. to *Historical Account*.

100. For a more detailed analysis of the portrait, see Pierrot, "Our Hero"; and Rainsford, *Historical Account*.

101. See Youngquist and Pierrot, introd. to *Historical Account*, ixxxviii–xl.

102. Rainsford, *Historical Account*, 183, 5.

103. Ibid., 155, 153, 195, 156.

104. On the ethics of vengeance in the French Revolution, see Wahnich, *In Defence of the Terror*.

105. Wahnich, *In Defence of the Terror*, 203.

106. See Bongie, "Juste Chanlatte and the Unsettling."

107. Fouchard, *Les marrons du syllabaire*, 11.

108. Jenson, "Living by Metaphor," 73.

109. Ibid., 87.

110. Southey, "Introduction, with Observations," 87.

111. Krug, *Fugitive Modernities*, 18.

112. In the last line of Ralph Ellison's *Invisible Man*, the unnamed protagonist, speaking from his subterranean hideout, famously asks, "Who knows but that, on the lower frequencies, I speak for you?" (581).

113. Derrida, *Of Grammatology*, 158.

114. Halttunen, "Humanitarianism and the Pornography."

115. Bongie, *Friends and Enemies*, 117.

116. Jenson, *Beyond the Slave Narrative*, 10.

117. [Dessalines], "Jean-Jacques Dessalines to George Nugent."

118. "Extract from the Secret Deliberations of the Government of the Island of Hayti," *Times of London*, July 3, 1804, qtd. in Rainsford, *Historical Account*, 213.

119. Wahnich, *In Defence of the Terror*, 95, 97.

120. The proclamation was likely written in collaboration with one or several of his secretaries, among which were Louis Boisrond-Tonnerre, author of the Act of Independence and of *Mémoire pour servir à l'histoire d'Haïti* (1804), the first Haitian history of the Haitian Revolution; and Pompée Valentin Vastey, who later became Henry Christophe's foremost publicist. About these authors, see Daut, "Un-silencing the Past"; and Bongie, *Friends and Enemies*.

121. "Communication on the Intentions."

122. In 1803 Col. Charles Chalmers, a former inspector general of colonial troops, published his *Remarks on the Late War in St. Domingo*, in which he argued that "the temporary misfortunes sustained by France were occasioned by her impolicy, cruelty, or other causes totally independent of the power of her Black Enemies, whose strength, as stated, is utterly inadequate to render them independent of that empire, or of any other much less formidable power" (iv). Rainsford takes him to task in his book *Historical Account*.

123. See Gourgaud, *Talks of Napoleon*, 112.

124. See Jenson, "Reading between the Lines," 161–194.

125. See Alderson, "Charleston's Rumored Slave Revolt."

126. See Lachance, "Repercussions of the Haitian Revolution," 209–230.

127. See Egerton, *Gabriel's Rebellion*.

128. Qtd in Simon P. Newman, "American Political Culture," 83.

129. Drexler and White, "Constitution of Toussaint," 59.

130. As late as 1812, the Aponte conspiracy in Cuba was seen through the prism of the Haitian Revolution. See Childs, *1812 Aponte Rebellion in Cuba*.

131. "Constitution of Hayti," 310.

132. Cugoano, *Thoughts and Sentiments*, 17. That the Haitian revolutionaries might have actually read Cugoano is not so far-fetched: Antoine Diannyère's translation of his pamphlet for the Société des Amis des Noirs in 1788 could well have found its way into the hands of Julien Raimond, to cite but one islander with direct connections to the *société*. Cugoano, *Réflexions sur la traite*.

133. Madiou, *Histoire d'Haïti*, 3:178.

CHAPTER 4. FEAR OF A BLACK AMERICA

1. Jefferson, *Notes on the State of Virginia*, 147.

2. White, *Encountering Revolution*, 2.

3. Woertendyke, "Haiti and the New-World Novel," 234.

4. Clavin, *Toussaint Louverture*, 11–13.

5. See Roediger, *Wages of Whiteness*, 59–60.

6. "Negro Plot."

7. See notably *Salem Gazette*, September 6, 1831. The original article was published in the *Richmond Commercial Compiler*.

8. See Gray, *Confessions of Nat Turner*, 8.

9. Obadele-Starks estimates the number of slaves introduced illegally into the United States between 1808 and 1863 as between 192,500 and 786,500. *Freebooters and Smugglers*, 9–10.

10. Brooks, "Early American Public Sphere." She notably mentions these African American authors' works: John Marrant's *Sermon to the African Lodge* (1789), Prince Hall's *Charges to the Lodge* (1792–1797), and Absalom Jones and Richard Allen's *Narrative of the Proceedings of the Black People during the Late Epidemic in Philadelphia* (1794).

11. Ibid., 82, 73.

12. Ibid., 85.

13. See Litwack, *North of Slavery*, 75.

14. See Jones, "Birthright Citizenship."

15. Wilson J. Moses, *Afrotopia*, 47.

16. Segal, *Rebecca's Children*, 64.

17. Discussing the etymology and evolution of the meaning of redemption in Jewish thought, Rawidowicz argues that in time "the vision of redemption became more national than before, narrower and more restricted but also more concrete and bloodier, because redemption, by its very nature, is blood-drenched. . . . Redemption, then, is initially linked with blood, the blood of the individual, of the family, and of the tribe. Later, an abstract, spiritual meaning developed from the word or concept *goel: geulah*, redemption as national liberation, redemption of the people." Rawidowicz, *Israel, the Ever-Dying People*, 66.

18. Hall, *Charge*, 11–13.

19. Hinks, *To Awaken My Afflicted Brethren*, 30–40.

20. Although Walker never mentions Cugoano, it seems likely he was familiar with his book, as it was discussed twice in the pages of the *Freedom's Journal* on May 18, 1827, and November 21, 1828. In each case, the short paragraph about Cugoano is copied almost word for word from Abbé Grégoire's *De la littérature des nègres*, translated and published in New York by David Bailie Warden in 1810 as *An Enquiry concerning the Intellectual and Moral Faculties, and Literature of Negroes*. See Cassirer and Brière, preface to *Cultural Achievements of Negroes*, ix.

21. Wilson J. Moses, *Black Messiahs and Uncle Toms*, 38.

22. Howard-Pitney, *African American Jeremiad*, 12, 13.

23. Wilson J. Moses, *Black Messiahs and Uncle Toms*, 32.

24. Walker, *Appeal to Coloured Citizens*, 79, 18.

25. "Original Communication."

26. Walker, *Appeal to Coloured Citizens*, 23, 33, 2.

27. "To the Honourable," 23, 25.

28. See Hinks, *To Awaken My Afflicted Brethren*, 91–92.

29. Walker, *Appeal to Coloured Citizens*, 76.

30. On black Christianity and black settler colonialism, see Sylvester A. Johnson, *African American Religions*, 159–209.

31. Walker means only white people when he addresses "Americans" in his text, for example, when he writes, "I ask you, O! Americans, I ask you, in the name of the Lord, can you deny these charges?" or "I tell you Americans! that unless you speedily alter your course, *you* and your *Country are gone!!!!!!* For God Almighty will tear up the very face of the earth!!!" *Appeal to Coloured Citizens*, 16, 45.

32. Ibid., 73.

33. Ibid., 71.

34. Hinks, *To Awaken My Afflicted Brethren*, 119–120, 134–152.

35. Walker, *Appeal to Coloured Citizens*, 71fn.

36. Acting of his own accord in seeking out Haitian president Boyer for support in the emigration scheme, Dewey lost his job at the ACS, who saw this alternative to the Liberian plan as a direct attack against them. See Dixon, *African America and Haiti*, 35–45.

37. See Horne, *Confronting Black Jacobins*.

38. Ibid., 62–63.

39. On Ohio, see Walker, *Appeal to Coloured Citizens*, 73, 77. On refugees to Canada, see Litwack, *North of Slavery*, 72–73.

40. Walker, *Appeal to Coloured Citizens*, 24. On Stephen, see chapter 3. For the received view on Protestantism and King Henry I, see Griggs and Prator, *Henry Christophe and Thomas Clarkson*, 63–73; for a revisionist take, see McIntosh and Pierrot, "Capturing the Likeness," 141.

41. Walker, *Appeal to Coloured Citizens*, 63.

42. See Blouet, "Slavery and Freedom." See also Horne, *Confronting Black Jacobins*, 154.

43. See Leonard L. Richards, *Gentlemen of Property and Standing*, 150.

44. Birney, "Letter of Hon. J. G. Birney," [129].

45. "James G. Birney," 260.

46. Lovejoy and Lovejoy, *Memoir*, 12.

47. "Abolition," 2.

48. Channing, *Letter of Dr. William E. Channing*, 7.

49. "Mr. [Robert] Sutherland to Major Rainsford," WO/1/75, British National Archives, Kew., fols. 41–44.

50. Beard, *Life of Toussaint L'Ouverture*, vi.

51. Daut, *Tropics of Haiti*, 22.

52. "L'Écrivain qui aborde un terrain vierge, qui, le premier, compulse et réunit des documents qu'aucune main n'a touches, qui ouvre une voie que nul n'a essayé d'ouvrir." Saint-Rémy, *Vie de Toussaint-L'Ouverture*, vii–viii.

53. Beard, *Life of Toussaint L'Ouverture*, 23, 36n, 110.

54. Redpath, preface to *Toussaint L'Ouverture*, v.

55. Nicholls, "Work of Combat." On the origins of Nicholls's concept in nineteenth-century racialized history, see Daut, *Tropics of Haiti*, 19–29.

56. Phillips, "Toussaint L'Ouverture," 468. This version of the speech was delivered in December 1861.

57. Phillips, "Toussaint L'Ouverture," 475–476.

58. Ullman, *Martin R. Delany*, 3.

59. Delany, *Condition, Elevation, Emigration, and Destiny*.

60. See Levine, *Martin R. Delany*, 83.

61. Walker, *Appeal to Coloured Citizens*, 86n.

62. Chiles, "Within and without Raced Nations," 339, 330.

63. See, notably, "Sad Intelligence from Hayti."

64. See, for example, "Haytian Emigration"; and "Haytian Emigration in Canada."

65. "Haytian Emigration in Boston."

66. McGann, introd. to *Blake*, xxv.

67. Rameau et al., "Slavery in America."

68. Delany, *Blake*, 40, 291, 313. Researchers have been unable to locate copies of the first four issues of the *Weekly Anglo-African* for May 1862, in which the announced final chapters of the novel were likely published.

69. See Gardner, *Master Plots*.

70. Delany, *Condition, Elevation, Emigration, and Destiny*, 181.

71. Crane, "Lexicon of Rights," 527.

72. Chiles, "Within and without Raced Nations," 345.

73. Delany, *Condition, Elevation, Emigration, and Destiny*, 181–182.

74. Sylvester A. Johnson, *African American Religions*, 234.

75. Doolen, "Be Cautious," 156–157.

76. Shelby, "Two Conceptions of Black Nationalism," 667.

77. See Tal, "That Just Kills Me."

78. Walker, *Appeal to Coloured Citizens*, 37.

79. McGann, introd. to *Blake*, xxiv–xxv.

80. See Childs, *1812 Aponte Rebellion in Cuba*.

81. On Narciso Lopez's ill-fated attempt at taking over Cuba, see Lazo, *Writing to Cuba*.

82. Buchanan, Mason, and Soulé, "Ostend Manifesto."

83. See Sibylle Fischer, *Modernity Disavowed*, 42.

84. Childs, *1812 Aponte Rebellion in Cuba*, 147.

85. Childs, "Black French General Arrived," 150.

86. Trouillot, *Silencing the Past*, 96.

87. Clymer, "Martin Delany's Blake," 727. Soulé's letter itself reproduces older terminology: the alarmist image of the fire next door evokes Burke's "On the Overtures of Peace," in which he called on the Roman "law of civil vicinity" to promote England's right to intervene against the French Revolution (54).

88. Clavin, *Toussaint Louverture*, 11–13.

89. Delany, *Blake*, 258.

90. Bolívar, "Thoughts on the Congress," 170.

91. On the place of race in Haitian constitutions, see Gaffield, "Complexities of Imagining Haiti." In Haitian *kréyol*, the term *blan* literally means "white" but designates non-Haitians of any skin color.

92. Dayan, *Haiti, History, and the Gods*, 15.

93. Sundquist, *To Wake the Nations*, 173.

94. Marx, *Eighteenth Brumaire of Louis Bonaparte*, 158.

95. Hugo, *Napoléon le Petit*, 35, 130, 132.

96. Marx, *Eighteenth Brumaire of Louis Bonaparte*, 9.

97. Dayan, *Haiti, History, and the Gods*, 13.

98. Gobineau, *Inequality of Human Races*, 48, 49.

99. Van Evrie, *Negroes and Negro "Slavery"*, 114, 160, 166–167. For more on Van Evrie, see chapter 5.

100. See "Letter from Hayti."

101. "What Shall Be Done?"

102. Delany, *Blake*, 289.

103. Seraille. "Afro-American Emigration to Haiti," 187.

104. *Weekly Anglo-African*, January 19, 1861.

105. Prince Hall founded the first black Masonic lodge in Boston in 1775; Walker joined Boston's African Lodge in 1826 (see Hinks, *To Awaken My Afflicted Brethren*, 70); Delany helped found the black Freemason Saint Cyprian Lodge in Pittsburgh in 1847 (see Levine, *Martin R. Delany*, 25–28).

106. See Anderson, *Imagined Communities*, 82.

107. Doyle, *Freedom's Empire*, 6.

108. Behn, *Oroonoko*, 56, 59.

109. Delany, *Blake*, 196.

110. Ibid., 21, 200.

111. Ibid., 231, 232, 238, 239.

112. McGann, introd. to *Blake*, xxiv.

113. The subhead for this section is drawn from the following quote: "It is a difficult thing for a white man to learn what a colored man really thinks . . . ; because, generally, with the latter an additional and different light must be brought to bear on what he thinks; and his thoughts are often influenced by considerations so delicate and subtle that it would be impossible for him to confess or explain them to one of the opposite race. This gives to every colored man, in proportion to his intellectuality, a sort of dual personality; there is one phase of him which is disclosed only in the freemasonry of his own race." [James W. Johnson], *Autobiography of an Ex-colored Man*, 19.

114. Delany, *Blake*, 127.

115. Baker, *Blues, Ideology and Afro-American Literature*, 114.

116. Delany, *Blake*, 115.

117. Doolen, "Be Cautious," 162.

118. Delany, *Blake*, 127, 110.

119. Ibid., 249n.

120. Wallace, "Are We Men?," 412.

121. Clavin, *Toussaint Louverture*, 132.

122. Sheller, *Citizenship from Below*, 160. See also Mentor, *Histoire de la franc-maçonnerie*.

123. Sheller, *Citizenship from Below*, 161. On antiquity-inspired representations of Lady Columbia, see David Hackett Fischer, *Liberty and Freedom*, 33–34. See also Jenna Gibbs, "Celebrating Columbia," 17–51.

124. Sheller, *Citizenship from Below*, 165.

125. Delany, *Blake*, 10.

126. Ibid., 194.

127. Nyong'o, *Amalgamation Waltz*, 101.

128. Weheliye, *Habeas Viscus*.

129. Spillers, "Mama's Baby, Papa's Maybe," 67, 80.

130. Delany, *Blake*, 313.

131. Ibid., 263.

CHAPTER 5. AMERICAN HERO

1. Rable, *But There Was No Peace*, 95.

2. Plessy v. Ferguson, 163 U.S. 537 (1896).

3. See Painter, *Exodusters*.

4. Sylvester A. Johnson, *African American Religions*, 253.

5. See Knadler, *Remapping Citizenship* and the Nation, 124.

6. Gatewood, *Black Americans*, 16–21, 24–25.

7. Sylvester A. Johnson, *African American Religions*, 251

8. Angell, *Bishop Henry McNeal Turner*, 244.

9. Chauncey, *Gay New York*, 113. On Roosevelt, the West, and the cult of the "strenuous life," see Vorpahl, "Roosevelt, Wister, Turner and Remington."

10. The myth is often called "southern rape complex." For a history of the term and evolving scholarship on this phenomenon, see Sommerville, *Rape and Race*.

11. Warren, *What Was African American Literature?*, 7.

12. David Brown, *Southern Outcast*, 3.

13. Helper, *Impending Crisis of the South*, v, 178–183.

14. Helper, *Nojoque*, v, 15.

15. Guyatt, "Future Empire of Our Freedmen," 97.

16. Griggs, *Imperium in Imperio*, ii.

17. Coleman, *Sutton E. Griggs*, 18.

18. Griggs, *Imperium in Imperio*, 2, 183, 262.

19. Coleman, *Sutton E. Griggs*, 70.

20. Knadler, *Remapping Citizenship* and the Nation, 144–145.

21. Griggs, *Imperium in Imperio*, 191, 194.

22. Ibid., 214.

23. Du Bois, "Talented Tenth," 62.

24. Griggs, *Imperium in Imperio*, 196, 207, 227.

25. Ibid., 245.

26. Gruesser, *Empire Abroad*, 45.

27. Griggs, *Imperium in Imperio*, 252.

28. Hagan, *This People's Navy*, 188.

29. See Gruesser, *Empire Abroad*, 40.

30. Griggs, *Imperium in Imperio*, 226, 93, 173, v, 175–176.

31. Williamson, *New People*, 94–100.

32. Griggs, *Wisdom's Call*, 119, 120, 122.

33. Van Evrie, *White Supremacy and Negro Subordination*, 150, 262.

34. Ibid., 262, 150; Hodes, "Sexualization of Reconstruction Politics," 404.

35. Griggs, *Imperium in Imperio*, 77.

36. Ibid., 131–132, 134–135.

37. Coleman, *Sutton E. Griggs*, 50–51.

38. On rape as a white supremist terrorist practice, see, notably, the testimonies in "Woman's Lot."

39. Knadler, *Remapping Citizenship* and the Nation, 157.

40. Griggs, *Imperium in Imperio*, 134.

41. Freedman, *Redefining Rape*, 74, 82.

42. Chauncey, *Gay New York*, 113, 10, 13.

43. Ibid., 132.

44. Spillers, "Mama's Baby, Papa's Maybe," 68, 77; Griggs, *Imperium* in Imperio, 145.

45. Griggs, *Imperium* in Imperio, 137.

46. Spillers, "Mama's Baby, Papa's Maybe, 70, 80.

47. Kramer, "Imperium in Imperio," 13.

48. See Griggs, *Wisdom's* Call, 71, 265.

49. Du Bois, *Souls of Black Folk*, 3

50. See Hodes, "Sexualization of Reconstruction Politics."

51. Freedman, *Redefining Rape*, 8.

52. Williams, "War in Black and White."

53. Kirshenbaum, "Vampire That Hovers over Carolina."

54. Sundquist, *To Wake the Nations*, 397.

55. Gunning, *Race, Rape, and Lynching*, 75, 51.

56. Chesnutt, *Marrow of Tradition*, 109, 59, 57, 109–111.

57. Gunning, *Race, Rape, and Lynching*, 76.

58. Chesnutt, *Marrow of Tradition*, 294.

59. Ibid., 112–114.

60. Wells-Barnett, *Red Record*.

61. Ibid., 117.

62. Ibid., 167.

63. Kilgore, "Cakewalk of Capital," 69.

64. Chesnutt, *Marrow of Tradition*, 233–234.

65. David Garland, "Penal Excess and Surplus Meaning," 807, 808.

66. René Girard, *Violence and the Sacred*, 13, 12.

67. Ibid., 817.

68. Gunning, *Race, Rape, and Lynching*, 76.

69. Kilgore, "Cakewalk of Capital," 70.

70. Chesnutt, *Marrow of Tradition*, 195.

71. Gunning, *Race, Rape, and Lynching*, 70.

72. Chesnutt, *Marrow of Tradition*, 321.

73. Gunning, *Race, Rape, and Lynching*, 76.

74. Jewett and Lawrence, *American Monomyth*, 176, 179.

75. Gavaler, "Ku Klux Klan and the Birth," 5.

76. Wister, "Evolution of the Cow-Puncher," 606, 603–604, 615, 617.

77. In his 1906 novel *Lady Baltimore*, Wister follows the protagonist, a northerner, as he spends some time in the South and is gradually convinced that in the new, post-Reconstruction Union, "the black must take orders from the white," living in a state "between equality and slavery" (206).

78. Vorpahl, "Roosevelt, Wister, Turner and Remington," 294.

79. Silber, *Romance of Reunion*, 192.

80. Wister, *Virginian*, 12.

81. Cawelti, *Adventure, Mystery, and Romance*, 221, 222.

82. Wister, *Virginian*, 433, 434, 436.

83. Knadler, *Remapping Citizenship* and the Nation, 120.

84. See Woodson, "Waring Family," 101. Waring notably wrote President Woodrow Wilson from Harlem to complain about the new administration's unfulfilled promises of positions for African Americans. Yellin, *Racism in the Nation's Service*, 107–108.

85. Woodson, "Waring Family," 105.

86. Waring, *As We See It*.

87. Jewett and Lawrence, *American Monomyth*, 170.

88. Knadler, *Remapping Citizenship* and the Nation, 5.

89. Kanzler, "'Race' and Realism," 340; Kawash, *Dislocating the Color Line*. Prasad notes a similar structure in two French Romantic novels describing slave rebellions: Victor Hugo's *Bug-Jargal* and Prosper Mérimée's *Tamango*. See *Colonialism, Race*, 142–144.

90. Waring, *As We See It*, 47, 11, 12.

91. Ibid., 91.

92. Ibid., 120, 171.

93. Bryant, *Victims and Heroes*, 84–87.

94. Waring, *As We See It*, 128.

95. Wister, *Virginian*, 147.

96. Waring, *As We See It*, 162.

97. Ibid., 61, 115, 105.

98. Ibid., 128.

99. Du Bois, "Atlanta University," 197.

100. Iriye, *Pacific Estrangement*, 159, qtd. in Gallicchio, *African American Encounter*, 15.

101. Waring, *As We See It*, 229.

102. Ibid., 230.

103. See McClintock, "No Longer in a Future Heaven"; Bryant, *Victims and Heroes*, 84.

104. Waring, *As We See It*, 231.

105. Ibid., 231, 233.

106. Jewett and Lawrence, *American Monomyth*, 51.

107. Waring, *As We See It*, 5, 7.

CONCLUSION

1. Pickens, "Hayti," 232–233.

2. Ibid., 233, 235, 237.

3. See Byrd, "Experiment in Self-Government," 200–205.

4. "Haiti to Be Seized."

5. "Negroes Plan to Take Haiti."

6. "Haiti to Be Seized."

7. See Suggs, "Response of the African American Press," 73–74.

8. Plummer, "Afro-American Response," 131.

9. *Negro World*, August 2, 1919, qtd. in Cronon, *Black Moses*, 46.

10. Gray, *Confessions of Nat Turner*, 20, 3.

11. Allmendinger, *Nat Turner and the Rising*, 63.

12. Warner, *Authentic and Impartial Narrative*, 31. See also Allmendinger, *Nat Turner and the Rising*, 105.

13. Allmendinger, *Nat Turner and the Rising*, 63.

14. [Higginson], "Nat Turner's Insurrection," 174.

15. Allmendinger, *Nat Turner and the Rising*.

16. Bernier, *Characters of Blood*, xx.

17. Spillers, "Mama's Baby, Papa's Maybe," 80.

18. Krug, *Fugitive Modernities*, 193.

WORKS CITED

"Abolition." *Charleston Courier*, August 12, 1835.

Aercke, Kristiaan P. "Theatrical Background in English Novels of the Seventeenth Century." *Journal of Narrative Technique* 18, no. 2 (1988): 120–136.

Airey, Jennifer L. "Lucrece Narratives: Rochester, Lee, and the Ethics of Regicide." In *The Politics of Rape: Sexual Atrocity, Propaganda Wars, and the Restoration Stage*, 111–146. Newark: University of Delaware Press, 2012.

Alderson, Robert. "Charleston's Rumored Slave Revolt of 1793." In Geggus, *Impact of the Haitian Revolution*, 93–110.

Allmendinger, David F., Jr. *Nat Turner and the Rising in Southampton County*. Baltimore: Johns Hopkins University, 2014.

Anderson, Benedict. *Imagined Communities: Reflections on the Origin and Spread of Nationalism*. 1983. Reprint, London: Verso, 2006.

Andrade, Susan Z. "White Skin, Black Masks: Colonialism and the Sexual Politics of *Oroonoko*." *Cultural Critique* 27 (1994): 189–214.

Angell, Stephen Ward. *Bishop Henry McNeal Turner and African-American Religion in the South*. Knoxville: University of Tennessee Press, 1992.

Appian. *The Civil Wars*. In *Appian's Roman History*. Vol. 3, translated by Horace White. 1913. Reprint, Cambridge: Harvard University Press, 1964.

Aravamudan, Srinivas. Introduction to *Obi: or, The History of Three-Fingered Jack*, edited by Srinivas Aravamudan, 7–52. Toronto: Broadview, 2005.

———. *Tropicopolitans: Colonialism and Agency, 1688–1804*. Durham: Duke University Press, 1999.

Ardouin, Beaubrun. *Études sur l'histoire d'Haïti: Suivies de la vie du général J.-M. Borgella*. 11 vols. Paris: Dézobry et Magdeleine, 1853–1860.

Aristotle. *Aristotle's Politics*. Translated by Benjamin Jowett. Oxford: Clarendon, 1916.

———. *The Nicomachean Ethics*. Translated by H. Rackham. Cambridge: Harvard University Press, 1982.

"Art IV. An Historical Account of the Black Empire of Hayti . . . by Marcus Rainsford." *Annual Review and History of Literature* 4 (1805): 219–228.

"Art. VII. *West-Indian Eclogues.*" *Monthly Review* 77 (1787): 283–284.

Ashcraft, Richard. *Revolutionary Politics and Locke's Two Treatises of Government.* Princeton: Princeton University Press, 1986.

Asín, Jaime Oliver. *Vida de Don Felipe de África, Príncipe de Fez y Marruecos (1566–1621).* Granada: Editorial Universidad de Granada, 2008.

Ayres, P. J. "The Revision of *Lust's Dominion,*" *Notes and Queries* 17 (1970): 212–213.

Baker, Houston A., Jr. *Blues, Ideology and Afro-American Literature: A Vernacular Theory.* Chicago: University of Chicago Press, 1984.

Barbault-Royer, Colonel [Pierre-François]. *Du gouvernement de Saint Domingue, de Laveaux, Vilatte, des agents du Directoire.* Paris: Debray, 1797.

Barère, Bertrand. *Rapport sur les crimes de l'Angleterre envers le peuple français, et sur ses attentats contre la liberté des nations, fait au nom du Comité de Salut Public.* Paris, 1794.

Bartels, Emily C. *Speaking of the Moor: From Alcazar to Othello.* Philadelphia: University of Pennsylvania Press, 2008.

Barthelemy, Anthony G. *Black Face, Maligned Race: The Representation of Blacks in English Drama from Shakespeare to Southerne.* Baton Rouge: Louisiana State University Press, 1987.

Beach, Adam R. "Global Slavery, Old World Bondage, and Aphra Behn's *Abdelazer.*" *Eighteenth Century* 53, no. 4 (2012): 413–431.

Beard, John R. *The Life of Toussaint L'Ouverture, the Negro Patriot of Hayti.* London: Ingram, Cooke, 1853.

[Beard, John R.]. *Toussaint L'Ouverture: A Biography and Autobiography.* Boston: Redpath, 1863.

Beatty, Paul. *The Sellout.* New York: Farrar, Straus and Giroux, 2015.

Beaumarchais, M. de. *La folle journée, ou le mariage de Figaro.* Lyon, 1785.

———. *The Follies of a Day; or, The Marriage of Figaro.* Translated by Thomas Holcroft. London, 1785.

Behn, Aphra. *Abdelazer; or, The Moor's Revenge.* 1676. In Hughes, *Versions of Blackness,* 29–116.

———. *Oroonoko; or, The Royal Slave: A True History.* Edited by Joanna Lipking. 1688. Reprint, New York: Norton, 1997.

Bell, David Avrom. *The Cult of the Nation in France: Inventing Nationalism, 1680–1800.* Cambridge: Harvard University Press, 2001.

Belsey, Catherine. "Tarquin Dispossessed: Expropriation and Consent in the Rape of Lucrece." *Shakespeare Quarterly* 52, no. 3 (2001): 315–335.

Bénot, Yves. "Diderot, Pechméja, Raynal et l'anticolonialisme." *Europe* 405–406 (1963): 137–153.

Bergstrom, Carson. "Form and the Pleasures of Interpretation: Reading William Collins's Persian Eclogues." *anq: A Quarterly Journal of Short Articles, Notes, and Reviews* 26, no. 4 (2013): 235–245.

Bernier, Céleste-Marie. *Characters of Blood: Black Heroism in the Transatlantic Imagination.* Charlottesville: University of Virginia Press, 2012.

Biondi, Martha. *The Black Revolution on Campus.* Berkeley: University of California Press, 2012.

Birney, James G. "Letter of Hon. J. G. Birney." *Liberator*, August 16, 1834.

Blouet, Olwyn Mary. "Slavery and Freedom in the British West Indies, 1823–33: The Role of Education." *History of Education Quarterly* 30, no. 4 (1990): 625–643.

Bolívar, Simón. "Thoughts on the Congress to Be Held in Panama." In *El Libertador: Writings of Simón Bolívar*. Edited by David Bushnell. Translated by Fred Fornoff, 169–170. Oxford: Oxford University Press, 2003.

Bongie, Chris. *Friends and Enemies: The Scribal Politics of Post/Colonial Literature*. Liverpool: Liverpool University Press, 2009.

———. "Juste Chanlatte and the Unsettling (Presence) of Race in Early Haitian Literature." *mln* 130, no. 4 (2015): 807–835.

Botkin, Frances R. "Revising the Colonial Caribbean: 'Three-Fingered Jack' and the Jamaican Pantomime." *Callaloo* 35, no. 2 (2012): 494–508.

Boussuge, Emmanuel. "La présentation de *L'Écueil du Sage* aux Comédiens-Français." *Recherches sur Diderot et sur l'Encyclopédie* 47. October 9, 2012. http://rde.revues.org/4925.

Bowers, Fredson. *Elizabethan Revenge Tragedy, 1587–1642*. Princeton: Princeton University Press, 1940.

[Boyle, Roger], Earl of Orrery. *Parthenissa, That Most Fam'd Romance*. 2nd ed. London, 1676.

Brenner, Clarence D. *L'Histoire nationale dans la tragédie française du XVIIIè siècle*. Berkeley: University of California Press, 1929.

Brette, A[rmand]. "Les gens de couleur libres et leurs députés en 1789." 2 parts. *La Révolution française: Revue d'Histoire Moderne et Contemporaine* 29 (October–November 1895): 326–345, 385–407.

Brooks, Joanna. "The Early American Public Sphere and the Emergence of a Black Print Counterpublic." *William and Mary Quarterly* 62, no. 1 (2005): 67–92.

Brown, David. *Southern Outcast: Hinton Rowan Helper and the Impending Crisis of the South*. Baton Rouge: Louisiana State University Press, 2006.

Brown, Laura. "The Romance of Empire: *Oroonoko* and the Trade in Slaves." In *Ends of Empire: Women and Ideology in Early Eighteenth-Century English Literature*, 23–63. Ithaca: Cornell University Press, 1993.

Brown, William Wells. *Clotel; or, The President's Daughter: A Narrative of Slave Life in the United States*. London: Partridge and Oakey, 1853.

Brownmiller, Susan. *Against Our Will: Men, Women and Rape*. New York: Simon and Schuster, 1975.

Bryant, Jerry H. *Victims and Heroes: Racial Violence in the African American Novel*. Amherst: University of Massachusetts Press, 1997.

Buchanan, James, John Y. Mason, and Pierre Soulé. "The Ostend Manifesto." *American History Leaflets*. October 18, 1854. http://xroads.virginia.edu/~hyper/hns/ostend/ostend.html.

Budgell, E. *Memoirs of the Lives and Characters of the Illustrious Family of the Boyles*. London, 1737.

"Buonaparte in the West Indies." *Anti-Jacobin*, October 1803, 200.

Burdett, William. *Life and Exploits of Mansong, Commonly Called Three-Finger'd Jack, the Terror of Jamaica in the Years 1780 and 1781*. London: Neill, 1800.

Burke, Edmund. "On the Overtures of Peace." In *Thoughts on the Prospect of a Regicide Peace: In a Series of Letters*, 1–81. London: Owen, 1796.

Burnett, Anne Pippin. *Revenge in Attic and Later Tragedy*. Berkeley: University of California Press, 1998.

Byrd, Brandon R. "An Experiment in Self-Government: Haiti in the African-American Political Imagination, 1863–1915." PhD diss., University of North Carolina, Chapel Hill, 2014.

[Byron, George Gordon]. *Ode to Napoleon Buonaparte*. 4th ed. London, 1814.

Camier, Bernard, and Laurent Dubois. "Voltaire et Zaïre, ou le théâtre des Lumières dans l'aire atlantique française." *Revue d'Histoire Moderne Contemporaine* 54, no. 4 (2007): 39–69.

Campbell, Mary B. *Wonder and Science: Imagining Worlds in Early Modern Europe*. Ithaca: Cornell University Press, 1999.

Carey, Brycchan. *British Abolitionism and the Rhetoric of Sensibility*. London: Palgrave Macmillan, 2005.

———. "A Stronger Muse." In *Ancient Slavery and Abolition: From Hobbes to Hollywood*, edited by Edith Hall, Richard Alston, and Justine McConnell, 125–152. Oxford: Oxford University Press, 2011.

Carlyle, Thomas. *On Heroes, Hero-Worship, and the Heroic in History: Six Lectures. Reported, with Emendations and Additions*. London: Fraser, 1841.

Casellas, Jesús López-Peláez. "The Enemy Within: Otherness in Thomas Dekker's *Lust's Dominion*." *sederi, Yearbook of the Spanish and Portuguese Society for English Renaissance Studies* 9 (1998): 203–207.

Cassirer, Thomas, and Jean-François Brière. Preface to *On the Cultural Achievements of Negroes*, by Abbé Grégoire, ix–xlviii. Boston: University of Massachusetts Press, 1996.

[Castiglione, Baldassare]. *The Courtyer of Count Baldessar Castilio Diuided into Foure Bookes: Very Necessary and Profitable for Younge Gentilmen and Gentilwomen Abiding in Court, Palaice, or Place, Done into Englyshe by Thomas Hoby*. London: Seres, 1561.

Cauna, Jacques de. "De Bréda à Cormier: Famille et proches, Dessalines esclave de Toussaint." In Cauna, *Toussaint Louverture, le grand précurseur*, 107–114.

———. "Dessalines esclave de Toussaint?" *Outre-Mers: Revue d'Histoire* 374–375 (June 2012): 319–322.

———. *Toussaint Louverture et l'indépendance d'Haïti: Témoignages pour un bicentenaire*. Paris et Saint-Denis: Karthala/SFHOM, 2004.

———. *Toussaint Louverture, le grand précurseur*. Bordeaux: Sud-Ouest, 2012.

Cawelti, John. *Adventure, Mystery, and Romance: Formula Stories as Art and Popular Culture*. Chicago: University of Chicago Press, 1977.

Chalmers, Colonel [Charles]. *Remarks on the Late War in St. Domingo, with Observations on the Relative Situation in Jamaica, and Other Interesting Subjects*. London, 1803.

Channing, William Ellery. *Letter of Dr. William E. Channing to James G. Birney*. Cincinnati: Pugh, 1836.

"Chap. XI." *New Annual Register for Year 1802* 23 (1803): 366–386.

Chatterton, Thomas. "Heccar and Gaira: An African Eclogue." In *A Supplement to the Miscellanies of Thomas Chatterton*, 53–59. London, 1784.

Chauncey, George. *Gay New York: Gender, Urban Culture, and the Making of the Gay Male World, 1890–1940*. New York: Basic Books, 1994.

Chesnutt, Charles W. *The Marrow of Tradition*. Boston: Houghton Mifflin, 1901.

Childs, Matt D. *The 1812 Aponte Rebellion in Cuba and the Struggle against Atlantic Slavery*. Chapel Hill: University of North Carolina Press, 2006.

———. "'A Black French General Arrived to Conquer the Island': Images of the Haitian Revolution in Cuba's 1812 Aponte Rebellion." In Geggus, *Impact of the Haitian Revolution*, 135–156.

Chiles, Katy. "Within and without Raced Nations: Intratextuality, Martin Delany, and Blake; or, The Huts of America." *American Literature* 80, no. 2 (2008): 323–352.

Clare, Janet. *Drama of the English Republic, 1649–1600*. Manchester, UK: Manchester University Press, 2002.

Clavin, Matthew J. *Toussaint Louverture and the American Civil War: The Promise and Peril of a Second Haitian Revolution*. Philadelphia: University of Pennsylvania Press, 2010.

Cleves, Rachel Hope. *The Reign of Terror in America: Visions of Violence from Anti-Jacobinism to Anti-Slavery*. Cambridge: Cambridge University Press, 2009.

Clymer, Jeffory. "Martin Delany's Blake and the Transnational Politics of Property." *American Literary History* 15, no. 4 (2003): 709–731.

Coleman, Finnie D. *Sutton E. Griggs and the Struggle against White Supremacy*. Knoxville: University of Tennessee Press, 2007.

Colley, Linda. *Britons: Forging the Nation, 1707–1837*. New Haven: Yale University Press, 1992.

Collins, John Churchton. *Bolingbroke: A Historical Study and Voltaire in England*. New York: Harper and Bros., 1886.

Collins, William. Preface to *Persian Eclogues*, by William Collins. London, 1742. https://scholarsbank.uoregon.edu/xmlui/bitstream/handle/1794/4064/collins2.pdf?sequence=1.

"Communication on the Intentions of the Black Government on the Appointment of a Governor-General for Life." *Times of London*, July 23, 1804.

"Constitution of Hayti." *Cobbett's Political Register*, August 24, 1805.

Coogler, Ryan, dir. *Black Panther*. Burbank: Walt Disney Studios, 2018.

Correspondance des déportés de Saint Domingue, à l'occasion du mouvement révolutionnaire du 30 Ventose, an 4e, au Cap. 7 Pluviose Year V. N.p., 1796.

Cotterel, François-Frédéric. *Esquisse historique des principaux évènemens arrivés à Saint Domingue depuis l'incendie du Cap jusqu'à l'expulsion de Sonthonax: Leurs causes, leurs effets; Situation actuelle de cette colonie, et moyens d'y rétablir la tranquillité*. Paris, 1798.

———. *Le Gouvernement de Saint Domingue peint par lui même, ou mémoire de l'ordonnateur Henry Perroud, sur l'événement du 30 ventôse au Cap, contre le Général Vilatte et les hommes de couleur, avec quelques réflexions préliminaires à leur mémoire justificatif*. Rochefort: Jousserant, [1797].

———. *Santhonax et Laveaux repoussés par leurs commettants, ou prévue des nullités de la députation de Saint Domingue pour l'an IV*. Paris: Marchands de Nouveautés [1797].

Cowper, William. *Poems*. Vol. 1. London, 1808.

———. *The Poems of William Cowper*. Edited by John D. Baird and Charles Ryskamp. Vol. 3. Oxford: Clarendon, 1995.

Crane, Gregg D. "The Lexicon of Rights, Power, and Community in *Blake*: Martin R. Delany's Dissent from *Dred Scott*." *American Literature* 68, no. 3 (1996): 527–553.

Craton, Michael. *Testing the Chains: Resistance to Slavery in the British West Indies*. Ithaca: Cornell University Press, 2009.

Cronon, E. David. *Black Moses: The Story of Marcus Garvey and the Universal Negro Improvement Association*. 1955. Reprint, Madison: University of Wisconsin Press, 1969.

Cugoano, Ottobah. *Réflexions sur la traite et l'esclavage des nègres, traduites de l'Anglais d'Ottobah Cugoano, Afriquain, esclave à la Grenade et libre en Angleterre*. Translated by Antoine Diannyère. London: Royer, 1788.

———. *Thoughts and Sentiments on the Evil and Wicked Traffic of Slavery and Commerce of the Human Species, Humbly Submitted to the Inhabitants of Great-Britain*. Edited by Vincent Carretta. 1787. Reprint, New York: Penguin Classics, 1999.

Curran, Andrew S. *The Anatomy of Blackness*. Baltimore: Johns Hopkins University Press, 2011.

Curran, Stuart. *Poetic Form and British Romanticism*. New York: Oxford University Press, 1986.

Daut, Marlene L. *Tropics of Haiti: Race and the Literary History of the Haitian Revolution in the Atlantic World, 1789–1865*. Liverpool: Liverpool University Press, 2015.

———. "Un-silencing the Past: Boisrond-Tonnerre, Vastey, and the Re-writing of the Haitian Revolution." *South Atlantic Review* 74, no. 1 (2009): 35–64.

Davis, Gregson. Introduction to *Virgil's Eclogues*, i–xx. Translated by Len Krisak. Philadelphia: University of Pennsylvania Press, 2010

[Day, Thomas, and John Bicknell]. *The Dying Negro, a Poem*. 3rd ed. London, 1775.

Dayan, Joan. *Haiti, History, and the Gods*. Berkeley: University of California Press, 1998.

[Dekker, Thomas]. *Lust's Dominion; or, The Lascivious Queen*. 1601. Edited by J. Le Gay Brereton. Louvain: Librairie Universitaire, 1931.

Delany, Martin R. *Blake; or, The Huts of America*. Edited by Jerome McGann. Cambridge: Harvard University Press, 2017.

———. *The Condition, Elevation, Emigration, and Destiny of the Colored People of the United States and Official Report of the Niger Valley Exploring Party*. 1852. Reprint, Amherst: Humanity Books, 2004.

Dellarosa, Franca. *Talking Revolution: Edward Rushton's Rebellious Poetics, 1782–1814*. Liverpool: Liverpool University Press, 2014.

Derrida, Jacques. *Of Grammatology*. Translated by Gayatri Chakravorty Spivak. Baltimore: Johns Hopkins Press, 1976.

[Dessalines, Jean-Jacques]. "Jean-Jacques Dessalines to George Nugent, 13 May 1804." MS 72. National Library of Jamaica. *Haiti and the Atlantic World*. https://haitidoi.com/2015/10/26/dessalines-reader-13-may-1804/

———. "Proclamation: Jean Jacques Dessalines, Governor General, to the Inhabitants of Hayti." In *New Annual Register; or, General Repository of History, Politics, and Literature, for the Year 1804*, 192–195. London, 1805.

Dillon, Elizabeth Maddock. *New World Drama: The Performative Commons in the Atlantic World*. Durham: Duke University Press, 2014.

Dixon, Chris. *African America and Haiti: Emigration and Black Nationalism, in the Nineteenth Century*. Westport: Greenwood, 2000.

Dollimore, Jonathan. *Radical Tragedy: Religion, Ideology, and Power in the Drama of Shakespeare and His Contemporaries*. 3rd ed. Durham: Duke University Press, 2003.

Doniger, Wendy. *The Bedtrick: Tales of Sex and Masquerade*. Chicago: University of Chicago Press, 2000.

Doolen, Andy. "'Be Cautious of the Word 'Rebel'": Race, Revolution, and Transnational History in Martin Delany's *Blake; or, The Huts of America*." *American Literature* 81, no. 1 (2009): 153–179.

Douglass, Frederick. *The Heroic Slave*. 1853. In *Three Classic African-American Novels*, edited by William L. Andrews, 23–69. New York: Mentor Books, 1990.

Doyle, Laura. *Freedom's Empire: Race and the Rise of the Novel in Atlantic Modernity, 1640–1940*. Durham: Duke University Press, 2008.

Drexler, Michael J., and Ed White. "The Constitution of Toussaint: Another Origin of African American Literature." In *A Companion to African American Literature*, edited by Gene Andrew Jarrett, 59–74. Malden: Wiley-Blackwell, 2010.

Dryden, John. "Heads of an Answer to Rymer." In *The Works of John Dryden: Prose, 1668–1691; An Essay of Dramatick Poesie and Shorter Works*, 185–194. Berkeley: University of California Press, 1971.

Dubois, Laurent. *Avengers of the New World: The Story of the Haitian Revolution*. New Haven: Belknap, 2005.

Du Bois, W. E. B. "Atlanta University." In *From Servitude to Service*, 153–197. Boston: American Unitarian Association, 1905.

———. *Souls of Black Folk: Essays and Sketches*. Chicago: McClurg, 1903.

———. "The Talented Tenth." In *The Negro Problem: A Series of Articles by Representative Negroes of Today*, 31–75. New York: Pott, 1903.

Dubroca, Louis. *The Life of Toussaint Louverture, Chief of the French Rebels in St Domingo*. London: Symonds, 1802.

[Duchosal, Marie-Émile Guillaume]. "Reprise de *Spartacus*." *Journal des Théâtres* 19 (Frimaire an 3ème de la République [December 9, 1794]): 81–89.

Dziembowski, Edmond. *Un nouveau patriotisme français, 1750–1770: La France face à la puissance anglaise à l'époque de la guerre de Sept Ans*. Oxford: Voltaire Foundation, 1998.

Earle, William. *Obi; or, The History of Three-Fingered Jack*. Edited by Srinivas Aravamudan. Toronto: Broadview, 2005.

Edwards, Brent Hayes. *The Practice of Diaspora: Literature, Translation, and the Rise of Black Internationalism*. Cambridge: Harvard University Press, 2003.

Egerton, Douglas R. *Gabriel's Rebellion: The Virginia Slave Conspiracies of 1800 and 1802*. Chapel Hill: University of North Carolina Press, 1993.

Ellison, Ralph. *Invisible Man*. 1952. Reprint, New York: Vintage International, 1995.

Eversole, Richard. "Collins and the End of the Shepherd Pastoral." In *Survivals of Pastoral*, edited by Richard F. Hardin, 19–32. Lawrence: University of Kansas, 1979.

Fantham, Elaine. "*Stuprum*: Public Attitudes and Penalties for Sexual Offenses in Republican Rome." In *Roman Readings: Roman Responses to Greek Literature from Plautus to Statius and Quintilian*, 115–144. Berlin: De Gruyter, 2011.

Farr, James. "Locke, Natural Law and New World Slavery." *Political Theory* 36, no. 4 (2008): 495–522.

———. "So Vile and Miserable an Estate...': The Problem of Slavery in John Locke's Political Thought." *Political Theory* 14, no. 2 (1986): 263–289.

Fawcett, John. *Songs, Duets, and Choruses, in the Pantomimical Drama of Obi, or Three-Finger'd Jack: (Perform'd at the Theatre Royal, Hay Market) to Which Are Prefix'd Illustrative Extracts, and a Prospectus of the Action*. London: Woodfall, 1800.

Fergus, Claudius K. *Revolutionary Emancipation: Slavery and Abolitionism in the British West Indies*. Baton Rouge: Louisiana State University Press, 2013.

Ferguson, Moira. "*Oroonoko*: Birth of a Paradigm." *New Literary History* 23, no. 2 (1992): 339–359.

Figlerowicz, Marta. "'Frightful Spectacles of a Mangled King': Aphra Behn's *Oroonoko* and Narration through Theater." *New Literary History* 39, no. 2 (2008): 321–334.

Fischer, David Hackett. *Liberty and Freedom: A Visual History of America's Founding Ideas*. Oxford: Oxford University Press, 2005.

Fischer, Sibylle. *Modernity Disavowed: Haiti and the Cultures of Slavery in the Age of Revolution*. Durham: Duke University Press, 2004.

Florus, Lucius Annaeus. *Epitome of Roman History*. Translated by Edward Seymour Forster. 1929. Reprint, Cambridge: Harvard University Press, 1947.

Fludernik, Monika. *Towards a "Natural" Narratology*. New York: Routledge, 1996.

Fouchard, Jean. *Les marrons du syllabaire*. 1953. Reprint, Port-au-Prince: Deschamps, 1988.

———. *Le théâtre à Saint Domingue*. Port-au-Prince: Imprimerie de l'Etat, 1955.

Fowler, Joanna. "Dramatic and Narrative Techniques in the Novellas of Aphra Behn." *Women's Writing* 22, no. 1 (2015): 97–113.

Franklin, Benjamin. "From Benjamin Franklin to Anthony Benezet, 22 August 1772." In *January 1 through December 31, 1772*, edited by William B. Willcox, 269. Vol. 19 of *The Papers of Benjamin Franklin*. New Haven: Yale University Press, 1975.

Freedman, Estelle B. *Redefining Rape: Sexual Violence in the Era of Suffrage and Segregation*. Cambridge: Harvard University Press, 2013.

French, Peter A. *The Virtues of Vengeance*. Lawrence: University Press of Kansas, 2001.

[Fréron, Elie Catherine]. "Lettre VII: Spartacus." *L'Année Littéraire* 4 (1760): 145–166.

Fryer, Peter. *Staying Power: The History of Black People in Britain*. London: Pluto, 1984.

Futrell, Alison. "Seeing Red: Spartacus as Domestic Economist." In *Imperial Projections: Ancient Rome in Modern Popular Culture*, edited by Sandra R. Joshel, Margaret Malamud, and Donald T. McGuire Jr., 77–118. Baltimore: Johns Hopkins University Press, 2001.

Gaffield, Julia. "Complexities of Imagining Haiti: A Study of National Constitutions, 1801–1807." *Journal of Social History* 41, no. 1 (2007): 81–103.

Gainot, Bernard. "Le général Laveaux, gouverneur de Saint Domingue, député néojacobin." *Annales Historiques de la Révolution Française* 278 (1989): 433–454.

Gallicchio, Marc. *The African American Encounter with Japan and China*. Chapel Hill: University of North Carolina Press, 2000.

Gardner, Jared. *Master Plots: Race and the Founding of an American Literature, 1787–1845*. Baltimore: Johns Hopkins University Press, 1998.

Garland, David. "Penal Excess and Surplus Meaning: Public Torture Lynchings in Twentieth-Century America." *Law and Society Review* 39, no. 4 (2005): 793–833.

Garraway, Doris. *The Libertine Colony: Creolization in the Early French Caribbean*. Durham: Duke University Press, 2005.

———. "Print, Publics, and the Scene of Universal Equality in the Kingdom of Henry Christophe." *L'Esprit Créateur* 56, no. 1 (2016): 82–100.

Garrigus, John. *Before Haiti: Race and Citizenship in French Saint Domingue*. New York: Palgrave Macmillan, 2006.

Gatewood, Willard B., Jr. *Black Americans and the White Man's Burden, 1898–1903*. Urbana: University of Illinois Press, 1975.

Gavaler, Chris. "The Ku Klux Klan and the Birth of the Superhero." *Journal of Graphic Novels and Comics* 4, no. 2 (2013): 1–18.

Geggus, David Patrick. "The Bois Caïman Ceremony." In Geggus, *Haitian Revolutionary Studies*, 81–92.

———. *Haitian Revolutionary Studies*. Bloomington: Indian University Press, 2002.

———, ed. *The Impact of the Haitian Revolution in the Atlantic World*. Columbia: University of South Carolina Press, 2001.

"Genius of True English-Men." *English Broadside Ballad Archive*. Misc. 133434, Huntington Library. London, 1680. Accessed February 12, 2017. http://ebba.english.ucsb.edu/ballad/32210/xml.

Gibbs, Jenna M. "Celebrating Columbia, Mother of the White Republic." In Gibbs, *Performing the Temple of Liberty*, 17–51.

———. *Performing the Temple of Liberty: Slavery, Theater and Popular Culture in London and Philadelphia, 1760–1850*. Baltimore: Johns Hopkins University Press, 2014.

Girard, Philippe. *Toussaint Louverture: A Revolutionary Life*. New York: Basic Books, 2016.

Girard, René. *Violence and the Sacred*. Baltimore: Johns Hopkins University Press, 1979.

Glick, Jeremy Matthew. *The Black Radical Tragic: Performance, Aesthetics, and the Unfinished Haitian Revolution*. New York: New York University Press, 2016.

Gobineau, Arthur de. *The Inequality of Human Races*. Translated by Adrian Collins. New York: Putnam and Sons, 1915.

Goggi, Gianluigi. "Diderot-Raynal, l'esclavage et les lumières écossaises." *L'Esclavage et la traite sous le regard des Lumières*, edited by Jean Mondot. *Lumières* 3 (2004): 53–93.

Gould, Philip. *Barbaric Traffic: Commerce and Antislavery in the Eighteenth Century Atlantic World*. Cambridge: Harvard University Press, 2003.

Gourgaud, Gaspard. *Talks of Napoleon at St. Helena with General Baron Gourgaud*. Translated by Elizabeth Wormeley Latimer. Chicago: McClurg, 1904.

Gragnon-Lacoste, [Thomas Prosper]. *Toussaint Louverture*. Paris: Durand et Pedone-Lauriel, 1877.

Gray, Thomas R. *The Confessions of Nat Turner, the Leader of the Late Insurrection in Southampton, Va*. Baltimore, 1831.

Grégoire, M. [Henri]. *An Enquiry concerning the Intellectual and Moral Faculties, and Literature of Negroes*. Translated by David Bailie Warren. Brooklyn, 1810.

———. *Mémoire en faveur des gens de couleur ou sang-mêlés de St.-Domingue, et des autres isles françoises de l'Amérique, adressé à l'Assemblée Nationale*. Paris: Belin, 1789.

Griggs, Earl Leslie, and Clifford H. Prator, eds. *Henry Christophe and Thomas Clarkson: A Correspondence*. Berkeley: University of California Press, 1952.

Griggs, Sutton E. *Imperium in Imperio: A Study of the Negro Race Problem*. Cincinnati: Editor, 1899.

———. *Wisdom's Call*. Nashville: Orion, 1911.

Gruesser, John Cullen. *The Empire Abroad and the Empire at Home: African American Literature and the Era of Overseas Expansion*. Athens: University of Georgia Press, 2012.

Gunning, Sandra. *Race, Rape, and Lynching: The Red Record of American Literature: 1890–1912*. New York: Oxford University Press, 1996.

Guyatt, Nicholas. "'The Future Empire of Our Freedmen': Republican Colonization Schemes in Texas and Mexico, 1861–1865." In *Civil War Wests: Testing the Limits of the United States*, edited by Adam Arenson and Andrew R. Graybill, 95–117. Oakland: University of California Press, 2015.

Habib, Imtiaz. *Black Lives in the English Archives, 1500–1677: Imprints of the Invisible*. Burlington: Ashgate, 2007.

Hagan, Kenneth J. *This People's Navy: The Making of American Sea Power*. New York: Free Press, 1991.

"Haiti to Be Seized by Negroes," *Morning Herald*, May 18, 1903.

Hall, Prince. *A Charge, Delivered to the African Lodge, June 24, 1797, at Menotomy: By the Right Worshipful Prince Hall*. N.p., 1797.

Halttunen, Karen. "Humanitarianism and the Pornography of Pain in Anglo-American Culture." *American Historical Review* 100, no. 2 (1995): 303–334.

[Hawkesworth, John], *Oroonoko, a Tragedy, as It Is Now Acted at the Theatre-Royal in Drury-Lane*. London, 1759.

Hayne, Victoria. "'All Language Then Is Vile': The Theatrical Critique of Political Rhetoric in Nathaniel Lee's *Lucius Junius Brutus*." *elh* 63, no. 2 (1996): 337–365.

"Haytian Emigration." *Weekly Anglo-African*, September 28, 1861.

"Haytian Emigration in Boston." *Weekly Anglo-African*, November 16, 1861.

"Haytian Emigration in Canada." *Weekly Anglo-African*, October 10, 1861.

Helper, Hinton Rowan. *The Impending Crisis of the South: How to Meet It*. New York, 1857.

———. *Nojoque: A Question for a Continent*. New York: 1867.

Herder, Johann Gottfried. *Auch eine Philosophie der Geschichte zur Bildung der Menschheit*. N.p., 1774.

Hersch, Seymour. "On James Farr's 'So Vile and Miserable an Estate.'" *Political Theory* 16, no. 3 (1988): 502–503.

[Higginson, Thomas]. "Nat Turner's Insurrection." *Atlantic Monthly* 8, no. 66 (1861): 173–187.

Hill, Christopher. "The Norman Yoke." In *Puritanism and Revolution: Studies in Interpretation of the English Revolution of the 17th Century*, 46–111. 1958. Reprint, New York: St Martin's Press, 1997.

Hinks, Peter P. *To Awaken My Afflicted Brethren: David Walker and the Problem of Antebellum Slave Resistance*. University Park: Pennsylvania State University Press, 1997.

Hodes, Martha. "The Sexualization of Reconstruction Politics: White Women and Black Men in the South after the Civil War." *Journal of the History of Sexuality* 3, no. 3 (1993): 402–417.

Hoffmann, Léon-François. *Le Nègre romantique: Personnage littéraire et obsession collective*. Paris: Payot, 1973.

Horne, Gerald. *Confronting Black Jacobins: The United States, the Haitian Revolution, and the Origins of the Dominican Republic*. New York: Monthly Review Press, 2015.

Howard-Pitney, David. *The African American Jeremiad: Appeals for Justice in America*. 1992. Reprint, Philadelphia: Temple University Press, 2005.

Hughes, Derek. "Rape on the Restoration Stage." *Eighteenth Century* 46, no. 3 (2005): 225–236.

———. *The Theatre of Aphra Behn*. New York: Palgrave, 2001.

———. *Versions of Blackness: Key Texts on Slavery from the Seventeenth Century*. Cambridge: Cambridge University Press, 2007.

Hugo, Victor. *Napoléon le Petit*. Bruxelles, 1852.

Hulme, Peter. *Colonial Encounters: Europe and the Native Caribbean, 1492–1797*. London: Methuen, 1986.

Hunnings, Leanne. "Spartacus in Nineteenth-Century England: Proletarian, Pole and Christ." In *Remaking the Classics: Literature, Genre and Media in Britain 1800–2000*, edited by Christopher Stray, 1–19. London: Duckworth, 2007.

Iriye, Akira. *Pacific Estrangement: Japanese and American Expansion, 1897–1911*. Cambridge: Harvard University Press, 1972.

"Jamaica, a Poem, in Three Parts." 1777. In *Caribbeana: An Anthology of English Literature of the West Indies*, edited by Thomas W. Krise, 328–339. Chicago: University of Chicago Press, 1999.

"James G. Birney." *Liberator*, December 26, 1835.

James, C. L. R. *The Black Jacobins: Toussaint Louverture and the San Domingo Revolution*. 1961. Reprint, London: Vintage Books, 1989.

Jefferson, Thomas. *Notes on the State of Virginia*. Philadelphia, 1788.

Jenson, Deborah. *Beyond the Slave Narrative: Politics, Sex, and Manuscripts in the Haitian Revolution*. Liverpool: Liverpool University Press, 2011.

———. "Living by Metaphor in the Haitian Declaration of Independence: *Tigers and Cognitive Theory*." In *The Haitian Declaration of Independence: Creation, Context, and Legacy*, edited by Julia Gaffield, 72–92. Charlottesville: University of Virginia Press, 2016.

———. "Reading between the Lines: Dessalines's Anticolonial Imperialism in Venezuela and Trinidad." In Jenson, *Beyond the Slave Narrative*, 161–194.

Jewett, Robert, and John Shelton Lawrence. *The American Monomyth*. Lanham: University Press of America, 1988.

[Johnson, James W.]. *Autobiography of an Ex-colored Man*. Boston: Sherman, French, 1912.

Johnson, Sylvester A. *African American Religions, 1500–2000: Colonialism, Democracy, and Freedom*. New York: Cambridge University Press, 2015.

Jones, Martha S. "Birthright Citizenship and Reconstruction's Unfinished Revolution." Forum: The Future of Reconstruction Studies. *Journal of the Civil War Era* 7, no. 1 (2017): 10. Accessed July 15, 2018. https://journalofthecivilwarera.org/forum-the-future-of-reconstruction-studies/birthright-citizenship-reconstructions-unfinished-revolution.

Kanzler, Katja. "'Race' and Realism: Vision, Textuality, and Charles Chesnutt's *The Marrow of Tradition*." *Zeitschrift für Anglistik und Amerikanistik* 57. no. 4 (2009): 339–353.

Kawash, Samira. *Dislocating the Color Line: Identity, Hybridity, and Singularity in African-American Narrative*. Stanford: Stanford University Press, 1997.

Kemble, Frances Anne. *Journal of a Residence on a Georgian Plantation in 1838–1839*. New York: Harper and Brothers, 1863.

Kent, R. K. "Palmares: An African State in Brazil." In Price, *Maroon Societies*, 170–190.

Kilgore, John Mac. "The Cakewalk of Capital in Charles Chesnutt's *The Marrow of Tradition*." *American Literature* 84, no. 1 (2012): 61–87.

Kirshenbaum, Andrea Meryl. "'The Vampire That Hovers over Carolina': Gender, White Supremacy, and the Wilmington Race Riot of 1898." *Southern Cultures* 4, no. 3 (1998): 6–30.

Knadler, Stephen. *Remapping Citizenship and the Nation in African-American Literature*. New York: Routledge, 2010.

Korngold, Ralph. *Citizen Toussaint*. Boston: Little, Brown, 1944.

Kowaleski-Wallace, Elizabeth. *The British Slave Trade and Public Memory*. New York: Columbia University Press, 2006.

Kramer, David. "Imperium in Imperio: Sutton Griggs's Imagined War of 1898." *War, Literature and the Arts* 25 (2013): 1–21.

Krug, Jessica A. *Fugitive Modernities: Kisama and the Politics of Freedom*. Durham: Duke University Press, 2018.

Kubrick, Stanley, dir. *Spartacus*. Beverly Hills: Bryna Productions, 1960.

Lachance, Paul. "Repercussions of the Haitian Revolution in Louisiana." In Geggus, *Impact of the Haitian Revolution*, 209–230.

Lacroix, Pamphile de. *Mémoires pour servir à l'histoire de la révolution de Saint Domingue*. Paris: Pillet Aîné, 1819.

[Laplace, Antoine de]. *Oronoko, ou le Prince Nègre*. Amsterdam, 1745.

La Porte, Abbé de. "Lettre XI. SPARTACUS, tragédie de M. Saurin." *L'Observateur Littéraire* 2 (1760): 241–256.

Las Cases, Emmanuel-Auguste-Dieudonné de. *The Life, Exile, and Conversations of the Emperor Napoleon*. 2 vols. London: Colburn, 1835.

[Laveaux, Etienne de] *Saint Domingue: Compte rendu par le général Laveaux à ses concitoyens, à l'opinion publique, aux autorités constituées*. Paris, 1797.

Laveaux, [Stephen], and Henry Perroud. "To the United States, Commercial Towns, the Merchants and Captains of the Continent of America and the Danish Islands." *Greenleaf's New York Journal*, May 20, 1796, 3.

Lazo, Rodrigo. *Writing to Cuba: Filibustering and Cuban Exiles in the United States*. Chapel Hill: University of North Carolina Press, 2005.

[Le Blanc, Abbé]. *Lettres d'un François*. Vol. 2. La Haye: Neaulme, 1745.

Lee, Nathaniel. *Lucius Junius Brutus: Father of His Country; A Tragedy*. London, 1681.

Lemieux, Jamila. "*Django Unchained*: A Dark Buddy Comedy about Slavery and Rape?" *Clutch Magazine*. Accessed February 12, 2017. www.clutchmagonline.com/2011/06/django-unchained-a-dark-buddy-comedy-about-slavery-and-rape/.

Leslie, Charles. *A New History of Jamaica: From the Earliest Accounts, to the Taking of Porto Bello by Vice-Admiral Vernon*. London, 1740.

"Letter from Hayti." *Weekly Anglo-African*, August 10, 1861.

Levine, Robert S. *Martin R. Delany: A Documentary Reader*. Chapel Hill: University of North Carolina Press, 2003.

Lipking, Joanna. "Confusing Matters: Searching the Backgrounds of *Oroonoko*." In *Aphra Behn Studies*, edited by Janet Todd, 259–284. Cambridge: Cambridge University Press, 1996.

Litvack, Frances. *Le droit du seigneur in European and American Literature*. Birmingham: Summa, 1984.

Litwack, Leon F. *North of Slavery: The Negro in the Free States, 1790–1860*. Chicago: University of Chicago Press, 1961.

Livy (Titus Livius). *The History of Rome*. Book I. Translated by Benjamin O. Forster. Cambridge: Harvard University Press, 1919.

Locke, John. *Two Treatises on Government*. London: Churchill, 1690.

Loftis, John. Introduction to *Lucius Junius Brutus*, by Nathaniel Lee. Edited by John Loftis, xi–xxiv. Lincoln: University of Nebraska Press, 1967.

Long, Edward. *The History of Jamaica; or, General Survey of the Antient and Modern State of that Island*. 2 vols. London: Lowndes, 1774.

Lorde, Audre. "The Master's Tools Will Never Dismantle the Master's House." In *Sister Outsider: Essays and Speeches*, 110–114. Berkeley: Crossing Press, 1984.

Lovejoy, Joseph C., and Owen Lovejoy. *Memoir of the Rev. Elijah P. Lovejoy; Who Was Murdered in Defence of the Liberty of the Press, at Alton, Illinois, Nov. 7 1837*. New York, 1838.

Lynch, Kathleen M. *Roger Boyle, First Earl of Orrery*. Knoxville: University of Tennessee Press, 1965.

MacPherson, C. B. *Political Theory of Possessive Individualism*. Oxford: Oxford University Press, 1962.

Madiou, Thomas. *Histoire d'Haïti*. 3 vols. Port-au-Prince: Courtois, 1847–1848.

Malone, Josephine. *Peter Newby: Friend to All Mankind; a Study of His Life and Poems and Friends*. Aylesford: Saint Albert's Press, 1964.

[Mandar-Argeaut], *Quelques éclaircissemens sur les troubles survenus dans le département du Sud de Saint Domingue, en fructidor an 4ème (août 1796 vieux style)*. Hambourg, 1797.

Marcellesi, Laure. "Louis-Sébastien Mercier: Prophet, Abolitionist, Colonialist." *Studies in Eighteenth-Century Culture* 40 (2011): 247–273.

Markley, Robert. "Sentimentality as Performance: Shaftesbury, Sterne, and the Theatrics of Virtue." In *The New Eighteenth Century: Theory, Politics, English Literature*, edited by Felicity Nussbaum and Laura Brown, 210–230. New York: Methuen, 1987.

Marx, Karl. *The Eighteenth Brumaire of Louis Bonaparte*. Translated by Daniel De Leon. Chicago: Kerr, 1907.

McClintock, Anne. "'No Longer in a Future Heaven': Gender, Race and Nationalism." In *Dangerous Liaisons: Gender, Nationalism, and Postcolonial Perspectives*, edited by Anne McClintock, Aamir Mufti, and Ella Shohat, 89–112. Minneapolis: University of Minnesota Press, 1997.

McGann, Jerome. Introduction to *Blake; or, The Huts of America*, by Martin R. Delany. Edited by Jerome McGann, ix–xxxii. Cambridge: Harvard University Press, 2017.

McIntosh, Tabitha, and Grégory Pierrot, "Capturing the Likeness of Henry I of Haiti (1805–1822)." *Atlantic Studies* 14, no. 2 (2017): 127–151.

McKeon, Michael. *The Origins of the English Novel, 1600–1740*. Baltimore: Johns Hopkins University Press, 1987.

Mentor, Gaétan. *Histoire de la franc-maçonnerie en Haïti: Les fils noirs de la veuve*. Pétionville: FOKAL, 2003.

Mercier, Louis-Sébastien. *Astræa's Return; or, The Halcyon Days of France in the Year 2440: A Dream*. Translated by Harriot Augusta Freeman. London, 1797.

———. *L'An 2440, rêve s'il en fût jamais*. Amsterdam: Harrevelt, 1770.

———. *Memoirs of the Year Two Thousand Five Hundred*. Translated by W. Hooper. Vol 1. London, 1772.

Mignolo, Walter D. "Afterword: What Does the Black Legend Have to Do with Race?" In *Rereading the Black Legend: The Discourses of Religious and Racial Differences in the Renaissance Empires*, edited by Margaret R. Greer, Walter D. Mignolo, and Maureen Quilligan, 312–324. Chicago: University of Chicago Press, 2007.

Miller, Christopher L. *The French Atlantic Triangle: Literature and Culture of the Slave Trade*. Durham: Duke University Press, 2008.

Milton, John. *The Tenure of Kings and Magistrates*. Edited by William T. Allison. 1649. Reprint, New York: Holt, 1911.

Montesquieu, Baron de. *Montesquieu's Considerations in the Causes of the Grandeur and Decadence of the Romans*. Translated by Jehu Baker. 1734. Reprint, New York: Appleton, 1889.

———. *Persian Letters*. Translated by John Davidson. London: Gibbings, 1899.

Moreau de Saint-Méry, M. L. E. *Description topographique, physique, civile, politique et historique de la partie française de l'isle Saint-Domingue*. Vol. 1. Philadelphia, 1797.

Morgan, Charlotte E. *The Rise of the Novel of Manners: A Study of English Prose Fiction between 1600 and 1740*. New York: Columbia University Press, 1911.

Moses, Diana C. "Livy's Lucretia and the Validity of Coerced Consent in Roman Law." In *Consent and Coercion to Sex and Marriage in Ancient and Medieval Societies*, edited by Angeliki E. Laiou, 39–81. Washington D.C.: Dumbarton Oaks, 1993.

Moses, Wilson J. *Afrotopia: The Roots of African American Popular History*. Cambridge: Cambridge University Press, 1998.

———. *Black Messiahs and Uncle Toms: Social and Literary Manipulations of a Religious Myth*. University Park: Pennsylvania State University Press, 1982.

[Mulligan, Hugh]. "The Lovers: An African Eclogue." *Gentleman's Magazine* 54 (January 1784): 199–200.

———. "The Lovers: An African Eclogue." In [Mulligan], *Poems Chiefly on Slavery*, 23–31.

———. *Poems Chiefly on Slavery and Oppression, with Notes and Illustrations*. London: Lowndes, 1788.

———. "The Slave: An American Eclogue." In [Mulligan], *Poems Chiefly on Slavery*, 1–7.

[Muralt, Béat-Louis de]. *Lettres sur les Anglois, les François, et sur les Voiages*. [Geneva: Fabri and Barrillot], 1725.

"Negroes Plan to Take Haiti." *Plain Dealer*, May 17, 1903.

"The Negro Plot: Copy of a Circular from the Governor of the State of South Carolina." *Alexandria Herald*, August 10, 1822.

Newman, Gerald. *The Rise of English Nationalism, a Cultural History 1740–1830*. New York: St Martin's Press, 1987.

Newman, Simon P. "American Political Culture and the French and Haitian Revolutions." In Geggus, *Impact of the Haitian Revolution*, 72–89.

Nicholls, David. "A Work of Combat: Mulatto Historians and the Haitian Past: 1847–1867." *Journal of Interamerican Studies and World Affairs* 16, no. 1 (1974): 15–38.

Nyong'o, Tavia. *The Amalgamation Waltz: Race, Performance, and the Ruses of Memory*. Minneapolis: University of Minnesota Press, 2009.

Obadele-Starks, Ernest. *Freebooters and Smugglers: The Foreign Slave Trade in the United States after 1808*. Fayetteville: University of Arkansas Press, 2007.

Obenson, Tambay A. "I've Read Tarantino's 'Django Unchained' Script and, Well, It's Not Nat Turner's Revolt." *IndieWire*, May 9, 2011. Accessed February 12, 2017. http://blogs.indiewire.com/shadowandact/ive_read_tarantinos_django _unchained_script_and_well_its_certainly_not_nat.

"Observations sur le Spartacus de Saurin, et sur le jeu de Larive dans cette tragédie: Second extrait." *Journal des Théâtres* 23 (Frimaire an 3ème de la République [December 13, 1794]): 97–103.

Oldfield, J. R. "The Eighteenth-Century Background." In *Popular Politics and British Anti-slavery: The Mobilisation of Public Opinion against the Slave Trade, 1787–1807*, 7–69. London: Routledge, 1998.

"Original Communication." *Freedom's Journal*, April 25, 1828, 38.

Pagden, Anthony. *The Fall of Natural Man: The American Indian and the Origins of Comparative Ethnology*. Cambridge: Cambridge University Press, 1987.

Painter, Nell Irvin. *Exodusters: Black Migration to Kansas after Reconstruction*. 1976. Reprint, New York: Norton, 1986.

Parker, Nate, dir. *The Birth of a Nation*. Burnaby, B.C.: Bron Studios, 2016.

Patterson, Orlando. "Slavery and Slave Revolts: A Sociohistorical Analysis of the First Maroon War, 1665–1740." In Price, *Maroon Societies*, 246–292.

Peabody, Sue. *"There Are No Slaves in France": The Political Culture of Race and Slavery in the Ancien Régime*. New York: Oxford University Press, 1996.

[Peele, George]. *The Battle of Alcazar*. London: Edward Allde, 1594. Chiswick: Malone Society Reprints, 1907.

[Perroud, Henry]. *L'Ordonnateur de Saint Domingue au ministre plénipotentiaire et consuls de la République auprès des Etats-Unis d'Amérique*. Cap. 10 Germinal Year 4 (March 30, 1796). Accessed July 16, 2018. http://gallica.bnf.fr/ark:/12148 /bpt6k58043162.r=.langEN.

———. *Précis des derniers troubles qui ont eu lieu dans la partie du Nord de Saint Domingue, adressé au ministre de la Marine et des Colonies*. Cap-Français: P. Roux, 26 Germinal Year 4 (April 15, 1796). Accessed July 16, 2018. https://archive.org /details/prcisdesdernieooperr.

Phillips, Wendell. "Toussaint L'Ouverture." In *Speeches, Lectures and Letters*, 468–494. Boston: Lee and Shepard, 1884.

Pickens, William. "Hayti." *Yale Literary Magazine* 68, no. 7 (1903): 232–238.

Pierrot, Grégory. "'Our Hero': Toussaint Louverture in British Representations." *Criticism* 50, no. 4 (2008): 581–607.

Plummer, Brenda Gayle. "The Afro-American Response to the Occupation of Haiti, 1915–1934." *Phylon* 43, no. 2 (1982): 125–143.

Plutarch. "Crassus." In *Plutarch's Lives*. Vol. 3, edited by T. E. Page, E. Capps, and W. H. D. Rouse; translated by Bernadotte Perrin, 313–423. 1916. Reprint, London: Heinemann, 1932.

Poitevin, Kimberly. "Inventing Whiteness: Cosmetics, Race, and Women in Early Modern England." *Journal for Early Modern Cultural Studies* 11, no. 1 (2011): 59–89.

Popkin, Jeremy D. *You Are All Free: The Haitian Revolution and the Abolition of Slavery*. Cambridge: Cambridge University Press, 2010.

Powell, Philip Wayne. *Tree of Hate: Propaganda and Prejudices Affecting United States Relations with the Hispanic World*. 1971. Reprint, New York: Basic Books, 1985.

Prasad, Pratima. *Colonialism, Race, and the French Imagination*. New York: Routledge, 2009.

Price, Richard. *Maroon Societies: Rebel Slave Communities in the Americas*. 1979. Reprint, Baltimore: Johns Hopkins University Press, 1996.

[PUCPDDLM]. *Observations d'un habitant des colonies sur le "Mémoire en faveur des gens de couleur: Ou sang-mêlés, de Saint Domingue et des autres isles françoises de l'Amérique" adressé à l'Assemblée Nationale par M. Grégoire, curé d'Emberménil, député de Lorraine*. December 16, 1789. *Gallica.fr*. Accessed May 12, 2012. http://gallica.bnf.fr/ark:/12148/bpt6k57904669/.

Rable, George C. *But There Was No Peace: The Role of Violence in the Politics of Reconstruction*. 1984. Reprint, Athens: University of Georgia Press, 2007.

Raimond, Julien. *Rapport de Julien Raimond, commissaire délégué par le gouvernement français aux isles-sous-le-vent, au ministre de la Marine*. Cap Français: Roux, 1797.

Rainsford, Marcus. *An Historical Account of the Black Empire of Hayti*. Edited by Paul Youngquist and Grégory Pierrot. 1805. Reprint, Durham: Duke University Press, 2013.

Rameau, S., Dulievre, Halle Aime, A. Dubrenil, D. Prosper Faur, et al. "Slavery in America: How Can It Be Abolished? Letter from Hayti." *Weekly Anglo-African*, April 27, 1861.

Rawidowicz, Simon. *Israel, the Ever-Dying People, and Other Essays*. Edited by Benjamin C. I. Ravid. Cranbury: Associated University Presses, 1986.

Raynal, [Guillaume-Thomas], Abbé. *A Philosophical and Political History of the Settlements and Trade of the Europeans in the East and West Indies*. Translated by J. Justamond. 2nd ed. Vol. 3. London: Cadell, 1776.

———. *Histoire philosophique et politique des établissements et du commerce des Européens dans les deux Indes*. 6 vols. Amsterdam, 1770.

———. *Histoire philosophique et politique des établissements et du commerce des Européens dans les deux Indes*. 2nd ed. 7 vols. La Haye: Gosse Fils, 1774.

"Réclamation des nègres libres, colons américains." *Le Moniteur Universel* 6 (November 29, 1789): 22.

Redpath, James. Preface to *Toussaint L'Ouverture: A Biography and Autobiography*, by John Relly Beard, iii–vi. Boston: Redpath, 1863.

Reid, Roddy. *Families in Jeopardy: Regulating the Social Body in France, 1750–1910*. Stanford: Stanford University Press, 1993.

Review of "West Indian Eclogues." *General Magazine and Impartial Review* 1 (1787): 199–200.

Richards, Jennifer. "Assumed Simplicity and the Critique of Nobility; or, How Castiglione Read Cicero." *Renaissance Quarterly* 54, no. 2 (2001): 460–486.

Richards, Leonard L. *"Gentlemen of Property and Standing": Anti-Abolition Mobs in Jacksonian America*. Oxford: Oxford University Press, 1970.

Rigaud, André. *Mémoire du général de brigade A. Rigaud, en réfutation des écrits calomnieux contre les citoyens de couleur de Saint Domingue*. Aux Cayes, [1797].

Roach, Joseph. *Cities of the Dead: Circum-Atlantic Performance*. New York: Columbia University Press, 1996.

Roediger, David R. *The Wages of Whiteness: Race and the Making of the American Working Class*. 1991. Reprint, London: Verso, 1999.

Rogers, Ibram H. *The Black Campus Movement: Black Students and the Racial Reconstitution of Higher Education, 1965–1972*. New York: Palgrave Macmillan, 2012.

Rogers, Katherine M. "Fact and Fiction in Aphra Behn's *Oroonoko*." *Studies in the Novel* 20 (1988): 1–15.

Rojas, Fabio. *From Black Power to Black Studies: How a Radical Social Movement Became an Academic Discipline*. Baltimore: Johns Hopkins University Press, 2007.

Rose-Millar, Charlotte. *Witchcraft, the Devil, and Emotions in Early Modern England*. London: Routledge, 2017.

Rushton, Edward. *Poems*. Liverpool, 1806.

[Rushton, Edward]. *West-Indian Eclogues*. London: Lowndes, 1787.

Russell, Trusten Wheeler. *Voltaire, Dryden and Heroic Tragedy*. New York: Columbia University Press, 1946.

Rymer, Thomas. *The Tragedies of the Last Age Consider'd and Examin'd by the Practice of the Antients, and by the Common Sense of All Ages*. London, 1678.

"Sad Intelligence from Hayti." *Weekly Anglo-African*, August 31, 1861.

Saint-Lambert, Jean-François de. *Ziméo*. In *Les Saisons, poème*, 226–259. Amsterdam, 1769.

Saint-Rémy, Joseph. *Vie de Toussaint-L'Ouverture*. Paris: Moquet, 1850.

Saurin, [Bernard-Joseph]. Preface to *Spartacus, tragédie, par M. Saurin de l'Académie Françoise*, vi–xv. Paris: Duchesne, 1769.

———. *Spartacus, tragédie, par M. Saurin de l'Académie Françoise*. Paris: Prault, 1760.

Scott, A. O. "The Black, The White and the Angry." *New York Times*, December 25, 2012: C1.

Scott, David. *Conscripts of Modernity: The Tragedy of Colonial Enlightenment*. Durham: Duke University Press, 2004.

Seeber, Edward D. "Oroonoko in France in the XVIIIth Century," *PMLA* 51, no. 4 (1936): 953–959.

Segal, Alan. *Rebecca's Children: Judaism and Christianity in the Roman World*. Cambridge: Harvard University Press, 1986.

Seraille. William. "Afro-American Emigration to Haiti during the Civil War." *Americas* 35, no. 2 (1978): 185–200.

Shakespeare, William. *The Tragedy of Titus Andronicus*. Edited by Elmer Edgar Stoll. 1593. Reprint, New York: Macmillan, 1913.

Shaw, Brent D. *Spartacus and the Slave Wars: A Brief History with Documents*. Boston: Bedford/Saint Martin's Press, 2001.

———. "Spartacus before Marx: Liberty and Servitude." *Princeton/Stanford Working Papers in Classics*. Version 2.2. November 2005. www.princeton.edu/~pswpc /pdfs/shaw/110516.pdf.

Shelby, Tommie. "Two Conceptions of Black Nationalism: Martin Delany on the Meaning of Black Political Solidarity." *Political Theory* 31, no. 5 (2003): 664–692.

Sheller, Mimi. *Citizenship from Below: Erotic Agency and Caribbean Freedom*. Durham: Duke University Press, 2012.

Silber, Nina. *The Romance of Reunion: Northerners and the South, 1865–1900*. Chapel Hill: University of North Carolina Press, 1993.

Simanga, Michael. *Amiri Baraka and the Congress of African People: History and Memory*. New York: Palgrave Macmillan, 2015.

Sommerville, Diane Miller. *Rape and Race in the Nineteenth-Century South*. Chapel Hill: University of North Carolina Press, 2004.

Southerne, Thomas. *Oroonoko: A Tragedy as It Is Acted at the Theatre-Royal, by His Majesty's Servants*. London: Playford, 1696.

Southey, Robert. "Introduction, with Observations on Uneducated Poets." In *Attempts in Verse by John Jones, an Old Servant*, edited by Robert Southey, 1–168. London: Murray, 1831.

Spengemann, William. "The Earliest American Novel: Aphra Behn's *Oroonoko*." *Nineteenth-Century Fiction* 38 (1983–1984): 384–414.

Spillers, Hortense. "Mama's Baby, Papa's Maybe: An American Grammar Book." *Diacritics* 17, no. 2 (1987): 64–81.

Spurr, John. "Shaftesbury and the Seventeenth Century." In *Anthony Ashley Cooper, First Earl of Shaftesbury, 1621–1683*, edited by John Spurr, 1–25. London: Ashgate, 2011.

Starke, Catherine Juanita. *Black Portraiture in American Fiction: Stock Characters, Archetypes, and Individuals*. New York: Basic Books, 1971.

[Stephen, James]. *Buonaparte in the West Indies; or, The History of Toussaint Louverture, the African Hero*. 3 parts. London: Hatchard, 1803.

Stephens, M. D. [James Stephen]. *The History of Toussaint Louverture: A New Edition, with a Dedication to his Imperial Majesty the Emperor of all the Russias*. London: Butterworth and Sons, 1814.

Suggs, Henry Lewis. "The Response of the African American Press to the United States Occupation of Haiti, 1915–1934." *Journal of African American History* 87 (2002): 70–82.

Sundquist, Eric. *To Wake the Nations: Race in the Making of American Literature*. Cambridge: Harvard University Press, 1992.

Sypher, Wylie. *Guinea's Captive Kings: British Anti-Slavery Literature of the XVIIIth Century*. New York: Octagon Books, 1969.

Tal, Kali. "That Just Kills Me: Black Militant Near Future Fiction." *Social Text* 20, no. 2 (2002): 65–91.

Tarantino, Quentin, dir. *Django Unchained*. Los Angeles: Weinstein, 2012.

Thomas, Susie. "This Thing of Darkness I Acknowledge Mine: Aphra Behn's *Abdelazer; or, The Moor's Revenge*." *Restoration: Studies in English Literary Culture, 1660–1700* 22, no. 1 (1998): 18–39.

Thompson, Ayanna. *Performing Race and Torture on the Early Modern Stage*. New York: Routledge, 2008.

———. "When Race Is Colored: Abjection and Racial Characterization in *Titus Andronicus* and *Oroonoko*." In Thompson, *Performing Race and Torture*, 51–74.

Thorndike, Ashley H. *Tragedy*. Boston: Houghton Mifflin, 1908.

Tissier, André. *Les spectacles à Paris pendant la Révolution: Répertoire analytique, chronologique et bibliographique*. Genève: Droz, 2002.

Todd, Janet. *The Secret Life of Aphra Behn*. New Brunswick: Rutgers University Press, 1997.

Tomko, Michael. "Abolition Poetry, National Identity, and Religion: The Case of Peter Newby's *The Wrongs of Almoona*." *Eighteenth Century* 48, no. 1 (2007): 25–43.

Tomlinson, Tracey E. "The Restoration English History Plays of Roger Boyle, Earl of Orrery." *Studies in English Literature* 43, no. 3 (2003): 559–577.

"To the Honourable the Senate and House of Representatives of the United States." *African Intelligencer* 1, no. 1 (1820): 23–27.

"Toussaint Louverture." *Annual Register for the Year 1798*, 1800, 249.

Trouillot, Michel-Rolph. *Silencing the Past: Power and the Production of History*. Boston: Beacon, 1995.

Turner, James Grantham. "'Romance' and the Novel in Restoration England." *Review of English Studies* 63, no. 258 (2012): 58–85.

Ullman, Victor. *Martin R. Delany: The Beginnings of Black Nationalism*. Boston: Beacon, 1971.

Van Evrie, John. H. *Negroes and Negro "Slavery": The First an Inferior Race, the Latter Its Normal Condition*. New York: Van Evrie, Horton, 1861.

———. *White Supremacy and Negro Subordination; or, Negroes a Subordinate Race, and (So-Called) Slavery Its Normal Condition*. 1867. Reprint, New York: Van Evrie, Norton, 1870.

Vaughan, Virginia Mason. *Performing Blackness on English Stages, 1500–1800*. Cambridge: Cambridge University Press, 2005.

["Voici, sur Toussaint"]. *Le Moniteur Universel* 110 (20 Nivôse Year 7 [January 9, 1799]): 448–449.

Voltaire. "A M. Saurin." *Oeuvres complètes*, 12:73. Paris: Didot, 1876.

———. *Brutus*. In Voltaire, *Dramatic Works*, 1:225–311.

———. "A Discourse on Tragedy: In a Letter to Lord Bolingbroke." In Voltaire, *Dramatic Works*, 199–223.

———. *The Dramatic Works of Mr. De Voltaire*. Vol. 1. Translated by Rev. Mr. Francklin. London, 1761.

———. *Essai sur les moeurs et l'esprit des nations et sur les principaux faits de l'histoire*

depuis Charlemagne jusqu'à Louis XIII. 2 vols. 1769. Reprint, Paris: Garnier
Frères, 1963.

———. *A Philosophical Dictionary from the French of M. de Voltaire.* Vol. 6. London,
1824.

———. *The Philosophy of History.* Glasgow, 1766.

Vorpahl, Ben Merchant. "Roosevelt, Wister, Turner and Remington." In *A Literary
History of the American West*, edited by J. Golden Taylor and Thomas J. Lyon,
276–302. Fort Worth: Texas Christian University Press, 1987.

Wahnich, Sophie. *In Defence of the Terror: Liberty or Death in the French Revolution.*
London: Verso, 2015.

Walker, David. *An Appeal to the Coloured Citizens of the World, but in Particular,
and Very Expressly, to Those of the United States of America.* 3rd ed. Boston, 1830.

Wallace, Maurice. "'Are We Men?': Prince Hall, Martin Delany, and the Masculine Ideal in Black Freemasonry, 1775–1865." *American Literary History* 9, no. 3
(1997): 396–424.

Walvin, James. *England, Slaves and Freedom, 1776–1838.* Houndmills: Macmillan,
1986.

Waring, Robert Lewis. *As We See It.* Washington D.C.: Sudwarth, 1910.

Warner, Samuel. *Authentic and Impartial Narrative of the Tragical Scene Which Was
Witnessed in Southampton County (Virginia) on Monday the 22d of August Last,
When Fifty-Five of Its Inhabitants (Mostly Women and Children) Were Inhumanly
Massacred by the Blacks!* New York, 1831.

Warren, Kenneth W. *What Was African American Literature?* Cambridge: Harvard
University Press, 2011.

Waters, Hazel. *Racism on the Victorian Stage: Representation of Slavery and the Black
Character.* Cambridge: Cambridge University Press, 2007.

Weheliye, Alexander. *Habeas Viscus: Racializing Assemblages, Biopolitics, and Black
Feminist Theories of the Human.* Durham: Duke University Press, 2014.

Wells-Barnett, Ida B. *The Red Record: Tabulated Statistics and Alleged Causes of
Lynching in the United States.* Chicago, 1895.

"West-Indian Eclogues." *Critical Review* 64 (1787): 434–435.

Whaley, John. *A Collection of Poems.* Cambridge, 1732.

[Wharton, Philip, Duke of]. *True Briton*, June 3, 1723.

"What Shall Be Done with the Slaves?" *Weekly Anglo-African*, November 23, 1861.

White, Ashli. *Encountering Revolution: Haiti and the Making of the Early Republic.*
Baltimore: Johns Hopkins University Press, 2010.

Williams, Rachel Marie-Crane. "A War in Black and White: The Cartoons of Norman Ethre Jennett and the North Carolina Election of 1898." *Southern Cultures*
19, no. 2 (2013): 7–27.

Williamson, Joel. *New People: Miscegenation and Mulattoes in the United States.* Baton Rouge: Louisiana State University Press, 1995.

Wilson, Kathleen. *The Island Race: Englishness, Empire and Gender in the Eighteenth Century.* London: Routledge, 2003.

Wister, Owen. "The Evolution of the Cow-Puncher." *Harper's* 91, no. 544 (1895):
602–616.

———. *Lady Baltimore*. New York: Macmillan, 1906.

———. *The Virginian: A Horseman of the Plains*. New York: Macmillan, 1902.

Woertendyke, Gretchen. "Haiti and the New-World Novel." In *The Haitian Revolution and the Early United States*, edited by Elizabeth Maddock Dillon and Michael Drexler, 232–249. Philadelphia: University of Philadelphia Press, 2016.

"A Woman's Lot." In *Black Women in White America: A Documentary History*, edited by Gerda Lerner, 149–215. 1972. Reprint, New York: Vintage Books, 1992.

Woodbridge, Linda. *English Revenge Drama*. Cambridge: Cambridge University Press, 2010.

Woodson, Carter Godwin. "The Waring Family." *Negro History Bulletin* 11, no. 2 (1948): 99–107.

The Wrongs of Almoona; or, The African's Revenge. Liverpool, 1788.

Yellin, Eric S. *Racism in the Nation's Service: Government Workers and the Color Line in Woodrow Wilson's America*. Chapel Hill: University of North Carolina Press, 2013.

Youngquist, Paul, and Grégory Pierrot. Introduction to Rainsford, *Historical Account*, xvii–lvi.

Zurcher, Amelia. "Serious Extravagance: Romance Writing in the Seventeenth Century." *Literature Compass* 8, no. 6 (2011): 376–389.

INDEX

Abdelazer (Behn), 15, 21, 36–40, 48, 49
abolitionism, 16, 20, 66, 67, 88–89; ameliorist, 81, 84, 85, 89, 121, 135; American,
129, 131, 133, 138, 139–145, 154, 160, 166,
167, 183; American Anti-Slavery Society,
139; black, 161; English, 97, 128, 137, 141,
143; French, 97, 103; Société des Amis
des Noirs, 97; Society for Effecting the
Abolition of the Slave Trade, 97; white,
89, 144, 154
—poetry of, 16, 54, 73–79, 88–89, 113–114,
117, 122; eclogue genre in, 73–75, 78, 79,
81; elemental trope in, 76, 79, 81, 86, 124,
128, 156
—rhetoric of, 78, 84, 139, 146, 160; discovery mode in, 18, 141, 142, 144; sensibility in, 78, 80
Affair of 30 Ventôse Year IV, 16, 100; as racialized conflict, 105–109
Africa: Africanization, 149, 152; Africanness,
57, 120; American literary representation
of, 50, 41, 135, 156, 202–203; emigration
to, 135–136, 145–146, 171; European
literary representation of, 25, 27, 41, 43,
56, 64–65, 67–68, 78–82, 89; genius of,
76–77, 78, 106
African Eclogues (Chatterton), 73–75
American Anti-Slavery Society, 139
American Colonization Society, 136, 137,
139, 227n36
American Revolution, 116, 158, 170

anciens libres, 100, 110, 120. *See also* gens de
couleur; mulatto
Anglo-Saxon: freedom and race myth, 9, 12,
154, 186, 188–189; race, 170, 171, 190, 200
Aponte, José, 149, 225n130
*Appeal to the Coloured Citizens of the World,
An* (Walker), 134–138
aristocracy. *See* nobility
Aristotle, natural hierarchy theory of, 5, 32–
33, 35, 36, 42, 48. *See also* nobility
As We See It (Waring), 17, 191–198, 204

Banneker, Benjamin, 169, 170
Barbault-Royer, Pierre-François, 107
Beard, John Relly, 141–143
Beaumarchais, 82–84, 87, 218n117
Behn, Aphra, 19, 20, 21, 36–40, 64, 112, 154,
155; *Abdelazer*, 15, 21, 36–40, 48, 49. See
also *Oroonoko* (Behn novel); revenge
Biassou, 99
Bicknell, John, 76–78, 93; *The Dying
Negro* (with Day), 76
Birney, James G., 139, 140
Birth of a Nation (Griffith), 188
Birth of a Nation (Parker), 202–204
Black Laws, 132, 139
Black No More (Schuyler), 174
Black Panther (comic book), 204
Black Panther (film), 202, 204–207
Black Panther Party, 205, 207
Black Power, 12, 103, 170

Prosser, Gabriel, 158; Gabriel's Rebellion, 125, 130

race: categories, 94–95, 98, 103–105, 126, 167, 174, 229n91; concept, 13–14, 21, 25–26, 29, 38, 64, 96; purity in, 65, 143, 152, 158–159, 174, 175, 188; scientific racism, 8, 65, 88, 95–96, 103, 152, 166, 173–175. *See also* blackness; whiteness

Raimond, Julien, 95, 97, 98, 104, 107

Rainsford, Marcus, 101, 159; *An Historical Account of the Black Empire of Hayti*, 111, 116–119, 141

rape: of Belton, 177; in *Blake*, 160–161, 175; definition of, 4, 50, 87; in *Django Unchained*, 8, 11; English treatment of, 59, 82; in *Imperium in Imperio*, 176–178; in *Lust's Dominion*, 39, 49; in *Oronoko*, 63; in *Oroonoko*, 50, 57; *raptus*, 3, 87; southern narrative on, 166, 175, 180, 181, 186, 188; *stuprum*, 3; terror through, 8, 11, 84, 131, 160, 176–178; in *West Indian Eclogues*, 81–82, 86–89. *See also* Lucretia

Raynal, Guillaume-Thomas, 89; *Histoire philosophique et politique des établissements et du commerce des Européens dans les deux Indes*, 9, 10, 16, 92–110 passim, 112, 113, 117, 123–124, 137, 138, 140, 142–143, 205. *See also* Louverture, Toussaint; Spartacus

Reconstruction, 17, 164, 169, 175, 180, 198, 199–200

Red Shirts, 164, 181. *See also* Ku Klux Klan

Redpath, James, 143–145, 153

Remus, 69

Republican Party, 180–181, 191

revenge: in *Abdelazer*, 37, 39, 40; in *As We See It*, 166, 194, 195, 197; black on white, 72, 75, 108, 118, 143, 166, 174, 175, 203–204; definition of, 5, 35; in *Django Unchained*, 11; French, 75; in *Imperium in Imperio*, 172, 174, 175, 176; Lucretia and, 3, 70, 186; in *Lust's Dominion*, 25, 27, 30; in *The Marrow of Tradition*, 182, 183; mulatto, 14, 103, 143, 174–175, 199; in *Oronoko*, 19, 20–21, 40–46, 49, 50; in *Parthenissa*, 33; poetic trope of, 76–80;

85; in *West Indian Eclogues*, 84–88; in western, 7–8, 190, 194

revenge drama, 10–11, 15, 21–24, 26, 40, 46, 50, 51; black villains of, 23, 45, 49, 50, 98, 180, 194, 205

Rigaud, André, 100, 103, 105, 107, 109, 110, 172

Robespierre, Maximilien, 53

Rochambeau, General Donatien-Marie-Joseph de, 118

Rome, 32, 52, 56, 58, 60, 68–69, 87, 96, 180, 191, 199; foundation myth of, 69–70, 88; national sentiment in, 70

—Republic of, 3, 4, 9, 53, 59, 161; birth of, 3, 59, 70, 186: civilizational model, 54–55, 68, 70, 74, 91, 115

Romulus, 3, 4, 69

Roosevelt, Theodore, 166, 188

Rushton, Edward, 54, 79–84, 86–89, 160

Russo-Japanese War, 196

Russwurm, John, 133

Rymer, Thomas, 38, 45

Saint-Domingue, 9, 91–116 passim, 124–125, 129–130, 133–134. *See also* Haiti

Saint-Lambert, Jean-François de, 68

Saint-Rémy, Joseph, 142, 143

Santo Domingo, 92, 99, 125, 153

Saurin, Bernard-Joseph, 71, 73; *Spartacus*, 15–16, 21, 31–34, 53, 68–72, 89, 111

scapegoat, 23, 50, 185

Schuyler, George, 174

sensibility, 53, 57–58, 73, 75, 78–81, 121

settler colonialism, black, 136, 171, 172

Seven Years War, 60, 66, 89, 115

Shaftesbury, Anthony Ashley Cooper, Earl of, 35, 36, 212nn60–61

Shakespeare, William, 22–23

skin color, 38, 41, 65

slave revolt, 2, 8, 9, 35, 40, 54, 84, 98–99, 112–113, 116, 148; in abolitionist literature, 16, 78, 80–82, 85, 88, 112–113, 156; in Americas, 5–6, 14, 15, 72–73; in Jamaica, 125; in *Oroonoko*, 19, 21, 46–48, 50; in *Parthenissa*, 32, 33, 34; in *Spartacus*, 69; in United States, 125, 130, 140. *See also* Turner, Nat

slavery, 50, 53; abolition in Saint-Domingue,